FREDERICK WALKER

Commandant of the Native Police

Paul Dillon

Connor Court Publishing

Published in 2018 by Connor Court Publishing Pty Ltd

Connor Court Publishing Pty Ltd
PO Box 7257
Redland Bay QLD 4165
sales@connorcourt.com
www.connorcourtpublishing.com.au

Phone 0497-900-685

Printed in Australia

ISBN 978-1925-501-957

Front Cover Image: Tracker, Courtesy Mitchell Library SLNSW

CONTENTS

Preface	5
What have I got to apologise for?	7
Chapter 1—Birth of a Nation	23
Chapter 2—Native Police	41
Chapter 3—Assessment of Native Police	71
Chapter 4—Dismissal	101
Chapter 5—Aborigines caught and killed	119
Chapter 6—Walker, the Civilian	143
Chapter 7—In Search of Burke and Wills	165
Chapter 8—Frederick Walker's Journal	181
Chapter 9—Telegraph Line	251
Chapter 10—Letters to the Press	281
Chapter 11—Native Police Operational Correspondence	345
Bibliography	475

Preface

Leonardo da Vinci said: "Art is never finished, only abandoned." In view of the earlier private edition of this work, this opportunity has allowed me to review the archival material once again to achieve greater accuracy and precision in its reproduction and quotation throughout the book but more particularly, in Chapter 11. Furthermore, this fortuity has perhaps, allowed me to sharpen and clarify the general thrust of the dissertation contained herein.

Paul Dillon

Courtesy QSL

Frederick Walker circa 1820 to 1866

What have I got to apologise for?

I believe this book has its genesis way back in the Keating era. I found the man particularly offensive in his attitude to what I would call the core Australian values that ran through the old, pre-multicultural Australia, the familiar elements of ancestry, religion, politics, class and culture. My family arrived in Melbourne, Australia in 1857 as unassisted Catholic settlers from Cork, Ireland and have lived and worked here ever since. The city of my birth seemed very homogeneous. It was a comfortable time to live, surrounded by the jovial and cheeky paddymelon faces of old Australia; not like the current prickly and spiky times of political correctness. Coming from a very ordinary background with a very ordinary education, I identified with the Labor party. I took an interest in politics at the time; Communists still stood for parliament and spoke at rallies, and I was fascinated by the claims of the Communists who spoke of the exploitation of the Australian worker and more surprisingly, Aborigines. All the workers I saw every day, and there were many of them, seemed happy enough, and on occasion they did strike. I went to school with aboriginal children and I also knew the local South Seas Islander families. As far as I could see nothing was out of place except for the self-evident divide between the boss and the worker. I used to enjoy listening to Mr Menzies' election speeches on the radio as he was constantly heckled by professional agitators. He never resorted to having them evicted but used his wonderful skill at putting them down, which I relished. They would yell, "What about the workers?" and he would reply, "You never had it so good," and would give some statistical quote to back up his repartee.

Whitlam, who I voted for, seemed at the time to be persuasive, believable, energetic and competent, yet after he was elected he fell upon the body politic of Australia in a frenzy and tore it to bits, smashed it to smithereens. He acted like a junkie gagging for an executive fix. He turned out to be a sophist, a destroyer of the Australian way of life;

what was his kink?[1] Gough Whitlam's handing over of the land to Vincent Lingiari,[2] was a disgraceful kick in the guts to all the white pioneers who had gone before and sacrificed their manhood for the advancement of the nation; imagine Ian Smith or Dr Verwoerd doing such a thing. Whitlam should have been charged with *indignité nationale*. The impact of Whitlam has been profound and from his election one can trace the downfall of the Australia that I once knew, where the serried ranks of Anzac veterans were Aussie to a fault both in look and mind, when it was once comfortable to walk around the place without the gawks from a freshly downloaded shipment of new Australians who prop and yaw, if glanced at even for a moment. To my mind, when Labor had a majority of members with a predominately Irish Catholic background, it stood for a fair go but at all times putting the nation's interest always at the forefront. The rise of communism, particularly after the Second World War, led to a bitter conflict for the control of Labor. Irish Catholics moved away from Labor while Labor did its best to purge the movement of these members. At the same time, Australia saw an ever-expanding economy that, by the mid 1960's, had led to full employment and it would be fair to say that the Australian workers never had it so good. Yet the party was lost in the wildness and tangled in a useless and sterile debate over Vietnam, holding itself out as a hater of all forms of colonialism. Of course, Whitlam went on to release PNG from the colonial grip of Australia thus mocking the Kokoda campaign.

Whitlam always argued he was for the independence of Australia. Patriotism is the last refuge of a scoundrel, and among the reforms he made, which broke the back of Australia, was dismantling the last drawbridge against the barbarians by the closing off of all routes of appeal from the High Court to the Privy Council. The Privy Council (Appeals from the High Court) Act 1975 marked the final step in the process of excluding appeals to the British Privy Council from decisions of the High Court of Australia. "Australia's nationhood requires that its judicial system should be entirely free from the supervision of the courts of

1 For an alternative view see Noel Pearson's eulogy at Whitlam's funeral.

2 Has there been any advancement? Look at the Kalkarindji and Dagaragu 2007 Howard intervention.

another country."[3] Not so, the existence of appellate superintendence provides a necessary impetus towards caution. Those who are supervised must always keep in the back of their minds, at least, the possibility that their opinions will be reviewed, reversed and adversely remarked upon.[4]

When the Queen goes, which these devils draped with the flag of our country are calling for with their forked-tongues, then Australia will drift into chaos like all republics. The Queen and the Privy Council are a check and a balance that any major machinery of government requires. They have a restraining effect on the excesses of any government bereft of reason and seeking to overthrow the natural order, as Whitlam ultimately tried to do; a Mr Hyde prowling the corridors of power, looking for every last vial of ayes to slake a thirst for wanton legislative profligacy, gone troppo. I remember that daunting image well. He bestrode the House like a monstrous Cyclops, decimating all we held sacred, churning the parliament till it reeked of bedlam and strange notions; debauching our nationhood till we have become what we are today.

Whitlam made this outlandish and outrageous statement in 1972:

> Aborigines — There is one great group of Australians who have been denied their basic rights to the pursuit of happiness, to liberty and indeed to life itself for 180 years – since the very time when Europeans in the New World first proclaimed those rights as inalienable for all mankind. In 1967 we, the people of Australia, by an overwhelming majority imposed upon the Commonwealth the constitutional responsibility for Aborigines and Torres Strait Islanders. A Labor Government will over-ride Queensland's discriminatory laws. To ensure that Aborigines are made equal before the law, the Commonwealth will pay all legal costs for Aborigines in all proceedings in all courts. We will establish once and for all Aborigines' rights to land and insist that, whatever the law of George III says, a tribe and a race with an identity of centuries – of millennia – is as much entitled to own land as even a proprietary company — legislate to prohibit discrimination on grounds of race, ratify all the relevant United Nations and I.L.O. Conventions for this purpose,

3 EG Whitlam, Second Reading 27 May 1975.

4 Melbourne University Law Students' Society Sir Anthony Mason Lecture 1996 6 September 1996 A F Mason from Trigwell To Teoh, The Hon Justice Michael Kirby AC CMG.

> and set up conciliation procedures to promote understanding and co-operation between aboriginal and other Australians.[5]

In looking at the above statement, the first point is that Aborigines were never slaves or bonded servants.[6] Later they were regulated and controlled by legislation. They still are; the only difference is that the legislation is a conduit to lavish largess on them. The fact that they remain under discriminatory legislation is of their choosing. Whitlam used the words Aborigines and Australians as if they were interchangeable and have the same meaning. Then in the final declaratory sentence he switches back to saying "between aboriginal and other Australians." Even those who might agree with the thrust of my argument would not accept that they are interchangeable and the dissidents most definitely would not. Of course, that is one of my grievances; Aborigines do not accept that they are Australian. This then becomes a matter of definition, of which I will have more to say. Then Whitlam said that Aborigines have been denied their basic rights to the pursuit of happiness, to liberty and indeed to life itself for 180 years. He may be right but so have I and my family as Catholics since 1857. Catholic schools received little or nothing in the way of grants or direct aid to further the education of a great group of Australians. Moreover, the statement is a deliberate untruth. The people who made such an outlandish statement[7] continued to keep slaves without a single scruple falling from their waistcoats.

The 1967 referendum gave the Commonwealth the power to make laws pursuant to Section 51, subject to the Constitution, for the peace, order, and good government of the Commonwealth with respect to (xxvi) the people of any race,[8] for whom it is deemed necessary to make special laws. The race power, to my mind, is to control and regulate the subject race. Up until the election of Whitlam, Australia had a white Australia policy,[9] effectively, the country was raceless or monoracial. Post WWII

5 Aborigines, Gough Whitlam, Australian Labor Party Delivered at Blacktown, NSW, 13 November 1972.

6 Not to be confused with Pacific Islanders.

7 United States Declaration of Independence, 4 July 1776. 1865 slavery abolished by the Thirteenth Amendment.

8 These are the deleted words: other than the aboriginal race in any State.

9 Immigration Restriction Act 1901.

migrants of non-British background were not officially concentrated[10] but did so of their own volition and became visible to some extent as a result of this.[11] The race power was used by the Whitlam Government to positively discriminate in favour of Aborigines and Torres Strait Islanders. It is important to keep in mind that Torres Strait Islanders are culturally and genetically Melanesian people, as are the people of Papua New Guinea. They are distinct from the aboriginal people of the rest of Australia, and are generally referred to separately.[12] The Whitlam Government established schemes whereby Aborigines and Torres Strait Islanders could obtain housing, loans, emergency accommodation and tertiary education allowances. It also increased funding for the Aboriginal Legal Service enabling twenty-five offices to be established throughout Australia.[13] Ponder this if you will, in the same parliament Kep Enderby, who got the Racial Discrimination Act passed, said fellow parliamentarians would surely agree that all human beings are born free and equal in dignity and rights and that any doctrine of superiority based on racial differentiation is scientifically false, morally condemnable, socially unjust and dangerous and without any justification.[14]

The next step in Whitlam's profligacy was the introduction of the Racial Discrimination Act. Whitlam had no specific head of power under the Constitution like section 51. What he did here, as he said above, was to use the executive power of the government to ratify all the relevant United Nations and I.L.O. Conventions for this purpose. This was a unilateral act done by the Whitlam government purporting to exercise it eternal affairs powers under the Constitution; not seeking the approval of the parliament and certainly not seeking approval from the people, and then legislating to give effect to the conventions in Australian domestic law. Under Whitlam, Australia had gone from a virtually racially neutral community to one where a) any ethnic or racial group could migrate to Australia, b) legislation was enacted to benefit and enhance two

---

10 There were some migrant reception centres for non-English speakers.

11 Carlton, the 'Little Italy' of Melbourne, and Leichhardt, its equivalent in Sydney.

12 https://en.wikipedia.org/wiki/Torres_Strait_Islanders

13 This is not a complete list, merely an example.

14 Second reading speech: House of Representatives, 13 February 1975 p 1.

specific racial groups and c) the majority, who were born here — Australians, were now to be prosecuted for any offensive behaviour (politically incorrect) because of race, colour or national or ethnic origin. Australia had gone from being, "G'day, how ya goin, mate?" to "Salam alaikum" or "Namaste". The original race power should have been seen as merely a power to control and regulate but it has been used to advance and enrich a small ill-defined group in the community which naturally enough has engendered envy and resentment based on a perception that the benefits are undeserved and unearned. To administer and control this double-headed monster, Whitlam created two bureaucratic industries, Aboriginal Affairs and Human Rights. This body is remarkable in that it was set up to protect the government's favoured and biased racist legislation. It is a law enforcement body not of sworn constables but of political police who operate to control and regulate the majority should they question the merits or fairness of the use of the race power. You often hear the dumber members of the Labor parliamentary party saying Australia has a mixed economy; they mean a private sector, subjected, not just to the vicissitudes of the market but rigorously policed for conformity to government red and green tape, and a government sector such as the above two, which operate unfettered in La La Land. Once you create a demand, which Labor did, you get a supply; the growth in numbers and funding for immigration and Aborigines has been impressive, if not frightening. Hence the need for a code of conduct for the host body (Australians), the Racial Discrimination Act, and a law enforcement agency to prosecute the host body (Australians) for non-compliance, Human Rights Commission, then a cover story to disguise the whole apparatus, which rounds everything off with a policy of multiculturalism.

Of course, the real irony of this tragedy is, and it is but a small piece of the rubble that Whitlam and his ilk have left behind, the fact that the code of political correctness that is laid out in the Racial Discrimination Act only survived in the High Court when challenged in the case of *Koowarta* v. *Bjelke-Petersen*[15] by the vote of Mr Justice Lionel Murphy

[15] [1982] HCA 27; narrow majority of four to three, Murphy part of the majority.

aka Senator Lionel Murphy.[16] Speaking at a legal convention in 1963, where there was discussion of a proposal to create the Federal Court of Australia, Mr E G Whitlam QC, later Prime Minister, said "that judges who interpret and apply statutes should be appointed by governments responsible to the parliaments which passed those statutes, and that, on principle, federal judges should interpret and apply federal laws."[17] Harmless enough, but Whitlam being who he was, perhaps, equally ominous, not only must justice be done; it must also be seen to be done. Murphy was a reprehensible individual of the first water. Whitlam, the mouse that roared; his 1972 speech was caked with pledges of lolly and folly for everyman and his dog, which all came tumbling down in a heap of egg shells like Humpty Dumpty on 11 November 1975.

To give some balance to this seemingly unfair criticism of Labor, I turn to Malcolm Fraser. If he had gone to Cambridge and been a little older, I might have suggested he was a sputnik orbiting the Cambridge Five. He had all the hallmarks of the squattocracy but he was red right down to his underwear. For a man who so assiduously dismantled Whitlam's Medibank yet left Whitlam's race legislation intact: there's the knavery of the man. However, where Fraser really let the country down was in the introduction and administration of the Lebanese Concession.[18] These issues are too painful to dissect; it's like cutting up your old faithful dog only to find it riddled with turpitude.

The drover's dog was elected Prime Minister from 11 March 1983 to 20 December 1991. His contribution to the race debate no doubt was wide and brim full and the merits of it are yet to be seen but in 1989, Bob Hawke cried over the Tiananmen Square massacre and allowed 42,000 Chinese students to stay in Australia. The students subsequently brought in large numbers of family so that the 42,000 swelled to an estimated 100,000, the biggest wave of Chinese migration since the gold rush of the 1850s.[19]

---

16 As Attorney-General in the Whitlam Government, Senator Lionel Murphy introduced the Racial Discrimination Bill in the Senate on three occasions, November 1973, April 1974 and October 1974 and failed.

17 (1963) 36 ALJ 308 at 327.

18 *The Australian*, 24 November 2016 Gerard Henderson.

19 *Sydney Morning Herald* (SMH) Children of the revolution 26 December 2003.

The final calamity of the Egyptian scourge was the redoubtable Paul Keating, Prime Minister from 1991 to 1996. Agitating in the north of the country was a man who wanted a wee piece of land, so it appears, where he could carry on some traditional Melanesian gardening although his domicile was the bright lights of Townsville and he had left the island paradise as a small boy. This scratching about by him, seemed to threaten the then Queensland government and out of an abundance of caution they passed the Queensland Coast Islands Declaratory Act 1985 (Q) which was thought to put an end to the mumblings of this malcontent. Out of this dream for a yam patch arose a call of, "I was robbed" which, believe it or not, the sleeping giant in Canberra heard. He awoke, looked around and in that split second of fate picked up the Racial Discrimination Act 1975 and KO'd Queensland, and then asked the plaintiff what was his cause? *Mabo [2]* was the result. Like the curate's egg, *Mabo [2]* was good in parts. You cannot say *Mabo [2]* is plain sailing; it is not. It is dissentious and rough, it deceives and cogs, and ducks with forensic nods and winks and apish courtesies to legal concepts and texts of doubtful value. A plain lawyer could not partake of the fair without suffering a bilious night of distemper and colic with spectral flashes of fee simple, fee tail, deodands, tenure, and copyholder, as well as Boschian images of Australian colonial atrocities pulsating in quick succession. Dawson J, a straight shooter when it came to the settlement of Australia, gave a sane appraisal of the situation and came to a common-sense decision:

> 79. In my view, the conclusion is inevitable that, assuming the native inhabitants of the Murray Islands to have held some sort of rights in the land immediately before the annexation of those islands, the Crown in right of the Colony of Queensland, on their annexation, exerted to the full its rights in the land inconsistently with and to the exclusion of any native or aboriginal rights. It did so under the law which it brought with it. It did so from the start by acting upon the assumption (which was also the assumption lying behind the relevant legislation) that there was no such thing as native title and that the Crown was exclusively entitled to all lands which had not been alienated by it: lands which were designated as Crown lands.

Brennen J held on the weirdest of views that Native Title to land survived the Crown's acquisition of sovereignty and radical title. The rights and privileges conferred by native title were unaffected by the Crown's acquisition of radical title but the acquisition of sovereignty exposed native title to extinguishment by a valid exercise of sovereign power inconsistent with the continued right to enjoy native title. Deane and Gaudron JJ relied upon Brennan J's legal concept of a radical title, in others words a Clayton's. However, rather than sticking to the script, launched into an outpouring of colonial atrocities against Australian Aborigines when the case involved Murray Island and then added a postscript giving a limp-wristed justification for their immoderate views. The evidentiary judge, Moynihan J was restricted to Murray Island; he did not hold a hearing into mainland Australia. Reading a few left-wing works appeared to have justified this outburst by Deane and Gaudron JJ. Toohey J also relied on Brennan J's concept of a radical title. He too could not refrain from launching into an uncalled-for attack on Australian settlers. Mason CJ and McHugh J agreed with the reasons for the judgement of Brennan J and with the declaration which he proposed. A brief could not stomach too much of *Mabo [2]* without a firkin of milk of magnesia. The reason the High Court went feral over *Mabo [2]*, no doubt has its genesis in the euphoria of the times but to my mind the difficulty arose in that firstly, appeals from the High Court had been cut off and that meant the court was unsupervised and free to pick up any so-called persuasive authorities it saw fit, or to put it this way, as there was an absence of any prior decision of its own or any prior decision of any appellate court in Australia, this then left the High Court to define the common law relating to native title for Australia which Whitlam had pursued while in government as best he could. Secondly, the Commonwealth Attorney-General did not intervene even though he had a statutory right to intervene in constitutional matters before the High Court: Judiciary Act 1903 (Cth) s 78A.[20] As far as I can see, little or no comment has been devoted to the absence of the federal Attorney-General in *Mabo [2]*. This may be of interest:

> Granting what you have said about the need for the Court to consider the generality of the application of the Mabo decision to

20 Long title of *Mabo [2]*: *Eddie Mabo and Celuia Mapo Salee and Sam Passi and David Passi and James Rice who bring this action on their own behalf and on behalf of the members of their respective family groups* v. *The State of Queensland and The Commonwealth of Australia.*

> the mainland of Australia, would you care to express a view as to whether it was justified in pursuing that line in the absence of any representation from either Aboriginals or non-Aboriginals from the mainland of Australia? It appears to me that the Court made that decision and that application in the total absence of any representation from persons greatly affected.
>
> In the Mabo decision, the High Court did not purport to decide any particular claim of native title in respect of any land other than the Murray Islands. What it did was declare certain principles.[21]

Keating kept out of the matter for reasons that one may only speculate about but it meant the court could not sound out the Commonwealth on matters of law or policy. It left the court to make value judgments about matters on which the Commonwealth may have assisted. Although *Mabo [2]* was directed to how an individual state might extinguish native title by the application of land law in line with the Racial Discrimination Act, no consideration was given to how the Commonwealth may extinguish native title on land held by a state. Obvious sources of power for the Commonwealth are the race power, the defence power and or the external affairs power. However, the real reason in my mind is that it allowed Keating to wake up one morning virginal, totally surprised but more importantly, blameless for the legislative handiwork of the High Court. The High Court unshackled from the Privy Council simply made law, or did it go further than the ever-present threat of judge-made law and act as the legislative arm of government and declare a government policy[22] the law?

> Pressure on courts to make law is where the interests now pressing for recognition are covered by the existing body of precepts, but the court believes that social and ethical ideas about their proper accommodation have changed since these precepts were formulated. There is no better example than the decision of the High Court in Mabo v Queensland [No 2] where a majority of the Court held that indigenous title to land survived the colonisation of Austra-

21 Crommelin "Mabo: The Decision and the Debate" Papers on Parliament No. 22, February 1994.

22 A policy that carried with it not only a new legal concept but the condemnation of all those who had acted in good faith on the now defunct principle of terra nullius.

> lia by the Crown in 1788, notwithstanding that the Privy Council had not accepted that view a century earlier in Cooper v Stuart. The majority in Mabo held that the extinguishment of indigenous rights and interests, based upon the doctrine of terra nullius, was justified by a policy which has no place in the contemporary law of this country. Judges are not in the business of repudiating the past, although sometimes, as Mabo [No 2] and R v L show, they must repudiate rules developed in earlier times when those rules have become out of touch with contemporary notions of justice.[23]

Balanced against this view is the following:

> At one level, the policy arguments for the High Court's recognition of native title seem to be overwhelming. The linchpin of the decision was what Brennan J described as the 'unjust and discriminatory' refusal of the previous law to 'recognise the rights and interests in land of the indigenous inhabitants of settled colonies'. Although the judgments devote relatively little time to the policy justification for transforming the common law, it is clear enough that the Court considered that the prior occupation of Aboriginal peoples carried its own moral and legal force, demanding recognition by the common law. There is also a good deal of what Professor Webber describes as 'the jurisprudence of regret' in the judgments. This is reflected in the view expressed by Deane and Gaudron JJ that two centuries of oppression and conflict had dispossessed, degraded and devastated the Aboriginal peoples and had left a national legacy of unutterable shame. There is no denying the powerful force of this reasoning, which has commanded widespread, although by no means universal acceptance in Australia. The question, however, that the judgments in Mabo do not explicitly address is this: why was it appropriate for the High Court to adopt the doctrine of common law native title two centuries after the commencement of European settlement and in the face of established legal principle to the contrary? It is, after all, one thing to recognise the strong moral claim of aboriginal peoples to native title; it is quite another for the High Court to decide that it, rather than the elected Parlia-

---

23 The Australian Bar Association Conference, London, England 5 July 1998 Democracy and The Law The Hon Justice M H McHugh AC.

> ment, should recognise that moral claim.[24]

The Mabo decisions gave rise to considerable controversy. Now, if the reader will pause and reflect for a moment, he or she, I hope, will see the gambit of the game played by Whitlam from 1972 when he was elected; a) he closed off the Privy Council, b) imported foreign laws into the domestic law, Racial Discrimination Act 1975, and c) then legislated for Native Title where he could. When the challenges came, as he knew they would he provided the blockers, which allowed the High Court a free hand to pick up and run with his concept of native title. There were of course, Privy Council cases that would have, if followed by the High Court, prevented the Court from holding *terra nullius* did not apply to Australian real property or land law such as *In re Southern Rhodesia* and *Cooper* v. *Stuart.*

Mabo [2] allowed Keating to deliver his Redfern speech which was nothing more than a diabolical harangue against the pioneers of Australia, a denunciation on a scale unheard-of until the rise of the authoritarian know-all. He thought the High Court had delivered some monumental victory or a cathartic or messianic revelation. It did nothing of the sort. Moreover, he read the judgment of Deane and Gaudron JJ as a legal seal of approval for the leftist view of the settlement of Australia which *Mabo [2]* was not. Deane and Gaudron JJ had wandered into an area in which they had no business to be. They had heard no evidence on the settlement of Australia and were not sitting as arbiters of the facts.

This is what he said but more importantly, he did not say or warn the electorate that he would introduce the Native Title Act to implement *Mabo [2]* nationwide:

> We need these practical building blocks of change. The Mabo Judgement should be seen as one of these. By doing away with the bizarre conceit that this continent had no owners prior to the settlement of Europeans, Mabo establishes a fundamental truth and lays the basis for justice. It will be much easier to work from that basis than has ever been the case in the past. For that reason alone,

24 Sackville, Ronald, "Why Do Judges Make Law? Some Aspects of Judicial Law Making" [2001] UWSLawRw 5; (2001) 5(1) University of Western Sydney Law Review 59.

> we should ignore the isolated outbreaks of hysteria and hostility of the past few months. Mabo is an historic decision; we can make it an historic turning point, the basis of a new relationship between indigenous and non-Aboriginal Australians.[25]

Paul Keating's election speech for the 1993 election said the following. Again, he did not warn the electorate he would introduce the Native Title Act based on *Mabo [2]*:

> This Government has long spoken of the need to address the historic and continuing injustice done to Australia's indigenous people. Over the years, a great deal of money has been spent and a great deal of good will expanded, but the Aboriginal and Torres Strait Islander people continue to suffer the consequences of two centuries of injustice, prejudice and neglect. Any Government that I lead will be determined to complete the process of reconciliation Labor has begun, and at last return to the indigenous people of Australia the dignity, social justice, health, opportunity and living standards to which all Australians are entitled. To fail in this is to betray not just the Aboriginal people, but ourselves, all that we profess to believe, everything Australia stands for. We are determined not to fail this time.[26]

He was elected in 1993 and as Prime Minister at 3.38 pm on 16 November 1993 he introduced the Native Title Bill inter alia:

> Today is a milestone. A response to another milestone: The High Court's decision in the Mabo case. The High Court has determined that Australian law should not, as Justice Brennan said, be frozen in an era of racial discrimination. Its decision in the Mabo case ended the pernicious legal deceit of terra nullius for all of Australia—and for all time. The court described the situation faced by Aboriginal people after European settlement. The court saw a conflagration of oppression and conflict which was, over the following century, to spread across the continent to dispossess, degrade and devastate the Aboriginal people. They faced deprivation of the religious, cultural and economic sustenance which the land provides and were left as intruders in their own homes.

---

25 Delivered in Redfern Park by Prime Minister Paul Keating, 10 December 1992.

26 Paul Keating, Australian Labor Party delivered at Bankstown, NSW, 24 February 1993.

> To deny these basic facts would be to deny history — and no self-respecting democracy can deny its history. To deny these facts would be to deny part of ourselves as Australians. This is not guilt: it is recognising the truth. The truth about the past and, equally, the truth about our contemporary reality. It is not a symptom of guilt to look reality in the eye — it is a symptom of guilt to look away, to deny what is there. But what is worse than guilt, surely, is irresponsibility. To see what is there and not act upon it — that is a symptom of weakness. That is failure.[27]

As I have said, his take on the *Mabo [2]* judgment is a dishonest misreading of the judgment. But to a bully in the throes of kicking his fag, rationality can hardly be expected. Of course, Tom Brown grew-up and gave poor old Flashman his comeuppance. So too Keating went to the scrapyard.

Mabo [2] did not give sovereignty nor was it retrospective and it only applied to Murray Island. Moreover, it simply said, prior to the arrival of the British, the natives had a land title of some communal type and until and unless specifically ousted it remained on foot. However, the onus of proof was on the claimant. Be that as it may, Labor has displayed the mentality of a sneakthief in this whole sorry saga. The author of this sad story no doubt was Whitlam. No leader of recent times with his level of intellect has ever had to endure years, not only in opposition but forced to endure the dementia of Evatt and Calwell. His over-active mind must have plotted and schemed a thousand times as he listened to and suffered the fools about him; and I am sure the 1967 referendum on Aborigines caused him to draw all sorts of schemes. Like the imperious stag that he was, his vainglorious antlers got caught in the tangle of political chicanery and thus he was felled by his opponents. Whatever solution is proposed to the aboriginal question then both political parties should learn from the above that it must be home-grown and derive from the people and by the people, not imposed by some left-wing view of colonialism. Where a society has had at its core a Judeo-Christian belief system on which the foundations of the society are built and manifested in its laws, and members of that society have acted in good faith in the advancement and furtherance of that society on the basis of those laws, then

[27] HR Hansard Tuesday, 16 November 1993 page 2877.

fundamental changes to those laws which cannot be described as meeting improved conditions but would, if implemented, not only destroy an existing principle but in fact introduce a new principle for conducting daily societal activities and where future members of that society are taught that the old concepts were wrong, bad and discriminatory, then such changes must be made by a public vote clearly demonstrating that the majority require these core values to be changed. As I said above, if laws are going to be made on the race power which favour and/or enrich the subject race; they need first of all to define strictly the membership of the race to the satisfaction of the majority of the those excluded who must pay the taxes for the largess to be distributed to the favoured race.

BLACKS ATTACKING AN OUT-STATION. [See Page 3.]

Courtesy of Illustrated News

Blacks attacking an out-station

1

Birth of a Nation

Once a upon a time, a man called Bennelong of the Eora people saw Captain Cook sail by and wondered what he was doing? When Cook did not stop, Bennelong thought no more about it; then sometime later, he heard on the bush telegraph that Captain Cook had been doing the rounds of London saying he had discovered Australia. Bennelong thought about this and said, "Dat can't be true because we already knowed we're 'ere. Dat Captain Cook plenty humbug." "Nebba mind," he thought, "E's no more worri." Then many seasons later, Captain Arthur Phillip turned up with his family and said he had moved into a place called Port Jackson. Bennelong thought to himself, "Why does this white man want Eora kuntri for his sit-down kuntri? We nebba asked him to come 'ere."

So, my dear reader that is how the story of Australia began. Of course, what Bennelong did not know was that on 22 August 1770, Cook landed on Possession Island, and claimed the entire coastline that he had just explored as British territory.[28] With the arrival of Arthur Phillip together with his instructions from George III on 21 January 1788, the Crown had taken possession of its Territory of New South Wales and its Dependencies, and we know possession is nine tenths of the law. In setting up a penal colony or settlement, what would be best practices for carrying out such a project? Perhaps the first step might be an environmental planning and assessment study to take into consideration the impact to the environment and the community of the proposed development or land-use change; detailing the impact to both natural and human environments. A fair-minded person would, of course, accept

[28] Cook's voyage was initially to observe the transit of Venus from Tahiti; then he was to look for the southern continent and if found, annex it, and report on its products and inhabitants.

that Captain Cook's survey of the East Coast of Australia, conducted from the Endeavour in 1770, was a more than an adequate examination and estimation of the conditions of both the natural and human environments as they then existed in New South Wales, which was in keeping with the best practices of the day.[29] In writing this book there were many imponderables to consider and perhaps the most obvious was, did anyone think to ask the Aborigines what they thought of the occupation of the country. The question is mildly absurd because Cook made every attempt to parley with the indigenous people he found along the coast but he received no coherent answer from them, either because they failed to understand him or his presence had no significance to them or they saw no issue in his questions and actions; perhaps, their silence or failure to respond signalled that they did not care or were accepting or acquiescing of the white man's presence. Captain Cook observed:

> There are no chiefs, and the land is divided into sections, occupied by families, who consider everything in their district as their own. Internecine war exists between the different tribes, which are very small. Their treachery, which is unsurpassed, is simply an outcome of their savage ideas, and in their eyes is a form of independence which resents any intrusion on THEIR land, THEIR wild animals, and THEIR rights generally. In their untutored state, they therefore consider that any method of getting rid of the invader is proper.[30]

Of course, it would be wonderful to go back to the beginning and asked the leaders of the then First Nation what they wanted in return for allowing the British to set up a settlement in Australia.[31] If one was to ask the current bunch of illustrious leaders, they would probably put forward the following conditions for a lease of Australia:

---

29 For a contra or different view see para 35 of Deane and Gaudron JJ *Mabo [2]*, which is obiter dictum anyway.

30 http://gutenberg.net.au/ebooks/e00043.html#ch8. Each tribe comprising from twenty to sixty of them. They acknowledge no particular Chief as being superior to the rest. The tribes would be much more numerous were it not for these barbarous and inhuman sacrifices, *The Life and Adventures of William Buckley*, by J Morgan, MacDougal, Tas. 1852 p 66.

31 This sentence is an example of how modern history is written about aborigines by introducing anachronistic questions and then answering them with modern concepts and language, hypophora at its grossest.

> Term of lease 99 years with an option for a further 99 years; on signing the lease an immediate payment or a fine of twenty billion in gold sovereigns; the First Nation to retain sovereignty over the lands and oceans of and pertaining to Australia and the said sovereignty will not be diminished, reduced or limited by the lease; the First Nation to have complete and total ownership and control over all things animate or inanimate in the seas and on the land and above or below the ground; the First Nation to receive annually fifty percent of the gross profits generated by the lessee; each First Nation citizen to be given a pension for life according to his needs and status; each First Nation citizen to be given free education, free health, etc. & etc. Moreover, neither the First Nation nor its members shall be liable to any form of taxation or conscription by the lessee. Disclaimer: should the party of the first part, the First Nation find that they have under quoted in regards to the above lease of the said Australia then on notice from the First Nation the lease will become null and void and a further lease more favourable to the First Nation will be entered into forthwith.

As amusing as the above may seem, the reality is as follows: the 2014 Indigenous Expenditure Report was released on December 12, 2014 reporting a total spend for 2012-2013 of $30.3 billion, accounting for 6.1 per cent of total direct government expenditure. Total estimated expenditure per person across all government programs in 2012-13 was $43,449 per Aboriginal and/or Torres Strait Islander compared to $20,900 for non-Aboriginal Australians.[32] This sort of public spending has gone on for years under Labor, welfare ad infinitum.[33]

The birth of a nation is a phenomenon. Profound yes, but it does not require an in-depth metaphysical analysis of the whys and wherefores of its conception and physical delivery. In the case of Australia, the Kingdoms of Great Britain and Ireland were acting according to the

---

32 Steering Committee for the Review of Government Service Provision, 2014 Indigenous Expenditure Report.

33 Labor policy: Come in, what would you like, my house, my job? We've got plenty; Labor will write you a cheque, no worries.

doctrine of discovery or exploration pursuant to international law.[34] Moreover, they had social problems in regard to a section of their population, namely, the criminal classes. A humane solution had to be found to the overcrowding of prisons. A policy of executing convicted felons no longer seemed meritorious; something more humane was needed. Commuting a sentence of death to transportation for the term of one's natural life seemed eminently more preferable to hanging a felon by the neck until dead. Accordingly, steps were taken to set up a penal colony in the Territory of New South Wales and its Dependencies. The landing and disembarkation of Governor Phillip and his party onto the Territory of New South Wales immediately brought into existence a colony. This act of entry by Governor Phillip made lawful by his authorised instructions from the Crown of Great Britain and Ireland is the basis of the legitimate sovereignty of Australia. In the course of this settlement, an interaction arose between indigenous groups of people already present in the same territory. The analysis or description of that interaction should cause no difficulty provided records were kept of that contact. However, Australian history has been plunged into an internecine dispute among historians which has now claimed the lofty title of History Wars. The conflict seems petty when looked at from the point of view of the challenges that faced the colony, which were overcome and a thriving democratic, first world country has arisen in its place. However, one group did not respond to the challenges facing it and thus did not thrive and withered on the vine. Of course, there has been social engineering in the creation of Australia. Like many countries, Australia brought in coolie labour to work and overcome what appeared to be difficult production costs in certain industries like mining and sugar cane. These coolie races then appeared to assume a threatening posture to the pioneer white race and thus were deported and prevented from entering the country evermore.[35] Although the original native class has withered and appeared as if it had almost vanished, there has arisen in

---

34 This concept is hotly discredited by the UN and other anti-colonial bodies, but their argument is a post facto political fabrication based on Marx's ideas from his writings on British colonialism in India and the emerging Cold War doctrine of recruiting post-colonial nations to the Soviet bloc in the UN.

35 Immigration Restriction Act 1901.

its place a mestizo class who are claiming the pedigree of the original native class and asserting that they stand in the footsteps of the long lost indigenous race. This cannot be right but the assertion is driven by the modern concept of reparations for past perceived political wrongs.

> ... having mated and intermarried with Europeans and with Japanese, Chinese, Filipino and Malay fisherman and pearl divers in the north the population both full blood and miscegenated is increasing rapidly. ... physically and/or culturally it is a different kind of population that is increasing. Aborigines are becoming other than they were. Quite soon, anthropologists will speak of the "Aborigines" and their culture in a strictly historical sense.[36]

Australia was never invaded. Australia arose *ex nihilo* from nothing. The act of settlement was not in furtherance of an ideology but a phenomenon. The pioneers improved the country so as to live more comfortably. Abophiles have assiduously asserted that they have found dishonourable motives and hidden genocidal blueprints in the detritus of Australian history. They have become obsessed with conspiracy theories behind every event in the calendar of settlement. Regrettably, this approach to Australian history lacks merit; is unconvincing in its argument, and divisive in its effect. Aborigines, in situ, cannot be categorised without bringing down on the head of the poor scribe an avalanche of abuse and hatred, if you do not conform to the party line. Moreover, the publisher may incur the sanctions of the Racial Discrimination Act. Voltaire[37] might sound his lofty principles but unchained, heartfelt thoughts allowed to wander across the page in barefaced, black ink need to keep Keats close by.[38] However, in the scheme of things, it is fair to say Aborigines were a Stone Age people. In classifying their economy, Marx's theory of history is more than fair, a primitive form of communism: shared property, no concept of ownership beyond individual possessions like tools, weapons, wives; hunter and gatherer, survival is a daily struggle; and a proto-democracy, no concept of leadership other than best warrior.[39]

36 *Encountering Aborigines: A Case Study: Anthropology and the Australian Aboriginal* by Kenelm Burridge Pergamon Press Inc 1973 p 65.

37 I disapprove of what you say but will defend to the death your right to say it.

38 Fools rush in where angels fear to tread.

39 No concept of diplomacy either.

From the Toynbeean perspective of challenge and response, the Aborigines of Australia had lived in an environment which provided all too readily the means of sustenance, and thus, they had faced no serious challenge and remained in a cultural stasis. On the current upbeat view of pre-history in Australia, this stasis extended over 65,000 years. When at last, a serious challenge in the form of white settlement in 1788 did confront the Aborigines of Australia, which carried within it the germ of opportunity for them, what was their response? The response required from the Aborigines was vision, leadership, and action to meet the encounter and create a basis for their survival and, hopefully, their prosperity.

It is from this challenge that so much historical debate nay, heat has arisen. One side of the debate is drawn from the politics of Marxism[40] seeing only the cruelty, crimes, injustices, and exploitation of the collision of the two cultures; not wanting to see the meeting of the two cultures as a steady process of osmosis; only wanting to portray it as a brutal state of war, redolent of the Vietnam War[41], where the policy was search and destroy and the rules of engagement were: for operations in areas beyond the settled districts, shoot anything that moved, and in populated areas, shoot individuals who were either armed, dressed in war paint or behaving in a disorderly fashion. Whereas the early settler accepted the challenge, the burden was picked up and carried through to the success that Australia is today.

What then might we call the other side of the collision who are generally known as squatters? Why capitalists,[42] as Marx would rightly say. The total numbers of licensed occupants of the stations in the Sydney District in 1848 was 1,041; the estimated quantity of land occupied by these squatters was 54,821 square miles; the average quantity of land occupied by each squatter was 53 square miles or 34,000 acres; the quantity of stock depastured upon these runs was horses 17,000, cattle 644,000,

40 A modern theory much discredited; nevertheless, clung to by feeble minded scribes.

41 Most of the early commentators were brought up on the Vietnam War, which, in the West, was a classic ideological conflict between the left and the right.

42 Market economy, Private property, Bourgeois democracy, Wages, Imperialism & Monopolistic tendencies.

sheep 2,358,000, totalling 3,019,000 animals; and the amount of money paid to the Crown, in license fees, for one year's occupancy of these magnificent runs, was £18,812.[43] The squatters, at all times, believed and acted according to the prevailing law and founding principles of the colony, genuinely and firmly accepting the sovereign as the fountainhead of all law and the source of their legitimacy.

What can be said about the Aborigines? I suspect whatever one might say will be considered too little. Then, perhaps, it might be too much. In researching my family history, one of them was a founding member of the Fenians who the British took quite seriously and perhaps set up as a result of the Fenian threat, the Royal Irish Constabulary, a very efficient police force. However, the point is this, many have tried to characterise the Fenians. The *Spectator* said the following:

> Its (Fenian) leaders are such mean people, a schoolmaster, a tailor, a news agent, a fifth-rate journalist, and a discharged sergeant. But rather than laugh at such a mean lot, as most Englishmen have done to date, one needs to remember the Indian mutiny which was started by ignorant sepoys in circumstances where they had no chance of winning. It is their ignorance that makes them dangerous because they are unpredictable and not amenable to the normal ways of diplomacy or war. If they were men of education, or standing, or wealth, a politician would have some basis for calculation. They can reason, or argue, or concede, or at worst, coerce; with O'Connell, it was possible to deal by compromise. But no man can anticipate even in thought the course these Fenian leaders would adopt. They are capable of rebelling in a county in which they have not a hundred followers, of trying to seize Cork and defeat its garrison with a squad of half-drilled peasants, of hurling their followers barehanded on to men armed with Enfield rifles. Therefore, the Fenians are formidable, not indeed to the Empire, but to the peace and good order of certain Irish counties. They are contemptible, their means are trifling, and their organization is ludicrously defective; why arrest fifty or sixty obscure fools for talking treason and drilling with big sticks?[44]

---

43 *SMH* 15 April 1848 p 2.

44 *Spectator*, Fenianism—Its Danger and Its Remedy, 30 September 1865, p. 4. Please note I have précised this article-author.

Well I hate to suggest it, but if one substituted Aborigine for Fenian, perhaps one would obtain a colonial view of how the squatters and the administration saw the Aborigines. If I may be permitted to extract one element from the above, then it would be that the Aborigines were unpredictable and not amenable to the normal ways of diplomacy or war and formidable, not indeed to the Empire, but to the peace and good order of parts beyond the settled districts. If the Aborigines thought about the encroachment of their territory, why did they not conciliate?[45] There was a total failure to respond in a meaningful way. There was a total failure to communicate on their behalf with the Governor. I would put it this way, trial and error and experience had taught the Aborigines that their way of life was successful therefore why change? They were the top predator. To date they had beaten all other predators. Furthermore, in hand-to-hand combat, the Aborigine was the better warrior. Aborigines had the self-assurance of an aggressor. A more generous white man perhaps, would have agreed with them, but he would have added the proviso, yes, you win and prosper, but you are pagans suckled in a creed outworn.[46] I doubt very much that the Aborigines of the time would have accepted that analysis of their way of life and as a consequence the rebuttal would have been a spear or a nulla nulla. My view is that each side was entrenched in their positions of self-justification and that each side believed they had right on their side. Therefore, collisions took place between settlers and Aborigines as Governor FitzRoy described them.

I do not, for one moment, accept that the conflict between the settlers or indeed, the government of the day and the Aborigines even when it became physical and involved killing people, black or white, was a war of any kind. First of all, the government did not have a policy of aggression against the Aborigines and did its best to discourage it and, on one occasion, took the executive steps necessary to have accused white persons charged with the murder of Aborigines, tried and on conviction, hanged. However much, historians may wish to downplay this event, I

45 See Reynolds, *The Other Side of the Frontier*, UNSW Press 2006 for an alternative view, p 120. Also note, in 1831, thirteen chiefly rangatira from the north island of the NZ met at Kerikeri and sent a letter to King William IV asking for help to guard their lands.

46 I am not referring to religions. I am referring to a way of life, society, or lifestyle.

believe it signalled a significant warning to all whites that taking the law into their own hands when dealing with Aborigines was done at their own peril. I hasten to add; did whites think badly of Aborigines? Yes. Did they agitate for their removal? Yes. Did they agitate for the control and regulation of Aborigines? Yes. And did they seek to have Aborigines punished for breaches of white man's law? Yes.

What about the Aborigines, did they make war? There is a consensus among many historians, who might be categorised as left-wing, who argue they did?[47] I cannot warrant that the Aborigines did not have in their mind conflict against the white settlers. What conflict resolution strategies did the Aborigines have? On the face of it, Aborigines saw violence as the one and only way to resolve conflict[48] and from the point of view of efficiency, violence is swift and final; attributes most arbiters see as desirable. Whether it was fair and equitable is perhaps not relevant that far back in time; it took the English legal system a long time to develop the jurisprudence of Equity. It is one thing to be an armchair freedom fighter. Terrorists are not backyard amateurs but highly skilled operatives, consider 9/11. Compare and contrast Pearl Harbour with 9/11. 9/11 is remarkable because the perpetrators used American hardware to attack and destroy American assets on the American homeland. How brazen was that? Firstly, Aborigines had no surplus (food or weapons), no bureaucracy, no inventory, no strategy, no high command, no order of battle, no troops, and no transport; you can whistle Dixie all you like and play the trumpet till ya blue in the face but there was no warfare. Frederick Walker gave this example of aboriginal tactics: "The blacks being on the ranges attempted to kill them by throwing stones down on the dismounted police but these missiles, however unpleasant to whites under such circumstances, are perfectly harmless when used against the Native Police." How Palaeolithic can one get? The killing of whites by

---

47 Unhealthy political correctness amongst this group appears to have caused them perhaps, to unfairly oppose research that disputes their own ideas about the history of aborigines and so called white violence.

48 In the Arnhem Land, we have been documenting rare depictions of fighting and are able to show that there has been a long tradition of warrior art. Taçon, P. and Chippindale, C. (1994) Australia's Ancient Warriors: Changing Depictions of Fighting in the Rock Art of Arnhem Land, N.T., Cambridge Archaeological Journal, 4(2), pp. 211–248.

Aborigines was idiosyncratic: breach of contract, tribal law, payback, food, murder, pleasure, revenge, insults, self-defence, trespass, accidentally, to obtain goods, and maybe, other reasons still unknown. They gave the appearance of fighting a war because it was done on their terms, and as I have said, in a one-on-one situation, most white men had no chance whatsoever against marauding Aborigines. As they were British subjects and their actions had no meaningful policy behind them, they were seen therefore as acts of violence by the individual and thus amenable to civil authority namely the police. Aborigines were never a threat to Her Britannic Majesty's government at Westminster, they were never a threat to the Government Resident at Moreton Bay and they were never a threat to the Governor in Sydney. On the borders of the unsettled districts, they could skirmish, hold corroborees, sing and kill and mutilate whites and their livestock to their heart's content, and that was the limit of it. Left-wing authors write romanticised historical works about heroic aboriginal battles akin to Marathon which according to these authors were regularly waged with the white foe being driven off and aboriginal borders re-secured. This heady mixture of boys' own triumphs and dastardly whites wiping out whole tribes in reprisals could, if not watched carefully, lead to the whites taking Australia by conquest. That would put an end to native title if this view ever became the received consensus of aboriginal resistance to colonisation. These battles need to be toned down. Let us assume for the sake of argument that they did conduct a war. They certainly conducted a no holds-barred campaign. Of course, the apologists will counter with the tit for tat rule. However most importantly, the Aborigines never attempted a settlement of any kind in which they set out their demands and or their grievances. In other words, the Aborigines threw away an opportunity to respond to the white invitation to grow and prosper with the white expansion. Let us now look at how it was resolved? If it was war, then the only category that Aborigines could fall into was that of a belligerent making them enemies of the Queen and beyond the reach of British domestic law. Furthermore, my view is that if there was a war, a state of armed conflict, then the Aborigines lost the war and as a result became prisoners and forfeited any territory they may have held. If that is the case, then the rhetoric about the history of Aborigines from the time of the settlement of Australia by Australians becomes even more prone to woolly thinking than it already is. Some may argue that my approach ignores the reality and is based on a definitional approach: if the Aborigines by definition had no conceptual and organisational capacity to wage war, then there was no war. Unlike most commentators, I have tendered my evidence, see Chapter 11. The ability to make war comprehends an ability to make peace and secure one's national integrity and borders by treaty. Aborigines, in my view, never sued for peace, each group learning nothing from their collective experience of dealing with white settlers. Their actions were a meaningless destruction of settlers' assets. By meaningless I mean, not amenable to analysis, without policy, random and opportunistic, criminal in nature.

If settlement was, as I argue, one of gradual exchange which I call the Cook exchange, then it is a process that involved first giving the Aborigines the protection of the British domestic law and trying to reach an accommodation with them in their adjusting to the colonial economy and its rules and regulations. It was not the old confrontationist approach of who owns that particular piece of land, where the first person says, "I want this land." The second person says, "No, you can't have it, it's mine." The first-person replies, "Where did you get it?" The answer, "From my father." "Where did he get it?" "From his father." "Where did he get it?" "From his father." "Where did he get it?" "He fought for it." "Well, I'll fight you for it."

I have postulated elsewhere that the aboriginal culture endemic to Australia prior to white settlement was clearly a Palaeolithic hunter-gatherer society which, as a consequence of no real challenges, remained in a cultural stasis for something like 65,000 years. However, when challenged by European settlement, failed to respond to the challenge and faded away. This hypothesis in itself would be sufficient but certain historians, in reviewing the settlement of Australia, are asserting that it was a brutal form of genocide, and one rather much abused indicator employed by this school of thought is to showcase the alleged genocide by constructing crude causality lists. Now you cannot have a causality list unless you have a population, and given that these historians use modern anachronistic terms and concepts like total war[49] then one must go beyond combatant numbers to population figures. The logic is simple,

---

[49] Including germ warfare by use of the smallpox; a recent novel vector has been alleged, chicken pox.

if the native population can be shown to be high then the constructed causality lists will be high also and thus give the impression of uncontrolled aggression against the "legitimate defenders of their territory". When looking at the Palaeolithic hunter-gatherer certain characteristics remain fixed, a short lifespan, say, a median age of 35 years for men and 30 years for women;[50] the best explanation for the relatively short [Palaeolithic] lifespan is the combination of stresses of nomadism, climate, and tribal warfare. One other dynamic in Palaeolithic populations is that such populations have a low-density rate per square kilometres of tribal territory. In other words, animal reproduction rates in the wild determine or influence the density rate of the hunting population living at one person per x square kilometres. Whether hunters needed a margin of safety (not over hunting) is another issue, further limiting density rates. Moreover, it would seem to me that aboriginal society appeared to have been rather stable, putting aside the Bradshaws, the last Ice Age[51] and the extinction of the megafauna; if so, then population densities throughout the continent must never have risen to a level where the society became threatened by an ever-expanding population which in turn would have produced a response to this challenge and created either a ruling elite or some other form of society or perhaps extinction.[52] The population must have always remained static and at a low level of density thus never threatening the abundant supply of food available and what appears to be the leisurely effort needed to obtain it.[53]

After looking at the literature, there seems to be a lot of high rollers out there and to date they appear to have taken over the craps table. Without canvassing the field, there is the received wisdom of John Mulvaney who estimated the pre-1788 Aborigine population at 800,000 and a reduced population of 200,000 at 1890. That is a solid kill rate of 75% of the population, impressive by any standards. Now it doesn't stop there.

Professor Ben Kiernan is director of the Genocide Studies Program

---

50 This would mean low birth rates; Morrill says, *very few children, seldom exceeding four*, 17 Years Wandering Among the Aborigines.

51 *Journal of Archaeological Science,* Volume 40, Issue 12, December 2013, pp 4612-4625.

52 Perhaps like Rapa Nui.

53 *Stone Age Economics* by Marshall Sahlins, Aldine Atherton Inc, 1972.

at Yale University. He argues (2002:177) that "the Aboriginal rights issue emerged slowly against a backdrop of genocide". He notes that the Aboriginal population is estimated to have fallen from 750,000 in 1788 to 31,000 by 1911, with most deaths due to introduced diseases, but, according to historian Henry Reynolds, with perhaps another 20,000-killed resisting white occupation between 1788 and 1901."[54]

Others have argued that by 1933 the population had fallen to either 117,000 or 70,000. Take ya pick. Within this period, the reader is asked to accept that the major killer is not the usual suspects such as white diseases and substances of addiction together with low reproduction rates but gun play on the part of the whites and their hired gunslingers, the Native Police. In this regard, you have a choice, Mr Reynolds with a causality list of dead from the range warfare of 20,000 or Mr Ørsted-Jensen, with a causality list of 65,000 dead. These figures are listed as murders. They seem so absurd that I have had difficulty in accepting them as sane and reasoned conclusions from, it is said, empirical historians writing an archivally based narrative.[55] My point is this, if smallpox and other diseases reduced the Aboriginal population to 200,000 or lower by 1890 and white diseases continued to not only kill Aborigines but reduce their birth rate significantly, then there cannot have been a population pool big enough for the whites to have gone out and intentionally shot Aborigines on a continuous basis. The numbers were simply not there to sustain this level of killing, which is extremely inefficient because the victims did not expose themselves to such activity voluntarily.

It might be as well to take a break from the morbidity and mortality figures and reflect on the following:

> Historian David Henige has argued that many population figures are the result of arbitrary formulas selectively applied to numbers

54 *Aboriginal Australia*: An Economic History of Failed Welfare Policy Laura Davidoff and Alan Duhs University of Queensland June 2008 p 5.

55 "I think we have to allow the possibility of such arguments, in Australia as well as Germany and the former Soviet Union, though it is clear that legitimate revision can tilt over to offensive apologetics." Macintyre, Stuart, 'On 'fabricating' history', *Evatt Journal*, Vol. 3, No. 4, June 2003. Macintyre is pulling the old chestnut out by calling his opponents Holocaust deniers; an honest and accurate review of history is legitimate.

> from unreliable historical sources. He believes this is a weakness unrecognized by several contributors to the field, and insists there is not sufficient evidence to produce population numbers that have any real meaning. He characterizes the modern trend of high estimates as "pseudo-scientific number-crunching." Henige does not advocate a low population estimate, but argues that the scanty and unreliable nature of the evidence renders broad estimates inevitably suspect, saying "high counters" (as he calls them) have been particularly flagrant in their misuse of sources.[56]

There are of course, lower, aboriginal population figures such as, pre-1788 of 300,000[57] and 150,000 by 1908.[58] These figures give poor kill rates when a balance has to be made between disease and firearm deaths by whites and their allies. I will try to deal with the firearm deaths of Aborigines elsewhere in the book but at this point I will briefly deal with the effect of introduced diseases. It is beyond question that contact between the First Fleeters and the Aborigines would have led to infectious diseases overtaking the Aborigines and reducing their numbers significantly. The principal pathogen has been identified as smallpox and I see no need to challenge that and other pathogens would have equally contributed to the mortality and decline of the Aborigine population together with the knock-on effect of low reproduction rates.[59] The main epidemic for Aborigines is said to be the time of the First Fleet and then a further outbreak in the Bathurst area in 1828-1830. The main culprit for the outbreak, of course, has to be the English. Much effort has gone into proving how they carried out their clandestine biological warfare but it appears to me that the pedlars of this school of thought are like all dumb cops, who look no further than the ever-present rule of thumb, the killer is always a known associate of the deceased, voila, the English. It was in fact those damn Frenchies who were anchored at Botany Bay immedi-

---

56 https://en.wikipedia.org/wiki/Population_history_of_indigenous_peoples_of_the_Americas

57 1930 Yearbook.

58 1908 Yearbook.

59 There is a theory that female aborigines were sought and traded by the low or criminal classes of the Colony as their only sexual outlet. This resulted in these women, on occasion, in returning to their tribes being killed by the tribe. The net effect would be to reduce reproductions rates even further.

ately after the arrival of the First Fleet, who infected the Aborigines with smallpox.[60] A rather more elaborate theory has been put abroad by Judy Campbell which appears to have a good deal of credibility about it.[61]

The following two surveys suggest to me that Australia never had a large population of Aborigines for the obvious reasons that reproduction rates would have been very low not only because of low fertility issues but also because of the hair-trigger nature of aboriginal society to resort to violence to resolve all disputes, both male and female. Lancelot Edward Threlkeld, Ebenezer, Lake Macquarie, NSW, wrote to the Colonial Secretary, 30 December 1837 as follows:

> The disappearance of so many of the Blacks, in this District, induced me to address a letter to His Excellency the Governor, stating the circumstance, and requesting the loan of the Official Returns of the Black Natives throughout the Colony, for the years 1835, 1836 and 1837, in order to ascertain whether the decrease was merely local, or general.
> An ABSTRACT from the Official General Returns of the Black Natives, taken at the Annual Distribution of the Government Donation of Blankets, to each Tribe, within the four divisions of the Colony, for the Years 1835, 1836, 1837.
>
> | | |
> |---|---|
> | South and South Western District, from Sydney to Twofold Bay | 422 |
> | Western District, Bathurst, Wellington Valley | 127 |
> | North and North Western District, from Sydney to Port Macquarie | 1220 |
> | Home District, Sydney and Windsor inclusive | 825. |
>
> Total Individuals 1835 — 2094;
> 1836 — 1528;
> 1837 — 1531.
>
> The last, but not the least, cause to mention, as occasioning the rapid diminution of the Aborigines of this Territory, is far above the control of mortal man, and not confined to the limits of the Colony. He who "increaseth the nation," or "destroys that there shall be no inhabitant," has visited the Land; and the Measles, the Hopping-cough, and the Influenza, have stretched the Black victims in hundreds on the earth, until, in some places, scarcely a

60 It was generally accredited by the Medical Gentlemen of the Colony on its first establishment, that the smallpox had been introduced among the Natives by the crews of the French ships then lying in Botany Bay. *Sydney Gazette* 14 October 1804 p 2.

61 *Invisible Invaders*, Judy Campbell MUP 2002.

Tribe can be found.[62]

The Guardian of Aborigines, 27 March 1854 published the following returns, "Aborigines in Portland Bay District 31 December 1853 — 599; Gippsland number of Aborigines 1843 — 1800, 1853 — 131 and February 1854 — 126; Yarra tribe 1852 — 39, 1853 — 36; Western Port tribe 1852 — 20, 1853 — 17."[63]

Large populations mean either a very large area to range over or the opposite, concentration in small areas. The paradigm does not fit either. If large rivers such as the Nile, Tigris-Euphrates, Indus and Yellow saw the beginning of civilisations, then, perhaps the Murray-Darling may have been conducive to a concentration of Aborigines and some form of intensification of living conditions, not so. Concentration brings some form of social control and regulation in an organisational sense. The Aborigines of the day had no such skills or concepts.[64] Furthermore, perhaps Dunbar's number may also have been a limiting factor in keeping populations low. The 1849 State of Aborigines report for the District of Lower Darling recorded as follows: "Estimated numbers 1500, in eight tribes residing chiefly in the Dumosa scrub at the back of the Lachlan; identical with blacks on the Upper Darling."[65] The following report also lends weight to this theory: "the Commissioner of Crown Lands, Mr Rolleston, advised the number of aboriginal tribes in the Darling Downs District: 7 tribes (Upper and Lower Condamine, Gowrie, Jimbour, Mooney, Lower Macintyre and the Severn River), 100-150 in each tribe, uppermost of 1000 altogether."[66] The following may add a dimension to the debate about aboriginal population densities in Australia (excluding Tasmania and Torres Strait):

---

62 Report of the Mission to the Aborigines at Lake Macquarie, New South Wales., December 30, 1837, Original Documents on Aborigines and Law, 1797-1840 (Online Resrouce: http://www.law.mq.edu.au

63 *Letter from Victorian Pioneers*, Ed by TF Bride LLD, Government Printer Melbourne 1898, pp 79-80.

64 "He went on to explain they had no written language and made guttural sounds with limited expression. They couldn't teach their language only by imitation and memory assisted by their wants." James Morrill, op cit.

65 QSL Reel A2.20 p 361.

66 QSL Reel A2.22 p 407.

According to Mr Parker's estimate, by a census, taken partly in 1843, and partly in 1844, the total number of the Aborigines throughout the District west of the River Goulburn is 1522. This District runs westward to the South Australian frontier and north from Mount Macedon and Mount William to the Murray. The tribes on the banks of the Murray, still very numerous, are not included. Mr Watton, in the district or country around Mount Rouse, comprising about 20,000 square miles, estimates the numbers of the Aborigines at 2,000. That proportion of the territory of New South Wales that may in a general sense he termed "occupied," extends over an area of about 320,000 square miles, and may be estimated to contain about 15,000 Aborigines. Allowing 80,000 square miles of this area to Port Philip, and assuming Mr Robinson's estimate of 5,000 Aborigines, there will be one Aboriginal inhabitant to each 16 square miles (41.44 square kilometres) for that District, and 1 to 24 for the remainder of the colony; the average for all New South Wales being one Aboriginal inhabitant to 21⅓ square miles (55.25 km^2). Considerable numbers of the Aborigines were met with by Dr Leichhardt and his party on their route to Port Essington, more particularly throughout Northern Australia. The banks of the rivers of that locality appeared comparatively well inhabited, and the travellers encountered native fisheries, numerous wells of fresh water, and the remains of vegetable food prepared for preservation. Captain Sturt gives an interesting account of numerous tribes of Aborigines which he met with towards the central regions of Australia, thickly planted along the grassy banks of a large creek, the bed of which was about the size of the Darling. Judging from the comparatively numerous Aboriginal population in the earlier years of the colony, the present average ratio of Aboriginal inhabitants to extent of territory for the entire Australian continent might be anticipated greatly to exceed the very slender estimate, above, given for New South Wales. But the explorations of Captain Sturt, Mr Eyre, and other travellers, have made known the existence of such extensive tracks of sterile country, throughout central and Northwest Australia that it may be doubted if that estimate can be much exceeded.[67]

The Mulvaney pre-1788 population estimate gives a density of 3.2

67 *Geelong Advertiser and Squatters' Advocate* 26 August 1846 p 1.

Aborigine per 20 square kilometres[68]; on the other hand, a pre-1788 population of 300,000 gives a density rate 1.2:20 km^2. I have taken a view that the Aborigines were few in number and never over exploited their environment and lived in a relatively modest way with an entrenched mindset of not disturbing the status quo, inimical to change.[69] Of course, I like the high rollers cannot speak for the devastation brought about by cyclones and droughts that must have afflicted Australia from time immemorial.

68 800,000 divided by Australian mainland of 5,000,000 km^2 excluding deserts = .16:1 km^2 or 3.2:20 km^2.

69 I am corroborated as follows: "Kangaroos have developed a number of adaptations to a dry, infertile country and highly variable climate. … females will only conceive if enough rain has fallen to produce a large quantity of green vegetation."

2

Native Police

What precise factors or events caused or persuaded Governor FitzRoy to establish a Native Police presence in the Clarence River, Darling Downs, and beyond the district of Wellington, I suppose we will never know. In his message to the Council of 8 June 1848,[70] he said, "certain collisions, in parts beyond the settled districts, between the white inhabitants and the Aborigines, appeared to him to require immediate steps to be taken for their suppression." These collisions were not identified nor were they particularised as to the nature and type of collisions, nor any particulars regard loss of life, personal injury or property loss or damage to either side. The newspapers of the day related a number of incidents involving clashes between whites and Aborigines which may be examples of FitzRoy's collisions as they involved the death of whites and blacks and substantial loss and damage to the property of white settlers.[71]

The next step in the process was to pick an officer to lead this small corps of native police. However, for those who glean the long-abandoned fields of history, it can be slim pickings at times; therefore, one needs to be all the more mindful of the quality of the finds in the quest for Frederick Walker. The reader might not be surprised to know that in the small population of the then colony of New South Wales, circa 1850s, there were many people who bore the surname, Walker but what has been surprising was the fact that at least four people by the name of Walker had a confluence of association with the northern Native

70 See Chapter 11 for the full text.

71 Aboriginal casualties were not given because traditional identifiers such as name, tribe, etc. were unknown.

Police: Richard Walker[72], Frederick Walker, Robert George Walker and Alexander Walker. On occasion, researchers have lost concentration and confused or unintentionally missed the fact that they were dealing with the wrong Walker thus attributing all sorts of grandiose and fanciful antecedents to Frederick. The Walkers were not related either by blood or by association. The most common error is to confuse and mix the life and times of Richard with Frederick's.

There is no discoverable background as to how or why Frederick Walker was appointed as commandant of this small force other than the following:

> Our first notice of Mr Walker dates many years' back, when he was clerk of the court at Deniliquin. Indeed, you may say he was police magistrate and everything, being the most able and active man there. At that period the blacks were giving great trouble. They had extensive swamps filled with reeds in which to retreat when pursued by the settlers. A large party was at last organised, and Mr Walker showed such aptitude for command upon one occasion that he was by common consent made leader in-chief. By his exertions, the blacks were rendered quiet, and the stations in those parts were no more molested. It struck Mr A. Morris, then the owner of Callandoon, that native police such as had previously been established in Victoria, was the only force which would be serviceable, and he determined that Mr Walker, his old friend in the south country, was the best man to organise such a corps. Through the influence of Mr Charles Wentworth everything was arranged, and Mr Walker was appointed.[73]

Whatever the truth of the matter, it is on the record and was made almost contemporaneously with the events themselves, thus, its credibility must stand unchallenged. Perhaps the statement can be enhanced with the following observations. The Sydney papers show that on 13 August 1844, the barque *Ceylon*, 253 tons, Beazley, master, arrived from London

---

72 Richard Walker appears to have been a prisoner of the Crown and obtained a Ticket of Leave from 30 August 1844 while located at Maitland, Murrurundi, County of Wellington, NSW Gazette 3 September 1844 p 1095 and died 1857 at Surat, see NSW BDM 4464/1857.

73 Taken from a piece that appeared in the *Empire* 6 February 1865 p 3.

with general cargo and passengers, one of whom was F Walker.[74] Moreover, the Commissioner of Crown Lands, Murrumbidgee, NSW, Henry Bingham filed a return of the Border Police for the period 1 January to 31 December 1845, which recorded "Frederick Walker as a full constable appointed from 1 April 1844 by the authority of the Governor @ 3/- per day; period of service 1 January to 1 April 1845."[75] The learned Editors of the *Tumut and District Sesqui Centenary* booklet opined: "1845 A proclamation in the Government gazette set up the first Court House with Frederick Walker as Clerk of Petty Sessions."[76] The facts are that the NSW gazette of 22 December 1846 appointed Tumut as a place for the holding of Courts of Petty Sessions from 21 December 1846 and that Mr Walker was appointed Clerk on 5 January 1847.[77]

His Excellency the Governor appointed Frederick Walker, Esq., to be Commandant of the corps of Native Police, to be employed beyond the settled districts, in the Sydney district on 17 August 1848.[78] More surprising than this, is the fact that he was sworn in as an ordinary constable at the Police-office, Brisbane on 8 February 1848.[79] As if this was not enough in the way of appointments, he was appointed a magistrate on 4 August 1848[80] and a Justice of the Peace on 25 October 1851.

There were not, it appears, at this early stage of the development of Walker's Native Police any regulations, directives, rules of engagement, establishment statements or organisational charts. On 24 April 1849, Mr Walker, Commandant of Native Police, arrived at Warialda with a party of native police, after a journey of eleven hundred miles from the Ed-

---

74 *The Australian* 14 August 1844 p 2, *SMH* 14 August 1844 p 2, *The Weekly Register of Politics, Facts and General Literature* 17 August 1844 p 87, *The Shipping Gazette and Sydney General Trade List* 17 August 1844 p 150 & *The Dispatch* 17 August 1844 p 3.

75 SRNSW MFL [4/7321]. Perhaps he was recruited in the UK.

76 *Tumut and district sesqui centenary* Editors: R.H. Graham and H.D. Watson 1974 p 23; who appear to have got it wrong.

77 Government Gazette, 5 January 1847, Mr Frederick Walker appointed Clerk of Petty Sessions, Tumut; and also, at a later date, 30 April 1847, Wagga Wagga.

78 Government Gazette 18 August 1848 N° 89 p 1033.

79 *The Moreton Bay Courier (MBC)* 19 February 1848 p 2.

80 Government Gazette 8 August 1848.

ward River. Mr Walker found the large tribes of blacks on the Darling very friendly, with the exception of a few, who attempted to murder two of the troopers, 100 miles below Fort Bourke. It seems the policemen were looking for their horses, when two of them, named Geegwaw and Larry, encountered twelve blacks, who at first appeared friendly, but on a sudden one of them attempted to wrench the carbine out of Geegwaw's hands, and another threw a jagged spear at Larry, who had no carbine with him; Larry caught the spear, and immediately killed the black who was attacking Geegwaw. Most fortunately at this moment Mr Walker came up, with four more troopers, who immediately shot four of the hostile blacks. During the last three hundred miles of their journey the horses of the troopers were much distressed and exhausted for want of grass and water, owing to the continued drought, and some of the horses died. The last two hundred miles the party travelled on foot; and for seventeen days were without rations of any kind, and had to subsist on emus, kangaroos, native dogs, and sometimes fish and ducks.

The extent of the destruction of stock and other property on the Macintyre River can indeed only be estimated. Many valuable flocks and herds, which were taken there at a considerable expense to the owners, owing to the wanton ravages of the blacks, were dispersed in all directions throughout the country and could not be recovered nor restored to the rightful owners. Cattle that were rushed and speared have a dread of remaining on or returning to the runs where they have suffered.

Police information from the Macintyre revealed that the blacks had killed five head of cattle belonging to Mr Jonathan Young, and sent him notice that they were preparing another attack. He applied to the constables, and some of his neighbours joined him. The police party came up with a body of the blacks, but the only one they got near was the notorious Gibber, who murdered Mr Marks's boy some time ago, and also Mr Yeomans's bullock driver. For this man, they had a warrant, and they called to him repeatedly to stand, but Gibber would not, and came in contact with Mr Marshall of the Native Police whom he knocked from his horse senseless to the ground with his nulla nulla; Gibber was of course quickly despatched. The Police described him as the fiercest looking savage they had ever seen, standing full six feet high; on one foot, he had no toes, and on the other only two, of a peculiar form, like claws.[81]

No sooner had Walker taken up his position on the Condamine, then he became operational against the blacks for attacks on cattle. He went in pursuit and succeeded in defeating the combined blacks from the Lower Condamine, Fitzroy Downs, and the Dawson; the latter being the same who had murdered Mr A. Campbell's man. An idea may be formed of the force of the hostile blacks, from the size of their camp, where there were upwards of eighty "gunyas" of bark, besides many blacks camped without cover. Certain intelligence was obtained that the above party and a large number of Condamine blacks had congregated on Charley's Creek; they were to join up on Dogwood Creek, upwards of 200 warriors; and from there they were to proceed to attack the stations of Messrs Edwards, and Chauvel and Blyth. Mr Walker in consequence called on the squatters for assistance.[82]

Notwithstanding Walker's presence on the Condamine, the blacks broke out on the Burnett River and Wide Bay districts where they murdered a shepherd in the employment of Mr Archibald Campbell. The natives also attacked the station of Mr Taylor, and drove away all the men, who took refuge at the station of Mr Percival Stephen. The huts on the station were burned to the ground, and ten bales of wool, the property of Mr Thomas Windeyer, utterly consumed. Mr Windeyer was preparing to proceed in quest of the outlaws and was about to mount his horse for that purpose, when by some accident his gun exploded, and the contents lodged in the unfortunate gentleman's thigh, shattering the bone. Application had been made to Mr Walker for the assistance of the Native Police, but the Commandant had not felt at liberty to comply with the request.[83] Mr Walker, with the Native Police, had visited some of the stations on the Dawson, and had been very useful in restoring a degree of confidence to the labourers in that quarter, but still the real or affected dread of the blacks had the effect of making labour very scarce and dear.[84] The squatters all speak in high terms of Mr Walker's indefati-

81 *The Maitland Mercury and Hunter River General Advertiser* (*Maitland Mercury*) 9 May 1849 p 2.

82 *MBC* 22 September 1849 p 3.

83 *MBC* 8 September 1849 p 2.

84 *MBC* 13 October 1849 p 3.

gable exertions. It was argued in some quarters, given the size of the area, instead of one, there should be three parties, at least, of the same force, which might act in concert and thus intimidate the blacks.[85] Then to the west of Walker's headquarters at Callandoon, the blacks attacked the station of Mr Ogilvy on the Balonne, spearing his cattle, and dispersing them all over the country. On the same river, Mr Hall, out of a herd of 5000, could scarcely muster 2000.[86]

In view of Mr Walker's early success, *The Sydney Morning Herald* did a feature on him:

> The Sydney division, which has hitherto consisted of sixteen men, is to be increased to forty-six. The force is now in the country on the banks of the Macintyre, Condamine, and Dawson, in command of Mr R. P. Marshall,[87] Lieutenant of the first division. Mr Walker, the Commandant, and Mr Fulford, who has just been appointed Lieutenant of the second division, proceed in a few days to the Murrumbidgee, for the purpose of enlisting thirty additional men.
>
> We understand that the greatest benefits have accrued to the districts in which this force, small as it is in number, has been located. Where but a year since the shepherds dare scarcely leave their huts, and every person went about armed for fear of the blacks, all is now as quiet and settled as in the districts that have been occupied these twenty years, and it is now very uncommon to meet a person armed even when he is travelling from station to station. Much of the success that has attended the experiment in this district is doubtless to be attributed to the personal character of the commandant, Frederick Walker, Esq. Mr Walker has been in the colony about nine years, nearly the whole of which time he has passed in the bush, and having always been kind to the blacks, he soon won their confidence. He was recommended to the Government by several gentlemen who were acquainted with his character and habits, and his appointment as Commandant was certainly a most fortunate one.
>
> The whole of the sixteen men who were first enrolled are now

85 *MBC* 20 October 1849 p 2.

86 *MBC* 29 December 1849 p 4.

87 Marshall and Fulford both appointed Gov. Gazette, 8 January 1850.

> in the force. Their pay is three-pence a day, rations and clothing. Their clothes resemble the undress cavalry uniform. We consider the well working of this corps to be most important, not only as regards its efforts as a body of police for the far interior, but also in a philanthropic point of view, as it appears to hold out more hopes of permanently civilizing the natives, than any experiment that has yet been tried. The headquarters are to be at Callandoon, on the Macintyre River.[88]

In fact, the Native Police consisted of the commandant, two officers, and one sergeant, Thomas Whitmill, and forty-four troopers; Callandoon, on the Macintyre, became the headquarters, and of the two detachments, one on the frontier of the Wide Bay and Burnett districts, and the other on the Lower Condamine.[89] To recruit additional troopers, Walker, escorted by two black troopers, returned to the Murrumbidgee in early 1850, where he proceeded to enlist thirty sable recruits.[90]

Matters still remained unsettled in the Wide Bay and Burnett districts with the blacks murdering two men on Dr Ramsay's station called Cockatoo and also spearing the overseer and driving off about a hundred sheep.[91] In the following fortnight, a coolie shepherd, in the employment of Mr G. Sandeman, at Burrandowan was killed while out with his sheep, having been found speared in the back of the neck, and afterwards tomahawked. As the body was not stripped, nor any of the sheep taken away, the murder is believed to have been caused by revenge for the deceased having ordered some of the natives from his hut on the previous day, when they had been importuning him for flour, and upon which occasion they showed much violent conduct. Mr Haly's station had also been twice robbed of sheep by the natives. The press said that the settlers were crying loudly for the native police and declared that they would resist payment of the money from which the native police were maintained if their wants were not promptly attended to[92] and a third memorial, soliciting speedy protection by the native police of the Burnett distinct,

---

88 *SMH* 10 January 1850 p 2.

89 *MBC* 12 January 1850 p 4.

90 *The Goulburn Herald and County of Argyle Advertiser* 9 February 1850 p 5.

91 *MBC* 6 April 1850 p 3.

92 *MBC* 20 April 1850 p 2.

had been transmitted to his Excellency the Governor.

The Native Police, commanded by Lieutenant Marshall, went in pursuit of the blacks who had committed aggressions among the cattle for the last three months, (though for sheep and human life there appeared to be no fear). After following their tracks for four days, they came up with them in the neighbourhood of the Yulebah, or Horse-track River, where an engagement took place, when the natives were dispersed with some loss.[93] Press reports of the time suggested that on the Lower Condamine the blacks in that locality were now quiet. Stock of all kinds was doing well, for although rain was wanted in that part of the country generally, the herbage had vigorously withstood the long drought. There had been no sickness this season and those in want of stations could find good ones on the Lower Condamine. Furthermore, Mr Marshall and his corps of Native Police had returned to headquarters, for a refit and pay.[94]

Walker reported to the Colonial Secretary on 17 December 1849, what he considered the most efficient mode of making use of the Native Police force. This communication was tabled in the Legislative Council and then published by the press in June 1850.[95] His letter of 31 December 1849 to the Colonial Secretary on recruiting further volunteers for the Native Police in southern NSW was also tabled and published.[96]

The following accolade from the press must have lightened the load on the government over aboriginal depredations on the Macintyre and Condamine areas as well as having placed a feather in the cap of Walker.

> FEW more satisfactory documents have been laid before the Council than the report from Commandant Walker of the proceedings of the native police force of the Middle District since its formation, which we copied into last Wednesday's Mercury. The brief, business-like record of the proceedings of this corps, from its arrival at the Macintyre on the 10th of May 1849, to the close of last year, discloses an amount of service that is almost incredible, looking at the numerical strength of the force employed. The

93 *MBC* 6 April 1850 p 2.

94 *MBC* 1 June 1850 p 2.

95 *SMH* 15 June 1850 p 3.

96 *MBC* 29 June 1850 p 4.

> value of the services thus rendered to the parties located on the Macintyre, Condamine, and other portions of our north-western border, can hardly be over-estimated. Life and property in those previously disorganised districts have been rendered comparatively secure; and although in the skirmishes which have taken place between the police and the natives, some life has been sacrificed, the presence on our borders of a police force adequate to repress outrage and punish crime, under the command of a right-minded and efficient officer, cannot fail to be eventually as beneficial to the Aborigines as to the whites. When the native police force is augmented to the extent contemplated, Mr Walker appears to feel no doubt that he will be able to maintain peace and order in the Macintyre and Darling Downs' districts, and to bring the districts of Wide Bay, Burnett, and Maranoa, to the same state. The services which Mr Walker last year rendered, with the limited force then under his command, is an excellent guarantee for the performance of all he now promises. The Government and Legislature have acted most judiciously in providing for this extension of the native police force. The experiment of employing the natives as a border police has so far succeeded to perfection. In proportion to its cost, this is decidedly the most efficient and the most useful corps in our police department: whatever defects there may be in the character of the Aborigines, they evidently possess the qualities requisite for forming a gallant, manageable, and efficient half-military police.[97]

Balanced against the above favourable report was the following:

> IN our last, we published from the Council Papers a letter from Mr Walker, Commandant of the Native Police, in which that gentleman, after detailing various services rendered by the corps under his command, notifies that "a lieutenant and twelve men" were to be stationed "on the borders of the Wide Bay and Burnett districts." The letter is dated in December last, and we gather that the writer was then about to proceed to the Murrumbidgee district, for the purpose of raising levies of men to reinforce his parties. Since the date of that letter, complaints of the depredations of the blacks have been most numerous in the Wide Bay and Burnett districts, and several atrocious murders have been committed; yet not a single trooper of the native police has yet made his appearance in either of those districts. If the harassed and goaded employers,

97 *Maitland Mercury* 22 June 1850 p 2.

> indignant and horror-stricken at the slaughter of their men and the plunder of their establishments, venture to form themselves into a special police for their mutual protection, they have the disagreeable consciousness that they may thereby subject themselves to the outcries of the fireside philanthropists, and to an indictment in the Supreme Court; besides the losses to which they are liable by the neglect of their more legitimate avocations while performing the duties of the police. The settlers are by no means desirous of undertaking an office so onerous and so dangerous, especially while they contribute largely towards the maintenance of an authorised force for the performance of such duties. Therefore, it is that they complain of being deprived of public protection, while they are prohibited from protecting themselves their complaint is founded on reason and justice, and we apprehend that it must be considered too serious in its character to be slighted by the Executive Government.[98]

Things may have quietened down somewhat by 15 June 1850, but a man named James McKirk, a shepherd in the employment of Mr John McMillan, was killed by the blacks. An inquiry was held at Callandoon on 13 June 1850 before Messrs Greenway, Morris and Marshall JPs and the following evidence taken:

> George Crawford of Mr John McMillan's Station having been duly sworn deposes: I am overseer to Mr John McMillan, the 10th Instant one of the shepherds named James McKirk went out in the morning as usual with his flock. The sheep returned at night without him. After dark, I and others made search that night for him without success. Next morning, the watchman reported to me that twenty-five sheep were missing from the flock. Previously to counting the sheep, we had gone in search of the man and found him dead at a distance of about one-half mile from the hut. The deceased was much marked and bruised about the head and had in particular one large cut in the left side of his head apparently made by a tomahawk. The deceased had also other serve cuts on his face and his throat bore the appearance of violent compression from hands, the marks of fingernails being very plain. His trousers were hanging down about his boots. When the deceased left the hut, he had on an old cabbage tree hat well down, a scotch

98 *MBC* 6 July 1850 p 2.

> twill shirt, a blue serge shirt, a waistcoat of crop barred patterns, a pair of braces, a pair of moleskin trousers and a pair of common boots almost new. He also took with him a musket with a flint lock. When the body of the deceased was found, there was nothing on it but the trousers and boots. The musket was missing and all the rest of the clothing. There having been rain during the previous night to our discovering the body, I could not see any tracks in the neighbourhood of the body. One of the shepherds reported to me that on the same day deceased was killed he had seen two blacks named Jerry and Tommy. The shepherds who made this report to me is named Denis Kelly. About three weeks before the death of deceased, he reported to me that his life had been threatened by the blackfellow, Tommy named above. Denis Kelly, Edward Carlet and Thomas Griffiths were with me when we discovered the body of deceased. The station of Mr John McMillan on which I am overseer and on which the above circumstances took place is situated on one of the branches of the Weir two miles above Mr John McGeachie's Station on that river. George Crawford. Sworn before us at Callandoon this thirteenth day of June 1850. CC Greenway JP, A Morris JP & RP Marshall JP.[99]

The news of this murder having reached the Lieutenant of the Native Police, he started for Mr McMillan's station. This was the second murder within the last four months, committed by the same blacks. But for the native police, there would be no living in this part of the country. It was admitted by all hands that no body of men ever did their duty with more untiring zeal. The settlers from the Darling Downs to Wide Bay were constantly looking forward to the arrival of the Commandant, with the recruits from the River Murray.[100] This longing for the Native Police was well founded when it was reported that upwards of 500 blacks were encamped about the boiling places during the season; but the abundant food they obtained did not appear to have had a good effect upon them, for when the operations of the establishments ceased, they took possession of the sheep belonging to the butchers, and helped themselves. The Chief Constable of Wide Bay, with the assistance of the inhabitants, succeeded in rescuing most of the stolen stock. The natives appeared most mischievous in the neighbourhood of Maryborough, where considerable

99 QSA Series ID14733/86141.

100 *MBC* 13 July 1850 p 3.

fears of their violence were entertained and equal fear of the consequences of firing upon them in self-defence. The resident magistrate had to send for the whole of the Maryborough police to protect his house, as the blacks had sent a message that they wanted possession.

Notwithstanding the high levels of anxiety, it was reported that Commandant Walker, with forty native troopers were camped at Bangallo Creek, Murray River, on the route northward to the Macintyre, on 13 June 1850. Walker had been detained until 6 May waiting the receipt of accoutrements and clothing for his men, and on 13 May he started, having only taken seven days to accustom the horses to carry carbines and swords, dress and break in the men, &c. About the middle of September, Walker was expected to arrive at Callandoon, on the Macintyre with his party.[101] In the midst of all the activity, the government took the time to have the House vote for a £120 increase in the salary of the Commandant of the Native Police to £250 per annum, which passed without objection, and £500 for additional expenses for that corps.[102] During this laborious wait for the native police, the following murders were committed, Mr Gregory Blaxland,[103] of the firm of Forster and Blaxland by the aboriginal natives of the Burnett district. It appeared that the body of the deceased was discovered by his servants within two hundred yards of his head station; spear wounds and other marks of violence showing clearly that the unfortunate gentleman had met his death from the hands of the native blacks. Captain O'Connell, Commissioner of Crown Lands for the district, held an investigation, and came to the conclusion that the deceased had been treacherously murdered by the natives.[104] Then the murder of a shepherd named Dixon, from Mr J. S. Ferriter's station at Toomcul in the Burnett district, by the aboriginal natives. The unfortunate man was discovered buried beneath a log with his head completely smashed. His dog was found near him. The superintendent succeeded, by sending a dog round the sheep, in extricating about one half of the flock from the scrub where they had been secreted by the blacks.[105] The

---

101 *MBC* 29 July 1850 p 1.

102 *MBC* 27 July 1850 p 3.

103 He was the son of the Gregory Blaxland, 1778-1853.

104 *MBC* 31 August 1850 p 2.

105 *MBC* 14 December 1850 p 3.

native police reached the Upper Brisbane and Burnett just in time to meet a large assemblage of blacks, who had been driven from the Upper Burnett and Wide Bay and had commenced operations by killing a man at Colinton. Just the day before Commandant Walker with his troopers arrived at Mr Simon Scott's, the blacks had been amongst his fat wethers and driven a lot off. The men under the very prompt directions of the Commandant, were soon on their trail and came up with them, when, behold! There was a muster of about 300 poor innocent darkies. The little band of police, headed by their resolute Commandant, charged them, and the whole took to the scrub; but as soon as they reached it they showed battle, throwing their boomerangs and spears fast and thick. In spite of all, however, the troopers dismounted, drove the whole herd into the ridges, and recovered about fifty of the sheep. Nearly all the blacks that have been concerned in the murders in this and the surrounding neighbourhood were with this mob. Commandant Walker then proceeded to Wide Bay direct.[106]

It seemed to the press at the time that Walker presence in the Wide Bay district was not emphatic enough, for the press expressed regret to learn that the usefulness of that excellent corps was very much impaired by the great restrictions placed upon Mr Walker in his dealings with the lawless tribes of blacks, who had been assembled in large numbers to feast upon the bunya, and who spread themselves in all directions over the country in going to and returning form the bunya scrub. It was even anticipated by some as a probable contingency that the native police would have to be disbanded, if some greater discretion was not given to the officer in command; the nature and habits of the Aborigines rendered the procedure usually adopted by police officers against civilized whites impracticable and absurd in their cases. A strong representation on this subject was made to the Government.[107] Nevertheless, the Native Police continued their rounds to Mr Tooth's station, where the blacks had been spearing cattle, and then onto Mr Corfield's, where the blacks had again carried off some sheep.[108]

---

106 *MBC* 18 January 1851 p 2.
107 *MBC* 15 March 1851 p 2.
108 *MBC* 31 May 1851 p 3.

The western front appeared all quiet until it was reported that aboriginal natives in the pastoral district of Maranoa on 22 July 1851, amounting in number to four or five hundred, attacked the station of Mr Patrick McEnroe situated about twenty-seven miles from the station of the Commissioner of Crown Lands at Surat. The stock-keeper was out on the run and a man named John Carpenter, who was left in charge of the hut, observed that a native black woman, who had been in charge of the milking cows, turned them out of the stockyard and walked away herself, immediately afterwards, two native blacks appeared and caught hold of her. Carpenter went out with his gun, and walked towards the spot, when the blacks took shelter behind trees and he then returned towards his hut. At this moment, a native youth, called "Jemmy Hawk," who had been for some time living with the men at the hut, receiving his food from them in return for his services, called out to Carpenter not to be afraid, but to come on. At the same time about forty blacks appeared among the trees and while Carpenter was hastening to his hut, about fifteen or twenty more blacks jumped up from the creek on the other side of him and the whole of the natives pursued him to the hut. He succeeded, however, in reaching it and, having barricaded the door, opened the port-holes (which are usually made in huts on the frontiers, for the purpose of resisting the assaults of the natives), and laid the firearms on the table. From one of the port-holes he saw about five hundred blacks assembled on a ridge about a hundred and fifty yards from the hut. They were all fully armed and painted white. Carpenter levelled a gun and called upon them to stand off; but, after a short hesitation, they made a rush at the hut and surrounded it on all sides. They blocked up the port-holes before Carpenter had an opportunity of firing at them, but he stabbed one of them in the eye through a chink beside one of the holes. Finding that the blacks were now pressing upon the hut and observing that some of them were carrying off some meat, he fired and shot one dead. It appeared from the deposition of Carpenter that he was hardly[109] pressed, and with difficulty kept off the natives, some of whom climbed on to the roof of the hut, and set fire to the bark roofing. He kept firing at them as he could get an opportunity and shot four of them in all. The blacks then drew off to a distance of two or three hundred

109 Archaic, harshly.

yards, taking their dead and wounded with them, and the hutkeeper took advantage of the opportunity to extinguish the flames on the roof of the hut, when he heard a shot, and Charles Hunter, the stock-keeper, immediately afterwards came galloping in. It appeared that Hunter, on returning to the hut; had found about four or five hundred blacks around it, with a large lot of cattle and a horse amongst them. He immediately galloped towards them, and fired at them, and then hastened to the hut to ascertain the fate of Carpenter, who came out to meet him bringing the firearms. The hutkeeper required assistance to extinguish the fire, but Hunter was chiefly anxious to recover the horse from the blacks, as their escape depended upon that. Accordingly, he begged Carpenter to hold the hut for a short time and, charging the blacks amidst a shower of spears and boomerangs, succeeded in driving the horse from them to the hut where the other man mounted, and both rode off, leaving the hut in flames and the blacks in charge of the cattle. These facts were substantiated on oath before the Commissioner of Crown Lands, on the same day; a party was organized as soon as practicable to proceed in pursuit of the stolen cattle. The party followed the blacks and ascertained on their way that the cattle had been regularly slaughtered as they were required for use by the plunderers. The pursuers came up with the natives near the Grafton range and, after a conflict, in which four of the blacks were killed, succeeded in recovering 150 head of the cattle. Mr Walker, the commandant of the native police, had left Surat only the day before the attack was made on Mr McEnroe's station. He had a body of troopers with him and had done good service before leaving; but his horses were nearly exhausted, having travelled over from Wide Bay. As he had left Surat for Callandoon, a distance of about 120 miles, by a route not before traversed, it was considered useless to send after him.[110] Apparently, the native blacks, enraged at their late defeat and the re-capture of the stolen cattle were mustering in force, for the purpose of another attack and the few settlers in the district were taking such precautionary measures as they could for their protection.

To add to this never-ending catalogue of crime, another barbarous murder was committed by the aboriginal natives of the Burnett district. The victim was a Mr Street, who was depasturing some sheep of his

110 *MBC* 23 August 1851 p2.

own on Mr Trevethan's run. Mr Goode of the Burnett Inn gave details that the murdered man was beaten in a most barbarous manner by his murderers and that some of his sheep were driven off. Furthermore, the Aborigines drove away a flock of 1400 ewes from Mr Hay's station, and murdered the shepherd.[111] Then again, the aboriginal natives murdered a man, and his daughter about twelve years of age, on the station of Mr Wilkins, twelve miles from Gayndah. They re-commenced their old pranks of killing cattle and sheep in numbers, and the native police who ought to have been available to punish them, were most unwisely taken out of the district by their officers to Callandoon for the purposes of getting their clothing, a distance to and from at least 700 miles. There was strong public feeling against the Native Police and they were voted, as a body, worse than useless.[112]

In a debate on estimates in the House sometime in November 1851, the following observations were made:

> Mr Jones complained of inefficiency on the part of the police in the neighbourhood of Wide Bay and cited a letter in support of his assertion. It had been complained, he said, that these policemen, acting under some advice from the Attorney-General, refused to act in any case unless they had a warrant. The Aborigines of the north were a most numerous and powerful body, who required to be vigorously guarded against. They came in canoes and in large bodies from a place called the Big Sandy Island, across a sheet of water as smooth as Port Jackson. This island ought to be visited and examined.
>
> Mr Richardson thought that the last speaker must have been misinformed having always understood that this was a most efficient body of police. The only fault was that they were not sufficiently strong to cope with the aboriginal tribes.
>
> Mr Bigge also bore testimony to the efficiency of this body of police, particularly when the large tract of country over which they had to carry on their operations came to be borne in mind. The salary of the Commandant, he thought, ought to be made equal to that of the Provincial Inspectors of Police. At present, it was but £250.

111 *MBC* 6 September 1851 p3.

112 *MBC* 4 October 1851 p 2.

Mr Hughes likewise stated that the Native Police have proved very efficient. Depredations had taken place while the police were absent; but if there had been a sufficient body of them this could never have occurred. He had never before heard an imputation of inefficiency cast upon the Native Police, except an inefficiency arising from the smallness of their numbers.

Mr Wentworth also hoped that the salary of the Commandant would be increased to the same amount as that fixed for the Inspectors. The force was too small in its numbers. The proposed augmentation would increase the advantages accruing from the establishment, and would prove some safeguard to the troubled districts. He doubted not that the House would before long come to a conclusion in favour of a very large increase of this force, and an extension of its operations to those districts where, at present, there was but the ordinary constabulary.

The Attorney-General was glad to hear from so many members a confirmation of the belief which he had previously formed as to the efficiency of this body. He had given no opinion to this police different from that given to any other body. He had with his hon. colleague revised the code of regulations for the general bodies of police, and he was glad to perceive that these regulations were acting beneficially. In giving their opinions they could only act upon the law, and not change it.

Mr Jones had never meant to say that this police could not do their duty. What he meant was that, being under the impression that they were fettered by particular restrictions, they had shrunk from acting.

The Colonial Secretary said the corps had been a very useful one, and untrammelled with any such restrictions as were alluded to by the last speaker. They could not, however, act contrary to law, or make actual war upon the blacks, being bound to defend the latter as well as the whites. He admitted the merits of the Commandant, and it would be his duty to recommend to His Excellency the Governor-General the placing upon the estimates of a sufficient sum of money to meet the increase recommended by honourable members. (Hear, hear.) The sum moved for was then voted.[113]

113 *MBC* 6 December 1851 p 2.

Then disaster struck in the Burnett District, on or about late March 1852. The Aborigines re-commenced hostilities in this district, signalled by the death of Mr Adolphus H. Trevethan, one of the most extensive flock owners in the district. It appeared that the blacks turned up at the station in numbers, killed two Chinamen, and drove away 1700 sheep. Before Mr Trevethan was aware of this, they marched on the head station, some 500 strong, and with loud voices and gesticulations, demanded that Mrs Thompson, the wife of the overseer, should be given up to them. On this Mr Trevethan ran out of his hut, unarmed, to hold a parley. He was in the act of picking up some tobacco he had given them, which they threw with vengeance to the ground, when he was speared several times. The unfortunate man succeeded in getting back to his hut, where he expired after two hours. The blacks then drove away the whole of the rams, with the rest of the sheep. This station is the same as that on which Mr Street was killed some months ago. During last shearing, the blacks bailed up all the shearers and took the whole of their blankets, tea, sugar, quart and pint pots, and clothing away; the men not being able to resist for want of arms and ammunition. Rawbelle is not far from the headquarters of the Native Police, but unfortunately Lieutenant Murray with Isis division were out on the Dawson River, almost all to a man, from the Lieutenant downwards, were laid up with fever and ague. Lieutenant Marshall was at Ideraway with his division, his horses knocked up with excessive duty. Perhaps if greater resources had been available to the Native Police such as two horses for each trooper they may have been able to meet the heavy operational demand placed on them. The following is an eyewitness account of the Trevethan incident written by his nephew Richard Trevethan:

> Mr Street the settler was killed by the blacks. I was there for six weeks during which time the blacks attacked the station and took away some sheep, also some shearer's clothes but they did not kill anyone. A day later, 14 men, some on horseback and others walking. The morning Uncle Adolfus was murdered, he asked me to go to the outer station and bring in 1000 sheep to head station. I saddled my horse and went about 20 miles when I saw the blacks coming along the track over the range. I drove the sheep I had picked up from the run with some cows to the station 4 miles' ahead of me. Blacks had taken the station and killed all on it. There a short

distance I saw a woman and five white men and a black fellow moving towards me. I turned and made my way home. There Uncle was no more. He received 5 spears in him one in the stomach, two in the breast, one in the ear and in neck. He was unrecognizable. The blacks took away 2000 sheep and good many calves and lambs. Some were recovered. Some of the white men arrived and said it was dangerous to go down near the river where the horse was, as the blacks were in that direction.

However, I started off by myself and when half a mile away one of the men called out to me to stop and he would accompany me to look for a horse which we found. I saddled the horse and went down country to tell Uncle William of what had happened. I arrived at 7am and later after 8 miles riding I found Uncle with a bag on his back. I told him what had happened. He took it to heart very much. He gave me his horse and I rode 60 miles and set off a party to acquaint police who were 200 miles on the Dawson River where the blacks had committed a murder. The police were 6 weeks before they arrived.

Next day I returned to Rawbelle station. Uncle Adolfus was buried. Uncle William was up the river & when he returned he said I was the cause of his brother's death. He said a woman said I ought to have come home when I saw the blacks first before they attacked the station. It was not likely as I was going to drove the sheep and my head in the lion's mouth. I did everything for the best, and if I am blamed, it was not my fault. I told Uncle William I could not do what the woman said.

The police rounded up a lot of blacks and shot some of them, other were taken away and hanged. The row started when the blacks were working on the station of Mr Street next to Uncle's place. Uncle said he would sell out and go to Sydney so I would try my luck and go to Sydney. I got a horse and dray and made my way to Sydney. Richard Trevethan, Long Gully, Sandhurst, Victoria.[114]

With Lieutenant Marshall in the neighbourhood of Gayndah, he came in with four of Mr Gordon Sandeman's Chinamen, the ringleaders in a revolt, in which the Chinese shepherds left 28,000 sheep in the hurdles and fled the station. Marshall arrested the ringleaders, and persuaded

114 http://www.trevethan.net/Home.htm

the others back to their duty. The four mentioned were brought up at the Police Office, and fully committed to the next Brisbane assizes. A petition was circulated amongst the whole of the squatters in the Burnett district, for they are all employers of Chinese labour, praying his Excellency to appoint a Chinese interpreter to the Bench; the whole of their worships' attention has been taken up every Court day in deciding disputes between the celestials and their employers; and as they do not yet exactly understand the language, these trials are necessarily one-sided. The Bench therefore decided upon applying for a paid Chinese interpreter.[115]

As the relentless grind of tending flocks in a solitary and unfriendly wilderness went on, the slow march of progress brought little relief to the Burnett with the failure of the Native Police to track and apprehend the murderers of Mr Trevethan. Then there was the murder of Mr Clarke, nephew of and superintendent to F. W. Roache Esq. of the Dawson River. He was killed and his head severed with a tomahawk from his body.[116] The police returned to Rawbelle beaten; their horses broken hearted after fourteen day's absence. The Chinese remained troublesome. Messrs Lawson's Chinamen threatened Mr G. Sandeman's overseer, and one of them was brought to Court and bound over, as usual. Notwithstanding all the troubles with the blacks, sheep and stations in the district continued to fetch a very high price; Messrs Strathdee having disposed of 2000 ewes and two blocks of land at a price averaging 8s. 8d a head; and Mr Mocatta disposed of his run before shearing, at 10s. a head.[117]

As the carnage of European lives continued to be thrown away in the quest to go forth and multiply with their flocks in the Promised Land, the *Moreton Bay Courier* in September 1852 grew more and more desperate in its editorial musings and moaning:

> OPINION PIECE
>
> Now as to the Native Police, said to be one of our great grievances, no wonder you cannot come to any conclusion on the merits of the case, when I assure you there are not two squatters up here

115 *MBC* 17 April 1852 p2.
116 *MBC* 24 April 1852 p 2.
117 *MBC* 1 May 1852 p 2.

of the same opinion. Some think them beyond all praise, others beyond all blame. Others think they will do by and bye, when they have had more experience. A fourth part that if they were only more numerous; a fifth that if their numbers were smaller, and they were better drilled, they would do; a sixth advises their combination with an equal number of white policemen; a seventh says "Only give Walker his own way", and so on. You can hardly meet two parties of the same opinion. Some say this discussion in the papers, about the Native Police, is doing a great deal of harm; others that it is doing a great deal of good-as if the police had the least idea of what is the matter, or their officers cared one fig about what is said of them. Of this I feel persuaded, that the officers are zealous in the discharge of their duties, and over ready, at a moment's warning, to saddle up, and start to any place, at any hour, day or night. The men are a half-drilled, undisciplined body; and, like all Asiatics, slow, indolent, and licentious. It takes them a long time to prepare, a long time to saddle up, a long time to eat their meals, and a long time to clean their accoutrements. They are slow in their gait, awkward in their movements, and crippled in their boots. How they get on in action I am not able to state, but those who have seen them state that they are so hasty and impetuous when their blood is once up, that when ordered to charge they cannot halt. I feel satisfied they might be made a higher efficient body, if incorporated with plenty of European sergeants, carefully selected from the ranks of the English or Prussian army, not with privates promoted to the Police. This is, I believe, Mr Walker's idea. The difficulty lies in obtaining suitable men to engage for such a service. I have no doubt when Mr Walker comes down here himself we shall see a change for the better; if the squatters will co-operate, instead of grumbling and finding fault, and the Government will only allow him to carry out his own views, and if he has the courage to turn a deaf ear to all the trash that is written and said about himself and his brigade. There has been a talk about a Commission of Inquiry. Who this emanates from I do not know; but I feel assured that if ever it takes place it will end most triumphantly in favour of the police or opinions will be so adverse that it will be impossible to come to a conclusion. There appear to be two parties, the young, resolute, and strong; good shots, and good hands at taking camps, these are all against the Native Police, and are anxious for their disbandment, whilst the married men,

> the young men with a few sheep, striving to get on, are anxious to have the services of the blacks as shepherds. These, together with the lazy and indolent, who would sooner send the police than go themselves after the blacks when they commit depredations, are in favour of them. This is about the real state of the case.[118]

All the words in the world meant little or nothing neither to the Aborigines nor for that matter to the white settlers because the killings kept on happening with another barbarous murder committed by the blacks in the Burnett district, late July 1852. A young lad named Dawson, employed as a hutkeeper on an outstation belonging to Mr McKay, a few miles from the head station, was found by the shepherd, lying dead beside the creek, where he had apparently been washing when attacked. The tomahawk used in the slaughter was lying near the body, the murderers having left it in their hurry to plunder the hut, which they had stripped of the flour and other articles. The Native Police chanced to arrive at the station next day, but the matter remains unsolved.[119]

Tackling blacks may have been one dimension to the business of managing a sheep run but with the importation of coolie labour, the duties of the Native Police were perhaps widened by having to enforce indentures made between the squatters and the coolies. Mr Gordon Sandeman's station, where thirty-seven of these people were employed, fell into a state of rebellion, occasioned through a white man travelling from hut to hut, assuring them that they were fools to shepherd for four dollars a month, when Europeans were getting £1 a week. Acting upon this, they all struck work, and left their sheep in the hurdles for a whole day. The ringleader was, however, arrested and placed in handcuffs, and the remainder were only prevented from coming into Gayndah by the timely arrival of Sergeant Kerr of the Native Police, who accidentally called at the station, and by his co-operation managed to get them to take their flocks out. The Sergeant was engaged during three days in riding round this establishment, which extends forty miles in one direction and sixty in another. By his presence and demeanour, he succeeded in restoring order and confidence, thus rendering essential services to Mr Sandeman at a most critical juncture. It was not only in abandoning flocks to the

118 *MBC* 25 September 1852 p 3.

119 *MBC* 7 August 1852 p 2.

mercy of blacks and native dogs that made the Chinese objectionable but also for sheep killing. They, like the old hands, would not go short of meat so long as there was a fat wether in the fold. Consequently, their use as a cheap class of labourer was brought into serious question with the settlers, notwithstanding their low wages.[120] Commandant Walker must have expressed some sense of achievement when it was reported that his plan of allowing the Aborigines in had been completely successful on one station, where the proprietors, Messrs Strathdee, for some time past had 16,000 sheep herded and watched entirely by blacks, who were allowed the same rations as white men, supplied once a week. During some months of their employment not a single sheep had been lost. In fact, the Messrs Strathdee stated that they had always been able to obtain the services of the natives in this way.[121]

As the settlements grew, undeterred by the blacks continued rapine and killings, Walker's job grew ever greater in the need to cover and patrol the vast pastures the settlers sought to graze and prosper from; so, Walker went forth as the vengeance of the Lord and detached a party of the force under his command to the Pine River, where several outrages had been perpetrated by the aboriginal natives. He was not in a position to commit more police. The Moreton and Wide Bay division of the force was not yet organized, in consequence of a delay in furnishing the necessary saddlery and other accoutrements. It was proposed to despatch the original 4th section of Native Police to Brisbane, who were expected to arrive at Ipswich on 20 October 1852. As business connected with the force would require Mr Walker's presence at Ipswich, he had determined to go with this detachment to the Pine River.[122] The detachment of the Native Police consisted of twelve men, together with two orderly troopers and a sergeant under the personal command of Mr Walker, the commandant, who arrived in Brisbane on or about 5 November 1852 and was quartered in the police buildings, near the court house. In the afternoon, they were drilled in the court house square, and the manner in which they went through the military exercises, first with the carbine and subsequently with the sword, elicited the admiration of all who witnessed

[120] *MBC* 23 October 1852 p 2.

[121] *MBC* 23 October 1852 p 2.

[122] *MBC* 16 October 1852 p 2.

it. The men were young, active, and for the most part, well formed; and they had an appearance of intelligence and of military regularity which plainly showed that much care had been taken in their training. Mr Walker and detachment left for Pine River the next day with eighteen warrants against the aboriginal natives of the area. Some of these warrants were of old date, and many single ones contained the names of several blacks. Mr Walker, advised the press that some of the men in this section had been in the force ever since 1848 and were chiefly natives of the Murray and Edward Rivers. Mr Walker expected to remain in the district for about six weeks, and arrangements were made for the stationing of a division of the force, permanently between the Moreton and Wide Bay districts. It had not yet been decided whether the detachment would be stationed on the upper part of the Mary or the head of the Brisbane, but most probably it would be the latter. The permanent division would be composed of a mixture of recruits and older members of the force and would be under the command of Mr Marshall. The detachment's arms and accoutrements were in excellent order, and altogether they presented a very efficient appearance.[123]

The Pine River operation involved stripping and searching the scrubs for the tracks of the natives. They discovered their tracks, and then followed them on the next day towards Durundur, where they arrived on Monday evening. On 11 November, the Police under Mr Walker, accompanied by a stockman, proceeded in search of some of the blacks against whom warrants had been issued, and came upon the tracks of six natives, believed to be the party who had eluded the police two days before. Following these tracks, they came up with the blacks, who made their escape into a pine scrub, but not before one was wounded. The native guide who accompanied the police declared that Bidong, Burnett, Dargilbo, and Dulamany, four of the blacks said to be concerned in the murder of Mr McGrath's shepherd, and also another accused black named Wandai, brother of Dulamany, were amongst this party. The guide, whose name was Charley, also asserted that the before mentioned natives were those who had murdered some of the people belonging to Thomas King. On 13 November, the police came upon the camp of the blacks, and attempted to capture the parties charged, but the natives tried to break

123 *MBC* 6 November 1852 p 2.

through a police line under the command of native corporal, Larry who opened fire killing Wandai. Others were thought to have been wounded, but the scrub through which they escaped was too dark for this to be accurately ascertained. On their return to Durundur, next day, the police heard of the murder of Mr Balfour's Chinaman, and proceeded to that gentleman's station.[124] Arising out of the Pine River operation, a Sergeant and four troopers of the Native Police arrived in Brisbane on 25 November 1852 with two aboriginal natives, "Mickey" and "Billy Quart Pot," in custody on a warrant charging them with having been concerned in the robbery at Mr Gregor's station at the time when that gentleman was murdered six years ago. Ralph William Barrow, the native boy who was a witness in the case, was employed at the German's station.[125]

A small party of the Native Police, under the command of Mr Walker, the Commandant, arrived in Brisbane from Durundur, for the purpose of getting horses shod. The men had, as usual, conducted themselves in a very orderly and exemplary manner while walking about the town. The members of this force had been much employed of late in apprehending runaway Chinese, in which service they had been very active. Accounts from the Burnett district were more peaceable in their character than formerly, but on the Dawson, affairs were not so favourable; although it had been expected that the severe check given to the hostile blacks in the Dawson valley would have a good effect. At one station on the Burnett, 8000 sheep were being shepherded by blacks, and the natives were employed at many other stations on the Burnett and Auburn. The Wide Bay district might have been considered peaceable, were it not for the murder of a Chinese in the employment of Mr E B Uhr. The alleged murderer in this case was Durraggeree,[126] the native black acquitted of a charge of attempted murder, at the Brisbane Circuit Court, in consequence of the inability of the chief witness, Mr Furber, to attend. The Lower Condamine and McIntyre country was peaceable enough. Accounts from the Maranoa were unfavourable, but it was rumoured that the Native Police

---

124 *MBC* 4 December 1852 p 2.

125 *MBC* 27 November 1852 p 3.

126 Durrugguree, *MBC* 29 May 1852 p 2. R v. *Perriba and Durrugguree* [1852] NSWSupCMB 14.

had lately given the hostile blacks in that locality a lesson.[127]

Commandant Walker always moved his force in an orderly fashion, hoping to be in the right place at the right time so as to thwart the cunning blacks and beat them at their own game. Accordingly, it was reported in the press that: the 5th and 8th sections of the Native Police, under command of Mr Walker, arrived in Brisbane, 29 June 1853. The 5th, under the command of Sergeant Dempster, the best Sergeant in the force, proceeded to the Clarence district immediately. The delay in despatching a section to that district had been mainly caused by the fact that Mr Morisset, the subaltern who was to have commanded it, had not yet joined the force. The 8th section would proceed to Wide Bay, to relieve the 4th, who under the command of a native sergeant, had been patrolling that district, and had in custody a black named "Athlone," charged with murder. This 4th section was the first that came to Brisbane, and was spoken of as the most efficient in the service. The 1st section, which had been kept back as a reserve for an emergency, has been despatched by Mr Walker to the Port Curtis country, where two men, forming part of Messrs J. and N. Leith Hay's establishment, had been murdered by the blacks. Six men of the 2nd section had proceeded to Callandoon; the remaining six accompany Mr Marshall, the first Lieutenant, who was now in the Maranoa District, inquiring into some matters which the Commandant does not approve of. The 3rd and 6th sections were at Wandai Gumbal, on the lower Condamine. The 7th section was on duty patrolling the Burnett and the northern end of the Wide Bay district, where they will remain until the 30th June. The 9th section is dismounted, at Traylan, headquarters, Burnett River, being without saddles, arms or clothing. None of the newly appointed Sub-Lieutenants have yet joined the force, and the Commandant has had considerable difficulties to contend with in consequence of the absence of European assistants; the European sergeants being generally found not to answer. Mr Walker said some of his officers, as well as a large number of the men have been suffering severely from the fever and ague so prevalent on the Burnett River, and which, in many cases has assumed a form more like the jungle fever of India. On his arrival in Brisbane, the commandant was requested to make a demonstration on the outskirts of Brisbane, where

127 *MBC* 29 January 1853 p 3.

many of the blacks have within the last few days been committing robberies upon the suburban farmers. The immediate cause of those thefts was supposed to be the disappointment and annoyance of the natives at the non-arrival of the usual supply of blankets for issue to them on the Queen's Birth day. The blankets were applied for in due course, and their non-arrival was attributed to the scarcity of those articles in Sydney. But the blacks would not believe this, and, under the conviction that the Government Resident here was deceiving them, seemed very much inclined to vent their spleen in acts of outrage. Mr Walker accordingly proceeded down the river in the direction of Eagle Farm, with a party of his men, and although not furnished with any information upon which he could make arrests, it is hoped that the appearance of a protective force may have a beneficial effect. The whole force of the nine sections of Native Police consisted, nominally, of 100 men; but several vacancies had been caused by death, and many others temporarily exist through illness. Added to this, one section was virtually disabled for want of equipment. Mr Morisset and Mr Keen had arrived at Callandoon on 10 May, where they have remained, awaiting orders from the Commandant.[128]

With opening up of Port Curtis, more territory became available to settlers and without hesitation they moved in seeking to exploit the country and make their pile. But an inevitable skirmish took place between the blacks and the surveying party, who repulsed them effectually and they decamped. Mr Hay, who had stations about 60 miles to the southward, sent his teams with wool to Port Curtis. They were attacked by the blacks, who drove off the teamsmen, and tore open the bags, scattered the wool abroad and stole the bags. Mr Walker, the commandant of Native Police arrived with twelve troopers, and shot some of the blacks concerned in the robbery of Mr Hay's wool. In a private letter, he said, "I have seen no country so good as this for the last twelve months. I am very sanguine about its becoming a great place. The blacks require all the watching we can give them. The more I see of this country the more I like it. There is a good deal of swamp in the neighbourhood, which consisting of rich alluvial districts, renders the vegetation very coarse and rank. These swamps might be converted to rice cultivation. It is believed that most of the tropical fruits will grow there, although, by the meteorological table

[128] *MBC* 4 June 1853 p 2.

that has been kept by the expedition, the heat at present has not been so great as was anticipated. The heat is greatest at mid-day becoming much more temperate towards the afternoon. The arrival of the native police had imparted a great feeling of security. One gentleman connected with the party, who had much experience on the gold fields, expresses his conviction that the soil is highly auriferous. This is highly probable as the mountain range trends to north and we are informed that quartz is found there in large quantities."[129]

The new year of 1854 brought with it a continued need to patrol and intervene. Lieutenant Murray, the officer in command of the detachment at Port Curtis, advised that a sergeant and two troopers of the Native Police, who had been despatched to complete a marked tree line between Port Curtis and Traylan, were attacked by native blacks on 10 January while encamped and asleep, and had considerable difficulty in beating off their assailants. The Sergeant and one of the troopers were severely cut on their heads, and the other trooper received a spear wound in the chest. The men returned to Port Curtis, and were rapidly recovering. It is believed that the blacks who made the attack were not aware of the quality of their opponents but supposed them to be a travelling party of whites.[130] Mr Surveyor McCabe and a number of his staff at Port Curtis went out on duty one day, fully armed, and espied some blacks hunting. Panic struck at the sight of the blacks, the surveyor fled, followed by his party, who threw away their carbines in order to make the best use of their legs, and arrived in camp without any serious injury, beyond a broken shin or two in tailing over logs. The natives, not having the slightest hostile intention, brought the firearms to the settlement next day, and delivered them over to Mr Wilmott, the storekeeper, remarking, with much laughter, how frightened the white fellows were, and how they did run. Having discovered the weakness of the surveyor's party (about a score strong), the blacks in a few days came down in force, and proceeded to plunder the tent. The gallant surveyor, with his party, at ounce retired behind a big tree, where a 20 stand of arms were piled, and with a Colt's

129 This prediction was correct, refer Mt Morgan. *MBC* 10 December 1853 p 2.
130 *MBC* 25 February 1854 p 2.

revolving rifle[131] in his hand, observed with the greatest complacency the plunder of his tent, and remarked that "he was paid to measure, and not to fight." Fortunately, a sergeant of the Native Police passed by soon after this outrage, and immediately went in pursuit. Next day Lieutenant Murray, with his division, went out and recovered the whole property.[132]

Mr Kettle, of the firm of Kettle and Spinks, graziers on the Lower Condamine, was herding a flock of his sheep for one of his men, who were ill, when, on 5 February, he was attacked by aboriginal natives, who murdered him, stripped the body and carried off about 1000 sheep. The murder was not discovered until the 7th, when the Native Police started in pursuit of the murderers.[133]

The ebb and flow of skirmishes rushed across the frontier, breaking in and out, all over Walker's broad turf as he tried to sandbag the thin black line of terror. Large parties of blacks assembled in the Pine River neighbourhood, amongst them was "Billy Barlow," the native charged with the wilful murder of Mr McGrath's shepherd. In the vicinity of Brisbane, the natives mustered in large bodies. These consisted of blacks from the northern coast of the bay, called the "Ningy Ningy" tribe. Their object was revenge upon the Brisbane blacks who delivered up their great man Dundalli, who languished in the Brisbane gaol awaiting his trial on several charges of murder. These whoops and hollers along the Brisbane, caused much loss and annoyance to the settlers in the suburbs and much anxiety to those on the Pine River and Sandgate. The press called for Mr Walker's attention to the expediency of sending a detachment of the corps to Brisbane without delay. Large sums of money had been expended in the purchase of land at Sandgate, or Cabbage Tree Creek, and many persons were desirous of availing themselves of a supply of labour for the purpose of building at that place; but the dangerous character of the blacks in that vicinity deterred them, as the place is utterly without police protection of any kind. Most desirable improvements were thus retarded, and purchased land suffered to lay waste, for

131 Given the date, this would have to be the Colt Model 1839 Carbine, a percussion revolving smoothbore carbine not the Colt Model 1855 Revolving Carbine.

132 *MBC* 26 August 1854 p 2.

133 *MBC* 4 March 1854 p 2.

want of a few Native Police troopers, the press observed.[134] Moreover, the Native Police were, as was customary, withdrawn altogether from Wide Bay, at this season of the year. The blacks, for whom warrants had been issued against for a long time, re-commenced their criminal ways: horses and drays were robbed daily; surveyor's tents and settlers' gardens were taken over altogether. Then, a surveyor's servant was found tied to a tree. Mr Buchanan himself, when walking through Maryborough, narrowly escaped being speared. A traveller was murdered within a mile and a half of Mr Brown's station; the natives separated the man's arms, legs, &c from the rest of his body, and actually went to the trouble of burning parts of them.[135] Then Bribie Island was added to Walker's bailiwick on him receiving letters advising an investigation into the circumstances connected with the murder of the Pilots' men, Gold and Anderson at Bribie Island, had been held at the Police Office, Brisbane, before Capt. Wickham, Messrs Duncan, Ferriter and Buckley, Lieut. Geary, and Capt. Barney and that warrants had been issued for the Aborigines Jacky, Andy, and Billy Barlow.[136]

The above is an attempt to document and describe the operational activities of the Native Police under the command of Frederick Walker. Moreover, the narrative ends abruptly because Walker was relieved from duty on 21 September 1854. The above portrays a very active and fluid law enforcement theatre of operations. The impression is that Walker was always reactive rather than proactive. The nature of his bailiwick was wide and broad which, perhaps to use an analogy, was infected with a pathogen that would randomly flare up and erupt into violence and then for no apparent reason would fall dormant again.

134 *MBC* 26 August 1854 p 2.

135 *MBC* 26 August 1854 p 2.

136 *MBC* 4 November 1854 p 2.

3

Assessment of Native Police

I would have liked to have opened this chapter by announcing that the Native Police's core mission had, in partnership with the black and white residents, promoted a safe and inclusive community through crime prevention and law enforcement; and then to have gone on and said, the Native Police had met its operational goals etc., etc. Of course, that sort of language is a dead giveaway and is systemic of the modern approach to dealing with matters pertaining to aboriginal history and related issues.[137] I must, therefore, stress the following that in analysing Walker's native police in terms of structure, police powers and the application of those powers in the defined jurisdiction (geographic and demographic)[138] modern logic or rationality of whatever kind or persuasion must not be applied to the machinery of government pertaining in the colony of New South Wales at that time nor to the law enforcement activities of Walker's police. The concept of a native police force was not new. There was one already in the Port Phillip District. The record reveals that Governor FitzRoy had identified a situation that was not conducive to peace and good order in the northern parts beyond the settled districts of Sydney. He did not appear to want to know the cause of the collisions nor did he suggest that the conflict was one-sided; by using the word collisions, he appeared to suggest that both sides (white or Aborigine) were equally culpable. His solution was to set up a native police force to take preventive action.

Frederick Walker was chosen for the reasons I have given above in Chapter 2, and was asked to set up a corps of Native Police. This study covers the period 17 August 1848 to 21 September 1854. It is believed

137 "an attempt was made to employ black bush craft in the struggle against Aboriginal resistance" (Reynolds 1990:46).

138 "beyond the settled parts, in the Sydney district"

that Walker was born circa 1820 and although he could read and write, he appears unscholarly. However, legend has it that he was a superb bushman with an innate ability to communicate with and influence Aborigines. His only public administrative experience seems to have been as a constable in the Border Police and Clerk of Petty Sessions. From this rather humble bedrock, he was asked to call up, equip and train and then to ensure the operational readiness of a Native Police force to patrol the northern frontier which was something like 55,000 square miles of wilderness. He was to watch and ward not by the highways and byways of the jurisdiction but to boldly go where no white man had gone before. How was he to do this: patrol by horseback, run a police force from his saddlebag and sleep under the stars. Apart from the core functions, he had also additional subsidiary functions of administration, training, victuals, ammunition and powder, clothes, communications, remounts, supply and maintenance of equipment and horses and management.

Characteristics of the Jurisdiction

Remarks	Clarence	Darling Downs	Moreton	Burnett	Wide Bay	Maranoa
Murders	13	11	2	22	5	8
Population						
males	1116	1704	234	740	319	74
females	605	469	33	112	87	11
Area sq m	9760	25640	2460	7050	5255	12815
Aborigines	407	1068	103	294	219	534

The above table makes no pretence to be complete. It is provided as a quick snap-shot of the characteristics of the jurisdiction of the Native Police.[139] There may be a quibble taken with the population figures given for the number of Aborigines in each district. The exact number will nev-

139 Murders *MBC* 28 May 1853 p 3; Population & area NSW 1851 & 56 census; Aborigines 1:24 sq. miles, *Geelong Advertiser and Squatters' Advocate* 26 August 1846 p 1.

er be known but the numbers were always low. Comr Rolleston, writing to the Colonial Secretary on 24 March 1851 in the annual Report on the state of Aborigines in the Darling Downs District made this observation on the number of aboriginal tribes in the District: 7 tribes, 100 - 150 in each tribe, uppermost of 1000 altogether.[140] Moreover, as time went by, the jurisdiction grew such that Port Curtis should be added to the above table and the collisions between settlers and Aborigines continued.

The estimates for Native Police for the northern districts of 1854 - 1855 are slightly difficult to reconcile in that the source material, the newspapers, give varying amounts proposed to parliament on different occasions. It seems £8000 was eventually passed. However, it really was not the money, although as a side note, Walker's budget had grown from £1000 to £8000 per annum, which must suggest that the force was needed and effective.[141] Briefly the force was broken down for estimate purposes as follows: Clarence, McLeay, Moreton, Wide Bay, Burnett, Maranoa, Lower Condamine, and Callandoon Districts; Commandant at £400, two Lieutenants at £200 each, 3 Lieutenants at £180 each, one Acting Adjutant at £120, 5 sergeants at £50 each, 120 troopers at 5d a day and 5 Sub Lieutenants at £120 each and Provisions, Forage, and Contingencies at £5,515. Then there were the additional estimates for Arms, Ammunition, Clothing and Accoutrements of £2,550.[142]

Compare and contrast Walker's Native Police headquarters which consisted of, up until he was dismissed, the Commandant, adjutant, two native orderlies and a white private secretary paid for by Walker with a start-up allocation of £1000 against the recommendations put forward at the Select Committee on Murders on the Dawson River of 15 June 1858 which proposed a Native Police headquarters of a Commandant, Adjutant and Riding Master, Paymaster, Surgeon, Sergeant-Major, Saddle Sergeant, 2 Farriers, and 4 Rough-riders, with a start-up allocation of £30,000, and then ask yourself why Walker hit the grog and went troppo after six years of hard slog.

140 QSL Reel A2.22 p 407.

141 The estimates for 1846 for the Border Police for the half year ending 30 June 1846 was £11,798 17 1.

142 *MBC* 12 August 1854 p2.

Disposition of the Native Police 27 July 1854

Station	Officer	Section	Troopers	Remarks
Port Curtis	Lt Murray Sgt Humphrey Sgt Bungaree	No 1 No 10	1 Sgt 2 Cpl 7 Tprs 2 Tprs to their Sect	
Traylan	Lt Marshall	No 4 No 10	1 Cpl 4 Tprs 3MU 1 Tprs drays	1 Cpl 4 Tprs Sec 10 to join Cmdt
Rannes	SLt Keen	No 3	1 Sgt 2 Cpl 7 Tprs	Ordered to Traylan
Lower Burnett	SLt RG Walker	No 7	1 Sgt 2 Cpl 7 Tprs	To relieve Rannes
Marybor-ough		No 4	4 Tprs	Join Traylan
Yabber	Lt Bligh	No 8	2 Cpl 10 Tprs	Bunya, Moreton & WB
Clarence	Lt Morisset Sgt Dempster	No 5	1 Sgt 1 Cpl 8 Tprs	Sgt Dempster to Macleay
Wandai Gumbal	Lt Fulford Lt Irving SLt Nicol	No 2 No 6 No 10	1 Sgt 2 Cpl 8 Tprs 1 Sgt 1 Cpl 10 Tprs 5 Tprs	Waiting for Cmdt
Callan-doon	Cmdt	No 6 No 4 No 10	1 Cpl drill 1 Tpr Cmdt orderly 4 Tprs	For Wandai Gumbal
En Route	SLt Fortescue	No 9 No 1	12 Tprs 1 Tpr	Due Traylan 14th
En Route	Sgt Graham	No 5 No 2	2 Tprs 1 A/Cpl	Join Lt Morisset
En Route	Sgt A Walker	No 4	1 Cpl 1 Tpr	Join Traylan

Note: 119 Men - death of 1 man at Traylan caused a deficiency of 1. Supernumeraries: 2, Orderlies: Commandant and Lt Marshall; 2 postmen carrying Gayndah & Wide Bay mail. MU=medically unfit.[143]

[143] QSL Reel A2.30 pp 44-45.

The above gives an operational view of the force as it bestrode its geographical jurisdiction as at 27 July 1854. The above structure of the Native Police looks impressive but the corps was undermanned. Moreover, logistics depots should have been set up in each district with a remount/quartermaster sergeant so the troopers could return to patrol work quickly; fresh horses should have been available at all times. Furthermore, the uniform of the corps was unsuitable to the conditions of work and the nature of the climate apropos the evidence of Henry Hort Brown, Esq. MRCS:

> There was a certain amount of the venereal disease, but the principal diseases were epidemics such as influenza, mumps, &c., which with them is always of a most serious nature.
>
> I think not, on account of their style of clothing and artificial habits acquired; because they wear very warm clothing, which they throw off when they are in a state of perspiration, and otherwise live, to a certain extent, artificially. I would recommend a lighter suit of clothing, and as near an approximation to their natural habits of life as practicable.[144]

One of the difficulties in understanding Walker's Native Police is that they had no legal definition as to function and power. The name is not helpful. Most police forces generally have their function as part of their nomenclature such as Border, Traffic, Drug, Secret police etc. Moreover, as was noted earlier, they were not created by an Act of Council (Parliament) and thus, had no legislative definition but appeared to be an ad hoc extension of the Crown's coercive powers.[145] It is my view that this lack of definition has permitted most commentators to make very broad assumptions about Walker and the Native Police because on the face of it, there appeared no way of contradicting their assertions and conclusions by reference to an executive order or legislation. In the normal scheme of things, one would have expected Walker to have received from FitzRoy a letter of appointment setting out the terms and conditions of his appointment and the policy or legal framework within which he was to operate. An instrument of appointment is a legally binding document

144 1857 NSW Legislative Assembly SC "On The Native Police Force."

145 The Crown has power pursuant to the concept of "peace, order and good government" provision.

and an essential part of appointing a person to fill a senior public office. There was no letter of appointment, as Walker observed: "I would call your attention to the fact that I have never received any instructions as to what my particular duties were to be."[146]

This was Walker's response to FitzRoy's letter of 8 August 1849, which arose out of Walker's letter of Moanna, Darling River, 23 March 1849. FitzRoy had written on the margin: "Was Mr Walker on appointment informed of the instructions from home respecting the necessity of taking depositions in all cases of collisions with the Blacks?"

The Colonial Secretary replied: "Apparently not."

FitzRoy responded: "This should now be done, and he should be instructed to do so in this case, have reports and to transmit the depositions to the Attorney-General."

If Walker had been given a letter of appointment, what might it have contained? I submit that it may have been modelled on the letter of appointment given to Commissioners of Crown Lands and contained similar terms and conditions, among other instructions, as follows:

> The Governor having been pleased to appoint you Commandant of the Native Police, and also a Magistrate of the Territory, I do myself the honour to transmit to you the following powers, functions and authorities, relating to the office and command devolving on you in the former capacity, viz.: Among other duties etc, etc. You will discourage, by every means in your power, the practice so prevalent among stockmen of carrying fire-arms, or even of keeping fire-arms at their stations, unless deemed absolutely necessary for their protection.
>
> With reference to the duties devolving on you for the protection of the Inhabitants and of the Aborigines, I have the honour to inform you that you will be allowed a corps of Native Police. The general object of the establishment of the Police, is to keep the peace and order amongst all parties,[147] but, in an especial manner,

---

146 F Walker's letter, Macintyre, 16 October 1849.

147 Sec 10 of Crown Lands Unauthorised Occupation Act, 1839 2 Vic No 27, shall keep the peace in his district and protect all persons being therein … he shall make perambulations of his district …

> it has been established for the protection of the Aborigines, and to stop the atrocities which have been committed on both sides, between them and the settlers; and you will bear in mind, that the black inhabitants of this country are no less the subjects of Her Majesty than the whites; that all are equally amenable to the law and all equally entitled to its protection. In every case of violent death, therefore, an enquiry is to be held into the probable cause of it, whether the deceased were a white or a black person, and the parties to be dealt with as the case may require, and the proceedings on the enquiry immediately transmitted to the Attorney-General. With respect to the ordinary duties of a Justice of the Peace, which you will be called on to discharge, I am to inform you that the laws of England in force in this part of the colony and the Acts of the Governor and Council are equally applicable in the districts to which you are proceeding as to any other part of New South Wales.[148]
>
> You will endeavour by every means in your power to gain an influence over the Black population; and to take care that they are kindly treated by the Policemen. You will explain to the Blacks, the consequences which they will draw upon themselves by any acts of aggression on the whites, as well as the punishment the latter will be subject to for any misbehaviour to them.[149]

I don't intend to define the Native Police. Frederick Walker was answerable to no one other than the Governor General, himself, FitzRoy. The organisation was uniquely Australian; having all the attributes and characteristic of what early Australian life was about, simple, rough and bush driven with little regard to comfort, ceremony, brass buttons or the sabretache. Moreover, they were a user pay funded organisation; the squatters paid an annual licence fee to occupy their runs. Perhaps more than most citizens, the squatters saw a direct correlation between the fees they paid and the protection the Native Police provided. Furthermore, there is one other dimension to the force that needs to be dealt with and that is Walker recruiting troopers from southern myall blacks. Many a commentator has drawn some weak-minded comparison to the Royal

148 This sentence is taken from the letter of 12/9/1837 appointing Foster Fyans Police Magistrate, Port Phillip by Col Sec. VPRS 4/P0 unit 3, item Folder N°: 5.

149 NSW Government Gazette 28 Jun 1845 [Issue N° 52] p 657.

Irish Constabulary (RIC) which is nonsense; Fenianism and the RIC is a study of its own. Walker made the following observation: "In my opinion, also no blacks ought to be made use of as police in their own country as I know that if they are employed as such they will frequently attempt to avenge their own private animosities. The Sydney Native Police being now employed to the North and have no animosity."[150] In other words, because payback was so ingrained or entrenched in aboriginal society together with the hair-trigger quarrelsomeness of the race, Walker could not risk unauthorised violence against other Aborigines by his troopers. His recruitment principle had nothing to with white concepts of corruption, bribery, fixing, perjury, theft or favouritism, which plagues modern police forces. The Native Police were not police because they were not sworn and could not be sworn.[151] They were a type of auxiliary watch-keepers who were armed for self-protection. The organisation grew very rapidly, at a much greater rate than FitzRoy or Walker imagined. The demand was immense and the early public comment appeared to suggest that protection from Aborigines was something the early settlers longed for. The age-old policing question for governments is: what is the critical mass of police required such that a perceived balance is achieved between crime suppression and the community's level of comfort and security. Did the Native Police reach that level? It is a difficult task to assess the Native Police; virtually impossible given the dearth of modern conventional data that statisticians and social commentators would rely on to assess, evaluate and audit such an organisation not that that has deterred the ardour of some commentators. Perhaps the highest function of the force was crime prevention and order maintenance policing with a secondary or lesser function of arrest and clear-up rates. To do this, the Native Police were to patrol often and widely leaving the Aborigines with the fear that the police were looking over their shoulders and were likely to be on hand should they misbehave, which in turn would lead the Aborigines to believe they would suffer immediate punishment.

In the course of Walker's operational time as a police officer, comment was made regarding his police powers. On the one hand, they were considered too narrow for the job he was charged with and on the other,

---

150 F Walker to Hon Colonial Secretary (CS), 10 March 1851.

151 See the debate on the Aboriginal Natives' Evidence Bill, *SMH* 29 June 1849 p 2.

he was constantly reminded that his duties were to protect all parties as no one was above the law. The following quotes from the newspapers of the day reflect the different views on the nature of the law enforcement powers of the Native Police:

> Greater discretion was not given to the officer in command; the nature and habits of the Aborigines rendered the procedure usually adopted by police officers against civilised whites impracticable and absurd in their cases.
>
> It had been complained that these policemen, acting under some advice from the Attorney-General, refused to act in any case unless they had a warrant.
>
> The Colonial Secretary said the corps could not, however, act contrary to law, or make actual war upon the blacks, being bound to defend the latter as well as the whites.
>
> Their instructions are too limited to permit them to deal with tribes who are in an actual state of warfare against the whites. Against such persons, the power of military authority, instead of the functions of a civil constabulary, ought to be directed.

The Native Police were not a creature of an act of parliament nor does there appear to be any quasi legal directives regarding their conduct or powers from government. Walker was a Magistrate and a sworn constable who held civil authority. Often Walker is described as Lieutenant Frederick Walker. He never held a naval or army commission of whatever kind and thus never exercised any military authority or power at any stage of his career. It seems to me that FitzRoy relied on those broad powers of a magistrate and the common-law powers of a constable, which was to keep the Queen's peace, to watch and ward; the police oath:

> I, do swear that I will well and truly serve Our Sovereign Lady The QUEEN as a constable without favour or affection, malice or ill will until I am legally discharged that I will see and cause her Majesty's peace to be kept and preserved and that I will prevent to the best of my power all offences against that peace etc., etc. faithfully according to Law so help me God.

Moreover, a constable may with or without a warrant arrest anyone for a breach of the peace and in the case of a felony, actually committed or dangerous wounding whereby felony is likely to ensue, he may upon probable suspicion arrest the felon; and for that purpose is authorised (as upon a Justice's warrant) to break open doors, and even to kill the felon if he cannot be otherwise taken.[152] The following is a description by Walker of how he carried out his police powers:

> During the four years in which I have held the command of this force, it has never acted unless I knew that a felony had been committed and I had reasonable grounds of suspecting the offenders, warrants had been issued, or affidavits clearly pointing out the offenders, sworn to. In every case depositions, have been forwarded to the Attorney-General of the proceedings of the Native Police, when a death has occurred through their endeavours to put a stop to hostilities; and he is the best judge whether I have acted legally or not. At all events, I have always thought that I was right, morally and legally.[153]

If my analysis of the law is correct, and I am supported by Marie Fels, PhD thesis 1986, Chapter 5, then I am of the view that Walker and all the other white officers and NCOs of the Native Police acted within the law when carrying out their duties. There is some ambiguity with regards to the black troopers who probably had no standing *de jure*[154] but from a *de facto* view, the analysis would be. Provided they did not touch or interfere with a white man, then they would suffer no jeopardy for a white man could civilly and criminally prosecute the black trooper. Where the black trooper assaulted, or killed an Aborigine in the course of his duty as a trooper, then Walker would have argued, any peace officer may call on any of Her Majesty's subjects to assist him, and they might act in that case, whether they were constables or not and be excused or justified by the common law. Moreover, no Aborigine had standing to bring an action against any black or white person.[155] At best, he could make a complaint to a magistrate, where the matter went from there would depend, I imagine to what degree of corroboration he had from independent white witnesses and or the physical evidence. White officers were needed

152 Blackstone Laws of England.

153 Letter dated Callandoon, 1 March 1852 to Colonial Secretary.

154 Because they were not sworn and could not be sworn.

155 "the inconvenience arising from the evidence of the native troopers not being admissible", FW to CS, Warialda 1 May 1849.

not just for the customary duties of control and direction but they also carried the evidentiary burden as well, only they could give evidence in court and being sworn constables they enjoyed not so much as immunity from the law but a presumption they were carrying out their duties lawfully in the service of the community.

If the government had issued no directives to Walker on how the Native Police might carry out their role, then what sort of policeman was Walker? Police are not lawyers and are not required to be lawyers. A policeman needs to be able to detect a crime in the first instance and then to gather and preserve the evidence. The question of culpability is a matter for the court to decide. Walker seemed to have a reasonable common-sense approach to his task but it is clear he had two difficulties with the law. One was accessories to a crime and the other was whether it was good public policy to arrest and convict the whole tribe for the actions of a few tribal ringleaders. On 7 November 1850, he sought clarification form the Attorney-General on the following matter:

> The case is simply this: A large number of blacks are assembled together armed, cattle are killed and the remains found in all their camps; although the ownership cannot be sworn to positively. Sheep are stolen in large numbers and men are callously murdered. No man is identified as one of the murderers or thieves. The only evidence which can be obtained is that which my men and I can generally (almost always) track the aggressive party; but if it implicates anybody would it implicate any blacks who may have joined the party since the offence?

Now the above is a typical piece of confused prose from Walker but he seems to be talking about two crimes: murder and stealing, and when a third party joins the offender after the commission of the crime. In the case of murder, there are accessories to the fact and accessories after the fact. If a third party with knowledge of the murder, relieves, comforts or assists the felon e.g. by helping to destroy evidence such as weapons or other physical evidence used in the commission of a murder then they are classified as accessories after the fact and are equally liable before the law. In the case of stealing, if a third party on joining the tribe sat down and feasted on the dead stolen cattle knowing they were stolen then they would be guilty of receiving. Whether Walker got a reply to his request for clarification is unknown but if he did, it appears he never really appreciated the concept of accessories to crimes because in the case of Mickie set out in Chapter 5, he got into hot water again but this time with His Honour Judge Therry. The other point Walker had difficulty with, was holding the whole of the tribe culpable for the actions of a few of the dominant males in the tribe even if they were all present during the commission of a serious felony like attacking and killing settlers. Walker appears to suggest that if the principal parties to the crime were caught and punished then the rest of the tribe should be let off with a warning. Of course, in the strict sense of the law, no such arbitrary approach may be taken; all perpetrators must be tried and punished, if convicted. It is not up to the police to exercise such discretion.

Turning now to operational issues, the first observation most commentators make is to assert that Walker simply rode around the countryside shooting Aborigines at will for no other reason than that they had to be eliminated so the country could prosper.[156] Far from it and contrary to this gung-ho view, Walker was strictly supervised and did his best to avoid unnecessary killing of Aborigines. Although no official rules of engagement appear to have been issued to Walker, the following is a good example of his view on what they were:

> What the Governor wants from you is to make charcoles (sic, charcoals) quiet. He does not want them killed and he won't let white fellows do so. If they won't be quiet, you must make them that's all. But you will not shoot unless your officer tells you. Mind, if the charcoles begin to throw spears or nulla nullas, then don't you wait but close up (and) knock them down.[157]

This simple direction to the Native Police was followed by *Instructions to Sergeants when in Command of Detachments* of which the following is a clear example of Walker's views on how sergeants are to carry out their duties:

> It is however certain that occasionally the Sergeants will have to endeavour to apprehend persons who have committed felony during

156 Do I really need footnotes? Ipse dixit: Reynolds, Bottoms, Loos, Tatz, Ørsted-Jensen et al.

157 See Chapter 11.

> their absence. When the Sergeant holds a warrant, his duty is very clear, if he can identify the individual or has reasonable grounds to believe him to be the individual and if he must with resistance, he is justified in making use of force against the man he wishes to apprehend and any person assisting him. The Sergeant has no right to retreat. When he holds no warrant; if he can prove that a felony has been committed and that he has reasonable cause to suspect an individual, he is justified in using force if resisted. With white persons, it is not difficult to prove all this; but blacks are so much alike the evidence is generally so faulty that the Sergeants must be very cautious. The Commandant has frequently found that the statements made to him by individuals differed very widely from their affidavits when made on oath by the same persons. When a Sergeant sees, a felony being committed as a matter of course he is obliged to take all the offenders in charge. Also, if he sees an assault committed; but not if he hears of an assault having been committed. In any case the same law applies to blacks as it does to whites and if the Sergeants go beyond the law they do so at their own risk. A Sergeant has no power to disperse an illegally assembled body of men without an order of a magistrate or the Riot Act has been read, but if any of them commit a felonious act, he is bound to seize him; and any person assisting the offender does so at his own peril. Many persons will try to run the Sergeants to acts of aggression against the blacks and these persons would be the first to turn on them if they succeed in making them break the law. The blacks cannot be considered as men armed for illegal purposes, because their weapons are their principal means of obtaining food.[158]

Apart from individual issues that may have arisen whilst in the field this appears to be the full extent of the legal directives applied to the Native Police by Walker. There is an admission by Walker against his own interest that he was advised by the Attorney-General that whilst on the Macintyre his activities were illegal.[159] This of course has been exaggerated by some commentators to support the 'black armband view of history'. Without any particulars, it is difficult to know what the illegality was. In what appears to be the next letter in this sequence of correspon-

[158] See Chapter 11.

[159] FW letter of Callandoon, 7 November 1850, see Chapter 11.

dence, the Attorney-General appears to be suggesting that the Native Police officers when alleging Aborigines resisted, failed to state on oath the actual acts of resistance; the resistance must be palpable. What was this illegality, was it root and branch misconduct or merely procedural?

Turning now to the court of public opinion, unfortunately, that court will not have a representative from the target demographics, the Aborigines. As I have said in earlier chapters, the Aborigines for whatever reason chose not to enter into a dialogue with the government of the day but acted in a way that was suggestive to the white settlers that they were hostile and destructive towards the enterprises of the settlers. The difficulty in putting the aboriginal side of the argument or debate is that their language does not appear to allow for the expression of abstract thought in regards principals of governance and protocols for settlement nor do they possess a script by which they might represent their thoughts in their own language. Thus, there are lacunae in regards aboriginal treatises on settlement by whites. I have as far as I am concerned put only one label on the Aborigines and that is Stone Age hunter-gatherers with the received assets the scientific community allows people thus classified. I do not intend to make any value judgements about them or to adopt any modern ethical, moral or legal standards by which to judge them at this juncture. I merely observe that they existed in as much as the settlers did. They could reason from experience and empirical evidence as the white settler could and did. Yet Aborigines never responded to the settlers nor the Governor in way that might have allowed an accommodation of the practical problems the Governor faced with white settlers, who believed they had a right to graze their livestock on the open range. I have often wondered in writing this book why so much angst appears to have arisen out of pastoral settlement in colonial Australia. I have never yet read a book that denounced the expansion of Pax Romana.[160] The right of discovery and or exploration is an acknowledged tenet of international law. Governor FitzRoy understood that and sought to accommodate that demand, provided the settlers did no harm to the Aborigines nor interfered with their hunter-gatherer status and their sources of food and subsistence. The point was initially made by Earl Grey: "Leases are not

160 Some wag will quote Tacitus: "when … nothing remains but desert, they call it peace", and enlist a Hebrew.

intended to deprive the natives of their former right to hunt over these Districts, or to wander over them in search of subsistence, in the manner to which they have been heretofore accustomed, from the spontaneous produce of the soil."[161]

Therefore, it is difficult to put the Aborigine view, if they had one. They seemed entrenched in their concept that white people and their goods were just another natural phenomenon ripe for the picking as they had done for millennia. Moreover, I am prepared to admit that initially the Aborigines had success in adopting this approach. In Hollywood talk, John Wayne would say, every time you shoot an Indian another two popup. The reality for the Aborigines was that every time they killed a white man another two would popup, ad infinitum. Which, of course, they did and that is the crux of the matter. The modern commentator's approach to this dearth of material on the aboriginal side, and it is a position because they openly state they appear for and represent the aboriginal interest, is to put words into the mouth of Aborigines as if they were writing an historical novel and then quote the statement back with ingenuous fervour as the genuine aboriginal position on some important historical event.[162]

What of the Aborigines then? What level of culpability is to be award to this group of individuals who committed murder, armed robbery, arson and stealing just to mention a few. This issue is never addressed by the black armband brigade. They gloss over the question of aboriginal criminality and culpability and allege the actions of the white man were either nonlegal (having no basis in law), illegal (prohibited by law) or criminal. Perhaps what they mean to say is that since the entry and occupation of Australia was root and branch illegal; in fact, an act of hostility, then any and all actions by the Aborigines are justified or excused by the defence of the homeland principle. Of course, it is an absurd justification for the criminal behaviour of the Aborigines against the white settlers given *Mabo [2]*.

DEANE and Gaudron JJ. 5. The common law of this country

---

161 Despatch No. 24 Earl Grey to FitzRoy 11 February 1848.

162 "to use Aboriginal voices to tell the story;" the works of Reynolds and Libby Connors are a good source of this.

> had its origins in, and initially owed its authority to, the common law of England (162) Confirmed by 9 GEO IV c.83 (The Australian Courts Act 1828 (Imp)), s.24. Under the common law of England, a distinction has traditionally been drawn, for the purposes of identifying the law of a new British Colony, between colonies where British sovereignty was established by cession or conquest and colonies where such sovereignty was established by settlement or "occupancy"(163) See Blackstone, Commentaries, 17th ed. (1830) (hereafter "Blackstone"), vol.1, par.107. In cases of cession and conquest, the pre-existing laws of the relevant territory were presumed to be preserved by the act of State constituting the Colony but the Crown, as new Sovereign, could subsequently legislate by proclamation pending local representative government. The position was quite different in the case of a settled Colony. Where persons acting under the authority of the Crown established a new British Colony by settlement, they brought the common law with them. The common law so introduced was adjusted in accordance with the principle that, in settled colonies, only so much of it was introduced as was "reasonably applicable to the circumstances of the Colony"(164) Cooper v. Stuart (1889) 14 App Cas 286, at p 291; see, also, State Government Insurance Commission v. Trigwell [1979] HCA 40; (1979) 142 CLR 617, esp. at p 634; Blackstone, vol.1, par.107. This left room for the continued operation of some local laws or customs among the native people and even the incorporation of some of those laws and customs as part of the common law. The adjusted common law was binding as the domestic law of the new Colony and, except to the extent authorized by statute, was not susceptible of being overridden or negatived by the Crown by the subsequent exercise of prerogative powers.

If *Mabo [2]* is correct, then Aborigines who resisted the law of the colony were amenable and subject to the criminal justice system of the colony.

Newspaper Summary

Name	Paper	Date	Comments	Remarks
W Johnson	MBC	5 Oct 1850	NP FA Maranoa	OD see FW ltr 7/11/50
R Jones	MBC	14 Dec1850	NP FA Burnett & WB	OD see FW ltr 7/11/50
JS Ferriter	MBC	14 Dec 1850	Info only	None required
J & N Hay	SMH	24 Jan 1852	NP essential	Favourable
Melancholy	MBC	10 Apr 1852	NP failed to act	OD
W Forster	SMH	2 Apr 1852	NP failed to act, ret to HQ	OD
A Squatter	MBC	24 Apr 1852	NP failed to act	Opinion
A Squatter	MBC	1 May 1852	NP failed to act	Opinion
A Squatter	MBC	29 May 1852	NP failed to act	Opinion
Wangallibee	MBC	10 July 1852	Reply to Melancholy & A Squatter	Favourable
Fiat Justitia	MBC	17 July 1852	NP deserve great credit	Favourable

FA=failed to attend OD=operational decision NP=Native Police

Post 16 June 1852, date Walker's letter published in SMH

Name	Paper	Date	Comments	Remarks
Editorial	SMH	23 June 1852	NP doing good job	Favourable
Glee	MBC	7 Aug 1852	NP under equipped	Favourable
A Squatter	MBC	7 Aug 1852	Walker incompetent	Dislikes NP
Editorial	MBC	7 Aug 1852	Conflicting opinions	Inquiry needed
WHW	MBC	14 Aug 1852	NP doing good job	Favourable
Slandered	SMH	14 Aug 1852	NP failed to act	Opinion
Shadow	MBC	21 Aug 1852	NP failed to act	Opinion
W Foster	SMH	21 Aug 1852	NP serves friends	Opinion
WH Walsh	SMH	11 Sep 1852	NP failed to act	Opinion
Squatter	MBC	11 Sep 1852	NP inferior force	Opinion
A Squatter	MBC	18 Sep 1852	NP ineffective	Opinion
WHW	MBC	23 Oct 1852	NP effective	Favourable
Squatter	MBC	20 Nov 1852	NP ineffective	Opinion
Subscriber	MBC	11 Dec 1852	NP effective	Favourable
A Squatter	MBC	17 Dec 1852	NP threaten white female	Refuted by FW

The above tables are my summaries of the letters to the Editor and the reader may after reading them at Chapter 10 — Letters to the Press, make up his own mind as to the thrust and meaning of each of the letters as they relate to Walker and the Native Police. I have divided the newspaper criticism along the fault line the government created when they published Walker's letter of 1 March 1852, which appeared as follows: *SMH* 16 June 1852, *Maitland Mercury* 26 June 1852 and *MBC* 17 July 1852. Most of the letters to the Editor are signed with pseudonyms and in the real world of putting your money where your mouth is, they would be thrown out as unnamed complainants.[163] Moreover, Walker only once responded to these anonymous letters and that was when Lt Bligh was defamed, see letter: "A Squatter published *MBC* 17 December 1852". Walker advised the Colonial Secretary that this letter was written by James Marks, a notorious hater of the blacks and thus his word was of little value.[164] This being so, is it fair to infer that all the above letters signed "A Squatter" were written by James Marks? They sound and taste similar, and, if so, therefore, may be ignored or dismissed as written with mala fide intent. If so, the attack on Walker is unjustified given that the government failed to give him clear legal instructions and clear rules of engagement, failed to give him adequate bureaucratic and managerial support and, lastly, failed to give him sufficient troopers, horses and equipment. However, some historians have hung their hats on these epistles and I am sorry to say their reputations as well, which no fair-minded commentator would do. The letter from William Forster, Gingin, Wide Bay, 2 March; *SMH* 2 April 1852 p 3 deserves some study since the author has put his name to the letter unlike most of the others. Ultimately, Mr W Forster became a significant person in the colony of NSW. However, I feel I am entitled to put the following facts forward because they go to his credit as a complainant; appointed a magistrate in 1842, Forster was removed from the lists in 1849[165] after a shooting incident in which an

163 The nit-picking, paranoid, social justice, pro bono lawyer would argue an employer has standing to act on and investigate unnamed complaints as possible whistle-blowers.

164 See Chapter 11, F Walker's letter Traylan, 31/12/1853 to Hon CS Re: incident.

165 He wrote a letter to the *MBC* dated Warwick, 21 March 1849 claiming no reasons were given for his dismissal. I would describe the letter as a pompous piece of self-serving malarkey. *MBC* 31 March 1849 p 2.

Aborigine was wounded by Gregory Blaxland.[166] Gregory Blaxland was his nephew and partner in the firm of Forster and Blaxland, who was killed by Aborigines in August 1850 at their head station in the Burnett District. Mr Forster's letter seems to be firstly, an initial blast at Messrs Leith Hay for supporting the Native Police and then, secondly, an acerbic rant about the ineptitude of the Native Police in having failed to execute the arrest warrants arising out of the Blaxland incident: "whether the warrants I have alluded to above would be put in force, the answer was, that the matter was in the hands of the ordinary authorities."

This criticism was a common allegation against Walker and the Native Police. However, to understand such a species of warrant, it has to be remembered that the warrant must state the arrestee's full name and his physical description together with the charges made against the suspect among other specifications set out on the face of the warrant. The custom in the case of arrest warrants for white persons was to write on the back of the warrant the physical features of the arrestee such as: complexion, weight, height, hair, eyes, age and any identification marks such as, scars, tattoos, birthmarks, moles, etc. In the case of Aborigines, the white informants appear to have had difficulty in recognising the particular physical characteristics of an Aborigine perhaps, through lack of familiarity with them. Consequently, their warrants were left without this added information. It might be helpful to pause and consider Walker's view about the arrest warrants he was given: "I hold several other absurd warrants such as two for blacks, names unknown and no description." Before a constable can execute the warrant, he must be certain of the identity of the person he is about to arrest by virtue of the warrant. In this day and age, police have recourse to ID cards, photographs, fingerprints and DNA. Walker often asked the informant to accompany him so he could identify the suspect. Often, they would not assist the Native Police. My view is that Forster was embittered over the loss of his two servant boys, the Peggs and his partner Blaxland[167] to violent death by Aborigines and saw Walker as an incompetent, government stooge who

---

166 http://adb.anu.edu.au/biography/forster-william-3553/text5489

167 This work may be useful as an introduction to Forster's background. Frontier Violence in Gin Gin A History of Murder, Massacre and Myth by Renee Coffey B.A. Uni of Qld 1 June 2006.

would not act against the Aborigines. Moreover, one has to understand the circumstances of the interception for arrest. Walker's critics seem to give no weight to the fact that he had to confront myall blacks in the bush who were unlikely to wait about while Walker went through the ritual of an arrest.

Of course, the cause celebre was Walker's letter of 1 March 1852 to the Colonial Secretary. The letter is remarkable for a wide variety of reasons and I doubt that Walker realised that it would be used against him in the manner in which it was. The incident has the appearance of a comedy of errors or a particularly, nasty example of the old saying, give a man enough rope and he will hang himself. Walker was under no obligation or pressure to write the letter. There had been no press criticism against him. In fact, most of it was favourable through 1851 and early 1852. Walker's letter is a piece of gratuitous self-aggrandisement. At times, Walker showed great insight such as in his letter of 22 October 1851 where he says: "8. I am aware that others persons have through the press been amusing themselves at my expense, but the opinion of these persons I believe not, as I knew that they would hunt to death any public servant if they only had the power." In fact, the letter of 22 October 1851 was his first attempt to justify himself and his actions as Commandant of the Native Police in the face of public criticism. FitzRoy noted on the letter: "Commandant's observations appear reasonable & satisfactory – as long as he continues to perform the arduous & responsible duties with same zeal & efficiency, will have support of Government." I feel most people would have interpreted this response by the government as keep up the good work but most of all keep your head down.

The thrust of Walker's March 1852 letter was to portray the settlers or more precisely the squatters as the aggressors and nasty ones at that too; perpetrators of cruelty, revenge and rapacious behaviour as well driving the blacks away from their own land and preventing them from making a living. These allegations were doubly reinforced by Walker flaunting his familiarity with the Governor General by ending his letter thus: "His Excellency the Governor General has already shown that he has sufficient confidence in me." For a public official who must interact with his constituency on a daily basis and to have some degree of civility with them, it does not do to call them names or challenge their bona fides. Again, pause and reflect on Walker's situation: "The letter is brought to me at a station where everybody is hurrying about on his business no room or table is left for one half hour at my disposal and I have to refer back to papers. I consequently go into the bush; the troopers make a bark table and chair the answers are written and forwarded by an orderly." For the squatters, they saw themselves as the aggrieved party who had extended the milk of human kindness to the Aborigines only to have their kindness summarily cut off with swift and silent retribution in the form of spearings, clublings and axings. For a group who had more self-righteousness under their mattresses than money, this form of bad behaviour by the Aborigines could not be tolerated. Moreover, it was an outrage to have a jumped-up, uncouth know-all like Walker instructing them, the crème de la crème of society, on how to run their businesses but more importantly, how to conduct themselves with Christian forbearance.

Be that as it may, FitzRoy praised his protégé as follows:

> Sir, With reference to you letter of 1st March last reporting the cause of the difference that exists between yourself and certain of the settlers in the Northern Districts. I do myself the honour to inform you that his Excellency the Governor General entirely concurs in the views and opinions expressed by you relative to the policy that ought to guide the government and the Native Police Force towards the settlers and the Aborigines; and which I am to add you have hitherto carried out to the satisfaction of the government. I have etc. E Deas Thomson[168]

Maybe so, however, an avalanche of abuse and hostility descended on Walker as the letters reveal; summed up as follows: "It is unfortunate that the Commandant of the Native Police is personally obnoxious to many in this district. Had he been a popular man this correspondence would, probably, never have come before the public." Furthermore, a group of settlers from the Burnett wrote to the Colonial Secretary dated 24 July 1852 disputing Walker's letter of 1 March 1852.[169] Moreover, the letter was published by the *Sydney Morning Herald* on page 3 of the edition of 11 September 1852 under the name of Wm Henry Walsh and may be seen at

168 SRNSW 4-3860 Reel2818 p 494.

169 FitzRoy wrote on the margin: Mr Walker. Sufficient, I think to acknowledge the receipt of this. CAF 10/9.

Chapter 10. Walker's response to this letter is addressed to the Colonial Secretary and dated 20 October 1852, which may be seen in Chapter 11.

The Governor's comments on Walker's reply were:

> Report appears a perfectly satisfactory refutation of statements contained in letter referred to; but as inclusion of that letter was merely acknowledged does not appear to be necessary to take any steps which would only have the effect of continuing the controversy, CAF.[170]

The public complaints against him were waved aside by FitzRoy. It appears because they shared a mutual belief that the Aborigines had a birthright to a use of or a right to the land but nobody could articulate what that use or right was. Earl Grey seemed to think that it was simply a matter of remembering past times and restoring Arcadia where the shepherds and the natives had lived in harmony forever. Walker saw himself as a pedagogue where the disobedient and recalcitrant Aborigines were to be weeded out and the tribe then taught to live a semi dependent life on the squatter's run. Of course, nothing worked, except that Walker did wear the tribes down and a kind of peace settled over the northern districts.

How effective was Walker? What were his clear-up rates? These questions are hard to answer because halfway through his command, Chinese coolies were introduced to overcome the lack of agricultural workers in the northern districts. The Chinese were not amenable to shepherding and for some reason the Native Police were given the task of policing those Chinese who worked and operated in the pastoral industry. There exist no returns by Walker that show crimes reported and clear-up rates. He reported to the Colonial Secretary on a regular basis in the form of a general narrative outlining what broad activities the Native Police carried out in the jurisdiction. I have constructed the following table from those reports which shows the number of Aborigines killed by native police in carrying out operational activities.[171]

---

170 QSL Reel A2.24 p 675.

171 1849 to 1859, NP killed 102 aborigines, see "A Question of Necessity" The Native Police in Queensland by J Richards Submitted for Ph D Griffith University March 2005, Appendix 3.

Source	Location	K	W	Remarks
FW ltr 23/3/1849	Upper Darling	5		NP self defence
FW ltr 26/5/1849	Macintyre		1	NP self defence
FW ltr 12/7/1849	Carbucky	2	x*	NP resisting
FW ltr 10/3/1851	Corfield's Stn	?	?	Affray 28/12/50
FW ltr 10/3/1851	S Scott's Stn	?	?	Shoot out 29/12/50
FW ltr 1/8/1851	Maryborough	2		NP resisting
FW ltr 1/8/1851	Dawson	1		NP self defence
FW ltr 15/9/1851	Burnett/WB	1		NP escaping
FW ltr 31/12/1851	Maranoa	3		NP resisting
FW ltr 31/12/1851	Wallann Stn	1		NP resisting
FW ltr 31/12/1851	Mackay's Stn	2		NP escaping 2/10
FW ltr 31/12/1851	Mackay's Stn	2		NP escaping 7/10
FW ltr 31/12/1851	Tooth's Stn	1		NP escaping 1/12
FW ltr 5/1/1852	Fraser's Island	2		NP resisting
FW ltr 23/7/1852	Yamboukal	?	?	NP affray
FW ltr 4/10/1852	Trevethan's Stn	1		NP resisting 18/4
FW ltr 4/10/1852	Mackay's Stn	3		NP resisting 29/8
FW ltr 26/10/1852	Macintyre	5		NP resisting 20/10

** Number unclear, several wounded. See THE NATIVE POLICE AT CALLANDOON – A BLUEPRINT FOR FORCED ASSIMILATION? Mark Copland Griffith University, Qld Canberra, 9-10 December 1999.*

The above table is not the full story because one cannot be certain as to its accuracy and completeness. The above table records thirty-one (31) deaths which were either excused or justified by law. Why I believe these figures are, if not the total number, at least realistic is because in response to Walker's report of 31 December 1851, FitzRoy wrote on the margin of this letter: "Attorney-General to peruse letter as great many blacks reported killed by Police – trust depositions when received will prove these acts of severity to have been unavoidable." This close supervision by FitzRoy suggests to me that any large-scale raids or attacks by unauthorised parties of settlers would have drawn FitzRoy's attention and the matter would have been investigated. Therefore, I do not subscribe to the massacre theory of which there were at least three during Walker's time as Commandant of the Native Police. These alleged incidents are identified as follows: the Carbucky incident involving Walker, the Cedars incident and the Paddy's Island incident.

I have also examined Mr Walker's style of writing and vocabulary. I have done this because a number of commentators when dealing with Mr Walker have denounced him as being the principal agent of the government's apparatus to suppress and exterminate aboriginal natives. Some on such flimsy evidence as his statement: "I would have annihilated that lot." It is my contention that neither the government at Westminster nor the governor of New South Wales ever had a policy of suppression or extermination of Australian Aborigines; as time went by, a working policy was developed from the ground up with the aspiration that the Aborigines would integrate with the pastoral economy and become a useful part of it. Unfortunately, this policy was not spelt out or articulated in a coherent manner and was rendered unworkable because the Aborigines continued a campaign of attacks on the ever-expanding pastoral settlements of Australia. This policy was cobbled together by the governor and his advisers and by the time of Walker, the governor had picked up the novel idea of putting on the ground in the trouble spots a dedicated policing body to shield the frontier. Nobody had any idea really how it might work other than putting a protective force on the frontier to watch and ward. Walker was selected; as I have said, totally uneducated and unskilled in any of the English gentlemanly professions such as a Lord, a lawyer, a clergyman, an officer (Naval or Army),[172] or a don. His only claim to fame was as an Australian bushman, which in reality was all that was needed. However, because of class prejudice at the time, Walker was considered an uncouth buffoon, with a bigmouth and a haughty manner. His grammar was bad, his syntax appalling and his construction of sentences tortuous. What of his vocabulary? Grandiloquent, with a weakness for words with Latin roots, the meaning of which he had not the slightest idea.

---

172 EW Docker writing in the *Sunday Telegraph* of 25 August 1985 at page 144 said that Frederick Walker was a former officer in the Bombay Marines who had disgraced himself but had been allowed to go Australia in 1844. The British Library hold all records for Bombay Marines and no record of F Walker can be found between 1838 and 1848.

Examples

"encumbered with the horses, the horse was an encumbrance"

Why not say a hindered, impeded or a hindrance?

"attempting the dispersion and subjugation of the hostile tribes, dispersed and subdued the tribes that are now destroying this district"

Why not say divide et impera or divide and conquer? Dispersion has caused a great deal of angst among some commentators seeing it as a code word and proof of the secret plan for a final solution. Normally, it would mean to scatter or break up, for a harder meaning perhaps rout. Commentators need to remember the Riot Act which allowed police to disperse unlawful crowds of people with punitive force.

"iniquitous practice, infest the brigalows ..."

Both words nasty and judgmental, one moment accusing the settlers of being morally wrong and in the same breath equating the Aborigines to an infestation of the brigalow scrub.

"I would have annihilated that lot."

To destroy completely; hardly the sober words of a Commandant of Police. To my mind, Walker was prone to bouts of grandiose delusions arising out of his rapid elevation in the colonial service, his drinking and his foolish belief that the Governor relied on him for advice which was never the case.

"these persons stigmatise as injudicious. ... they would hunt to death any public servant ..."

Again, the use of exaggerated and inappropriate language that seeks to portray him as a victim of unfair criticism; a continuation of his delusional state of persecution and self-importance.

"vindictiveness against the blacks."

A repetition of the use of emotive words, perhaps retaliatory or punitive; even better would have been firmness against the blacks. Vindictiveness suggests spiteful revenge, which the settlers did not want. They wanted relief from the frequent attacks on their employees and livestock.

"to protest malignantly against an inference"

Once again, Walker portrays his paranoia by suggesting that any criticism of him was from ill will or malicious; it was never fair criticism.

"an infamous libel"

A familiar cliché, demonstrating that anything said against him is not fair comment but an infamous libel.

"Absurd warrants"

Judge Therry said, "his expression of several absurd warrants certainly seem to be a very unsuitable mode for this gentleman to express himself respecting warrants issued under competent authority;"

Again, Walker has adopted a form of language that given his position as head of a police force, created the impression of unprofessionalism bordering on incompetence. What he meant to say, it appears, was that the warrants were illegal and void for their uncertainty, lack of adequate description of the arrestee.

My view is that Walker's language is not a helpful tool to discern or prove he was either the father of or the perpetrator of a policy to eradicate or exterminate Aborigines because he was delusional most of the time either from alcohol or quinine which exacerbated his work-related anxiety and stress.

Speaking generally, Walker had a force of men who were capable of attacking Aborigines in the wild and going hand-to-hand with them; "1st section when I state that they average 5 feet 10 inches in height and 11st 5lb in weight." The one advantage he had was that his men had firearms, carbines. However, the weapons were cap and ball,[173] percussion muzzleloaders. To load them the trooper was required to stand upright and expose himself to danger; and placing a cap on the nipple, while on horseback or under combat stress was difficult. On the other hand, myall blacks did not fight in the open and they had foolproof weapons, unlike the black powder firearms of Walker's which could misfire. After

173 The cap on being struck by the hammer, ignites the powder which expels the ball, a solid missile discharged from the firearm, with the aim of hitting the target.

an initial volley of spears and other assorted throwing sticks, Aborigines would retreat to the closest thick scrub or decamp completely from the scene. Walker would then dismount and the tactics would be to make contact with the opposition who rarely hung around to skirmish. Only native police were capable of following myalls into the scrub, whites were not surefooted enough. His reports are replete with the all too familiar refrain that the aboriginal natives made off.

The following anecdote drawn from the time of Walker and featuring him in action may allow most people to make a reasonable assessment of the Australian frontier:

> As the natives continued hostile, we found it necessary to punish them for plundering Ross's camp, and several Murrumbidgee men came to our assistance, John Scott, the Jackson brothers, Williams an ex-barrister who lived with them, Lee, and Frederick Walker who brought with him two fine Murrumbidgee natives, Robin Hood and Marengo, who proved useful. These two blacks afterwards accompanied Walker to Queensland when he was appointed Commandant of the Native Police. Ross and I joined and made a party of eight mounted whites and two natives.
>
> These people evidently had gathered in this miserable camp to be out of harm's way, and of course we did not molest them. They assured Marengo they were not present at the raid on Ross's camp and professed much friendship and so on. We broke up any war spears found, but otherwise did not molest them; and Walker, to impress them I suppose, drew one of his holster pistols and fired at a dog close by but missed him. This set us laughing as we rode away.
>
> Our next search was along the River, and the second day we came upon a mob who shewed fight and there was some shooting. They had fired the grass around and it was difficult to see or follow them though they yelled enough. During the firing Robin Hood ran up to a native who was yabbering at the top of his voice and threw his arm round him and shouted to us, "God damn you, don't shoot my father!" Not so kind was Marengo, for I saw him drag a child from a log by the legs and swing him intending to knock his brains out, when we stopped him.
>
> The skirmish was soon over for the blacks had the river to dive

> into. One afternoon in a big bend of the river a mob of seventy to eighty native all painted and armed for a fight shewed up and came on in a semi-circle yelling and abusing us at the top of their voices and this time they did not skulk behind tress. Now we were in quite open ground and as the natives' reed spears thrown with the woomera would carry to seventy to eighty yards we went back a short distance to a large fallen tree with many broken limbs, and there we took our stand. As we were retiring to this tree the natives set up a great yell thinking, I suppose, we were retreating, and came on valorously until we opened fire, and some were hit. Then they took shelter behind any trees, showing only when throwing a boomerang or launching a spear, but they soon tired of that for none of their spears reached us. As a matter of fact, these reed spears are only dangerous at a distance when the blacks are cool, for when excited their marksmanship was very poor; nor was our shooting much more effective, for our smooth bore carbines and shot guns did not carry ball with any precision more than sixty to eighty yards. Bad as the shooting was, the natives did not stand long, but as usual bolted for the river and we after them, taking snap shots at heads as they came to the surface to breathe. I should here say we had to make our own cartridges, after fashion, and ram the ball on top. Our appliances for shooting in those days were very primitive.[174]

My view of most modern commentators on this period of conflict between Aborigines and the white settlers is that they have never operated a firearm let alone loaded and fired a black powder, percussion muzzleloader. I am left with the overwhelming impression that these commentators assumed every settler was armed with a John Wayne repeating rifle, six gun and modern ammunition that was smokeless and never misfired; and, moreover, that the settlers and native police rode horses of the quality Wayne rode and had Hollywood backup; and, furthermore, that the Aborigines charged in mass formation, which was far from the truth.

The final assessment of Walker can only be made by taking Frederick Walker out of the festering pustule of Moreton Bay as it then was and

---

[174] The Morey Papers, Ed Vivian R de Vaux Voss, Emu Park, Qld 10 February 1952 pp 24-31.

putting him up against the grand scheme of things. From time immemorial, philosophers have pondered the concept of dualism: mind and matter, nature and nurture, black and white, good and evil, yin and yang and nomadic versus sedentary. The sedentary peoples have tried all sorts of tricks, defences, tributes, treaties and all-out warfare against nomadic people, but never the twain shall meet it seems, as far as an acceptable outcome. When looked at clinically, farmer soldiers could never match nomadic warriors. However, farmers had made huge advancements in animal technology by domesticating animals and training dogs to guard and shepherd them. Could that technology be used against nomadic groups? The trick was to distil the paradigm from this technology and apply it against the nomads. This approach to dealing with threatening invaders or disruptive groups within or at the boundaries of society is to chant the old mantra, set a thief to catch a thief. The principle is straight forward. Since the nomadic warrior enjoys fighting and the recognition that goes with it, he is easily recruited as a mercenary at a very low cost; Native Police were paid 3^{d} a day[175] while white police were paid 5/6 a day, twenty-two times greater than the Aborigine. The benefits are as follows: the warrior can be counted twice, first as an addition to the settlers' forces and secondly, as a loss to the nomads. Then there is the economic gain in that the small outlay on his wages mitigates loss of life and his otherwise property damage through plunder or having to pay large subsides. Then there are the social gains, by bringing him into the fold, you are at best reducing his capacity to revert back and perhaps, have him, in turn, weaken the resolve of the tribe by his new learned manners and acquired property. The application of this principle only needs the right form of leadership of the newly acquired mercenaries. The Native Police when looked at through this abstraction perhaps, allows Walker to seen as just another patsy flattened on the anvil of national advancement. I don't believe Walker was an alcoholic who just threw away his rank and station in life. In modern terms, he would be described as suffering post-traumatic stress disorder but as I said, he has to be judged by the standards of his day and he was adjudged an alcoholic which allowed FitzRoy to discard him and continue the amaranthine game of trying to find the hidden se-

[175] The ration for each native trooper was 1 lb. of flour, 2 lbs. meat, ½ oz tea, ¼ lb. sugar, half a fig of tobacco, and ½ oz. soap, a day.

cret to frontier harmony. To me Walker sits in same pantheon as Breaker Morant, and TE Lawrence.

Perhaps the following might stand as a valediction to Frederick Walker JP:

> Its officers were chosen from men whose qualifications were supposed to be education, breeding, knowledge of drill and firearms, and ability to handle natives. Those were the written demands. The unwritten ones included the right to die unhonoured and unmourned, to ride in constant danger, and to suffer privation and hardship.[176]

[176] space.library.uq.edu.au/view/UQ:212740s00855804_1964_1965_7_3_508.pdf

4

Dismissal

The dismissal of Commandant Walker seems incongruous given the level of rapport he appeared to have had with FitzRoy. However, the record revealed he had two groups of critics who were prepared to use their power to remove him from the command of the Native Police. In the preceding chapter, I attempted to assess the operational effectiveness of the Native Police and although conventional data on which to assess such an organisation was difficult to collect, my view is that by and large the Native Police under Walker was effective and efficient in protecting the frontier outside the settled districts. So why would groups seek to get rid of Walker? It seems to me that Walker had a makeup that brought him into conflict with his peers usually by his publicly criticising them. From this far out when assessing Walker, I submit it is reasonable to tender Walker's letter of 1 March 1852 to the Colonial Secretary and his Circular to the Officers of the Native Police Corps dated 1 July 1854, which may be found at Chapter 11 as evidence of his willingness to provoke and antagonise those he worked with, such as colleagues and squatters. Both letters are rambling, self-serving diatribes against the squatters in the first instance and his officers in the second. Each letter received the approbation of FitzRoy which to the aggrieved parties would have been unreasonable given Walker's immensely narcissistic personality.

On 30 August 1854, the Legislative Council in considering Estimates resolved itself into the Committee of Supply:

> The Auditor General proposed the following for the Native Police force an increase of pay to 96 troopers, from 3d to 5d each per diem, £292 etc. Mr Flood thought this native police force should be placed under the superintendence of the Inspector General of Police. As long as this force was under the exclusive management of the commandant, there would be no certainty that the force received the pay and rations voted for them. As far as he could

hear, the character of the present commandant was not such as would warrant the confidence reposed in him. It was the subject of frequent complaints that if this officer were ever found sober; it was from the very good reason that he could obtain no drink.

Dr Douglass protested against the practice of making attacks on the personal character of public officers in the House. If complaints were justified, they should be made to the Executive, and not in a way which prevented any individual attacked from saying anything in his own justification. With regard to the system of distributing the rations, if it was under the sole superintendence of the commandant, he thought that the system was wrong. There ought to be an appeal open to the men.

The Colonial Secretary defended the conduct of the commandant, declaring that he believed him to be the most efficient person for the office in the country.

The Attorney-General expressed his belief that, if the commandant were a habitual drunkard, he was unfit for his office, or any other office; but he thought no indecency of conduct could exceed that of any hon. member of that House indulging, under cover of the privileges he enjoyed, in attacks on the private and personal characters of persons not present to defend themselves. He had had much correspondence with this officer, and had always found him an able officer, he had also had many complaints made against him, but they were mainly of a personal nature, but certainly they did not involve the charge now made against him. If any such charge could be substantiated, on due representation to the Government, the proper steps would be taken.

Mr Leslie defending the character of the commandant expressed his opinion that the discussion upon it was entirely irrelevant.

Mr Morris defended in strong terms the zeal of the officer in question and deprecated the discussion on his character which had taken place.

Dr Lang had been lately in the Northern Districts, (laughter) and in the course of his peregrinations he had heard that the officer whose character had been called in question was heartily devoted to his duty, and the wonder was how he contrived to manage his troops so well, when he appeared generally half-seas-over. (Laugh-

> ter) Considering that his services were deemed well performed, the House might be disposed to overlook his peccadilloes, yet he protested against any person being the recipient of the public money whose character as an officer was not unquestionable.
>
> Mr Suttor remarked that the Government time ought not to be taken up day after day in entertaining petty charges of such a nature. If any person had a complaint to make against a public officer, the Executive and not the House were bound to investigate it, unless the Executive refused to entertain the question, when it might be brought before the House; but there was no proof that such had been the case in the present instance.
>
> Mr Cowper differed from those honourable members who condemned the discussion relative to the character of the Commandant of Police, for so long as he had reason to believe that a public officer was a public delinquent, that officer should hear of it from him, and he would not vote money for such an officer. At any rate, in voting a sum of money they were bound to have regard to the trustworthiness of the individual to whom the money was entrusted, and he hoped after what had transpired that the Government would institute an inquiry into the charges preferred against their officer, and either clear up his character or dismiss him from the service.
>
> Mr Flood asserted that the recipient of public money for paying the aboriginal police ought not to be a reputed drunkard, and the question before the Committee was, whether, in the event of the allegation being true, the commandant was a fit person to be the recipient, and to have the appropriation of the public money. The vote was then carried.[177]

The above outburst in the House put Frederick Walker smack dab in the middle of a controversy that gave his detractors the opportunity to belittle and ridicule him. Walker's close friend, Augustus Morris, member of the Legislative Council and settler of Callandoon, wrote to Walker on 6 September 1854 from the Australian Club, Sydney:

> My dear Walker, I have only a moment to write to you. All sorts of charges are being made against you and your police, as see *En-*

[177] *SMH* 31 August 1854 p 4.

> *glishman*[178] of Saturday. The murder of the blacks there referred to was today brought before the Council by Cowper on a question to the Attorney-General who said he never before heard about the neglect but expressed his determination to leave no stone unturned to enquire into the matter. He has not written a letter to the Editor for his authority. The plot seems to thicken against you. That terrible failing, as I have warned you so often will I fear be the ruin of you. I intend to move Friday for a Select Committee to enquire into and report upon the general management of the Native Police. The Committee will be: Cowper-Leslie, Dobie-Mayne, Flood-Nichols, King-Russel & the Attorney-General. This the only course by which you can get justice and be brought face to face with your accusers. I will of course be the Chairman. I have just told the Colonial Secretary that I am writing to you to come. He will write by the steamer's next mail. You must not delay a minute. Bring with you the means of defending yourself and bring everything, the excessive charges of the settlers for rations and things. In fervent haste, yours sincerely A Morris[179]

The record also revealed a fragment of a further letter written by Morris to Walker on or about the same time as follows:

> … you are charged with being unfit to be entrusted with the ration money of the Police. It is said it ought to be done by contract. I know this to be nonsense. I wish you would provide me with the means of defending you as I have undertaken to do, when your (situation) comes under consideration. I will fight for you to the last but you must reform you must purge officers et al, risk charges. I send you the *Herald* but the papers never reveal the discussions in committee at any length. A tremendous onslaught was made on you. Lose no time in writing to me. I will in case I do not hear from you in time … every assistance for the Colonial Secretary's office. I wish you were here. Hoping that all these … matters may be of ulterior advantage to you. Believe me, yours sincerely A Morris[180]

Then the following proceedings were reported in the debates of the Legislative Council, on 7 September 1854, with reference to the Native

178 A Sydney newspaper which ran an article on 2 September 1854 accusing the Native Police of murdering aborigines.

179 QSA Series ID14733/86134

180 QSA Series ID14733/86134

Police. Mr Morris (Liverpool Plains) moved:

> 1. That a select committee be appointed to inquire into, and report upon, the general management of the Native Police.
>
> 2. That such committee consist of the following members, viz. Mr Cowper, Mr Leslie, Mr Dobie, Capt. Mayne, Mr Flood, Mr Nichols, Captain King, Mr Russell, and the Attorney-General. Mr Barker seconded the motion.
>
> The Colonial Secretary did not think that the course proposed to be pursued by the hon. member for Liverpool Plains was the correct one. He had stated on a previous evening that the Government would inquire into the charges against the Commandant of the Native Police, and, in his opinion, charges of such a nature as had been made against the Native Police ought to be investigated by the Government. He did not make these observations in disparagement of the Select Committee of the House, the value of those services he appreciated and acknowledged, and he promised that if the hon. member would withdraw his motion; an investigation should be instituted by the Government.
>
> Mr Morris, in deference to the expressed wish of the House, would withdraw his motion although he had no confidence in Government inquiries. Leave having been granted, the motion was withdrawn.[181]

On 19 September 1854, from the Australian Club, Morris wrote again:

> My dear Walker, I had intended to have sent you an outline of my speech in moving for a committee on your case, but I have been so busy that I have been unable to carry out the intention.
>
> The Government intend to order an inquiry on the spot into the management of your Force and I greatly fear that you will be sacrificed to the clamour against you. However well you may prove you have managed the Force, nevertheless your intemperance will be seized hold of as sufficient to dismiss you. I must say that I fear your Force is dreadfully disorganised, your officers and yourself do not stand to one another in the relation you ought. Now I have always warned you against intemperance, I always saw that the habit would be your stumbling block and the more merely that you had

[181] *SMH* 9 September 1854 p 10.

> deceived yourself into a belief that you scarcely ever exceeded.
>
> I hope you may re-establish your character and by the past correct the future. You will see by the papers what is said against you. There can be little doubt that your troop requires wholly to be reformed. From every side, they think there is discipline neither amongst officers nor men. I hope I shall hear from you before the General Estimates come in. Mark you thus, the Select Committee was refused for the reasons above mentioned, believe me. Yours sincerely A Morris.[182]

On 21 September 1854, the Colonial Secretary wrote to Walker as follows:

> Sir, In consequence of certain representations having been received from the officers under your command seriously affecting your character as an officer, His Excellency the Governor General has deemed it expedient to relieve you from duty until they can be duly investigated.
>
> 2. His Excellency directs me while communicating this information to instruct you to proceed to Brisbane where you will receive further instructions through the Government Resident there. I have etc. W. Elyard.[183]

On the same date, the Colonial Secretary also wrote to Lieutenant RP Marshall as follows. However, it should be noted that FitzRoy in approving the below letter wrote the following comments on the draft: "Approved. CAF 20th I think upon consideration it will form a dangerous precedent to suspend the Commandant upon ex parte statements of his subordinate officers. He can be informed that he is relieved from duty during the investigation and ordered to proceed to Brisbane where he will receive further instructions through the Govt Resident. Then Lt Marshall should be informed that, although under the circumstances it is not to be wondered at that he addressed himself direct to the Government instead of sending his letter through the Commandant, he should have furnished that officer with a copy of it in order that he might have had the opportunity of defending himself if it was with in his power to

182 QSA Series ID14725/86134

183 SRNSW 4-3862 Reel 2818 p 422.

do so. CAF 20th."[184]

> Sir, I do myself the honour to inform you that your letters tendering your own resignation and enclosing communications from the officers named in the margin (Lts Fulford, Murray, Irving, Nicol, R Walker & Sgt Dolan) containing statements against the Commandant of the Native Police and also tendering their resignations have been received and laid before the Governor General.
>
> 2. An investigation will be made into the circumstances referred to and the Commandant afforded an opportunity of furnishing such explanation as it may be in his power to do; but in the meantime, the resignation of yourself and the others of the corps cannot be accepted.
>
> 3. As the Commandant has been informed that he is to consider himself as relieved from duty during the investigation and that he is to proceed to Brisbane where he will receive further instructions through the Government Resident there. His Excellency requests that you as Senior Lieutenant will do what is necessary and may be in your power for keeping up the discipline of the native police force and that you will intimate to the several officers that they must be responsible for their own immediate commands so that the native troopers may not be let loose on the community pending His Excellency's decision on the case of the Commandant.
>
> 4. You will be good enough to acknowledge the receipt of this letter and to report the steps that you may take in consequence thereof.
>
> 5. I am however to remark that although it is not to be wondered at that you addressed yourself direct to the Government instead of sending your letter through the Commandant yet you should have furnished that officer with a copy of it in order that he might have had the opportunity of defending himself if it was in his power to do so. I have etc. W. Elyard.[185]

On 3 October 1854, Walker wrote a rather touching and prescient letter from Traylan to Sergeant Alexander Walker:

> Sir, It is with much regret I have heard that two men have been

184 QSL A2.48 p 104.

185 SRNSW 4-3862 Reel 2818 p 423.

killed on the Dawson notwithstanding the precautions I had taken.

2. I trust that upon the return of the men you tried all you could do to discover these murderers.

3. Whenever you go on duty yourself remember to give your orders in writing to whatever corporal you may leave behind.

4. I need not remind you to be cautious in carrying out the written instructions to sergeants.

5. I regret to state that it is probable I shall soon leave the force and most of the troopers resign with me. I will see that you are provided for. By next post you will receive your pay up to 30 September. I would send it over but not for Ferguson been absent.

6. Send me Dick and Jemmy with the light cart and my horses except Jundah which Orlando will keep. I remain etc. F Walker Cmd^t NP. Edward will want you to write a letter to me for him, which please send by the next post. He must sign it as well as Tahiti and Larry.[186]

On 14 October 1854, Walker, still at Traylan, replied to the Colonial Secretary:

Sir, I do myself the honour to state in reply to your letter of 21st September, N° 312 that my horses as stated in my letter of 25th Sept N° 54/23 are all knocked up but as I expected some here on the 21st I will then immediately start according to your instructions for Brisbane.

2. In the meanwhile, I am engaged with Mr Ferguson in making up the accounts. I have etc. F Walker Cmd^t NP

On 31 October 1854, FitzRoy noted on Walker's above reply: "Read. Capt. Wickham may be informed in order that he may report if Mr Walker does not arrive into Brisbane in due time. CAF 31st. Capt. Wickham 2 November 1854, 54/9848."[187]

On 25 October 1854, JC Wickham Govt Resident, Brisbane advised the Colonial Secretary: "Sir, With reference to your letter of the 23rd ultimo, No 54. 8216 enclosing letters from the officers of the Native Police

186 QSA Series ID 14725/86134

187 SRNSW NRS906 4/719.2.

Corps preferring charges against the Commandant of that Force, I do myself the honour to inform you that Mr Walker has not yet reached Brisbane."[188]

FitzRoy observed: "I consider that Mr Walker had not had sufficient time to comply with his orders, when this was written?"

When Walker had not arrived in Brisbane by 8 November 1854, Wickham again wrote to the Colonial Secretary and FitzRoy commented as follows: "Had sufficient time elapsed for Mr Walker to proceed to Brisbane after his second order to do so?"

The Colonial Secretary replied: "Yes, the letter instructing him to proceed to Brisbane left the office on the 27th September last. But see 54/9447 enclosed."

FitzRoy noted: "Nothing further need be done at present."

When the House again went into debate about estimates for the Native Police on or about 16 November 1854, the Colonial Secretary stated "that it was a matter of great regret with the Government, that a collision had taken place between the Commandant of the Native Police and his officers, and that in consequence, the whole of the latter had sent in their resignations, which might be considered a step which would involve the disbanding of the force. A commission had been appointed by the Government to inquire into the conduct of the Commandant; he had hoped that they should have been enabled to lay its report before the House; but he had not yet received any intelligence from the commission beyond the fact that Mr Walker, the Commandant of the Native Police force, had not yet appeared before them. The Commandant of the Native Police had not as yet been actually suspended, but he had been directed to attend on the Board at Brisbane, and in the meantime the command of the force devolved on the senior lieutenant of the force."[189]

On 1 January 1854[190] from Brisbane, Frederick Walker wrote to the Colonial Secretary enclosing a medical certificate, as follows:

---

188 SRNSW NRS906 4/719.2.

189 *SMH* 16 November 1854 p 4.

190 Should read 1855.

Frederick Walker to Col. Sec.

I do myself the honour to state that although no such intimation has been given to me, I am aware that the Board at this place has given a decision adverse to me and upon that I wish to make no remarks; but previously to this decision a circumstance took place of which I most grievously complain. Two troopers (Dick & Boonya James) of the N° 4 Section had accompanied me as orderlies, my one orderly Considine doing duty in the place of me and my other being dead. On the day, previously to the meeting of the Board when (page missing) Considine the four horses in the margin chestnut-Pussy Cat, brown-Wallibin, brown-Camelaroy & grey-packhorse, my three police saddles and return to me the private property taken at Brisbane.

His Excellency would oblige me by allowing Paul or Orlando I do not care which to accompany Considine as he would not be able to manage such a journey by himself. Considine has never been in any section and is new on the Dawson. In the meanwhile, I remain on the Logan at the stations of different settlers from whom luckily, I have received much kindness during my sickness and who have expressed much indignation at such a gross act of violence.

I would feel obliged by your letting me know whether His Excellency accedes to my request in order that I may write to Considine relative to some articles I left on the Dawson.[191]

Enclosure to Walker's letter:

H. Bell MD, North Brisbane, 22 December 1854

I hereby certify that Commandant Frederick Walker J.P. has been under medical treatment, for some day's past, suffering from nervous debility.

I am not much acquainted with this gentleman, having attended him for the first time a few days since, but I can state that a person in this condition may, in both walking and speaking, very much resemble a person directly under the influence of liquor.

The Colonial Secretary instructed on 19 January 1855 that a copy of Walker's letter be sent to Lt Marshall, A/Commandant for any observa-

191 QSL Reel A2.31 p 402.

tions he may wish to make regards Walker's comments. He also wrote to Frederick Walker on the same date as follows:

Col. Sec. to Frederick Walker, 19 January 1855

Referring to my letter of the 21st September last, informing you that in consequence of certain representations having been received from the officers under your command seriously affecting your character as an officer, his Excellency the Governor General had decided it expedient to relieve you from duty until they were duly investigated. I am mow instructed to inform you that a progress report has been received from a Board of Officers consisting of the Government Resident at Moreton Bay, the Crown Commissioner of that District and the Police Magistrate of Ipswich who had been appointed to enquire into the charges preferred against you.

2 The Board however found it expedient to discontinue the formal enquiry initiated before them for the reason alleged in their Report from which the following is an extract: In conformity with the instructions contained in your letter of the 23rd September last, we have the honour to inform you that the Board of Enquiry for investigating the charges preferred against the Commandant of the Native Police assembled at Brisbane on the 23rd November last for the purpose of making preliminary arrangements, the Commandant having already reported his arrival to Captain Wickham. Notice having been forwarded to the Acting Commandant Marshall to attend the Board with the necessary witnesses and their arrival being notified. The Board assembled again at 12 o'clock on the 19th instant to proceed with the inquiry when there (sic, they) were in attendance: Acting Commandant Marshall, Lieutenant Irving and Sub Lieutenants Nicol and Bligh. Commandant Walker failed to appear after waiting half an hour the Board proceeded with the examination of Marshall. Whilst so doing Mr Walker presented himself at the office (it being about one hour after the time appointed for the meeting) accompanied by some eight or nine of the Native Police, which he was most desirous to bring into the Court with him. This however being resisted they were left at the door, and Mr Walker took his seat evidently in a state of intoxication bordering on stupidity so at not even to recognise his first Lieutenant Mr Marshall who was sitting at his side, seeing the disgraceful condition of the Commandant the Board requested him to retire, this however he declined to do and conducted himself in such a haughty and insulting manner to

the Board that without removing him by force they had only one resource to adjourn the Court. This being done Mr Walker retired with the troopers and was proceeding with them across the river when Mr Marshall assisted by the officers in the presence of one of the Board prevented him, but the officers with the assistance of the Chief Constable secured their arms and accoutrements but not without some danger, as Mr Walker drew a sword and threatened Mr Irving. In the evening, the two troopers also returned bringing over their horses with them having left their drunken Commandant in disgust.

3 After examining the officers present as to the arrears of pay and rations alleged to be due to them, the Board postponed their further proceeding and reported as follows: (1) that Commandant Walker is in constant habits of intoxication, that render him totally unfit for any responsible post under government and particularly for that of commanding the Native Police. (2) that the accounts of the Native Police Corps are in such a state of confusion and the arrears due for pay and rations so heavy (as shown in an account for rations supplied by several persons for the use of the men marked a.) that in the opinion of the Board immediate steps should be taken to stop the appropriation of any further sums on Mr Walkers orders. (3) That Mr Walker is tampering with the police and endeavouring to render them disaffected to their officers and the Government, the Board have ample evidence under their own eyes, although they have no fear for the result.

4 Under the circumstances disclosed in this Report, His Excellency with the advice of the Executive Council has desired me to inform you that you are now dismissed from the office of Commandant of Native Police.[192]

Col. Sec. to Lt RP Marshall, 19 January 1855

Having laid before his Excellency the Governor General the report of the Board appointed to investigate the charges preferred against Mr Walker the Commandant of Native Police by the officers of that corps, I am instructed to inform you that under the disgraceful circumstances disclosed in that report. His Excellency with the advice of the Executive Council has been pleased to dismiss Mr Walker

[192] SRNSW 4-3862 Reel 2818 p 484. Please note the transcript of the inquiry may be seen at Chapter 11.

from the office of Commandant of Native Police.

2. His Excellency with the advice of the Council has also been pleased to direct that the position in a pecuniary point of view in which Mr Walker stands to the government should be immediately inquired into and reported upon by the proper officer in order to determine what further steps it may be necessary to take with respect to him. With this view, His Excellency has desired me to request that you will immediately endeavour to call in all outstanding claims on the government by reason of liabilities incurred by Mr Walker on account of the public service and in the meantime the officers of the corps will be paid the arrears which are apparently due to them.[193]

Col. Sec. to Lt RP Marshall, 9 February 1855

I do myself the honour to inform you that his Excellency the Governor General has been pleased to appoint you to be Commandant of the Native Police in the room of Frederick Walker Esq dismissed.[194]

In the end, the fall of Frederick Walker was a rather tawdry affair which reflected badly on the entire system. He was an ordinary man plucked from the backblocks of southern NSW, who seemed to possess remarkable skills as a bushman with a good deal of energy, and was asked to set up and run a law enforcement agency in a wilderness with little or no support from the community he was sent to protect against a formidable race of autochthons who would brook no interference with their way of life. What in the end was the cause of his downfall? Was his drunken appearance at the inquiry planned or psychotic? In other words, did Walker deliberately turn up drunk to sabotage the inquiry or was he non-compos mentis; or was a conspiracy hatched by the squatters to enlist RP Marshall to act against F Walker?

Does the following letter support any of the above propositions?

Francis Lear to Frederick Walker, 22 October 1854

I would be much obliged if you could get a run as proposed by yourself. I will leave the road as soon as you can get a run. I think stock will be low at the sale of the year and will be a good time to

193 SRNSW 4-3860 Reel2818 p 486.

194 SRNSW 43860 Reel 2818 p 492.

> purchase, if it should prove so.
>
> I give you authority to use my signature in obtaining the licence for the run. I hope I am not taking too much liberty in writing these few lines.
>
> If you should write please direct to B Gill, Ipswich.[195]

Conventional wisdom might suggest that the above letter was proof that Walker had seen the writing on the wall and viewed his dismissal as a fait accompli and consequently, had taken sober and mature steps to secure his future. However, it does not account for his outrageous behaviour at the Board of Inquiry. There is no doubt he had an alcohol problem because he lost his job as a result of being drunk and behaving in a gross and disrespectful manner but was there an underlying mental health issue? I don't believe Walker was a psychopath. It seems Walker had an impressive manner with people, perhaps charismatic, who engendered loyalty in some and resentment in others but he appeared to have found the minutia, the bureaucratic routine of his command beyond his control for want of attention to detail. He could command in the field but couldn't run a pie cart at home because he was delusional most of the time either from alcohol or quinine which exacerbated his work-related anxiety and stress.

My view is that the following from his mother's letter of early 1854 suggests Walker was ill: "Indeed, I am grieved to death to think of your hard situation, and above all of your bad health and what would I give to be able to afford you any relief and comfort my dear son. Your fate presses, son, on my heart as you may believe. The only thing I can possibly think of to benefit you is for you to get leave of absence and come to England and live quietly with us for a year."

H Bell MD gave the following medical opinion: "suffering from nervous debility. … but I can state that a person in this condition may, in both walking and speaking, very much resemble a person directly under the influence of liquor."

However, RP Marshall A/Cmd^{t} NP wrote back to the Colonial Secre-

195 QSA Series ID14733/86141.

tary on 6 February 1855[196] as follows about Dr Bell's certificate: "5. The medical certificate accompanying Mr Walker's letter states that he was suffering from nervous debility, a fact self-evident to everyone who saw him and I am sorry that Mr Walker should have rendered it necessary for me to state that I saw him at Brisbane on five or six different days and that on such occasions he was much intoxicated. After having known Mr Walker for five years, I could not be mistaken as to the state he was in."

On the other hand, counsel would be entitled to put the following to Marshal, who said in evidence on 2 December 1856: "... though I served for six years with Mr Walker, I do not think I spent as many as six weeks with him. I may, perhaps, have seen him exceed at a private dinner table, but I did not consider it part of my duty to take any notice of the circumstance."[197]

It is a matter for the jury to give what weight they will to Marshall's evidence, if they believe him, of course. Although modern medicine treats malaria with quinine, in the nineteenth century quinine was a patent medicine freely available over the counter, marketed in the powdered form of sulphate of quinine, and sold by the ounce to medicate fevers and ague. The directions for use were a couple of grains dissolved in water. Walker purchased an ounce, among other substances from John Row, Chemist, Sydney on 7 February 1854.[198] Quinine may cause vomiting, diarrhoea, abdominal pain, deafness, blurred vision, dizziness, spinning sensation and disturbances in heart rhythms. This is what Walker had to say: "... it is no joke shivering and shaking three or five hours one day and riding 25 miles the next. The cure is almost as bad, for the quinine quiet stupefies me."

Based on perusing his hotel accounts, it seems Walker was a heavy drinker of brandy and a heavy smoker as well. Furthermore, the diet of the corps was poor which leads me to conclude Walker probably suffered from regular indigestion and possible gastric reflux as well as the side

196 Walker was dismissed on 19 January 1855 so Marshall's letter is of little consequence in real time but does it help the reader form an opinion as to Walker's state of mind pre-facto?

197 NSW 1857 Legislative Assembly Select Committee into Native Police Force.

198 Row's bill was £10/14/- which as at the close of the inquiry remained outstanding, see Annex A.

effects from the quinine which can be serious. The role of Commandant of the Native Police was not an easy one. The Native Police were not an independent police unit operating behind enemy lines; periodically, returning to headquarters to be rested, refitted and remounted. It was a fully-fledged police force with a chain of command, which meant it had a headquarters and was required to maintain full accountability to the government of the day. A bureaucracy came with that level of police organisation. The only attempt Walker made as Commandant to alleviate his nonoperational workload was to hire at his own expense, a private secretary to handle the paper work. After reading the correspondence of Walker and the public criticism of him, and the fact that Walker drank to excess, it would be reasonable to assume that he may have been experiencing mental fatigue and high levels of work related stress. Moreover, the fact that Marshall was able to recruit the white officers to act in unison against Walker, the Commandant, suggests that Walker was isolated and probably paranoid as well. Marshall's letter of September 1854 setting out the complaints and allegations against Walker is unavailable; however, Marshall said at the 1857 Select Committee into the Native Police: "Complaints were made by the officers of his irregularities, drunkenness, and abuse to them, as well as his general irregularity in the management of the Force."

This potential act of mutiny can only have remained alive, if Marshall was given assurances that whatever the fallout might be, he would suffer no more than having to resign if Walker survived the investigations. Marshall also made the following comment at the 1857 Select Committee into the Native Police: "I would have complained to the Government before I did, but that I felt reluctant to do so individually. I did not feel confident in making any complaint against him, seeing the way in which he was supported. I know complaints have been made, and that his conduct was most glaring, although no notice was taken of it."

So, came to an end, a short but glorious career in the colonial service of New South Wales. The currency lad[199] all too quickly revealed his lack of breeding and thus failed the test as an officer and a gentleman.

---

199 I acknowledge the purists will have my guts for garters, but Walker really was a dinky-di Aussie.

The Bunyip aristocracy would not stand for some jumped-up, uncouth, roughneck, who, when offered the brandy decanter for a light refreshment, returned it empty and who had blackfellows for friends.

Date	*Name*	*Allegations*	*Wnt*	*Killed*	*Remarks*
6/11/1846	Millbong*	Self-defence	No	by Whites	Justifiable Homicide
1/12/1846	Horse*	M-Mr J Uhr	Y	by Whites	Resisting warrant
Oct 1846	Constable	M-Mr Gregor	Y	No	Nolle prosequi
Oct 1846	Constable	M-Mary Shannon	Y	No	Nolle prosequi
Sept 1847	Dundalli	M-William Boller	Y	Death penalty	Hanged 5/1/1855
21/9/1847	Make*	M-Mary Shannon	Y	Death penalty	Reprieved
20/10/1847	Perriha	GBH-G Furber	Y	No	Not guilty
20/10/1847	Durrugguree	GBH-G Furber	Y	No	Not guilty
27/5/1848	Omilly	M-Mr Gregor	Y	by W Police	A & R Police
27/5/1848	Omilly	M-Mary Shannon	Y	by W Police	A & R Police
27/5/1848	Omilly	M-William Boller	Y	by W Police	A & R Police
9/5/1849	Gibber	M-Mr Mark's boy	?	by N Police	A & R Police
9/5/1849	Gibber	M-bullock driver	Y	by N Police	A & R Police
9/7/1849	Darby	Killing cattle etc.	Y	by N Police	A & R Police
18/10/1846	Mickey*	M-Mary Shannon	Y	Death penalty	Commuted 7 years HL
6/2/1850	Nobody	M-a white man	Y	by N Police	Escaping police
30/8/1850	Unknown	M-G Blaxland	Y	by N Police	Resisting police
30/8/1850	Unknown	M-G Blaxland	Y	by N Police	Resisting police
29/3/1852	Davy	M-A H Trevethan	Y	Death penalty	Hanged 22/8/1854
15/10/1853	Sippy	M-female	Y	No	Nolle prosequi
11/11/1853	Sippy	Robbery w violence	Y	No	Guilty 3 years HL

A=assault, HL=hard labour, M=murder, N=native, R=resist, W=white, Wnt=warrant, Y=yes. *Millbong Jemmy; *Horse Jemmy* Make-a-light & * aka Mickie.

5

Aborigines caught and killed

(Please refer to table at page 118 whilst reading case histories.)

Millbong Jemmy: In 1832, with several others, he attacked two boat's crew, after beating them severely, proceeded to roast them on a fire. About 1840, he broke open the Government Mill to steal flour and stabbed Mr Thomson in the chest with a knife. He also attacked the Government Station at Eagle Farm.[200] He was at the death of Mr Gregor and his servant; Millbong Jemmy was the most active of the murderers. Millbong Jemmy, the principal in no less than five murders within a comparatively short space of time, was killed on or about 6 November 1846. This individual accompanied by a number of other blacks, after driving Mr Richards away from his station at Eagle Farm and finding himself hotly pursued, retreated across the Brisbane River to Doughboy Creek. He then appeared at a hut on the creek occupied by some sawyers, and demanded rations, which were given to him. Not being satisfied, he asked for more, and on being refused, attempted to rush the hut. At this critical moment, one of the sawyers and a bullock driver happened to return to the hut, when a contest commenced. Millbong Jemmy, armed with a waddie, struck one of the sawyers on the arm, and made him retreat to the hut. The party then brought his gun and shot him on the spot, two balls having penetrated the brain. He survived upwards of two hours. The other blacks, on seeing their ringleader fall, instantly decamped and made for the scrubs. The body of the black was brought on a dray to Brisbane the same morning, when an inquiry took place before

[200] MBC 2 January 1847 p 2.

the Police Magistrate.[201]

Horse Jemmy: At the Police office, 5 December 1846, an inquiry, at the instance of the Attorney-General, took place touching the death of Horse Jemmy, an aboriginal black, who was shot by one of the Government men on Major North's station, on the 1 December 1846, while resisting the execution of a warrant which had been granted for his apprehension. The Magistrates present were Captain Wickham, Dr Simpson, Lieut. Blamire, and Major North.

The first witness examined was a prisoner of the Crown, named Daniel Doyle, who deposed as follows: I am in the employ of the Government Agricultural Department. On 30 November, I was one of the persons who obtained the permission of the Government overseer, Mr Thomson, to proceed with John Lyndon and Joseph Reynolds to apprehend Horse Jemmy and two other blacks, for spearing Government cattle. I had likewise another warrant for Horse Jemmy, as the murderer of Mr Uhr.[202] At daylight, on 1 December, I went with my comrades to Mr North's station, and met a black named Charley, who told me that the camp of the natives was in the rosewood scrub that they were hunting wallabies, and that they intended shortly to shift their camp. I then proceeded with my companions to the scrub, Mr Francis North following afterwards on foot. When I reached the scrub, I found the blacks' camp. My two companions stayed behind at a distance of about 130 yards from the scrub. At the camp, I found Horse Jemmy, whom I knew well; and on sitting down I entered into a conversation with him. There were upwards of 200 blacks about the camp at the time. I asked him to come along with me to some sawyers, who were cutting cedar on

[201] *MBC* 7 November 1846 p 3.

[202] £40 REWARD. Subscription for the Apprehension of the Three Blacks Who Murdered Mr Gregor and Mrs Shannon; and also, for the Apprehension of the Principal in the Murder of Mr Uhr. A REWARD of £10 for each Black will be given to any party who apprehends the following Aboriginal Natives, viz.: Jackey Jackey, Dick Ben, and Moggy Moggy, the murderers of the late Mr Gregor and Mrs Shannon; and Horse Jemmy, the principal in the murder of the late Mr Uhr. Persons who approve of the above objects, are politely requested to forward their Subscriptions to J. Richardson, North Brisbane. November 27, 1846. *MBC* 28 November 1846 p 1.

the other side of the river. I promised him some flour to induce him to leave the camp. He left the camp with another black named John Mayhall and after proceeding forty or fifty yards, Horse Jemmy, in consequence of something that was said to him by Mayhall, declined to go any farther. I then told him that I had a warrant against him for the murder of Mr Uhr, and that he was my prisoner. I then laid hold of him and the other black. We struggled together, and I got thrown down. Mayhall got loose and threw a waddie, which knocked the hat off my head. I had pistols in my belt at the time, which were hidden by my blue shirt. Immediately afterwards Horse Jemmy released himself from my grasp and rose up. As he was going away, he turned round and looked at me. I then pulled out a pistol, while rising on my side, and discharged it at him. I fired because I heard the blacks yelling and thought if I did not do so, they would attack me, as they were answering Mayhall's cooeys. My companions, as I afterwards heard, fired in the air for the purpose of keeping the blacks off. When the attempt to capture Horse Jemmy took place I was between the blacks in the scrub, and Mr North and my own people. After Horse Jemmy was fired at, he ran for a short distance, when a vine caught him and stopped his further progress. I did not fire at him with the intention of taking his life; it was for fear that the other blacks would come upon me. He was not quite dead when myself and companions went to pick him up. After I had fired at Horse Jemmy, the two men came up first, and afterwards Mr Francis North with two of his men. We carried Horse Jemmy to Mr North's station, a distance of about two and a half miles. When we reached within 150 yards from the station he expired. Before I proceeded to apprehend the blacks, I was told that a reward had been offered[203] for their apprehension, and that a conditional pardon would be given to any prisoner of the Crown who effected the capture. I had not got the warrant for the apprehension of Horse Jemmy in my possession.

[203] Colonial Secretary's Office, Sydney 9th November, 1846. Twenty-Five Pounds Reward, or a Conditional Pardon. Whereas it has been represented to His Excellency the Governor, that Mr Andrew Gregor and a female servant in his employment have been recently murdered by the native blacks, at the Pine River, in the Moreton Bay District: Notice is hereby given, that a Reward of Twenty-five Pounds will be paid to any free person or persons who may secure and bring to justice the murderer or murderers, or if a Prisoner of the Crown, application will be made to Her Majesty for the Allowance to him of a Conditional Pardon. By His Excellency's Command, E. Deas Thomson. NSW Gazette 10 November 1846 N° 94 p 1406.

I knew there was such a warrant, and that Mr Thomson had it. This is all I know about it. James Reynolds was subsequently examined, and likewise John Lyndon, who corroborated the evidence of the first witness. Reynolds also stated that Horse Jemmy has long been known by the name of Waakoon Jemmy. It was also elicited during the examination of Lyndon that he had seen the name of Horse Jemmy in a warrant which was in the hands of Doyle, at Major North's.[204]

Constable: The aboriginals, Marney and Constable were forwarded to Sydney for trial at the Criminal Sessions; the former for spearing cattle on the Government run at Redbank and Constable with robbing Mr Gregor's hut after that unfortunate gentleman had been deprived of life by three of his companions.[205] On their arrival in Sydney, they were conveyed to the Gaol, and remained there until it pleased the Sydney authorities to liberate them, in consequence of the Attorney-General having declined to prosecute. The Government, it appears, very properly refused to incur the expense of sending them back to the district by the steamer and hit upon the more economical expedient of forwarding them overland. To enable them to travel with comfort, they were furnished with letters to the different officials, who gave them provisions, and instructed them how to proceed on their journey. When they reached Brisbane having been, according to their own account about two months on the road, they were asked how they liked Sydney? They replied it was "budgeree place, plenty meal, plenty flour, plenty tobacco, plenty everything." Mr Keck appeared to be held in friendly remembrance by them as the dispensator of some of the aforesaid benefits. Since their return, they have expressed their determination to "bail crammer" (act honestly) for the future; the meaning of which is, that they will neither steal anything while they are watched, nor tell a lie when the truth serves their purpose better. As soon as the tribe to which they belong became aware of their return, preparations were immediately made for a grand corroboree at Breakfast Creek, at which it was expected Messrs Marney and Constable would relate their adventures since their departure from the district. They have picked up a good deal of English and colonial slang

[204] *MBC* 6 February 1847 p 2.

[205] Constable, had been committed for trial by the Brisbane Bench in November 1846 upon a charge of being accessory to the murder of the late Mr Gregor and Mrs Shannon. *MBC* 27 March 1847 p 2.

on the road and have become acquainted with many of the fashionable customs and usages in Sydney; for instance, Constable on being asked "if his mother knew he was out," immediately put his thumb to his nose and told his interrogator to go to a place which shall be nameless. There is no doubt, however, that their ideas have been considerably enlarged by what they have seen in Sydney, and it is to be hoped they will profit by the lesson.[206]

Dundalli: Although ironed on the legs, his behaviour was most violent. He had assaulted his fellow prisoners and even declared his intention to murder one of them; he seized and attempted to overpower one of the turnkeys who was opening the ward door and who had to shout for assistance. He has since threatened the life of this man.[207]

> **Executive Council Proceedings, 12 December 1854**
>
> In the case of Dundalli capitally convicted at Brisbane on the 22nd November last before Mr Justice Therry of the murder of William Boller and sentenced to suffer death, the Council advises that the Law be allowed to take its course. M Fitzpatrick, Clerk [Margin note: approved FitzRoy GG.]
>
> **John Boman, Sheriff to Col. Sec., 14 December 1854**
>
> I have the honour to acknowledge the receipt of your letter of yesterday advising me that the aboriginal Dundalli is to be executed at Brisbane on the fifth day of January next, of which I have caused the unhappy man to be informed. [Margin note by Hon CS: Nothing further required.]

This aboriginal native convicted at the last Brisbane Circuit Court of the murders of Andrew Gregor and William Boller,[208] paid the just penalty of his crimes by the forfeiture of his life, in front of the gaol, on 5 January 1855. Prior to this the guilty man did not express much fear, but when preparation was made for erecting the gallows, he seemed to be aware that his case was almost hopeless; and when the executioner went into his room to pinion him, he cried and wailed piteously, appealing to all near for their help to save him. As, owing to the desperate character of this criminal, some resistance was expected, more than the usual

206 *MBC* 15 May 1847 p 3.

207 *MBC* 10 June 1854 p 2

208 Trials reported at *MBC* 25 November 1854 p 2.

precautions were taken to prevent an escape. A few Native Policemen, under Lieutenant Irvine, were on the ground with the town police, under arms, and a rope was passed through the cord that pinioned the culprit's arms; but he went up the ladder without the aid of force, continuing, however, to call upon the names of those who know him and crying out loudly in his own tongue when on the scaffold, to some blacks who were witnessing the execution from the ridge at the Windmill Hill, opposite the gaol. The preparations having been completed, at a signal from Mr Pront the Under Sheriff, the bolt was withdrawn and the murderer fell; but in consequence of some wretched bungling on the part of Green, the hangman, the feet of Dundalli fell firmly on the top of his coffin, beneath the gallows. A turnkey quickly drew away the coffin, but still the feet of the hanging man touched the ground, and the spectators were shocked by the sight of Green lifting up the legs of the malefactor and tying them backwards towards his pinioned arms, by the rope that passed through the pinioning. Death seemed to be almost instantaneous after the fall; but, richly as the blood-stained convict deserved the death he suffered, it was still a most sickening sight to behold the cool and butcher-like conduct of the hangman, made necessary by nothing but the grossest neglect. If anything could be more disgusting than this, it was the presence of large numbers of women, many of whom had brought their children with them! After hanging the usual time, the body was lowered down for interment. Thus, died one of the guiltiest and most incorrigible of the aboriginal natives of this quarter. His many crimes had long made him the abhorrence of the whites and it is to be hoped that his death will teach the blacks, who had been in the habit of looking up to him that our laws may overtake the guilty, however long the time since he first eluded his punishment.[209]

In the report of the execution of the aboriginal Dundalli, it was mentioned, that just before the cap was drawn over the wretched criminal's face, he cried out with a loud voice to some native blacks assembled on a hill opposite to the gaol and addressed them with much earnestness and rapidity. The Brisbane blacks generally agree that this appeal was made to his wife and other members of his own tribe, whom he called upon to take revenge of those Brisbane aboriginals and others

209 *MBC* 6 January 1855 p 2.

who had been instrumental in capturing him and lodging him in the watch house. There can be little doubt from the agreement of several statements, that that was the subject of the dying man's address; and he thus retained to the last moment that cruel ferocity of character which had so prominently marked his life. Notwithstanding the expression of many contrary-opinions, we hold to the belief that this public and terrible punishment of a notorious criminal, in the presence of some of his own people, must act as a salutary warning upon them, as, from the years of impunity which he had enjoyed, they must have believed that he could forever defy the terrors of our laws.[210]

Make-a-light: At the Brisbane Circuit Court, 14 November 1851 before Mr Justice Therry, Moggy Moggy, an aboriginal native, was indicted for wilful murder, for that he, with force and arms, at the Pine River, in the colony of New South Wales, did, on the 21 September 1847, feloniously, wilfully, and with malice aforethought, then and there inflict a mortal wound on William Boller, of which wound the said Wm. Boller lingered till the 27th September, and then died. The prisoner being called upon to plead stated, through Davis, the interpreter, that his name was not Moggy Moggy, but Make-a-light.

The Crown Prosecutor was then permitted to amend the indictment. Prisoner pleaded not guilty. James Davis, blacksmith, Brisbane, was duly sworn as interpreter. James Smith, sworn and examined: Has known the prisoner at the bar for seven or eight years. Saw him at the Boggo Scrub, near Brisbane, about that time, and employed him to strip bark off the trees; the prisoner was then called Moggy Moggy, but the whites called him Paddy; witness saw the prisoner about five years' at Bulimba, at two or three different times, and spoke to him; he said he had thrown away the name of Moggy Moggy, and was then called Ohangalee; remembered the murder of Boller, about four or five years ago, at the Pine River, which is about 35 miles from Brisbane, where Boller was sawing timber with witness and another man, William Waller; called him there Moggy Moggy, prisoner said his name was Ohangalee. Saw him first on a Sunday, at Pine River, with about fifteen or sixteen other blacks. Prisoner offered to give witness a bandicoot, which he refused to receive. Dundalli, a

210 *MBC* 13 January 1855 p 2.

black, asked Boller where the gins were; Boller replied they knew nothing of them; Boller and witness were sawing in the pit on the morning of the murder, when about eleven o'clock a number of blacks came; witness saw prisoner spear Boller in the shoulder as he was attempting to escape; he them endeavoured to escape himself; a black fellow struck witness with a waddy, when he recovered he tried to reach the hut, but was struck again with a waddy; saw Boller at the hut sitting with a double-barrel gun lying across his knees; witness told Boller to make his escape; they retreated out of the scrub, keeping Boller's gun to his shoulder; he asked the blacks why they owed him a grudge; saw the blacks afterwards go into the hut; witness helped to carry Boller on his back to Mr Griffin's station, 2½ miles off; Boller was removed to Brisbane hospital, witness saw him there three days afterwards; did not see him when he was dead, but saw his coffin, and attended at the funeral; deceased was a dark man, about 5 feet 6 inches high, and had a broken nose. The day of the murder witness returned to the hut in the afternoon and found everything taken away; saw one wound on deceased's shoulder, and one in his belly.

Cross-examined by Mr Purefoy, who, at the request of His Honour, had undertaken the prisoner's defence: Witness was sworn before Captain Wickham on the inquest of William Waller, who was killed at the same time, did not mention the prisoner's name Moggy Moggy, saw the prisoner about a year and a half afterwards at Kangaroo Point, did not inform the constables; saw him about four years after Boller's death in Brisbane Goal; first called him Moggy Moggy before the Magistrates when committed for trial, but in gaol called him Ohangalee; saw Boller speared about three yards from the pit; quite certain that the prisoner was the man who threw the spear; could pick him out of a hundred blacks.

Kearsey Cannan, Surgeon, Brisbane, sworn and examined, deposed, saw the deceased at Mr Griffin's at the Pine River, he was then unable to move, he had received several spear wounds, one in the belly, between the lower edge of the ribs and the hip, a dangerous wound; I saw him two days after at the hospital; saw him dying, he is since dead; he had a flat nose. Dr Ballow and Scott who were then at the hospital are since dead.

James Davis, the Interpreter, sworn and examined, deposed, that he had known the prisoner at the Bar for eighteen or nineteen years; he is about twenty-three years of age; saw him about five or six years ago about the settlement, with two or three of the Wide Bay blacks; had known him by the name of Paddy, and lately by the name of Make-a-light; never knew an Aborigine by the name of Moggy Moggy; think it a very hard thing to know one black from another.

Cross-examined by Mr Purefoy: Witness had lived among the blacks for fourteen years, and was well acquainted with their habits and customs; tribes will sometimes meet together to fight; has known blacks for five or six years, then be absent for a short time, and on returning he did not know them from change of dress and paint, and other means; never knew the prisoner by the name of Moggy Moggy; considers Wide Bay to be 200 miles, and does not believe that two or three blacks will come from thence here without coming with white men; does not know a black of the name of Dundalli; it is a most difficult thing to distinguish one black from another; he would not undertake to do it; the smallest number of blacks, witness had seen in a tribe was one hundred and fifty.

Mr Purefoy addressed the Jury for the prisoner, commenting forcibly on the evidence of the principal witness, Smith, and on the great improbability of his being able to identify the prisoner after the lapse of so many years. The learned counsel contrasted this evidence with that of Davis, the interpreter, who, after a residence of fourteen years amongst them, would not undertake to identify blacks, after being absent from them but comparatively a short time.

His Honour summed up with great care and the Jury after a few minutes' absence, found a verdict of guilty. Proclamation for silence having been made, his Honour the Judge proceeded in a most solemn and impressive manner to pass the awful sentence of death on the prisoner, expressing the deep feeling of distress he experienced in passing sentence of death within 24 hours on two beings in a state of heathen darkness. That whilst the blacks lived under the protection of the laws, the white man must be protected from assault and injury, and the law in this instance must be vindicated. His Honour further observed that this case like others would no doubt be considered at another tribunal, but he could hold out to the prisoner no hopes of mercy. Sentence of death was then passed in the usual form.[211]

Proceedings of the Executive Council on the 8 December 1851:

Executive Council Proceedings

In the case for Make a light an aboriginal native convicted before Mr Justice Therry at the late Brisbane Circuit Court of the wilful murder of William Boller, in September 1847, the Council advise that the sentence of death passed upon Make a light be respited, in order that further enquiry maybe instituted as to the identity of the prisoner; the judge who tried the case having stated his belief that the evidence on this head adduced at the trial was not satisfactory. M Fitzpatrick, Clerk of the Executive Council Office.[212]

GW Elliot, Sheriff to Col. Sec. 15 December 1851

I have the honour to acknowledge the receipt of your letter of the 13th instant, informing me that the sentence of Death passed on the aboriginal Make a light is not immediately to take effect but only respited till further ordered of which the unhappy man will be appraised.[213]

GW Elliot, Sheriff to Col. Sec. 23 December 1851

I have the honour to acknowledge the receipt of your letter of yesterday's date N° 289, informing me that the sentence of death passed upon Make a light will not be carried into effect.

2. The prisoner shall be informed of the above reprieve as early as possible[214]

Francis Bigge to Col. Sec. 29 January 1852

I have the honour to state that the Aborigine native generally known by the name of Moggy Moggy was tried at the Brisbane Assizes in November last for the murder of a sawyer of the name Boller and having been found guilty and sentenced to be hanged was subsequently pardoned in consequence I am informed as to doubts of his identity. Of the propriety of this step of course there can be no question, but as there is in existence in the Northern Districts a strong belief that this man was implicated in the

211 *SMH* 3 December 1851 p 4 and *MBC* 15 November 1851 p 2.

212 QSL Reel A2.23 p 370.

213 QSL Reel A2.23 p 373.

214 QSL Reel A2.23 p 372.

murder of Mrs Shannon and Mr Gregor at the Pine River some three or four years since, I would respectfully submit whether it is expedient to forward this man to the place where this crime was committed or to any district adjacent thereto such as the Wide Bay District where I understand he is to be forwarded by the first opportunity occurring. As he has not been forwarded from the gaol at Brisbane, I would submit whether it is not advisable simply to discharge him and not confer any special mark of favour which I am fully convinced would only embolden Aborigines of those districts and probably lead to further loss of life. Margin notes: inform Mr Bigge that steps to be taken with respect to liberation of this man determined after consultation with Mr Justice Therry & forwarding him to Wide Bay is not intended as any special mark of favour. CAF[215]

J C Wickham to Col. Sec. 29 March 1852

In accordance with the instructions conveyed to me, by your letter of the 23rd of last December relative to the case of Make a light, an aboriginal native, who was convicted at the last Brisbane Assizes of the wilful murder of William Boller. I now do myself the honour to inform you that, as there is no direct communication, either by land or sea between this district and Wide Bay. I consider that the best means of carrying out the recommendation of Mr Justice Therry "that the prisoner should be quietly sent to Wide Bay" would be to discharged him from prison to make the best of his way back to his own Tribe.[216]

After Make-a-light was reprieved from the sentence of death passed upon him for the murder of William Boller, and the two aboriginals who were charged with attempting to murder Mr Furber, were released from Brisbane Gaol, they were carried off in triumph to the camp near Breakfast Creek by the blacks in the neighbourhood of Brisbane, and drunken orgies were held in the evening, at which threats and defiance towards the whites were very freely circulated.[217]

Perrika and Durrugujree: aboriginal natives were indicted on a charge of wounding one George Furber, with intent to do him grievous

[215] QSL Reel A2.23 p 347.

[216] QSL Reel A2.23 p 345.

[217] *MBC* 5 June 1852 p 2.

bodily harm, at Mary River, in the month of October 1847. The prisoners, by James Davis, who was sworn to interpret between them and the Court and Jury, pleaded not guilty, one of them saying that he was a mere boy at the time the assault was said to have taken place. The deposition of Mr Furber was put in and read, as he was too ill to attend but it was so incomplete and unsatisfactory that the prisoners were discharged.[218]

Omilly: An inquest was held on the body of the deceased aboriginal on 29 May 1848, in an apartment connected with the General Hospital. The following is the evidence then adduced: Bobby Winter, an aboriginal-native: Knows the black man now lying dead; he is named Omilly. At the time of the murder of the late Mr Gregor and Mary Shannon witness was passing on his way to the camp and saw Omilly strike Mary Shannon on the back of the head with a tomahawk. (The above evidence was interpreted by Eugene Lucette, who was sworn by the Coroner.) James Smith: Knows the black now lying dead; has seen him twice before; does not know his name. The last time witness saw him was when his mate, William Boller, was murdered at the Pine River. Deceased struck witness with a waddie at that time and threw two spears at him. He also stole two of witness' blankets. James Ramsay: On 27 May 1848, witness was ordered by Constable Murphy to go to the blacks' camp to apprehend a man who was concerned in the murder of the late Mr Gregor and Mrs Shannon. Murphy told witness that a man named Lucette would point him out. On arriving at the camp an aboriginal, named Stephy Cullen, pointed out the place where the man was lying. Lucette said his name was Omilly. Witness then went to where he was lying and surrounded him. Lucette and witness went towards him at the same time; Lucette laid hold of him by the hair and said this is the murderer; witness then took hold of him by the leg and put handcuffs on his ankles; at the same time Lucette and Bobby Winter put a rope on him. At this time, he was struggling hard to make his escape. Lucette and some friendly blacks then took him up the hill; they carried him by the hands and feet. The deceased's friends now tried to rescue him, and threw spears and boomerangs, one of which pierced witness shoulder. Witness with the other constables were walking behind to keep off the hostile blacks, and witness did not discover that the man was dead until they arrived at

[218] *MBC* 29 May 1852 p 2 & *Empire* 11 June 1852 p 3.

the Police-office. Witness saw a rope round deceased's neck when they arrived at the cells.

Peter Murphy: Witness is acting Chief Constable. On 27 May 1848, witness was told by the Police Magistrate that one of the blacks concerned in the murder of the late Mr Gregor and Mary Shannon was in the aboriginal camp, and that witness should send out a party of constables to apprehend him. The Police Magistrate at the same time told witness that a man named Lucette would point him out. Witness sent out Constables Ramsay, Walker, Conroy, and Hoare. Witness met them in the town on their return. The blacks were carrying Omilly on their shoulders. Witness was then told that the man was dead. Eugene Lucette: On 26 May 1848, witness was told by a black gin that one of the late Mr Gregor's murderers was in the camp of the natives near the settlement. Witness gave information of the circumstance to the Police Magistrate, and with a party of constables proceeded on Saturday evening last to the blacks' camp to apprehend him. A black named Stephy Cullen pointed out the deceased as being the man. Witness then went into the camp with Bobby Winter, an aboriginal native, who immediately on seeing Omilly, said that's the fellow. Winter and witness then laid hold of him; witness then put a rope round his neck and under his arm, for the purpose of securing him, as he was making violent efforts to escape. The constable then, came up and put handcuffs round his ankles. A violent tumult ensued among the blacks; the friends of Omilly then tried to rescue him, and threw boomerangs and spears, one of which wounded a constable. The friendly blacks then laid hold of the rope, Omilly at the same time struggling hard to escape, and dragged him up the hill. Witness supposes that during the struggle Omilly's arm must have slipped out of the rope, and that he must have been strangled while making violent efforts to escape. Witness did not know that he was dead until he arrived in Brisbane. No more violence was used than what was necessary to apprehend the deceased.

The Coroner stated to the jury that, in the absence of any other medical gentleman, he had examined the deceased; the body bore the appearance of a person who had met his death from suffocation. There were no shot marks on it, nor any marks of blows. The Coroner also said he had examined the wound in the constable's shoulder and dressed it. The spear had traversed a space of about four inches. The jury immediately and without retiring, returned a verdict that the deceased had met his death while resisting the lawful apprehension of his person on a charge of murder.[219]

Mickey: On 1 December 1852, "Billy Quart Pot" and Mickey, the two native blacks apprehended by the Native Police on suspicion of having been concerned in a former outrage at the Pine River, were brought up for examination before Captain Wickham and Messrs Duncan and Ferriter. Ralph William Barrow, who has so frequently given evidence in connection with this subject deposed to having witnessed the attack on Mr Andrew Gregor's station in the month of October 1846, when that gentleman and Mrs Shannon were murdered.

The prisoner Mickey was there, but the witness did not know his name. The other black he did not know at all. He was not the person alluded to by the witness in his deposition of 1846, as "Quart Pot." The prisoner Mickey had no hand in the murders, but witnesses saw him carrying away some of the plunder. The prisoner had previously told witness that "Dundalli" and "Moggy Moggy" intended to murder Mr Gregor and do violence to the white woman. The prisoner "Mickey" cross-examined the witness, who, however, made no variation in his statement. The Bench discharged the prisoner "Billy Quart Pot," and called upon Mickey, with the usual caution, for any statement he wished to make. He replied that he had told Barrow before the attack—that it was done by salt water blacks—and that Barrow did not "pidna" (know) him, he (Barrow) being so young at the time. The Bench committed Mickey to take his trial for the robbery.[220]

Mickey, an aboriginal native, was indicted for stealing a quantity of flour, tea, and sugar, some blankets, and a pair of pistols, the property of one Andrew Gregor, at the Pine River, on 18 October 1846. Mr Gregor's station was attacked, and himself and Mrs Shannon, the wife of one of his servants, murdered. The prisoner was positively sworn to by one Ralph William Barrow, the sole witness, whose evidence could be admitted, as having been present on that occasion, assisting in carrying

---

219 *MBC* 3 June 1848 p 2.

220 *MBC* 4 December 1852 p 2.

away property. He was not one of those who actually struck the blows. The witness Barrow was much frightened, but being treated kindly by the Judge, he was brought to tell his story very plainly. Mr Fawcett, who with Mr Little appeared for the prisoners, cross-examined the witness, and elicited the fact that at the last examination at the Police Court he had asserted that two blacks named Mickey were present at the attack, whereas he now said there was only one. On reference, however, to his statement at the inquest, when his memory was fresh, his evidence then was found to agree with that now given. A statement of the prisoner was put in, wherein he so far confessed knowledge of the transaction that he said he had warned the witness Barrow of the intended murder. The Attorney-General, in opening the case, said that he had declined taking the course that was open to him, and indicting the prisoner for the murder, as there was only one witness to his identity, and the event was so long past. Mr Fawcett addressed the jury for the defence, but they found the prisoner guilty, and he received the sentence of six months' imprisonment with hard labour in Brisbane gaol.[221]

Mickey, an aboriginal native, was indicted for the wilful murder of Mary Shannon, at the Pine River, on 18 October 1846. The only evidence offered was that of Ralph William Barrow, who was a stock-keeper in the employ of Mr Andrew Gregor, on the day of the murder. He saw the prisoner and several other blacks come to the station and was only a short distance from the hut where Mary Shannon was; the door and windows were open, and he distinctly observed Dundalli and Tickpen (two aboriginals) attack and kill her, whilst Mickey was standing by aiding and assisting. The jury, after retiring for upwards of an hour, found the prisoner guilty. His Honour remarked that he should not pass sentence of death upon the prisoner. Judgment of death was recorded. The sentence therefore is left to the Executive.[222]

Justice R Therry to Col. Sec. 9 July 1853

In reply to your letter of the 9th ultimo. respecting a man named Mickie who was tried before me for murder at the late Brisbane circuit requesting me to state what amount of punishment I would propose, I beg to suggest that I consider seven year's hard labour

221 *SMH* 25 May 1853 p 2.

222 *Bell's Life in Sydney and Sporting Reviewer* 28 May 1853 p 2.

on the roads or other public works would be suitable commutation. The murder with the commission of which Mickie was charged was that of Mr Gregor and his servant committed so far back as 1846. Altho Mickie was present with a large number of other aboriginal natives and thereby became legally guilty as aiding and abetting in the commission of the crime, yet he does not appear to have taken any active part in the participation of the deed but was for the most part engaged in stealing flour and sugar from the store whilst the murder was perpetrated by others.[223]

JH Plunkett, Att-Gen to Col. Sec. 27 July 1853

I have the honour to acknowledge the receipt of your letter of the 23rd instant. transmitting the enclosed extract from the communication received from the Commandant of the Native Police, which relates to the case of the aboriginal named in the margin, Mickie who was convicted at the last Brisbane circuit court of the murder of Mr Gregor and also to other Aborigines against whom warrants are out and requesting my opinion thereon.

2. In reply, I beg leave to state that Mr Walker is mistaken in supposing Mickie was convicted as an accessory after the fact. He was convicted for aiding and abetting and being present at the time of the murder.

As the life of the convict has been spared (in the humanity and expediency of which I concur) I see nothing in the case of Mickie to call for further consideration at present. Margin note: Sentence may now be commuted in accordance with Mr Justice Therry's recommendation. CAF 2nd Aug.[224]

Extract

At the last Assizes at Brisbane a black of the name of Mickie apprehended by the Native Police was convicted for the murder of Mrs Shannon and Mr Gregor (I presume as accessary after the fact). Now it is certain that he did rob the hut after the murder, but you must understand that he was a mere boy at the time and that the murderer made every boy, woman and child carry away the property. I can give the Attorney-General a half a dozen more under the same warrant all I have to do is to go round the different

223 QSL Reel A2.23 p 361.

224 QSL Reel A2.23 p 357.

stations and take the boys who are tailing cattle, bullock driving or otherwise employed. There ought to be an amnesty for every one included in that warrant except Dundalli, who was actual murderer. I hold several of these absurd warrants such as for blacks, names unknown and no description. Signed Frederick Walker

Justice R Therry to Col. Sec. 8 August 1853

In reply to your letter of 22nd inst., transmitting the copy of an extract from the letter of the Commandant Native Police respecting Mickie in which case I recommended a commutation of punishment. I beg to remark that the gentleman observations on proceedings at Brisbane are founded on error. It is an erroneous and incorrect assumption on his part to assume that Mickie was indicted as an accessory after the fact.

He was indicted as an aider and abettor present at the time of the murder. The statement of Mr Walker that he can give the Attorney-General half a dozen men under the same warrant and his expression of several absurd warrants certainly seem to be a very unsuitable mode for this gentleman to express himself respecting warrants issued under competent authority; and as to his opinion that there ought to be an amnesty, I can only say I never heard of such a thing in cases of capital felony.

Mr Walker I apprehend would not have written such a letter as he has done if he knew that all who are present at a felony tho not actually aiding in the commission of the offence but are in such a situation as to be able readily to come to the assistance of others engaged in its commission the knowledge of which was calculated to give additional confidence to his companions, in contemplation of law, are aiding and abetting.

This was Mickie's case and that of the whole party who accompanied him. He was engaged plundering the stores whist others were engaged at the same time and at the same place in committing the murders. They were all ready to assist if necessary and were all aiders and abettors. No doubt there are shades and degrees of guilt in the participation each had in the commission of the crime and it is for this reason that I recommended the commutation in Mickie's case.

Mr Walker's letter does not in the slightest degree alter my opinion as to the propriety of that commutation and I venture further to

> suggest that Mr Walker's sympathy may be very commendable, it appears to me that the fate of Mr Gregor and his servant is not without some claim to sympathy too, and that it should not be too exclusively bestowed on those who break the law.[225]

The sentence of death recorded at the last Brisbane Assize, against Mickie, an aboriginal native convicted of murder, was commuted to seven years' hard labour on the roads.[226]

Gibber: Police information from the Macintyre, where they have been lately stationed, revealed that the blacks had killed five head of cattle belonging to Mr Jonathan Young, and sent him notice that they were preparing another attack. He applied to the constables, and some of his neighbours joined him. The police party came up with a body of the blacks, but the only one they got near was the notorious Gibber, who murdered Mr Marks's boy some time ago, and also Mr Yeomans's bullock driver. For this man, they had a warrant, and they called to him repeatedly to stand, but Gibber would not, and came in contact with Mr Marshall of the Native Police whom he knocked from his horse senseless to the ground with his nulla nulla; Gibber was of course quickly despatched. The Police described him as the fiercest looking savage they had ever seen, standing full six feet high; on one foot, he had no toes, and on the other only two, of a peculiar form, like claws.[227]

Darby: Since the engagement near Carbucky, the aboriginals appear to think that they cannot carry on their former depredations with impunity. Darby the most notorious of all the ringleaders has died from his wounds to which circumstances we may no doubt attribute much of the present quiet.[228]

Nobody: Lieutenant Marshall, captured, at Callandoon, McIntyre River, a blackfellow named Nobody[229], for whose apprehension there was a warrant issued, as being concerned in some murder of white men some time ago. The police were put in charge of him to bring him on

225 QSL Reel A2.23 p 350.

226 *MBC* 8 October 1853 p 2.

227 *Maitland Mercury* 9 May 1849 p 2.

228 SLQ Reel A2.19 pp 312-315.

229 See F Walker's letter of 9 November 1850 to Colonial Secretary.

here, but he became refractory and attempted to make his escape, when they found it necessary to fire upon him, which put an end to his existence.[230]

Douglas William Campbell's deposition, 9 November 1850

Douglas William Campbell of Callandoon, Postman being duly sworn deposes: I was present in January last when Lieutenant RP Marshall started two troopers in charge of Nobody for Warialda. Mr Marshall explained to Nobody that if he attempts to escape he would be shot. He was also warned by one or two of the aboriginal natives belonging to this neighbourhood who were present when he was sent away. DW Campbell. Sworn before me at Callandoon this ninth day of November 1850, A Morris JP[231]

Thomas Young's deposition, 19 November 1850

Thomas Young of Callandoon, Gentleman being duly sworn deposes: Sometime in January last, I saw two of the Native Police start with a prisoner, a black called Nobody. About six hours after their departure the two troopers returned and stated that their prisoner had twice attempted to escape from them and that on the third time they had shot him as he would have escaped into a scrub. At Mr Marshall's request, I accompanied him to the spot where the body lay about eight miles from Callandoon. The body was lying about four hundred yards off the road. It lay close to scrub too thick for any horseman to pursue a man on foot. The police shewed us the place where they stated that Nobody had twice attempted to escape and that he nearly pulled one of them, Yorky off his horse. I have no doubt that the report of the two troopers was correct. These two troopers are called Logan and Yorky. Thomas Young. Sworn before me at Callandoon this nineteenth day of November one thousand eight hundred and fifty. Frederick Walker JP.[232]

Unknown: murder of Mr Blaxland. The following is a communication from Wide Bay, published in the *Herald* of June 17. "We have just had a visit from a detachment of the Native Police under Lieutenant Marshall; they endeavoured to apprehend Boomer and Fireaway, two native blacks

230 Correspondent. *Maitland Mercury*, 6 February, see *MBC* 16 February 1850 p 4.

231 QSA Series ID14733/86134.

232 QSA Series ID14733/86141.

who killed Mr Blaxland on the Burnett some time ago, but they took the river and escaped, though it is supposed they were wounded."[233] Mr Marshall attempted to capture two of the murderers of the late Mr Blaxland, they however took to the river and it not being possible to apprehend them they were fired at and I believe both killed.[234]

Davy: Davy, an aboriginal native, was indicted for the wilful murder of Adolphus Henry Trevethan, at Rawbelle, in the Burnett district, on the 29 March 1852. There was only one witness in this case, the others being unaccountably absent, but the evidence given was very clear and distinct. James Carney deposed that he was a workman at Rawbelle on the 28 or 29 March 1852, and early in the morning a large number of blacks, about three hundred, came to the station. Mr Trevethan and five or six men went out, and Mr Trevethan, laying down his gun, called upon some of the blacks whom he recognised to put down their spears and come forward to parley with him. About half a dozen of them did so, and amongst them witness distinctly recognised the prisoner Davy, who was well known to him before, and had been frequently employed at the station. After some talk with them, Mr Trevethan went to the store and got some tobacco for them. They then asked for pipes, and Mr Trevethan procured some from the store. He went up to the half dozen blacks, and they surrounded him. In a few seconds afterwards witness, who saw no blow struck, observed Mr Trevethan come up to the hut with his hand on his breast, exclaiming "I'm dead; I'm dead." He had five spear wounds in his breast, three of which were near the heart, one in the right breast, and one in the abdomen. The blacks with whom he had been parleying were then running away to the main body, who were about three hundred yards off. Here they resumed their weapons, and finally they moved off. Mr Trevethan died in about two hours after he received the wounds. Witness saw no spears with the blacks when Mr Trevethan was talking to them, but several spears were afterwards found near the spot where he stood. The Attorney-General wished to put in evidence of the custom of the blacks to trail the spears with their toes, so that the grass may conceal them, but this was held inadmissible. The evidence of Walter Middleton was read, with the view of showing that

233 *MBC* 28 June 1851 p 3.

234 F Walker to Col. Sec. 1 August 1851.

another black, named Paddy, might have been mistaken for the prisoner; but the witness Carney, who knew both blacks, was firm in identifying the prisoner. The jury found the prisoner guilty, and his Honour passed sentence of death upon him, in the usual form.[235]

Execution. The aboriginal native Davy, convicted of the murder of the late Mr Trevethan, suffered the penalty of death on Tuesday morning, 22 August 1854, in front of Brisbane gaol. The Rev James Hanley visited the prisoner and appeared to have succeeded in making a considerable impression upon his mind. No clergyman however, attended him in his last moments. He walked out and ascended the scaffold without the least resistance. In a few seconds the fatal preparations were completed, and the unhappy convict died without a struggle. To the shame and disgrace of the town, a very large number of women and children were amongst the spectators. The murder for which he suffered was attended by the most aggravated circumstances, the unfortunate victim being at the very time engaged in making presents to the blacks, when they cruelly and treacherously deprived him of life. Davy was positively sworn to as one of the six who were concerned in this deed of blood; and if any doubt of his identity, could possibly have existed, it was removed by his own confession since his condemnation, that he was really present; although he strove to excuse himself by saying that he did not strike the blow. He was what is called a half civilised black, well known about the station, and probably affording the information upon which the plan of attack was arranged. It is impossible to reflect with indifference upon the taking away of human life; but surely the compassion and the protection of society are due to those who are exposed to such murderous attacks as these; and it is difficult to perceive the grounds upon which the *Free Press* considers that the mercy of the Executive should have been extended to this murderer. About fifty white men had been killed in these districts, without one such public example having been made, and in the very paper which puts forth this morbid sympathy; it was reported from Wide Bay details of the continued and barbarous outrages of the blacks to the northward. The Executive acted with proper firmness and judgment in carrying out the sentence of the law upon this occasion. The aboriginal natives had so frequently escaped the punishment of their crimes. That

235 *MBC* 27 May 1854 p 2.

they had begun to look upon the sentence of death as a mere bugbear and a farce.[236]

Sippy: The aboriginal native committed by the Callandoon Bench, for the murder of an unfortunate German woman at Messrs Easton and Robertson's station, arrived at Drayton on or about 1 October 1853, escorted by two mounted troopers and a Sergeant of the Native Police, who were bringing him down to Brisbane gaol.[237]

HE Easton to Colonial Secretary

You are perhaps aware that a murder has been committed upon this station by an aboriginal, called generally by Europeans, Sypey. A few facts illustrative of the character of Sypey may endeavour to prove to what extent the police are to blame in not proceeding against him long before this.

In October last, Sypey was employed by me at a lambing station where I was residing. One morning he decamped taking with him a complete suit of my own clothes. He then proceeded to a station of Mr Smiths about 10 miles off. After remaining there for two or three days he robs one of the gentleman's shepherds of his blankets and rations. About a month after this he again visits one of my shepherd's huts and robs him of his rations, razors and everything that he could lay his hands on. After this he proceeds to a station of a JW Young's about 15 miles from this. He there robs one of the huts of a gun and rations etc. etc. About a month after this he returns again to me and robs one of my huts of rations and whatever he could lay his hands on. His last act in his career of crime has been to butcher a fine helpless and unfortunate German woman. His next act remains perhaps it is one of murder. Up to the committal of his last crime no effort has been made to have this backfellow taken. On the two first charges just enumerated, I applied to Mr Walker in person for a warrant for the apprehension of Sypey. The statement of the Commandant was to this effect, that I had been robbed by Sypey of a suit of clothes.

The evidence I had to offer amounted to this. I was attempting to count down a flock of sheep in company with a white man and two Aborigines one of them being Sypey. On the morning in

236 *MBC* 26 August 1854 p 2.

237 *MBC* 1 October 1853 p 2.

> question when I got up I missed Sypey also my clothes with the assistance of the other black whom I put great faith in. I tracked Sypey to a scrub where I found his old clothes. The black that was with me pointed out the place where he had put on my clothes and showing me the track of my own boots. I offered to swear to this statement but I am sorry to say that Mr Walker considered that he could not grant me a warrant on such evidence.[238]

> **Frederick Walker to Col. Sec. 14 October 1853**
>
> … has already perceived that the reason why I did not act in the station clothed case was that Mr Easton brought me nothing but hearsay evidence. Sippy who is a boy of about 14 years of age is now in Brisbane gaol having been apprehended by the 2nd Section under Sergeant Graham.[239]

Martin Feeney Gaoler states: "On Thursday at 6 o'clock, principal turnkey mustered prisoners, saw prisoner then, all correct – after Muster, prisoners delivered to Robert Orr night turnkey – thunderstorm, five minutes before 8 o'clock principal turnkey reported prisoner Sippy had escaped – neighbourhood immediately searched by himself, Police & others – did not find prisoner. Wrote letters to Chief Constables of Ipswich, Drayton & Warwick notifying of escape – next morning started with one of Police & 6 black fellows in search – followed his track for 2 days when track lost, horse knocked up, returned after starting fresh party after him from Ipswich. Orr's duty to keep watch in front of cells – prisoner escaped by taking out brickwork where there was a hole for ventilation – looks into kitchen yard of Gaol, duty of turnkey Clinton to walk around yard every 10-15 minutes. Sworn before us this 14th day of November 1853 at Brisbane – W A Duncan JP, J E Barney JP."[240]

Sippy, an aboriginal, was charged with robbing one Robert Hardgrave of a mare and other property, at Moggill, on the 11 November 1853; using violence at the same time to the said Robert Hardgrave. The prisoner, who was confined in Brisbane gaol on a charge of murder, made his escape, and on his way up the country met the boy Robert Hard-

---

238 QSL Reel A 2.28 p 233.

239 QSL Reel A 2.28 p 230; see also Chapter 11, Frederick Walker to Col. Sec. 14 October 1853.

240 QSL Reel A2.27 p 480.

grave, whom he robbed of the mare he was riding, beating him at the same time very cruelly with sticks, and leaving him apparently dead. Dr Hobbs, who dressed the boy's wounds, deposed that there were seven cuts on his head, which bled profusely. The scars of some of the wounds were exhibited to the jury. The Attorney-General, in opening the case, stated that the charge of murder for which Sippy had been committed could not be sustained then, in consequence of the absence of material witnesses. The jury without hesitation found the prisoner guilty of robbery with violence, and he was sentenced to three years' hard labour in Darlinghurst gaol.[241]

Of course, the above is not the full story which will never be told anyway; it is a sample that allows the reader to view a slice of Australian history at one particular period of time. The following table is an attempt to show how the criminal justice system dealt with persons who committed capital felonies.

Persons Hanged 1848 to 1854

Race	Brisbane	Bathurst	Darlinghurst	Goulburn	Maitland	Newcastle
White	2	6	6	2	6	1
Aborigine	2	3				
Asian	1					

For Aborigines in the relevant period, at Brisbane, four were sentenced to death for killing white people, two were hanged and two escaped the gallows. Given the number of whites murdered by the Aborigines in the northern districts, the clear-up rate was poor. However, in the line of policing, Aborigines had a greater chance of being killed while being apprehended for a serious crime. Yet on the small sample we have, Aborigines seemed to have enjoyed the full panoply of the criminal justice system, due process, judicial review, ministerial review, commutation and in some cases reprieve as well as death.

---

241 *MBC* 27 May 1854 p 2

6

Walker, the Civilian

When the Board of Inquiry into Frederick Walker ended with a whimper, rather than a bang, those baying for Walker's blood called it a damp squib and wanted stronger action taken against Walker because of the widely-held belief that Walker had committed peculation and fraud on the Native Police. Perhaps the following, may indicate that some action had been taken against Walker: "An information having been laid in Sydney against Frederick Walker, late Commandant of the Native Police, and a warrant issued there for his apprehension, he was apprehended at Bromelton on the Logan River, on the 9th ultimo, by the Chief Constable of Ipswich, and, forwarded to Sydney, on a charge of embezzlement. The amount involved in this charge is believed somewhere about, £100."[242] The issue was cleared up in the Legislative Council's sitting of 10 October 1855 when the following statements were made:

> The ATTORNEY-GENERAL said the Commandant discharged his duties satisfactorily up to a certain time, when he fell off from the path of propriety by giving way to drinking habits. He appeared on two days in a state of intoxication before the Board of Enquiry, who of course recommended his dismissal. He was afterwards apprehended on the charge of embezzlement, but the evidence on which the warrant was issued was proved to be incorrect.
>
> The AUDITOR-GENERAL said there had been no irregularity in reference to the accounts of the Commandant with the Government. He did however send in his claims for 1s. 9d. per ration for his troopers, when he was paying 1s. 11d. There were therefore some outstanding accounts against him. This inattention was of course blameable. He was now giving his assistance in setting the accounts straight. When the whole matter was settled, a report could be brought up. Mr. Walker was not one of those who gave any security.[243]

242 *SMH* 9 October 1855 p 2.

243 *SMH* 11 October 1855 p 5.

From the information available, Walker seems to have gotten back in the saddle again and was:

Ridin the range once more
Totin his old .44
Where you sleep out every night
And the only law is right
Back in the saddle again
Whoopi-ty-aye-oh[244]

In other words, Mr Walker had taken up his new-found profession as a "run-hunter". In the retelling of the late Mr GP Serocold's life story, it was put his way:

> In 1857 Mr Frederick Walker, commandant of the Native Police, accompanied by a man named Wiggins arrived at Mr Serocold's station, Cockatoo Creek, with two black ex-policemen, on the lookout for new runs. That station had been taken up in 1846, and still remained the frontier station owing to the broken country adjoining it, which was full of blacks, who frequently killed men employed on it and then retreated into a country of rock and scrub where even the Native Police could not follow on horseback. Walker proposed to find a way through this broken country and to take up runs further to the north. Messrs Serocold and Mackenzie agreed to assist Messrs Walker and Wiggins, all sharing equally in any new runs found. Mr Serocold in his record said, It took a month to prepare the expedition, including packhorses and provisions of all kinds, and I saw the parties start well. After five weeks they returned, having taken up six runs on the Comet River, so called by the explorer Leichhardt. We sent in forms of application to the Crown Land Office in Sydney, and Mr Wiseman, as Commissioner, was ordered to report upon them. Later on, Walker and I met Mr Wiseman and crossed the Expedition Range and spent three weeks in going over the new runs. Part of the country had never been explored before, and one mountain at the head of the Comet River was named Mount Serocold after me. We lived on dried beef, damper, and tea with any birds we could shoot.[245]

Arising out of his visit to Cockatoo Creek and his work there as

244 Courtesy of Gene Autry.
245 *Morning Bulletin* (*MB*)17 September 1912 p 4.

a run-hunter, Messrs Walker and Wiggins were involved in an oft-told anecdote about a collision with Aborigines. This version appeared in the *Morning Bulletin* on 28 October 1922:

> On one occasion Mr Frederick Walker, the well-known explorer, paid a visit to Cockatoo Creek Station. He was accompanied by a Mr Wiggins and a New South Wales black boy named Jimmy Sandeman. They had been doing exploration work searching out new pastoral country and had been surrounded by the blacks at four o'clock in the morning. Knowing that the blacks were bad they had divided the night into three watches, Mr Walker taking the first, Jimmy Sandeman the second, and Mr Wiggins the third. The blacks crept upon them during Mr Wiggins's watch, and a blow on the head sent him to the ground, with a shattered skull, and there he lay until all was over. Mr Walker was grazed with a spear and received a blow from a nullah-nullah but was not seriously injured. Jimmy Sandeman got a blow, too, but struggling with his assailant he managed to grab Mr Walker's pistol and with it shot the leader dead, whereupon the blacks all ran away. The party then made for Cockatoo Creek, arriving at the station in about a fortnight.
>
> Mr Wiggins had then recovered his senses, but was still suffering, and it was not until the operation of trepanning was performed, either at Rockhampton or Gladstone, that he was restored to his former good health.
>
> The pistol that saved their lives was presented by Mr Walker to Mr Serocold, and by him it was given to Mr Pearce. It is a formidable looking old horse pistol, carrying the old fashioned "hat" or "belltopper" cap, and is quite heavy enough to crack even a black fellow's skull. It has been the constant companion of Mr Pearce on his many journeyings and always carried with a sense of security, which only a good firearm could give in those dangerous times. Many years afterwards Mr Pearce saw on the Leichhardt River the lonely grave of Mr Walker, who had perished there from Gulf fever.[246]

Perhaps the more accurate version might be that given by WH Wiseman, CCL of the Crown Lands Office Leichhardt, Cockatoo on 16 November 1857 when he wrote as follows:

246 *MB* 28 October 1922 p 11.

> In conclusion, I must also mention a fact shewing the insecurity of travelling in this country. Mr Frederick Walker and Mr Wiggins with their black boys were attacked at the very same hour of the same night the 27 October 1857 while encamped on the Comet River by a numerous party of savages. Mr Wiggins was knocked senseless by a waddy and Mr Walker speared in three places when he succeeded in shooting one man and apparently one of his black boys put the villains to the rout. He had great difficulty in reaching the nearest station though Mr Wiggins did almost not recover. Mr Frederick Walker is still bad from his wounds.[247]

On 27 October 1857, perhaps one of the most sanguinary outrages in the annals of Queensland history occurred when the Fraser family of the Hornet Bank station, Upper Dawson River were annihilated by the local tribe of Aborigines. This event in itself would have in modern times generated a massive surge in the provision of home security services. So, in some regards, it does not seem unreasonable for Walker, given his apposite experience and skills, to have offered his services as a security provider for the local isolated settlers. However, Walker remained the vindictive target of the officers of the Native Police and was the subject of a report by Lt John Murray of the Native Mounted Police Barracks, Port Curtis on 19 January 1858 writing to the Commandant of the Native Police, Wide Bay as follows:

> 5th. I have further the honour to state for your information that Mr Frederick Walker, late Commandant of the force has collected a number (seven) of the old discharged troopers and is patrolling the country with them. These men are under no control and it is difficult to say to what extreme they may go. I feel certain that while these men are allowed to roam about just as they please, it will be very difficult to keep troopers in the force especially their own countrymen. They have already persuaded one of my best hands (Toby) to join them. I would suggest that horses be provided by the government and the whole sent back to their own country in charge of an officer.[248]

This in turn led to Wickham, Government Resident, Moreton Bay writing to the Colonial Secretary on 5 March 1858:

---

247 SRNSW NRS906 4/719.2

248 SRNSW NRS906 4/719.2

> 4th. In the fifth paragraph of Lieutenant Murray's report he brings under notice the fact of Mr Frederick Walker the late Commandant of the Native Police having collected a number of the old discharged troopers and that he is patrolling the country with them, a circumstance which may lead to serious consequences as in frustrating the efforts of the Commandant and officers in keeping the men under control.
>
> Mr Walker has great influence with some of the blacks who were formerly under his command and who may be employed to entice the troopers to desert for the purpose of serving some private purpose. I would therefore beg to suggest that the attention of the Commissioners of Crown Lands in the Port Curtis and Leichhardt Districts should be called to the circumstance and instructed to take such measures as may be deemed by the government to be most desirable in putting a stop to such proceedings.[249]

However, Walker's new security service appeared to garner some support from the community as the following letters to the Editor show:

> … in fact, since Mr Fred Walker, in spite of his many faults, commanded the Native Police, it has been yearly getting from bad to worse, and seems still to persist in its backward course. Speaking of Mr Walker, I am sorry to hear that gentleman lately received three spear wounds from the blacks, and when almost dead raised himself and shot a black that was in the act of spearing his servant. It is a man of this stamp (barring the faults) we want, or none. An Inhabitant of The Northern Districts. Gayndah, November 27th, 1857.[250]
>
> The Native Police. Two native troopers, late of the native police, arrived here the other day, recruiting the discharged troopers of that corps, to form an independent or private troop, under the late commandant Walker. It is got up, and is to be supported by the sufferers from the non-efficient state of the present corps. I take but little heed of the statements given either for or against the present police by the numerous correspondents to different journals, knowing well the impossibility of satisfying all, and remembering the same feeling was shewn towards the gentleman who is now again brought into

249 SRNSW NRS906 4/719.2

250 *The North Australian, Ipswich and General Advertiser* (*North Australian*) 15 December 1857 p 4.

requisition. I look only to facts, and I have taken some little trouble to collect the following. I am not aware of any authentic record of the victims being kept, and what I give are only the murders that are distinctly remembered in these far north districts. It will therefore be much under the actual number, and I may have classed one or two wrongly. Distinctly remembered murders number 44, and 5 wounded, which I have classed or divided thus:

	Murdered	Wounded
Before the Native Police was established.	7	2*
During the time, Walker commanded the Native Police.	5	0†
During the time, Morisset and Marshall commanded, viz., to the present time.	32	3++
Total	44	5

**Messrs Tiverton, Streets, Blacksland (sic, Blaxland), 2 boys named Pegg, Wm. Eat, and an English woman, killed; 2 men at Blackslands (sic, Blaxlands), wounded.*

†McClaren, and 2 men with him; a man and his daughter, at Messrs Wilkin and Holt's, Yenda, killed.

++Five on the station of Wm. Young; a man travelling, murdered near Broom's, Agnes Vale; Furbar and his son-in-law; 2 men at Carlo O'Connel's; John Hillary at Cheval and Tolson's; a German woman on the Dawson; a boy at Mackay's, Dalgangale; 2 at Gigoomgan; 6 at Cardew's; and 11 at Fraser's killed. Mr Elliott speared; 2 men on Charlton's Run tomahawked and left for dead.[251]

So, great was the turmoil arising out of the Hornet Bank massacre that even Mr Walker suffered injuries as the following letter relates which was laid before the Legislative Assembly by Mr Martin:

Frederick Walker to Attorney-General

I do myself the honour to draw your attention to a former letter from me, in which I mentioned the illegal arrest of 'Tahiti' formerly my orderly. I now have to inform you that Tahiti was on the 28th April last, inhumanly murdered within one mile of Cockatoo, the residence of G. P. Serocold, Esq. JP, and that there is no doubt he was murdered by the ruffians under the orders of Mr Carr, officer

251 *MBC* 6 March 1858 p 2.

> of Native Police. This poor lad, who was about twenty-four years of age, had been with me at various periods since 1844, had always been noted for his pacific demeanour, his integrity, sobriety, and good conduct during eight years' service upon the river, and his only fault, for which he has been murdered, has been his strong attachment to me. So much did I value him, that when I left the police force, I left him my sword, sent to me by my mother, and which now has become the spoil of his assassins. I now request that you will be so kind as to inform me what steps the Government intend taking as regards this dastardly foul crime. I have written to my friends in England on the subject, and it will be brought before both Houses of Parliament—before the House of Commons by my cousin's husband, Grantly G. Berkeley; and my brother-in-law, Captain R. Yorke, N. B., will get Lord Hardwicke to bring it before the House of Lords.[252]

Moreover, the squatters of the Upper Dawson River were becoming quite stroppy in their dealings with the government of the day and the Native Police, allegations of gross incompetence were levelled at the officers of the Native Police; letters to the Editor appeared regularly spelling out the incompetence of the Native Police. Then Mr Pollet Cardew of Euroombah wrote to the Colonial Secretary on 19 November 1858 setting out in plain English what he saw as the wilful neglect of his property:

> Sir, I do myself the honour to draw your attention to the following statement and I feel convinced that you will perceive from it that my neighbour Mr Andrew Scott and I have been subjected to a great grievance.
>
> You are too well aware already that this station and that of Hornet Bank are the out most stations on the Upper Dawson and that this station has been the scene of nine murders within twelve months and that Hornet Bank has attained a melancholy notoriety on account of the awful massacre of that place.
>
> It should have been supposed that the government being aware of these occurrences would have given strongest orders to the officers of the Native Police to punish the murderers and repel all future attacks; and such orders I was informed those officers had received.

252 *MBC* 4 August 1858 p 2.

> Nevertheless, no attempt whatever has been made to effect either the one or other and to my neighbour and myself find ourselves at the expiration of twelve months as completely defenceless as former as regards any assistance from the government by whom we are so heavily taxed as we have previously.
>
> In consequence of the neglect on the part of the officers of Native Police, I have been put to the expense of £280 and Mr Scott £200 in paying and rationing extra armed watchman to protect the lives of our servants and our property. It is true that with exception of one occasion where two of my shepherds in April last were killed, I have been quite successful in repelling any attempt by the murderers to renew those outrages; but I consider it monstrous that we should be put to this ruinous expenditure and at the same time be subjected to such an enormous taxation and where £18,000 has been voted annually for the police force which as far as regards us has been a mere imposition.
>
> During the last twelve months, the only time the police have visited these scenes of murder and violence was in April last, and I have a party of police passed this place two days ago but what they are about I know not.[253]

This letter it appears was sent onto the Government Resident at Brisbane to obtain the views of Lt Morisset, Commandant of the Native Police who replied as follows on 20 January 1859:

> Sir, In reply to your instructions to me to supply you with any report on a letter addressed by Mr Pollet Cardew to the Honourable Colonial Secretary, dated 19 November 1858, complaining of the Native Police never having afforded Protection to his and a neighbouring station. I have the honour to state that immediately after receiving the appointment of Commandant I proceeded to the Upper Dawson and in consequence of the murders that had been committed on the Euroombah station, I stationed an officer with a detachment of Native Police there where they remained until I formed it absolutely necessary to remove them inconsequence of Mr Cardew and Mr Andrew Scott having organised an armed party consisting of a number of men whom I had dismissed from the corps for conduct which could not be overlooked and under the command of Mr F

[253] QSL reel A2.41 p 170.

> Walker late commandant of Native Police who made a boast that he had long sought an opportunity of injuring the Native Police force and that he now had a very good one. And so well carried on this determination of annoying the regular force that in two or three days he had persuaded the very best men in the force to desert and creates the greatest disaffection among the rest, and had I not taken the steps I did I should not have had a man left; moreover, the officers had to be most careful afterwards in keeping their men and those of Messrs Cardew and Scott from coming into collision which I know would only have ended in bloodshed as the troopers were greatly incensed at the taunting messages they were constantly receiving from the rival party. When Mr Walker found his attempts to induce them to desert were defeated. I may here mention that the influence Mr Walker obtained among the men was by making them the most extravagant promises which of course he never intended to fulfil.[254]

The paper trail suggests that the Colonial Secretary then spoke to the Attorney-General regarding F Walker's conduct as reported by Morisset and the Attorney-General then formed the view that Walker's conduct in operating a private security force was illegal. Consequently, the government then chose the office of the Chief Commissioner of Crown Lands to advise Walker that he must cease and desist his activities and disband his force. Accordingly, M Fitzpatrick, Secretary of the Department of Lands and Public Works, wrote on 19 January 1859 to the Chief Commissioner of Crown Lands:

> Sir, In forwarding the accompany papers respecting a force of disbanded Native Police Troopers reported as having been raised by certain squatters on the Upper Dawson and placed under the charge of Mr Frederick Walker late Commandant of the Native Police, I am directed to enclose to you a copy of a letter from the Secretary to the Crown Law officers conveying the opinion of the Attorney-General that under the circumstances described in the communications from the Government Resident at Moreton Bay and the Commandant of the Native Police, steps should be immediately taken to disband Mr Walker's force.
>
> 2. I am at the same time to request that you will instruct the Commissioner of Crown Lands for the Leichhardt District to proceed

254 QSL reel A2.41.

> according to the recommendations of the Attorney-General. I have etc. M Fitzpatrick. Margin note: Enclosed papers returned in accordance with the informal direction hereon. The Leichhardt Commissioner has been instructed. To WH Wiseman 28/1/1859.[255]

Wiseman from Euroombah, Upper Dawson replied as follows and included the attached statutory declaration from F Walker to the Chief Commissioner of Crown Lands, Sydney on 15 March 1859:

> Sir, In compliance with the instructions conveyed to me in your letter of the 20 January 1859 Nos 59/677 & 59/261, I do myself the honour to state that I left headquarters as soon as the state of the weather and roads permitted and that I arrived at Euroombah the station of Mr Pollet Cardew whereon Mr Frederick Walker resides on the 12th instant, a distance of 250 miles.
>
> 2. I lost no time in summoning Mr Walker who on my questioning him on the subject stated that of late he had not been out on patrol with these ex-troopers; that all of these were no longer under his orders and that those who were, were in the service of Mr Pollet Cardew regularly engaged as shepherds.
>
> 3. Mr Walker shewed me their agreements written and duly signed and witnessed wherein these troopers engaged to shepherd the sheep at £35 per annum wages. Mr Walker himself is engaged as overseer and has 10,000 sheep under his charge at a station, 20 miles distant from the head station and has these ex-troopers under him who of course carry arms as the district is still unsafe without them.
>
> 4. Mr Walker wrote and signed the declaration which I enclose. Mr W Cardew the superintendent at Euroombah confirmed these statements.
>
> 5. I proceeded onwards to Hornet Bank the station of Mr Andrew Scott where 5 others of the ex-troopers were engaged as shepherds. Mr Ross the superintendent was absent but saw one of the ex-troopers and read his agreement. He and four others are engaged as shepherds. I warned him against going out with his comrades under the orders of Mr Frederick Walker and told him that he would be put in handcuffs and sent to Sydney if he did. He promised to attend to what I said and to warn his comrades and as they all know me such

255 QSL reel A2.41 p 722.

warning may have effect. Mr Ross whom I saw next day at Euroombah wrote the declaration which I have the honour to enclose.

6. I trust that these declarations will be satisfactory. I did not attempt to obtain a deposition on oath as I did not find the men embodied and as from all I heard and saw I had reason to believe that these ex-troopers were really shepherding.

7. I informed Mr Frederick Walker of the opinion of the Attorney-General as to the illegality of his patrolling the District with an armed force. He attempted to deny his doing so saying that he only pursued those who were depredators and seemed to claim such right. I did not discuss the point with him but told him that I or any other Magistrate would execute the orders of government and arrest him if caught in the fact. He immediately disclaimed all intention of doing what was prohibited by the government.

8. I shall enclose an account of this with a copy of the Attorney-General's letter and of the Riot Act to the Bench of Magistrates of the Upper Dawson to enable them to take the necessary steps for the arrest of Mr Walker and his troopers in case at any future time they might go out patrolling.

9. I did not wish nor did I suppose I had the power legally to discharge these ex-troopers from Mr Cardew's service and from that of Mr Andrew Scott and order them to their homes. It is alleged by Mr Walker and maintained by the Government Resident at Gladstone that these ex-troopers were to have been taken back to their homes free of expense when their period of service should have terminated. I am inclined to think that some practical assistance was afforded but not sufficient probably but as these men are now in position to earn the means of returning if they desire and as some at the expiration of their agreements are to have as payment a horse and saddle perhaps they will then go home and thus put an end to all reclamation on that hand. I have etc. WH Wiseman CCL[d]

Euroombah, 14 March 1859

I Frederick Walker of Euroombah hereby solemnly declare that I am engaged as overseer by Mr Pollet Cardew of Euroombah in the District of Leichhardt that five men formerly troopers under my command when I was Commandant Native Police are now in Mr Cardew's employment under my orders, four are hired as shepherds and one is hired a stockman. I have this day shewn to Mr Wiseman the men's agreements and my sheep note book with the return of sheep herded by each man. These shepherds are all armed as they as well as myself occupy the sheep station exposed to the greatest risk leaving the European shepherds to take charge of the remainder of sheep nearer the head station. I further declare I have no wish to act at variance with the desire of the government and Mr Pollet Cardew has assured me of the same. Frederick Walker Witness to signature WH Wiseman JP.[256]

Parliamentary Papers, Correspondence in Reference to Mr F. Walker's Complaint of Aggression by the Native Police on Planet Creek.

Frederick Walker to Col. Sec. 3 April 1861

I do myself the honour to state, that on the 26th January 1860, I arrived on the spot on the Planet Creek, which I had fixed on as one of the stations of Mr Cameron: I was there met by eighty adult Aborigines, with their gins and children, and subsequently seventy more arrived. From that time to this these Aborigines have carried on with me and the other employees of Mr Cameron, a most friendly intercourse — several of them having, at different times, assisted in shepherding, driving my horse-team, cutting bark, washing the sheep, and otherwise making themselves as useful as possible, whilst the remainder have, as usual, carried on their hunting operations, without in any way interfering with, or injuring the property on the station. In June, the stock of Messrs Denison and Hope and Rolleston followed me, and under the charge of a Mr Sutton, occupied the station of Albinia Downs, when I, having left Gregg in charge of the stations already formed for Mr Cameron, removed to a spot exactly opposite Mr Sutton, but separated by a mile of scrub and the Brown (or Comet) River.

The blacks immediately expressed their desire to carry on the same friendly interview with Mr Sutton that they had established with me, and this was accordingly assented to, they, however, always camping on my side, near my tent.

When Mr Sutton's European servants abandoned him, the blacks shepherded his sheep, and they also otherwise assisted him in every

256 QSL Reel A2.41 p 721.

way in their power.

When Mr Rolleston visited his station, he expressed to me his delight with the perfect state of peace which existed, so much so, that single men travelled the roads without fear of molestation, frequently taking one of the blacks to show them a nearer track.

Suddenly, about the beginning of last month, this peace was broken by the native police under Mr Patrick, attacking and killing and wounding several of the friendly blacks at Mr Rolleston's station.

I have questioned Mr Patrick on the subject, but his answers are very unsatisfactory, and the whole transaction ought to be enquired into. The night of the 4th March, upon which the news first reached the head station of Mr Cameron, was one of much anxiety to me, for I had one man at a distance, with a flock of sheep, and the whole tribe of blacks were dreadfully excited, and accused me and all the Europeans with complicity in what they rightly termed — treachery.

I, however, pacified them by promising to apply immediately to the government and also to Mr Rolleston — for they believe, and I join in that belief — that Mr Sutton was a party to this rascally transaction. Since then a worse outrage has been attempted at the station of Mr Charles Dutton, a magistrate of the territory; but it was prevented by him. As that gentleman has applied to the commandant for an explanation, I refrain from entering into particulars. I would now, Sir, earnestly call upon the government to take measures for the protection of these blacks in future, and I would suggest that those measures should be immediate, or the result might be a collision betwixt the settlers and the native police.

Lt Wm Bligh to Col. Sec. 21 May 1861

In the absence of the Commandant, I have the honour to acknowledge the receipt of Mr Walker's letter reporting an attack on friendly blacks by the native police, under 2nd Lieutenant Patrick, which has been forwarded by you to the Commandant to be reported on.

I do myself the honour to inform you that I have just returned from a tour of inspection to the Comet River and am in possession of Mr Patrick's report concerning this alleged outrage. He states that the blacks came up to Messrs Denison, Hope, and Rolleston's station, and being ignorant of the presence of the native police, that some of their number, fully armed and without gins (a very dangerous sign) came up to the kitchen, before daybreak, and demanded sheep; that, becoming aware of his presence they went away; that he followed them to prevent outrage to the shepherds at the out-stations, and on coming up with a large number, they attacked him, and he was compelled to fire on them in self-defence; and this report coincides with the information I have received from different persons in that neighbourhoods, who are in every way as worthy of belief as Mr Walker, and who have acquired their information in the same way as he has, namely, from hearsay. Neither do the neighbouring squatters appear to be under any fear as to the consequences of Mr Patrick's proceedings, and with the exception of Mr Dutton, they, expressed their satisfaction at his general conduct as police officer.

With reference to the last paragraph of Mr Walker's letter, suggesting that the government should take immediate measures for the protection of the blacks in future, lest a collision should result between the settlers and the native police, I have the honour to state that no one but Mr Walker could for a moment entertain such a foolish idea: the squatters on the Comet are unanimous in desiring the protection of the native police, and even Mr Dutton himself told me that his opinion was, that the force was much required there, and that he should be happy to support, in every way in his power, any other officer than Second Lieutenant Patrick.[257]

The following letter appeared in *The North Australian, Ipswich General Advertiser*, 9 August 1861.

Frederick Walker to Attorney-General, 10 July 1861

I was much pleased to see in a report of a speech made by you, in the legislative Assembly that you stated it was the duty of magistrates to protect the Aborigines quite as much so as it was their duty to protect the Europeans.

This from the Attorney-General of the colony is a valuable admission, but I would ask you of what use are such truisms, when it is notorious that they are ignored in practice? At the Juandah massacre, the blacks who had been proven to the satisfaction of five magistrates to be innocent of any participation in crime were subse-

257 *The Courier*, 6 August 1861, p 2.

quently murdered, some in the verandah, some in the kitchen of a magistrate, who in vain remonstrated.

Two blacks who had by some whim been spared were then made to bury the victims, and one ruffian said to the other, what shall we do with the sextons? The answer was, shoot them; one was accordingly shot, why the other was spared, I know not, possibly the supply of cartridges was running short.

Again, when 'Tahiti,' a native of the colony of Victoria, who had faithfully served the government for eight years, was murdered, it was from the station of a magistrate that he was illegally taken in irons, and notwithstanding the urgent protest of that magistrate.

When, after the delay of ten months, the government caused an enquiry to be held, Mr Commissioner Wiseman, a magistrate, instituted a mock inquiry, and, — I dare him to controvert it, — did his utmost to screen the murderer. I am informed by a gentleman of known respectability that not long ago the bench of magistrates at the Condamine refused to entertain the claim of a black to a horse which had been given to him, upon the plea that the blacks were aliens, and could hold no property. Was it ever heard of before, proclaiming a man to be an alien in his own fatherland?

I could name other cases wherein magistrates, either through ignorance, or want of moral courage, have not extended to the Aborigines the protection they are by law entitled to; one magistrate told me, notwithstanding the repeated decisions of the judges of the Supreme Court, that the Aborigines were not British subjects, and not amenable to British law.

I know of but one case in which a magistrate has successfully resisted the slaughter of unoffending blacks; I allude to that of Mr Chas. B. Dutton, and in this case, I have heard his proceeding censured because his brother Henry threatened the officer of native police with his revolver. The public, however, I trust will applaud the act, for by so doing he made use of the only argument that could have succeeded and saved the station from being polluted by another crime. A strong feeling prevails that this state of things is connived at by the government, for it has been frequently reiterated that the proceedings of the officers of native police were ****** **** punitive instructions from Mr Charles Cowper. I believe, however, that a forced construction has been put upon those instructions; but even

> so, it is clear that the officer to whom they were addressed was unworthy of the confidence of the government.
>
> I fear that the government of which you are a member has been constantly misinformed upon these matters; but I hope now their eyes may be opened, and that means will be taken to put an end to an infernal system, which has already cast a deep stain upon the honour of this colony.[258]

In the above memoirs of Mr Serocold, Messrs Walker, Wiggins, Serocold and McKenzie took up runs on the Comet River. After these runs were successfully lodged and approved, it seems that they were then transferred as follows, to Fredk. Walker, Planet Creek, N° 1, 3, 4, 5, 6; and Clematis, N° 1, 2, 3, 4. The contractual basis of these transactions is not clear but it may be that Mr Walker transferred his licences to other runs to Messrs Serocold and McKenzie in return for Planet Creek and Clematis.[259]

It further appears, based on the following advertisement that Mr Walker may have liquidated his southern assets to expand his newly acquired northern assets:

> CAUTION. The undersigned having purchased from Mr Frederick Walker all his Cattle, branded FW near side of neck and FW near side ribs and his Horse Stock, branded WAL conjoined near shoulder, as well as his interest in the station known as "Balaro," in the District of Bligh. Cautions all parties against trespassing or removing stock therefrom without his consent. James F. Plunkett. Wargundy, 26th August.[260]

It can only be speculation as to the precise nature of the transactions and the scope of them that Walker involved himself in, but the record shows that on 14 June 1859, he agreed to sell and transfer all his right and interest in and to six blocks of country on the Planet, Comet and Brown known as Planet N° 1, 2, 3, 4, 5 and 6 to David Cameron. What is of interest, I believe, is the nature of the consideration Walker was to receive from Cameron for his interest in the said Planet runs. It was not money but a complicated style of living.

On 2 February 1861, Frederick Walker instructed his solicitors Macal-

---

258 *North Australian, Ipswich and General Advertiser* 9 August 1861 p 3.

259 *MBC* 17 July 1860 p 4

260 *SMH* 3 September 1861 p 1

ister & Scott to apply to the Supreme Court of Queensland for a præcipe for a writ of summons against Daniel Cameron for £2000, which perhaps suggests their contract of service had defaulted. Whatever the trouble was, it is unclear but the following advertisement appeared in the Sydney newspapers of December 1862:

> J and W. BYRNES and CO. have received instructions to dispose of the well-known PLANET DOWNS STATION, consisting of eleven blocks of country in the Comet River and Planet Creek, in the Leichhardt District of Queensland, together with 6000 sheep, about 1200 head of cattle, 80 horses, etc. Five of these blocks embrace both sides of the Planet Creek, from Expectation Range to the Comet or Brown River, with a frontage of five miles to the latter. The character of this country is undulating stony downs rich black soil, open box forests, clothed with a varied mixture of barley, blue and other favourite grasses, having proved eminently suited and healthy for sheep, both as regards condition and fleece. The improvements consist of
>
> HOMESTEAD
>
> A house of six rooms, lined throughout with calico, and having a good verandah. A store 30 feet by 16 feet, with verandah all round, embracing bedroom, office, meat room, &c, &c.
>
> WOOLSHED
>
> with lever press complete, split and log yards, and every convenience for shearing.
>
> WASH PEN
>
> complete of logs and split wood, water, soft and sweet, with depth of 16 to 18 feet.
>
> PADDOCK
>
> of 150 acres closed in; also, ring fence (of heavy posts) two heavy rails enclosing the whole Homestead, about 150 acres.
>
> GARDEN
>
> planted with bananas, pine apples, &c, &c.
>
> BAILING YARD and STOCK YARD
>
> Men's huts, &c.

> THE CATTLE STATION
>
> has huts, bailing yard, three stock yards, &c, &c.
>
> J. and W. B. and Co will cause the above to be offered at public auction in Sydney, on the 26 February 1863, should it not have been previously disposed of by private contract.[261]

On or about 21 January 1863, Dean and Co. announced that they had sold Planet Downs (Comet River, Queensland) with 6500 sheep and 1400 head of cattle, for £12,000. Then shortly thereafter, Frederick Walker inserted the following advertisement in the local Sydney papers:

> NOTICE. With reference to the advertisement of the sale, by Mr D. Cameron, of the Planet Downs Runs, I hereby, on behalf of Mr Frederick Walker, give notice that any person purchasing the same will do so subject to an equitable charge, which the said Frederick Walker has upon certain of the said runs to the extent of £2000. Thomas Bellas, attorney for Frederick Walker. Rockhampton, 6th February 1863, Witness W. G. Anderson.[262]

On or about 21 February 1863, Planet Downs, Comet River began trading under the name of Cameron and Sheridan. In the meantime, Walker filed a writ in Supreme Court of Queensland on 14 May 1863 against David Cameron. The matter came on for hearing in the Supreme Court at Brisbane on 12 February 1864 as follows:

> Demurrers, *Walker* v. *Cameron.*
>
> This was a demurrer to the defendant's pleas.
>
> The declaration stated that Frederick Walker sued Daniel Cameron upon an agreement entered into between them in writing, and dated the 14th June 1859, by which the plaintiff agreed to sell and transfer all his right and interest in and to six blocks of country on the Planet Downs to the defendant, and engage himself as superintendent to the defendant, and to use his utmost endeavours to protect the stock, for the term of two years. In consideration of the transfer, and at the expiration of the said two years, the defendant agreed to make over to the plaintiff 1000 ewes, shorn and in lamb, of the

---

[261] *Empire* 18 December 1862 p 7; also 19, 20, 22, 24, 25 & 26 December 1862 & January 1863.

[262] *SMH* 12, 16, 19, & 23 February 1863.

average owes on the station, a team of ton working bullocks with bows and yokes complete, one of the working drays of the station, one ton of flour, one chest of tea, 640lbs. sugar, and also two stock horses; and the defendant also agreed to pay £100 per annum with board and lodging, and to grant the plaintiff 10 per cent, on the branded increase of horses and cattle, and 5 per cent, of the weaned lambs whore the increase was above 50 per cent, and under 75 per cent., and 10 per cent, whore increase amounted to 75 per cent, In the event of the nonfulfillment of the agreement in its integrity, the amount to be allowed to the plaintiff was to be settled by arbitration, and a bill at 3 months was to be given by defendant. The defendant, on being satisfied with the transfer of Planet Downs, agreed to give plaintiffs bills at 3, 6, and 12 months, for £116 13s. 4d. each, and the plaintiff agreed to assign three "Crescent runs" contiguous to the Planet Downs as security for the repayment of the £350 advanced. In the event of his tender not being accepted the defendant was to withhold sheep to the value of £350 from the plaintiff. Subsequent to this agreement, and before any breach of it, it was agreed that the defendant should accept five instead of six of the Planet Runs, the agreement as regarded the rest being still in full force. And all conditions were fulfilled, and all things happened, and all times elapsed necessary for the plaintiff to maintain his action, yet that the defendant did not perform any part of the said agreement, and the plaintiff claimed.

To this declaration the defendant pleaded that all conditions were not fulfilled.

1. Because the plaintiff having been engaged as superintendent for two years left before the two years elapsed.

2. Because the plaintiff having been engaged as superintendent for two years was to give his utmost endeavours to protect the property and increase the stock of the defendant, but he left before the two years elapsed, and left the stock unprotected, and suffered the same to be lost, wasted, and decreased.

3. Because, having been engaged as aforesaid, he did not use his utmost endeavours to protect the stock.

To these pleas the plaintiff demurred on the grounds that the pleas do not allege that the conditions mentioned in the pleas were conditions precedent, and that the conditions alleged were not conditions precedent to the performance of the contract and could not be pleaded as such.[263]

Mr F Walker got judgment against Cameron for £2900 in damages.[264] The next step in this longwinded and complex saga was that Planet Downs, Comet River was put up for sale by the mortgagee, who presumably were Cameron and Sheridan as follows:

> Containing 11 blocks, country capable of carrying about 100,000 sheep, homestead, woolshed, huts, yards, paddocks, and every other necessary required for carrying on sheep farming. The property of Messrs Cameron and Sheridan.
>
> For Sale by order of the Mortgagee.
>
> The above valuable property is open for sale by private bargain up to the 20th instant, and if not disposed of by that time, will be advertised for sale by public auction on 4th April next. For further particulars, apply to J. and W. Byrnes and Co., Victoria Chambers, Pitt Street, Sydney.[265]

It was sold by Mr Brewster on 16 June 1864 on these terms, "the Planet Downs station, in the Leichhardt district, Queensland, together with 22,000 sheep, at 20s. per head; 1000 head of cattle, more or less, unmustered, for £1000; with stores, drays, working bullocks, taken for the lump sum of £1000; total amount of sale, £24,000."[266] Arising out of the above sale, the partnership of Messrs Cameron and Sheridan called in all claims against the partnership.[267] The next step by Walker was to obtain a Writ of Fi Fa, issued in the above suit of *Walker* v. *Cameron* against the above-named defendant, Cameron, for Planet Downs to be sold at auction by order of the Sheriff of Queensland, on or about Tuesday, the 9th day of August 1864, at Rockhampton. Cameron then declared himself insolvent and the estate of the said Daniel Cameron of Planet Downs,

---

263 *Courier* 13 February 1864 p 3. The court documents may be seen at Chapter 11.

264 *Maryborough Chronicle, Wide Bay and Burnett Advertiser* 28 April 1864 p 4.

265 *SMH* 3 March 1864 p 6.

266 *SMH* 16 June 1864 p 5.

267 Notice. All Claims against the Partnership firm of Messrs Cameron and Sheridan, of Planet Downs, Comet River, Rockhampton, Qld, must be forwarded to the undersigned signed as correct by Messrs Cameron and Sheridan. J. and W. Byrnes and Co., Pitt Street, Sydney. Sydney, 30 June, 1864. *Empire* 2 July 1864 p 1.

was on the 8th day of September 1864 placed under Sequestration by W. H. Wiseman, Esquire, a Commissioner for accepting the surrender of Insolvent Estates.

Pattern 1840 Constabulary Carbine
Makers: Tower, Birmingham Gun Makers; Caliber: .653 inch, 17 bore; Bore: smooth;
Barrel Length: 26.0 inches; OA Length: 42.5 inches; Weight: 6lb 15 oz
Type of Action: percussion muzzle loader, single shot; Sights: foresight only

7

In Search of Burke and Wills

In 1860–61, Robert O'Hara Burke and William John Wills led an expedition of 19 men from Melbourne to the Gulf of Carpentaria in the north, a distance of around 3,250 kilometres (approximately 2,000 miles). At that time, most of the inland of Australia had not been explored and was completely unknown to the European settlers. After six months without receiving word from the Burke expedition, the media began questioning its whereabouts. Public pressure increased and on 13 June 1861, the Exploration Committee agreed to send a search party to look for Burke and Wills and, if necessary, offer them support. In all, six expeditions were sent to search for Burke and Wills, two commissioned by the Exploration Committee, three by the Royal Society of Victoria and one by the Government of South Australia. The Victorian Relief Expedition was led by Frederick Walker.

The Exploration Committee met on the afternoon of 4 July 1861 to discuss, among other matters, a proposal put forward by a Mr A Morris. He proposed that the committee should endeavour to obtain the assistance of Mr Frederick Walker, commandant of the native police of New South Wales some time before the separation of Queensland:

> This gentleman was well known as an excellent bushman in the northern districts and had a greater knowledge of the character of the natives of Australia and had acquired greater influence with large numbers of them, than any other person ever attained. While he was cautious to guard against surprisal, yet he had methods of gaining their confidence, even on a first interview, which was quite remarkable. Mr Morris was satisfied, if Mr Walker got on the tracks of Mr Burke, or any other white man, that he (Mr Walker) would induce the wild Aborigines to assist in finding the missing person. Mr Walker had, for the last five or six years, employed himself in selecting runs for different parties, and in acting as protector to outside squatters; in

> both capacities, he had been eminently successful, and with scarcely, if ever coming into unfriendly collision with the native tribes.
>
> He had just returned from the head of Cooper's Creek (the Victoria of Mitchell), where he discovered several tributaries hitherto unexplored, and also obtained traces of the lamented Leichhardt's party, whose fate, either on his outward or inward journey, Mr Walker could undoubtedly solve. Mr Walker had in his employment five or six aboriginal natives from the Murrumbidgee district, who, through all changes of fortune, had remained faithful to him for ten or twelve years, and who had qualities for the work proposed which white men do not possess. He had also ten or twelve horses, accustomed to travel and feed together. With the aid of maps, Mr Walker was quite competent to lay down his route correctly, and to do everything towards making known the geography of the country over which he may pass.
>
> Should the committee determine to seek Mr Walker's cooperation, they should send their communications through the Queensland authorities at Rockhampton, with a request to forward them to Mr Walker, who, if not in Rockhampton, will be heard of at a Mr Dutton's station, in the neighbourhood. After some debate, the committee adjourned until the following day at two o'clock.[268]

The following day after much debate, ultimately, the following motion was carried unanimously: "That, subject to the approval of the Government, Mr Walker be requested to organize and take charge of a contingent party from Rockhampton, and that Professor Neumayer be requested to accompany the steam-sloop *Victoria* to co-operate with Captain Norman in adopting measures to secure the objects in view, and to take the command of a second land party at Carpentaria, should such be deemed desirable on the arrival of the *Victoria* there."[269]

In Melbourne, the fate of Burke was the all exciting theme. Mr Howitt and party had started. Professor Neumayer went to the Gulf of Carpentaria with the steamer *Victoria* and was to take command of a land party. Frederick Walker was to be offered the command of the land party that was to proceed from Rockhampton. The search for Burke was to

---

268 *The Argus* 5 July 1861 p 5.

269 *The Argus* 6 July 1861 p 5.

be the primary object of both expeditions. Despatches were sent by the Sydney steamer from Melbourne, to Captain Mayne, the Auditor-General of New South Wales, requesting him to communicate with Mr Walker, and have him forthwith, equip an expedition which should start from Rockhampton. It was proposed that it should consist of nine persons, and the estimated expense was £900. The following telegram was sent to Captain Mayne, which explained the purport of these despatches:

> As honourable secretary to the Exploration Committee of the Royal Society, I have to inform you that it was resolved to day to send Mr Walker should that gentleman accept the offer, to search for Mr Burke, and to join *HMCSS Victoria* at the Albert River. Mr Morris states that you would cooperate with Mr Walker, and make arrangements that men and horses should be in readiness at Rockhampton to start on the shortest notice. Will you kindly do so by the earliest opportunity? Full written instructions will be forwarded to you for transmission to Mr Walker, by the honourable the Chief Secretary by Monday's Sydney post and the Victorian government intends to request you to take the full management of that portion of the expedition of search which is to start from Rockhampton. (Signed) John Macadam, MD[270]

The *Rockhampton Bulletin and Central Queensland Advertiser* of the day was mildly sensitive to any perceived criticism of F Walker when it ran the following:

> The *Courier's* Sydney correspondent endeavours to cast a slur on the Inland Expedition from Rockhampton in search of Burke, by insinuating that Mr Walker, who has been requested to take command of the party, will give more attention to "run-hunting" than to the object of the expedition. We have been requested to state that this is totally untrue. The only grounds for this insinuation appear to be that Mr Walker has been previously engaged in searching for runs. His experience in this occupation eminently qualities him for the work in which he is now to be engaged, and the fact of his being well known as an excellent bushman has led to his being selected for this purpose. Mr Walker is now in town, preparing for a speedy departure.[271]

270 *The Courier* 18 July 1861 p 4.

271 *Rockhampton Bulletin and Central Queensland Advertiser* 17 August 1861 p 2.

The Victorian Government's steam sloop-of-war, *Victoria*, arrived in the bay early on Saturday morning 10 August 1861, and at the bar about 1.30 pm. Captain W. H. Norman came up to Brisbane in the *Breadalbane*, and had an interview with his Excellency the Governor during the evening. The *Victoria* made a splendid passage from Melbourne. She left Queenscliff on the morning of the 5th instant, and steamed with light winds to Cape Howe, where the wind freshened and became stiff, and she performed the remainder of the distance to Cape Moreton under sail. Captain Norman had put into the bay to see the party to be fitted out by the Surveyor-General, Mr Gregory; his equipment, and also stores for Mr Walker's party which were shipped on board for transport by the *Firefly*. The *Victoria* also took on 40 tons of coal. After leaving the bay she proceeded direct to the Gulf of Carpentaria, accompanied by the *Firefly*. The *Firefly*, brig, transport to the *Victoria*, arrived at Moreton Island about an hour after the latter vessel passed up. She sailed from Melbourne on 31 July.[272]

The *Rockhampton Bulletin and Central Queensland Advertiser* of 24 August 1861 stated that Mr Walker's party was to take its departure that morning, and furnished the following:

> The Queensland Government having contributed £500 towards the expenses of the undertaking, arrangements have been made for an additional land party, to be fitted out under their direction. The leadership has been confided to Mr Landsborough, and this party will go onto the Albert River in the steamer *Victoria*, the special work assigned to them being to search the creeks around the Gulf of Carpentaria. We do not anticipate that much will be affected by this party, with only £500 to pay their expenses.
>
> Captain Norman, of the *Victoria*, takes command of the whole when they meet at the Albert, and on their return, Mr Walker will take charge of the horses, &c, belonging to the Queensland party, and bring them over land to Rockhampton.
>
> Mr Walker starts this morning, and he has kindly furnished us with the particulars respecting his expedition, and the intended route. The committee leave him wide discretion, as circumstances alone can determine the best course to be pursued. He is directed, howev-

272 *The North Australian, Ipswich and General Advertiser* 13 August 1861 p 2.

er, to make for the Albert River with as much despatch as a general search on the way will permit. For their guidance, Commander Norman, has furnished the following signals:

Each evening at 1 pm a gun will be fired; at 8.30 pm, a signal rocket; & at 9 pm a blue light. The same signals will be used by the *Victoria's* boat in the river. Mr Walker's party consists of:

Frederick Walker, leader.
Macalister, assistant.
Richard Houghton (in charge of horses).
John Horsfeldt (in charge of stores).
Natives.
Patrick from the Edward River
Harry "
Jingle "
Walter "
Rodney Murray River
Coreen Jemmy from Billibong
Jemmy, from the Comet River (a supernumerary).

The natives, the last-named excepted, are those who Mr Augustus Morris mentions as having, in prosperity or adversity, for twelve years stuck to Walker.

The party is partly armed with Terry's breech-loading rifles, and partly with double barrelled guns (superior). They are also supplied with a number of excellent fowling pieces, with Ely's patent wire shot cartridges. Mr Walker first starts for Dutton's station, where he loads the horses, with the exception of a few that carry some articles which cannot be procured up the country. From Dutton's he proceeds to his tree, marked 29 over a Maltese cross, on the Victoria, or Backoo River.[273] So far, the route is familiar both to him and his men; and as they know all their camps they can get their horses into proper drill. From thence they will make for the heads of the Gilbert, crossing the heads of the Alice, and probably those of the Lind and Thomson rivers. Mr Walker believes that the Flinders will be found to take its rise in the high ranges at the head of the Gilbert, and therefore he may possibly follow that river down until he crosses Gregory's track.

273 Barcoo River.

> He intends marking all his camps FW over half-moon, cut with a chisel and every tenth camp will also have the date. He has told Captain Mayne that he will average fifteen miles per diem from the date of leaving Dutton's and he will take, six days to reach that station from Rockhampton; consequently, Captain Norman may expect him in sixty days from the date of departure from Rockhampton. Should he not arrive by that time, or within ten days of it, Captain Norman may rest assured that he is on Burke's track. No fears need be entertained of the safety of his party, as the natives he takes with him have before been with him for eighteen days together, without any provisions whatever, excepting what they got from hunting, and he takes with him five months' provisions, and will therefore be able to supply Burke's party should he fall in with them. Mr Walker says that his men never suffer from scurvy, as he knows how to prevent it making its appearance and, relative to the point, he wishes Captain Norman to take with him a barrel of dried apples, and some beef, preserved with sugar, for the homeward route.

On 14 April 1862, the *Argus* produced a critique of Mr Walker's outward expedition:

> A careful perusal of the journals of Mr Frederick Walker, the leader of the expedition which started from Rockhampton overland for the Gulf of Carpentaria, for the purpose of discovering some traces of Burke, will impress the reader very favourably as regards the qualifications of that gentleman for the enterprise he undertook; the courage, coolness, and caution, he displayed in carrying it out, and the sagacity and fidelity exhibited by his aboriginal companions. The distance traversed from the time Mr Walker's party left the remotest out-station in Queensland, until he reached the depot on the Albert River, was equal to that which intervenes between Cooper's Creek and the Gulf of Carpentaria. The country penetrated appears to have presented many obstacles to progress, before which ordinary travellers would have recoiled, and on two occasions Mr Walker was brought into contact with powerful bodies of hostile natives, with whom, in the first instance, he entered into a deadly engagement; while, in the second, owing to his ammunition running short, he was obliged to oppose strategy to force. The first encounter with the natives occurred upon the 30th of October last, when a formidable body of Aborigines, armed with spears, bore down upon the intruders, and detached about thirty from the van to charge the Europeans.

Fortunately, the latter were armed with Terry's breech-loaders, and were thus enabled to keep up such a rapid and steady fire, that the blacks were placed *hors de combat* before they could approach within 150 yards, so as to make their spears available. Twelve of the thirty were killed, and most of the others wounded, the main body immediately retreating in dismay. This attack seems to have been wholly unprovoked on the part of Mr Walker and his companions, and on Sunday, the 1st of December, when camped on the Leichhardt River, the blacks again assumed the offensive. One of the Aborigines accompanying the expedition, ascended a tree, and found the enemy "stretching out in a half-moon, in three parties." This move, observes Mr Walker, "which my men term stock-yarding, is, I believe, peculiar to blacks throwing spears with a woomera, the object being to concentrate a shower of spears. It was one long familiar to me, and I directed Mr Macalister to charge their left wing. The result was that the circular line doubled up, the blacks turned and fled. Their right wing, which was, I think, the strongest mob, got over the river, and were off; but their centre and left wing suffered a heavy loss." A few days afterwards, Mr Walker and an aboriginal named Jingle had to ride for their lives, when making an excursion from the camp, their retreat upon which was intercepted by the natives.

In a letter addressed to Captain Norman, Mr Walker expresses a hope that the government of Victoria will pay to the families of his aboriginal companions the moderate stipend which he had promised them; and on the arrival of the men in Melbourne, would either provide them with a passage to Rockhampton, or give their families the means of re-joining them in Victoria; failing which, Mr Walker requests "that any remuneration which might he intended to be made for his own services, should be appropriated to carry out his guarantee, as his men have, for so many years, considered his promise as sacred." Mr Walker need entertain no uneasiness on this score. To the admirable conduct and unswerving fidelity of his aboriginal followers we are greatly indebted for the success and safety of the expedition, and their services will neither be overlooked nor grudgingly rewarded.

Mr Walker's exploration has made us acquainted with a large tract of country lying to the westward of the district explored by Leichhardt, between the 18th and 24th parallels of south latitude, and the 140th and 147th degrees of east longitude. Most of the numer-

> ous watercourses discovered appear to have been of an intermittent character and to be fed by the violent thunder showers which occur in those regions during the summer months; and the whole face of the country undergoes a magical transformation in the course of a few days. Broad rivers roll their tumultuous waters through channels previously dry, the adjacent flats are converted into shallow lakes, vegetation springs up with amazing rapidity, and Captain Norman mentions that, upon a plot of ground off which the dry grass had been burnt, he measured, ten days after a tropical shower, blades of fresh grass which were ten inches in length. Although Mr Walker's overland journey was effected at nearly the hottest period of the year, he seems to have found sufficient water for the use of his party, together with an abundance of feed; and the magnitude of some of the streams which circulate through that part of Australia in the rainy season may be estimated from the fact that the bed of the Weelgar River (latitude 20 deg. 16 min.) measured 111 yards from the foot of one bank to the other. The heat in the shade is described as ranging from 100 deg. to 110 deg. during the day, but the nights were delightfully cool, and, strange to say, refreshing breezes sprang up from the SW, or towards the centre of the continent.

Mr Walker, the explorer, addressed the following letter to the *Rockhampton Bulletin and Central Queensland Advertiser* on his return from his search for Bourke and Wills:

> Sir, In your issue of this date you print an extract from the *Sydney Morning Herald*, dated June 20th. The writer of the article in question says properly, that Landsborough must have crossed the Barkly River; but as to that river being reported by Landsborough to be navigable, I doubt, as he is too good a bushman to make such a blunder. Next the writer of the article in the *Sydney Herald* states, that if the Barkly emptied itself into Lake Torrens, it must have been crossed by Burke. Now the Barkly is a separate watershed from any flowing to Lake Torrens, and consequently Burke and Wills could not have crossed it until after they had left their depot that unfortunate depot on Cooper's Creek. Subsequently Burke and Wills did cross the Barkly. Wills marks it in his map as a permanent watercourse latitude 23 0 45, and longitude 140. Within a few hours, Burke and Wills crossed another river, which they called the Burke. Where I left the Barkly, at my N° 27 camp, it is placed on my map latitude 20.45, longitude 144.8. If the writer of the article in the *S M Herald* will

> compare these notes, he will find that Burke did cross the Barkly, and soon after the Stawell. He wants to know what becomes of this river. I am surprised that he cannot see that the Barkly flows into the same lake which Stuart sighted on its western side, and which he alludes to at the end of the article in question. There is another point in that article which requires correction. I never said that I saw Leichhardt's trails on the Barkly. I saw them on the water shed of the Thompson, as I showed you by my map; but I did learn from the blacks on the Barkly that white men had gone down that river many years before. As for the Barkly dwindling into small dimensions, that I believe to be out of the question. In one of my conversations with you, I mentioned that the heads of the Leichhardt River flowing into the Gulf of Carpentaria, had not yet been accounted for; and yet it is evident that they take their rise in ranges SSE from where Gregory crossed that river, not far from the head of the Cloncurry of Wills, which is a tributary of the Flinders. The corresponding watershed on the south side of the range must flow into the Barkly, and will therefore increase that river, not cause it to dwindle away. I remain, Sir, yours truly, Frederick Walker. Rockhampton, 6th July 1862.[274]

The *Empire* of the day saw Walker's exploits as that of a gun-toting cowboy who had lost sight of his ideals:

> We regret that the same cannot be said of Mr Frederick Walker's expedition. That gentleman started from Rockhampton in August last; and after occasionally touching on Leichhardt's tracks; and after passing over splendid pastoral country, watered by fine rivers reached Captain Norman's camp at Carpentaria early in December. On several occasions during his journey he was enabled to open communications with the natives, from whom he received much valuable information with reference to the character of the country and the course of its streams, A most remarkable circumstance noted by him is that, while some of the Aborigines spoke a language known on the Comet River, others on the shores of Carpentaria, were unintelligible to all but a black from the southern districts of New South Wales. Several of them spoke of a large party that had passed many years before, evidently alluding to Leichhardt's party, and some of the natives had iron tomahawks, and even a broad axe. It was on the twenty-sixth of November that Burke's return trail was struck, on

[274] *SMH* 22 July 1862 p 5

the Flinders' River. By this track, Mr Walker turned back south from Carpentaria, after recruiting his supplies.

It has been already indicated that this traveller was far more unfortunate than Mr Howitt in his transactions with the natives. It will be desirable to bear in mind that the tribes on the coast are of a much more warlike and resolute disposition than the Aborigines in the inhospitable country between the Darling and Cooper's Creek; but even this fact scarcely affords a satisfactory excuse for what is revealed by Walker's journal. On the 30th of October, a large party of natives assembled near the camp, and evidently resented the presence of the travellers at a spring of water, the only one near, showing, themselves in their war paint, and armed with formidable spears. A portion of Mr Walker's party charged the blacks, firing at them with revolvers, and we are told that twelve natives were killed and that the whites remained masters of the spring. On the 6th of November, another encounter took place, when one Aborigine was killed; and on the first of December, a number of natives having been observed at some distance from the camp forming themselves into a half-moon, in three parties as if for the purpose of attack. Mr Walker directed Mr Macalister to charge their left wing. The result he says was that their line doubled up, and that the blacks turned and fled. Their right wing he adds, which I think, was the strongest mob, got over the river and were off; but their centre and left wing suffered a heavy loss. Really it would appear that we were reading the despatch of an invading general, rather than one from a peaceful traveller engaged in a work of humanity. Mr Walker has long been known to have a weakness for military operations, and on proper occasions he may have done good service in this way but he appears to have imported the spirit of the dragoon somewhat unnecessarily into the business intrusted to him in his late expedition.[275]

Exploration of the Interior, Landsborough's Diary:

February 6, today I had the good fortune to get Lieutenant Woods to assist me with my work. He made a beautiful tracing from the sketch I had made to show my route to the SW. The sketch was made solely by dead reckoning. I wanted to take notes from Mr Walker's journal and chart of his route from Rockhampton, but as he told Captain Norman that no one was to be allowed to do so, I was not permitted

275 *Empire* 18 April 1862 p 2.

> to make them. Having agreed with Captain Norman to return to the depot tomorrow, I was, having letters to write and preparations to make for the next expedition, in a continual bustle.[276]

The following letter to the Editor was Mr F Walker's response to Landsborough's above statement:

> Sir, Upon the first appearance in print of Mr Landsborough's statement that I had left instructions that he should not see my map, the *Rockhampton Bulletin* very properly remarks that, as I was under the orders of Captain Norman when I reached the Albert River, it was not likely that I should give him instructions. Upon my outward route, I made two maps, marked up every evening, one on a scale of eight miles to the inch, and the other marked down on Gregory's map. When I gave the copy of the former, with the journal to Captain Norman, I asked him whether he would show them to Mr Landsborough. He replied that, as they were given to him for his Excellency the Governor of Victoria, to be laid before the Royal Society, he was not at liberty to show them to anyone, but at my request there would be no objection to Mr Landsborough inspecting the copy of Gregory's map, with my route marked on it, which I had given to Captain Norman for his own use. Notwithstanding, Mr Landsborough repeats his unfair statement, and in your article of the 11th September, you appear to take it for granted. Mr Landsborough well knows that, besides the reason assigned to me, Captain Norman had another one, which would prevent him from showing him my large map. I remain, Sir, your obedient servant, Frederick Walker, Bauhinia Downs, October 14th.[277]

At the annual meeting of the Royal Geographical Society, at Burlington House, London on 20 July 1863, the president, Mr R. Murchison, presented a gold watches to Mr William Landsborough, and to the representatives of Mr John McKinlay and of Mr Frederick Walker, for their successful explorations in Australia. Mr Landsborough was present and pointed out on the map the route taken by the expedition of which he was a member, as it was described by the president.[278]

It seems that Walker missed out on the Victorian government's lar-

276 *SMH* 8 September 1862 p 2.

277 *SMH* 30 October 1862 p 2.

278 *Courier* 21 July 1863 p 3.

gess to those who helped look for Burke and Wills:

> For some weeks past Mr Walker, who took such a prominent part in exploring the northern parts of this territory three years ago in search of Burke and Wills, has been residing in Brisbane. This gentleman, as will be remembered by our older colonists, acted for some years as Commandant of the Native Police, and performed the services allotted to him in a manner which gained credit to himself. By him reports were regularly, at least so far as was practicable, sent to the Attorney-General, of what had transpired; but even he, it appears, has been abused through the efforts of persons who have since had reason to be grateful to him for the admirable charts of the country through which he travelled, which were made by him, and which have on all occasions been freely offered when their inspection could be of assistance. For instance, the journal published by Mr Bourne was founded on the notes and maps lent to him by Mr Walker — so at least we are informed.
>
> In consideration of the valuable services rendered by Mr Walker, the Geographical Society of London presented him with a watch; about two years ago, but which has never yet been received by that gentleman. The Victorian Exploration Society have also neglected to reimburse him for the expenses he incurred in fitting out his contingent party, and thus after enduring years of fatigue, and facing difficulties inseparable from penetrating into an unknown territory, Mr Walker's claims have been entirely ignored. In Victoria, the survivor of Burke's party has been liberally provided for. For Mr Howitt, who headed a contingent party, suitable provision has been made. The exertions of Sturt and McKinlay have been liberally recognised. Mr Walker remains alone as regards an undeserving neglect.[279]

Twelve months after the Royal Geographical Society of London had awarded Mr Frederick Walker, a gold watch in recognition of the services he had rendered to the colony as an explorer, through some mistake, was sent to Adelaide instead of to Queensland, and there it remained until his Excellency the Governor of Queensland interested himself in the matter and communicated with the South Australian Government. On 20 June 1864, the long-lost watch was handed over by Mr Herbert to Mr Walker, and thus that gentleman has received the first acknowledgment

279 *Courier* 22 February 1864 p 2

of the valuable aid he gave to the cause of exploration. Inside the case of the watch was the following inscription: "The President and Council of the Royal Geographical Society of London to Frederick Walker, for his successful exploration in Australia, May 25th 1863."[280]

After Walker received his gold watch from the Royal Geographical Society of London the *Empire* saw fit to re-instate Walker and to commend him as well:

> We are glad to hear that it is the intention of the Government again to employ the services of an old and valued servant of this colony, Mr Frederick Walker. What particular service is now required from that gentleman has not transpired, but we believe that it is connected with the formation of telegraphic communication with India and thence to the mother country. The mission is a most important one. There are now so many new people in Queensland that it is probable that Mr Walker's services are known to only a few old residents. In this money-making community, we are always glad to pay a tribute to an open-hearted, generous man, who has throughout a long career done all for others and nothing for himself. Our first notice of Mr Walker dates many years' back, when he was clerk of the court at Deniliquin. Indeed, you may say he was police magistrate and everything, being the most able and active man there. At that period, the blacks were giving great trouble. They had extensive swamps filled with reeds in which to retreat when pursued by the settlers. A large party was at last organised, and Mr Walker showed such aptitude for command upon one occasion that he was by common consent made leader in-chief. By his exertions, the blacks were rendered quiet, and the stations in those parts were no more molested. Next, we heard of Mr Walker as commandant of the Native Police force about 1848 or 1849. The blacks on the Macintyre River had nearly driven the settlers from the country, and sixteen men were killed within a few miles of each other. It struck Mr A. Morris, then the owner of Callandoon, that native police such as had previously been established in Victoria, was the only force which would be serviceable, and he determined that Mr Walker, his old friend in the south country, was the best man to organise such a corps. Through the influence of Mr Charles Wentworth everything was arranged, and Mr Walker was appointed. He always had, and still has, a singular power of gaining the affections of the blacks and making them obey him, and also is a

280 *Sydney Mail* 25 June 1864 p 5.

> good bushman. He sought out in the southern parts of New South Wales such men as he judged would suit his purpose, and then made his first great journey. He brought the men right up the Darling, then almost an unknown country, and arrived with them at Callandoon, without meeting with any severe mishap. He there turned his horses to rest and went to work with his men on foot; in less than three months the country was quiet, and the stockmen's lives were safe; then followed the active exertions made on the Balonne and the Dawson.
>
> The work was always done, and without cruelty. Mr Walker some years ago retired from the command of the native police and spent some time in exploring the country about the Comet River, having crossed Expedition Range. He was nearly killed by the blacks on this occasion; he received several severe wounds and had a hard fight for his life. His journey to Carpentaria in search of poor Burke and Wills is well known, and it is therefore necessary to touch upon that subject. He most deservedly received for that service the thanks of the Queensland Parliament, and also a handsome testimonial from the Geographical Society of London no slight honour. We are finally indebted to the labours of Mr Walker for the settlement of the Flinders River, and a vast portion of our northern territory, whereby we have acquired a great increase of revenue.[281]

Then the following business transpired in the Legislative Assembly of Queensland on 9 August 1864:

> Mr Douglas moved the following resolution: "That the thanks of this House be given to Mr Frederick Walker, for his services as an explorer in Northern Australia." He would briefly call the attention of the House to a few facts in connection with Mr Walker's explorations. In August or September 1861, fears were entertained for the safety of the expedition under Burke and Wills; and at that time, it was determined by the Victorian Government and the Royal Society that an attempt should be made to ascertain the fate of the explorers. In due course two parties were fitted out and left Queensland, and the results which attended the explorations of these parties were now a matter of history. Mr Landsborough, escorted by the screw-steamer *Victoria*, went with his party by sea to the north, and then started overland across the country, and reached Menindee,

281 *Empire* 6 February 1865 p 3.

and eventually Melbourne. The result of the other overland expedition, which popularly was not considered so successful, was the subject of the resolution which he now brought before the House. He considered that the merits of the leader of that expedition had been overlooked. Mr F. Walker had been sent out at the instance of the Royal Society of Victoria, and the colony of Queensland had voted no sum of money in aid of his expedition. None of the expenses of the expedition had been defrayed by this colony. He left on the 17th October 1861, and, starting from Mitchell's Victoria, went to the Gulf of Carpentaria. On the 7th December, according to his journal, arrived at the depot on the Albert. On arriving at that place, he had ascertained that Burke had been in the neighbourhood, and his (Mr Walker's) party had seen tracks of camels. Mr Walker communicated at once with Captain Norman and Mr Landsborough; and he (Mr Douglas) would here revert to a statement which had gained circulation, to the effect that Mr Walker had refused to Mr Landsborough an inspection of his maps, on the occasion of his meeting him at the northern river. This statement was a misrepresentation of circumstances, and he (Mr Douglas) held in his hand a letter from Captain Norman to Mr Walker, denying any such statement. In a geographical point of view, Mr Walker's expedition, although he did not succeed in assisting the explorers, had been most satisfactory. His maps had been checked and were considered very correct and had proved of great use to subsequent explorers and occupiers of country. Since his explorations, the country from the Barcoo to Carpentaria had been to a great extent taken up, and that occupation had been facilitated by the land marks laid down in Mr Walker's charts. He (Mr Douglas) would desire to point out that the services of Mr Walker had never been formally recognised by the Queensland Government, although they had been recognised by the Geographical Society of Great Britain, who had voted him a gold watch. Mr Walker had been a volunteer in a very dangerous service and had hitherto reaped nothing but honour. Even previously to Separation Mr Walker had been of considerable service to the community. Mr Lilley seconded the motion.

Colonial Secretary conceived that there would be no difference of opinion as to the desirability of carrying the present motion. It would cost the colony nothing, and it was at least due to Mr Walker to place on record their recognition of his services. Mr Walker was in many respects a remarkable man. As an explorer, and in his management of the blacks, there was no man his superior in the colony; and the services he had rendered to the colony should at least be recognised. Should the Government desire hereafter to form an expedition for the survey of the eastern coast along the Gulf of Carpentaria and Cape York, no doubt a party could be placed at the disposal of Mr Walker at a moderate cost, and no man more suited for such a task could be selected. Up to the present time Queensland had done less than any other colony towards exploration; and upon such an object they might fairly expend a thousand pounds or two without being losers. (Hear, hear.) Motion put and passed.[282]

282 *Queensland Times, Ipswich Herald and General Advertiser* 11 August 1864 p 4.

8

F W Journal in search of Burke & Wills

I have kept no regular journal until the day upon which I left the Victoria River, and as the ground previously was nearly all well known to me, the following will serve as a sort of preface. I received Capt. Mayne's letter on the 6th August [1861]. I returned that day forty miles to Bauhinia Downs; stopped there the next day to arrange matters with my friend Mr Chas B. Dutton; sent Patrick to collect my men and gave directions to Jack Horsfeldt to cure the meat for the expedition. I then started for Rockhampton, but when I reached the Dawson I could not get the horses within twenty yards of the bank. Patrick cut a canoe and I crossed; finding Mr Govan at Rio, I exchanged horses with him. I rode his to Rockhampton and he, mine to his station. I hastened to get everything in readiness but found that only twelve horses had been purchased. With the assistance of my friends Mr Hutchinson and Captain Hunter I made up my lot in a few days and started the whole party out on Saturday, the 25th August.

Stopped till the next day partly to get the English mail and partly to hear what had become of the *Victoria* steamer. Captain Cottier, of the *Clarence*, told me that vessel, together with a brig, were to have started the day previous (Saturday) direct for the Albert River, without touching anywhere, so I was disappointed in my hopes of seeing Captain Norman before I started. Some delay took place owing to the heaviness of the ground on my way up to Mr Dutton's. We however managed to cross the Dawson safely; stopped two days at Mr Living's, taking in flour and sugar and arranging the packs, and two more days at Mr Dutton's, packing the meat and preparing everything in proper order for the final start, which, to my great joy, took place on the 7th September. The horses are not in as good order as I would wish, some are all right, but others look very seedy, and several have been griped. I must get them in proper trim before I can go ahead full speed. So, for the present short stages and good camps are the order of the day. And it is lucky I know the ground so well. When I reached Albenier Downs, the station of Messrs Hope, Dennistoun, and Rollestone, a mare was so ill I was obliged to leave her. I saw that if I wished to make anything of a journey I must have more strength in horses, especially as the pack saddles hurt the horses' ribs, and I had no spare ones to relieve them. I accordingly bought three from my friend Mr Patten, and four more from Messrs Davis and Allen. We now pushed on, but still only by moderate stages, as the horses were still much purged by the new grass. We reached Mr Macintosh's station on a creek flowing into the Nogoa.

On the 14th September 1861, spelled and the 15th; left the station, for good or otherwise on the 16th. Upon reaching the Nogoa, which I crossed on the 19th, I went to the north to hit Poma, which tributary of the Claude takes its rise at my pass over the main range; this is a great detour, but by this means I avoided the dense brigalow scrub which intervenes between the Nogoa River and the Salvator Lake and the pass. On the 20th we reached the beautiful Emerald Downs, on Poma Creek, camped there the 21st, and arrived at the foot of the pass and my old camp on the 23rd; the grass had caught fire from my camp and was now a fine sward; the horses were within a square mile in the morning, and as we got a good start did the twenty miles to my N° 30 tree on the Nivelle, in good time; nevertheless, one horse, evidently sick, gave in on the way and had to be left. We camped here the 25th; sent back for the sick horse, and I marked a tree FW/4. My first marked tree is on Emerald Downs, as that was new ground to me. The 26th we pushed down to the Nive and marked a tree N° 5. This is about five miles above my old N° 11 camp. The next day, 27th, crossed over to the Victoria, and camped N° 6, below my N° 29 tree. On the 28th, 29th, and 30th pushed down the Victoria by fair stages, the horses now rapidly improving.

On the 1st October 1861 moved down the river to another camp two miles farther, and at this camp marked FW/⌣/10, and RSV/3 Oct/1861. We spelled until the morning of the 7th October, long. 146° 1', lat. 24° 34'. Whilst camped here we searched for the L tree seen by Gregory, but as we had seen his 22nd (XXII.) tree on the north bank we searched on the same for the L tree, and it was not until the 5th, Jingle and Mr Haughton found it on the south bank. In the meanwhile, I had found another L tree 2 miles below our camp on north side, and 7 below the tree seen, by Gregory. I looked for an open road NNW but was checked by a dense almost impenetrable scrub of acacia. Mitchell calls the acacia "brigalow," but that is incorrect, for it differs much from it, and I have seen but two or three brigalow since we crossed the ridge dividing the Nive watershed from that of the Victoria. The blacks call this acacia "gorrt." Brigalow, they call "noorwool". A little below the second L tree I found I could pass round the termination of this scrub. I surmise that Leichhardt intended leaving the Victoria at the tree seen by Gregory; was stopped in his NNW course by the same barrier encountered by me and turned back to camp at the tree found by me, subsequently clearing the scrub where I rounded it. His track, if he had dry weather, would, on this basaltic soil, be soon obliterated. The horses, by the few days' rest here on the best grass the Australian colonies afford, got into fine condition, and it was a pleasure to see so many fine horses with their coats shining as if they had been stabled and well groomed.

Journal from 7 October to 7 December 1861.

Monday, 7 October 1861. There was much difficulty in catching the horses this morning, owing to their having improved so much during the last few days' spell. Walter and Harry returned with my letters this morning. Having at last got a start at 10.30, we first went 35° W of N to clear a scrub and passing by Leichhardt's second L tree; at the end of two miles I turned NNW, and kept this course for 15 miles, until we pulled up a small creek on a myall plain. The country has been to-day a succession of downs and plains intersected by narrow and open scrub of the acacia the blacks call "gorrt". Camp N° 11; rain at night.

Tuesday, 8 October 1861. A fair start at 8.30; course still NNW. At the end of 4 miles and ¾ we crossed a sandy creek with a large bed but no water; it was here running through sand hills, but lower down I could see it opened on the downs and plains we had been traversing all morning. One mile beyond this we killed an emu; the next 5 and a half miles brought us to another creek, but with a pool of water; luckily for the horses the first mile and a half was through open acacia scrub, the remainder plain. We now ascended a high downs ridge, surmounted by a belt of scrub; we reached the summit in three miles, still NNW. Here were fresh tracks of blacks. We reached the division of waters betwixt the Alice and Victoria. The first creek crossed to-day was no doubt that crossed by Sir Thomas Mitchell, and which he marks on his map as a deep rocky channel. Still NNW for three miles and a quarter more, crossing one plain, the remainder open scrub. We now turned N by W 10° for three miles, and N by E 10°, because Jingle thought a creek lay in that direction, for two miles and three quarters. The last five miles and three quarters has been sandy box country, clothed with a grass like knitting-needles. We camped without water at dusk; I was disgusted to find three packhorses missing. All hands at work to make a yard, in which we enclosed the horses for the night.

Wednesday, 9 October 1861. At daylight Patrick, Jemmy (Cargara), and Jingle started for the missing horses, and, to my great joy, brought them safe to the camp within half an hour. We now made haste to pack and started at 8 N by E 10° for 3 miles, when we found a pool of muddy or rather milky-looking water; the horses indulged in a good drink, and we filled two of our excellent water bags-last night we found the benefit of then. I now turned my course again NNW, which we followed for 4 miles, when I discerned symptoms of a watercourse trending N by E 10°. A very short distance showed I was right, and I followed it for 3 miles through a scrub, when it joined a larger creek, which flowed WNW. This creek I followed for 3 miles, to camp at a place sufficiently open and well grassed for my purpose. This creek had, after we came on it, received two tributaries from the NE, and had now abundance of water, possibly but not certainly permanent. One horse called the Artful Dodger gave some trouble by plunging pack and all into a deep water-hole; Mr Macalister and Mr Haughton got him out with some trouble. Camp N° 13. Except the last 6 miles, the ground was the same sandy box country, with the same grass as yesterday evening.

Thursday, 10 October 1861. This morning we would have made a fair start, considering the scrubby nature of the ground, but a delay took place, owing to Mr Macalister going in search of some horses, which were already found and close to camp; we started, therefore, as late as 10.15 am. The first mile and a quarter NNW 25 was through scrub; we then ascended a small range, and travelled over a tableland of sandy ground, with the same needle-like grass as yesterday. At the end of 5 miles we descended into a broad sandy creek, with reeds, and which had not long ceased running; I called this the Patrick, after one of my old comrades (aboriginal); another delay of an hour took place, owing to a flour bag having been torn. The Patrick now ran NNW 30°, and then NNW 25°; I therefore followed it for two miles and three-quarters; it now turned NW 45°, but I still followed it, for the heavy sandy ground and an oppressively hot day I saw was distressing to the horses; at the end of another two miles it turned NNW 25°, when a half mile's ride brought us to a long reach of water at which I camped, as the day's work was too much broken into. (Camp N° 14.) Thunder to the westward and southward. I suppose I am now about 9 miles from the Alice. When I left the Victoria, I lay down in pencil, on Mitchell's map, what I supposed to be the probable course of the Alice, also a tributary which exactly answered the creek we were on last night, and which I have now called the Macalister. The Patrick I fell in with 3 miles sooner than I anticipated, but its northerly course makes up for that. I hope to fall in on the other side of the Alice with a tributary coming from the NNW, probably from the north. Marginal note: Rodney, Jingle, and Jemmy (Coreen) being in the advance party to-day, saw very old tracks of horses, and apparently, mules, going down the Patrick. I much regret not having seen them, as they must have been Leichhardt's.

Friday 11 October 1861. Much trouble in collecting the horses this morning, as they have, for the first time, split up into four different lots. I started Mr Macalister at 10.30 am with thirty horses, but the remainder delayed me and Mr Haughton till 1.30. Mr Macalister had travelled NNW by compass, according to by instructions, and I pulled him up at a beautiful camp, on a small creek, with excellent grass. The country after the first 4 miles was all plains and downs, intersected by small belts of the gorrt (acacia) scrub. The last 5 miles was over very fine downs, clothed with that excellent grass I call rye (because it always grows near barley grass). From these downs, I saw the range, about 25 miles to the east; I was too late to mark the tree this evening, and accordingly marked it the next morning, but only with a N° 15, as I was in a hurry to get a start this cool morning.

Saturday, 12 October 1861. To-day we rode 15 miles NNW by compass, over fine very high downs; crossed two small creeks flowing from them N by W and camped at the head of a third. The range now lay about 20 miles east, and betwixt us and it there was a fine downy valley, evidently well-watered. Day cool and pleasant and horses doing well on the excellent feed. (Camp No 16) Marked as usual, FW/ᴗ. Latitude by observation, 23° 17' S, Night cool; thermometer at daylight 50°.

Sunday, 13 October 1861. Our course, NNW by compass, took us down the creek we had camped on, until it joined another water in several places. We crossed this creek, and at the end of 7 miles and a half from our camp we crossed a creek full of water, with a branch flowing to the SW. This I take to be the Alice. Hitherto we have been on fine downs all day. Within half a mile we crossed a tributary coming from the north, and in another mile another tributary; by keeping our course NNW, we again crossed the first creek, and at the end of 6 miles we came to a fine reach of water too tempting to pass, so we camped 4 miles back; in the first tributary, we saw the finest reach of water I have seen this side of the range, and at it was more than one black's camp. About 1 mile lower down than where we crossed the Alice, was a range on the right bank which I have named Mount Rodney, after one of my Murray men. As all the creeks meet there, I expect there must be a large quantity of water at the foot of it. (Camp No 17.) The two tributaries both flow through acacia (gorrt) scrub for the last 5 miles, but where we have camped the country is more open, with promise of improvement. It will be observed that we have seen very little permanent water; but by following down the watercourses into the valley which lay to our right the last two days, I would expect to find abundance.

Monday, 14 October 1861. Made an excellent start at 8.30; the first 2 miles the country was more thickly covered with the acacia than suited me, and as we now had hit the creek again, I crossed it and travelled parallel to it for 1½' 60° W of N by compass. The country now opened, and I resumed my NNW compass course. At the end of 2 miles crossed the other creek, and 2 miles more brought us to the summit of the downs ridge which separates the watershed of the Alice from that of the Thompson. Some low ranges were seen to the east about 5 or 6 miles off, and a small one on the downs to the west about 3 miles is probably where the two creeks we have left take their rise. Ten miles more over the downs, and as we descended stony plains, brought us to a beautiful river running W by N. This, which is no doubt, a tributary of the Thomson, I have called the Coreena. Mr Gregory, when he left the Thomson, says that river is formed by the small watercourse emanating from the sandstone ridges; had I swallowed that, I should not have ventured where I am now. Just ahead of us, about ten miles, we have seen the smoke of blacks travelling and burning the grass as they go (against the wind); they are evidently going up another river towards the range. This is splendid sheep country. I have no doubt that many of the holes in the Coreena are permanent; but it is not possible to tell which, as that river has not long ceased running. It floods occasionally about a quarter of a mile on each side, except where the downs approach the bank, which they do about 1½' above the Camp N° 18. The gum trees look as if drought were a complete stranger to them, so fresh and healthy looking are they.

Tuesday, 15 October 1861 This day was one of disappointment, for the boy Jemmy Cargara returned at 1.30 without three of the horses which he had been seeking since daylight. This is the first time he has failed. I now sent out three men on horseback, and they returned with the horses at three. Shortly after I had unsaddled the remainder, Coreen Jemmy and Patrick reported having seen the tracks of a considerable number of horses. I sent Mr Macalister, Mr Haughton, Jingle, and Coreen Jemmy, to examine them; they returned and reported there was no doubt of the tracks; that they were very old and had been there near a fine lagoon about 2 miles above my camp and in fine weather. Aneroid 29.5.

Wednesday, 16 October 1861. Made an excellent start at 8.30. We went NNW near 1 mile from camp; crossed a tributary creek; travelled over plains intersected with gorrt acacia scrub, one rather too closely timbered, the others open. At the end of 5 miles saw one large solitary myall tree; the next 5 miles through open acacia and narrow but long strips of plain brought us to a watercourse, a black's camp a few days old, and two nice little lagoons - one very promising looking; the remainder of the day was over sandstone ridges, clothed with a disagreeable needle grass. Four miles from the lagoons we crossed the well-marked tracks of a very large party going a little N of W. These tracks were very old and had been made in wet weather. They will be visible probably for years to come, whereas mine, made in dry weather, will be obliterated the first rainy season. At the end of 24 miles from camp, we came on the opposite declivity of the sandstone ridges, and from thence saw a high peak I have called Mount Macalister, being 5° north of west by compass, and another bluff mount which I have called Mount Horsfeldt, after my store-keeper. I now perceived why Leichhardt's tracks had been going west. He probably camped on the Coreena, above where my men saw the horse tracks; thence travelled parallel to my course, and being higher up on the ridges, saw the peak sooner than I did, and turned off towards it. I now saw I was getting too intimate with the dividing range and altered my course to NW by compass. One mile brought me to a small water-course, with many small pools of temporary water, and as there was a sufficiency of good grass, I camped. (N° 19) How is it that the blacks here have iron tomahawks? One has evidently a broad axe. The blacks on the Nive, who are much nearer the settlements, have only stone tom-ahawks - some very fine ones.

Thursday, 17 October 1861. Started at 7 o'clock. Went 3 miles NW by compass, when, having crossed a high ridge, we came on a river running to the S of W. This I believe to be the principal head of the Thomson. Here were seen the old tracks of horses; Leichhardt's camp was probably lower down on this river. We proceeded on the same course for 2 miles, passing betwixt two basalt ridges. I now for half a mile diverged to WNW to get on a plain, when I resumed the NW course for two miles over two basalt ridges. The basalt was injuring our horses' feet, and I turned again WNW to get on the plains. We crossed a creek in 2 miles more, and in another mile a ridge. I was now able to resume the NW course, and in three miles we hit a nice lagoon, and another head of the Thomson running SW betwixt these two, and going NNW was again the well-defined tracks of Leichhardt's party (he must have had a considerable quantity of wet weather.) He had no doubt from Macalister's Peak perceived he was on the verge of the desert and turned again to his old NNW course. At the end of another mile and a half, I turned 25° N of W to go to a peak rising off the downs. From this peak, which I reached in 3 miles and a half, I saw displayed before me an awful waste of endless plains. My man, Patrick, who ascended the peak with me, and who is accustomed to the immense plains of the Edward and Murrumbidgee, was struck with consternation, and he remarked to me, "There is no t'other side this country." Upon leaving this solitary peak, which I have called the Sentinel, I had to turn 10° W of N by compass. We passed betwixt two terminations of spurs, and in 4 miles, having crossed one ridge, we came to a gum creek running W by N. We searched in vain for water, and had to push on over the next ridge, and in 3 miles NNW we reached another creek with sufficient water for a day or two. I must stop here one day, for one of my horses gave in at the last creek, and three of the expedition horses within half a mile of this camp. The day has been oppressively hot.

Friday, 18 October 1861. This morning Mr Haughton and Rodney went back for my mare Nancy. They found her at a good lagoon within a quarter of a mile from where Jemmy (Coreen) had been looking for water. One of the expedition horses which knocked up yesterday is an impostor, for he has carried no load until the last three days as, without making a yard, we could not catch the brute. The other horses are apparently as fresh as the morning I left the Victoria River. Jingle and I took a ride for 3 miles down the creek which ran WNW through the plains. I found another long pool of water, but fast drying up. We went to the top of the next ridge to get a good view of the range. I must still, I see, keep 10° W of N by compass. I observed a high mountain in the direction, with a remarkable gap in it. If a large river running to the W does not rise thereabouts I am much deceived. I expect to cross Leichhardt's track again to-morrow; of course, whether we see it will depend upon whether he was still travelling in a rainy season or not. The ground dries up here very quick. The thermometer, from 12 to 2 pm, was 96° in the shade; the aneroid is 29.4. I marked a tree FW/20, and another near it RSV/18th Oct/1861. The tracks of three blacks were seen this morning; they had passed up a few hours before we reached this (Saturday) morning. I have been much misled by a watch I got in Rockhampton. I more than once found it had stopped when I compared it with my own, which I carry in its case packed in the pistol box. It now appears that this must have taken place when I was travelling, not after I had come into camp, as I supposed, for by observations taken from two different stars this morning our latitude 21° 50', 20 miles more north than my dead reckoning, which previously never differed from the observations more than three miles. We have travelled over some very good downs since leaving the sandstone. Near the ranges the grass is sufficiently thick, but as they slope down to the plain it gets thinner and thinner.

Saturday, 19 October 1861. Started at 8 and travelled so well that by 12.30 we had completed our 17 miles. We crossed some fine downs; at the end of the first 4 miles we crossed a creek running WSW, at the end of 2 more miles we crossed another creek running SW, and another mile and a half brought us to a third, which ran SSW: 3 more miles pulled up the last of the waters of the Thomson watershed. This one was running south. We were now rising fast, and we travelled 2 miles upon a plateau of downs. Seeing the gap, I have spoken of a little on my right, I altered my course from 10° W of N by compass, to north, and 3 miles more on the same plateau brought me to it. I now turned down the opposite fall 10° W of N by compass and in 3 miles pulled up a large creek running in three and sometimes more channels. This creek is running WNW and is evidently the beginning of a large river. Some very high mountains are now close to us to the north. The aneroid is now 29.2, or 29.19. The gap we have crossed could have been very little under the height of the main range; where we crossed it then the aneroid was 28.9. Camp N° 21.

Sunday, 20 October 1861. Sunday morning, thermometer at daylight, 66°. A horse of mine called Camelaroy, and an old stager, not being satisfied with the grass, took seventeen horses back with him to the old camp; we consequently did not get away until 12. I steered NNW by compass, for 12 miles over fine very high basaltic downs, but thinly grassed in some places: we passed a tributary of the creek or river we camped on last night and camped on a much larger head of the same river, which I have now called the Haughton, after my companion Mr Richard Haughton; the other head I have called the Camelaroy. We unfortunately disturbed three blacks, and thus failed in having an interview. They left very much worn iron tomahawks in this camp, and I have added three new ones to it. The hole here, though of great size and depth, is nearly dry. There does not appear to have been any of the heavy rains here which fell on the Victoria, as well as on the coast, in July and August.

There is no appearance of spring; the carrots, instead of being green like what they were on the Alice waters, have for the last few days been quite brown and brittle. A very high mountain, ENE from the camp (N° 22), I have called Mount Gilbee, after Dr Gilbee, who moved the resolution that I should lead this party.

Monday, 21 October 1861. Started at 8 o'clock; for the first 5 miles 30° W of N, when we crossed a tributary of the Houghton 2 and a half miles same course to the top of a scrubby spur of the range, on which Patrick shot a turkey. I now had to turn N by compass to get out on to a plain, in which we reached in 2 miles; turned then N by W 12 min. by compass and crossed another tributary of the Haughton. Here Nanny gave in; three of the men in vain looked-for water and we had to push on over a ridge for two miles and a half, when the mare would not go any further. I ran down a creek WNW for 4 miles, and then W by N for 4 more, being enticed on from point to point by the appearance of the gum trees, and the hope of finding water to bring Nanny on to it. I saw it was of no use, and turned NW for half a mile, and then N by W 10° for 2 miles, and N by W 8° for two miles more to the top of a gap in a mountain I have called Pollux; another to the east I called Castor. I had now a fine view of the country to the north, and with my glass saw gum trees across a plain about 5 miles off. One of the packhorses here gave in, and we had to leave it. We went down the slope of the downs for 3 miles N by W 10°, and then turned N by E 10° 2 miles, to some splendid reaches of water, evidently the back water of a large river. We had however to leave four more horses on the downs, and it was dark before we got our saddles off. The horses, parched with thirst, having had no water during a fearfully hot day, rushed into the water, packs and all; luckily no damage was done. A day's spell as a matter of course.

Tuesday, 22 October 1861. Three of the horses came in by morning, and Mr Haughton and Patrick fetched in the other two. Poor Nanny I must leave to her fate, in hopes she will return to the Haughton; luckily the nights are deliciously cool, and I gave her a bucket of water out of our water bags. Mr Haughton took water back to the horse we left at Mount Pollux. Jingle, in collecting the horses, to-day, saw the river, which he says is as big as the Dawson; we shall cross it to-morrow, and likewise another, which I think comes round a peak I saw from Mount

Pollux, bearing by compass, 12° E of North. Marked a tree FW/ᴗ/23. The downs here are well grassed, and if the climate is not too hot, this is as good sheep country as any in Australia. I have no doubt that permanent water is to be found near this, but that at our camp would not stand more than seven or eight months.

Wednesday, 23 October 1861. Made a very bad start, owing to the horses having split into so many different mobs; it was ten o'clock when we left the camp. Within half a mile NNW by compass we crossed the river, which is a sandy dry channel 90 yards wide; this is an immense width, considering how high we are, the aneroid standing at 29.15; 5 miles from the camp, on the same course, we crossed a large tributary, two-thirds of the width of the main river, which I have named the Barkly, after the Governor of Victoria. Two miles more NNW brought as to the top of a basalt ridge, and as a range was now in our way, I turned 32° W of N for two and a half miles to the top of another ridge, having crossed a small channel. I now turned 55° W of N for one mile, and then W for one mile to a small creek with two temporary water-holes and good grass. As I must cross the range, which I take to be a spur of the main range, I camped here, not wishing to attempt more to-day. I am glad to see the horses are as fresh again as ever. I hoped to cross Leichhardt's track, but we have seen no signs of it. As the Barkly is running NW I think it probable he followed it as long as it kept that course. I suppose this river, which I expect receives large tributaries from the north, is a principal feeder of Stuart's great lake, and that Eyre's Creek flows into it; if so, Burke must have pulled it up. (Camp No 24.). The thermometer this morning at daylight was 64°, this evening at sundown 86°. The aneroid 29.16. Night squally and aneroid rose to 29.25.

Thursday, 24 October 1861. I expected to make a good start this morning, but seven of the horses went some distance up the creek to some water, which Jemmy Cargara says he thinks is permanent; this delayed us until 9.30. When I got to the top of the range I found I was on an extensive I basaltic tableland. The aneroid stood at 28.9. The range, with a peak which I saw from Mount Pollux, stood in the midst of this tableland, and now bore 5° W of N by compass. Two very high mountains were seen about 18 miles off; one 10° E of N, and the other 20° E of N. The basalt was distressing to the horses, and we could not average two miles an hour. At the end of three and a half miles, 30° W of N, we were pulled up by a deep ravine with a large creek at the bottom. The ravine was lined with cliffs of basalt columns, and it was with some difficulty we found a slope of debris not too steep for our descent, and then great care had to be taken. On reaching the foot of the cliffs we ran down the creek for three miles W by N to a fine pool where we camped, having been five hours doing this short distance. I forgot to mark the tree at this camp. It ought to have been 25. The creek I have called the Jingle, after one of our men.

Friday, 25 October 1861 Made a fair start at 7.45 am I followed down the Jingle as I wished to clear the basaltic ranges if possible; this took me two miles WNW, four miles W by N 10°, 2 miles W, 2 miles W by S 12° and then 1-mile SW by W, brought us to a pool where we watered the horses; within half a mile W by N. We now joined the Barkly River, 1-mile W by N 10° to a bit of downs. I now saw that a spur of the same basaltic ranges must make the Barkly run WSW, and as there was no help for it I steered in that direction, crossing the river and camping at the end of 3 miles at a fine pool of water with good grass and open country. The beau ideal of a camp which I have marked FW/◡/26. The large tributary which I have called the Macadam, after the Secretary of the Victoria Exploration Committee, must have joined the Barkly at the back of a spur I see from here bearing 30° S of E. I had a view of both of them from the tableland, and then a plain separated them. We have had lots of pigeons at this camp; a lagoon about half a mile from here is reported by Rodney to be permanent; I shall probably see it to-morrow. The day has been very hot, and yet not oppressively so, owing to a wind which, although blowing from WSW, was, strange to say, cool. We have generally had cool breezes from the east hitherward, at night especially. After sundown, the thermometer was 100°. Aneroid 29.2.

Saturday, 26 October 1861. The horses were more scattered this morning than I expected, and I started Mr Haughton with one-half at 7.30 am and followed him with the remainder at 9 am. I overtook him at the end of seven miles WSW by compass and found him in vain endeavouring to get a parley with some gins who were crouching in the long grass on the bank of the river. I gave them some tomahawks, which gave them more confidence. One old lady who spoke a language of which

Jemmy Cargara understood a little, stated that she had seen men like me many years ago down the river; pointing WSW, she said another river joined it from the SE; this must be the Haughton; she also in pointing WSW repeated the words Cara Garee several times. I now turned NW by compass for 3 miles, but the basalt again made us turn S by W 10° 3 miles to a fine reach of water and fine feed for the horses. I determined to spell here a day before attempting the basalt, which "coûte que coûte" [at all costs], I must surmount if I wish to get to the north. Jingle having seen a little black boy near this, Mr Haughton went to the camp with three of my men, and where he fell in with three black men; they had with them one of the gins to whom I had given the tomahawks; this insured a friendly reception, and they returned to my camp with Mr Haughton. They gave us to understand by signs and by as much of their language as Jemmy Cargara could comprehend, that it was joined by another large river from the NE. If we went NW by compass after crossing that river we would go-over a range and then come to a river which ran NW into Careegaree, by which we conclude they mean the Gulf of Carpentaria; the other must be Stuart's great lake. The river I think and hope is the Flinders. These blacks have superior spears, thrown by a woomera. One of grasstree jointed was of immense length; another not quite so long had three prongs, one of which was barbed with a bit of bone fastened on with gum Thermometer 86° at sundown, at twelve to day it was 88°, and 100° at two and three pm Aneroid 29.21.

Sunday, 27 October 1861. The thermometer, at 1 am was at 68° this morning; the aneroid rose to 29.25, and subsequently to 29.32. Horses all in sight or nearly so at daylight. After twelve o'clock the aneroid went down to 29.19. Yesterday evening Mr Haughton and I ascended the range, at foot of which is this camp (No 27). We found that it was still the same tableland of basalt we have been skirting; however, by rounding this point, we get about two and a half miles NW of good ground, and then must encounter the basalt again. Day very hot. Thermometer in shade 102° at 2 pm, at 98° at 3 o'clock, at sundown 89°. The water at this camp no doubt stands a long time, but as at present it is only five feet deep, it cannot be deemed permanent, notwithstanding its great length. Jingle yesterday saw some large lagoons of permanent, or as he terms it, old water, on the south side of the river; and as there is a chain of such lagoons all along on that side under the downs no doubt many are permanent; on this, or the north side, there are waterholes similar to that at this camp whenever the spurs of the basalt tableland approach the river. Jemmy Cargara, in looking for the horses this morning, fell in with the blacks again, and among them was now an old man, who spoke some words of his language. He said he doubted whether we should find water for the horses in the first river we had to cross. There is, therefore, more than one yet running into the Barkly across our course. He told Jemmy that after crossing a river we should cross a range which came from Jemmy's country, meaning, of course, the main range. Lat. 20° 46', 1½ min diff. from dead reckoning.

Monday, 28 October 1861. Made an excellent seven o'clock start. After rounding the spur at No 27, we had five miles of fairground NW until we reached the top of the basalt: three and a half miles NW took us over this spur, the descent and a ravine in it being so broken as to cause me to fear some accident to the horses; luckily none took place, and seven and a half miles more NW over good undulating downs which we rode at 5 miles an hour, brought us to the first river, which I have called the Dutton, after my friend Mr Charles B. Dutton. The old black's doubts as to the water proved correct, and as Rodney, by digging, found some within a few inches of the surface, I determined to camp and make a pool for the horses. To supply 48 horses was no light undertaking, but all hands worked with a will. Coreen Jemmy made some wooden shovels; the first two were failures, but the third was a "chef-d'œuvre" [masterpiece], and before sundown the horses were all satisfied and had plenty to return to during the night. The small black ants here are such a nuisance that no one can sleep.

Tuesday, 29 October 1861. Started at 7.30 but only went five miles 39° W of N by compass, because we pulled up two nice pools of temporary water with good grass, and I do not deem it prudent to pass water after the warning we have received. Coreen shot a turkey, which gave us some excellent soup.

Wednesday, 30 October 1861. Started at 7.15. Went 30° W of N to a gap on a downs ridge, from thence saw a range ahead of us, reached the summit of it in seven miles, same course, having crossed two large creeks. We now travelled over this range, which was of red sandstone, of course, clothed with spinifex grass, for fire miles NW, and this brought us to a fine channel of a river, where we disturbed a black digging for water. We ran this river which I have called the Stawell, after the President of the Victorian Exploration Committee, for two miles, W by N compass, where Rodney found a beautiful spring waterhole, where we camped; the feed for the horses is also excellent. We had hardly unsaddled our horses, when the voices of blacks were heard. Jingle, Paddy, and Jemmy Cargara went down the river towards them, when to their surprise, they were addressed in Yarrinaakoo [Yagalingu], the language spoken by the blacks on the Comet, and told in angry terms to be off, and not to come there. My men resented this treatment, but fearing my disapproval should they fire on them, as they wished to do; they came back and reported to me that these blacks were "coola." We now heard them shouting in all directions, very evidently collecting the others who were hunting. In the meanwhile, we had our dinner. Shortly after they had collected what they deemed sufficient for their purpose, and we heard one party coming up the river, and another answering their calls from over the ridge near our camp. It was now time for us to be doing, so I directed Mr Macalister, Mr Haughton, Jingle, Paddy, and Coreen Jemmy to take steady horses and face the river mob, whilst Jack and Rodney, and Jemmy Cargara stopped with me to protect the camp and meet the hill party. The mounted party met about thirty men, painted and loaded with arms, and they charged them at once. Now was shown the benefit of Terry's breech loaders, for such a continued steady fire was kept up by this small party that the enemy never was able to throw one of their formidable spears. Twelve men were killed, and few, if any, escaped unwounded. The hill mob probably got alarmed at the sound of the heavy firing and did not consider it convenient to come to the scratch. The gins and children had been left camped on the river, and as there was no water there our possession of the spring was no doubt the "casus belli". They might have shared it with us had they chosen to do so. This unavoidable skirmish ensured us a safe night; otherwise I think there would have been some casualty in my party before morning, as they can throw their spears 150 yards. I marked a tree on one side FW/30; and on the other, RSV/30 Oct/1861. Thunder at night and a few drops of rain.

Thursday, 31 October 1861. The question now was, what water were we on, and had we crossed the main range or not. The river below our camp turned a little S of W. I started at 7.45 and went eleven and a half miles W by compass, over very good downs, with a skirt of scrub on our right and the river trees visible a long way on our left. I now turned WSW by compass for the sake of getting water, and in five miles pulled up, not the Stawell, but a river coming from the NE. Jingle and Paddy, Coreen Jemmy and Rodney, went to look for water, and as Jemmy Cargara said the river he had seen was running WSW, I crossed it and went for 2 miles in that direction, but seeing no appearance of gum trees, I turned SSW for 1 mile, and still no signs of a river. I now turned SE, and in 2 and a half miles came to the river, as there were no signs of the tracks of my men I ran it up NNE, until I came to where Jingle had been digging for water. It was now 5 o'clock, and I saw that we must camp. The men soon came up, and we succeeded in watering 16 horses that night. To-day a great mishap has occurred, two boxes with my candles and a half piece of bacon having been lost. Thunder at night and a little rain.[283]

Friday, 1 November 1861. The horses that had water over night returned with many of the others, and had poached up the ground all about the two holes we had made. All hands set to work and soon had made two good waterholes, at which the horses have been enjoying themselves throughout the day. Mr Haughton, Paddy, and Jemmy Cargara collected all the horses. The grass is very good here, and as we have now abundance of water we spell here to-day; to-morrow we must make another try for the main range. Yesterday evening I hit the Stawell below the junction of this, which my men called the Weelgar River. The Stawell now runs SW and is evidently a large contributor to the Barkly. There must, I think, be water somewhere near this, for we saw three ducks pass in the night, and the cockatoos are so numerous. Coreen Jemmy made to-day two such very good shovels that I have determined on carrying them with me for the future. The bed of the Weelgar River I measured 111 yards from the foot of one bank to the other.

Saturday, 2 November 1861. The horses are not mustered until 9.30, and as it was threatening rain I determined to give the horses another

283 *Argus* 15 April 1862 p 2.

day on this good grass. A discovery very annoying to me was made this evening, for I counted the horses and one was missing. Cool night.

Sunday, 3 November 1861. At 6 pm thermometer 97°. Men all day looking for lost mare. Paddy and Jingle went back to 30 camp and fetched my lost candles. Spring found down the river, latitude 20° 16', not one-mile difference from my dead reckoning. Cool night.

Monday, 4 November 1861. Men all day in vain searching for tracks of lost mare; I am now satisfied she never came from Camp 30, if she ever reached that. Paddy and Coreen Jemmy saw large pools of permanent water in the Stawell.

Tuesday, 5 November 1861. Horses these last mornings have been much scattered, coming in small parties to the water, and there camping until evening. This morning, as I expected great delay. I started Mr Haughton, Paddy, Coreen Jemmy, and Rodney, with all the horses that were packed, at 9 am The remaining six, and Jingle's horse, detained the remainder of the party until 3.15 pm It was dusk when we reached a tributary of the Stawell, at the end of 18 miles NNW; Mr Haughton had not, however, stopped here, and as we could no more see the tracks, we searched for a spot to dig for water, as he had all the water bags with him. The place we tried gave every symptom, but nothing beyond mud. There was no help for it, so, having tied up the horses, we tried to sleep, having first each swallowed a tin of apple jelly, which was a great relief, for we had eaten nothing since 6 am; Jack stated he would, however, be dead before morning. At 10.30, after a short sleep. I lit a match, and to my great joy found there was water in our hole, sufficient to give each a half-pint. At one, after another snooze, I found we could dip the pint pot, and I woke Mr Macalister, Jack, Jingle, and Jemmy Cargara, when everyone drank as much as he required. The night was quite cold.

Wednesday, 6 November 1861. At 5.45 we had packed up and were off on the tracks again, and within eight miles WNW pulled up the camp. Mr Haughton had got water in another tributary by digging. Some blacks had been encountered near the camp, who had attacked Paddy and Rodney, who were looking for water; one was killed by a shot from Paddy. All hands had now to go to work to enlarge the water hole, as the horses could not get sufficient; this was done and a fence erected on both sides, to prevent the horses treading down the sand banks. Mr Haughton stopped the greater part of the day by the hole, only letting in two horses at a time, until everyone was amply satisfied. Thermometer 104° in the shade at 3 pm, but a cool breeze from SW. (Camp N° 32). Coreen Jemmy's shovels are a great comfort.

Thursday, 7 November 1861. Had great delay in collecting the horses; we managed, however, to go 11 miles NNW by compass, over a tableland of red sandstone, after having crossed some downs near Patience Creek. I observed that rain had fallen not long ago, and the grass was green; but it made me feel very grateful when I found a small creek with abundance of water, and fine feed for the horses. The creek I have called Grateful Creek; nevertheless, we were obliged to abandon a horse to-day. My black men found some long reaches of water higher up the creek, which will last two or three months, and the knocked-up horse was left within one mile of the creek. (Camp N° 33) Barometer 29.11.

Friday, 8 November 1861. A good start, and notwithstanding the great heat, we managed to do sixteen miles NNW and three W by N down a creek here; however, we have no water. At first, we tried to dig where we camped, but as the water came too slow, Mr Macalister, Jack, Jingle, and Rodney went with me half a mile further down, and round a spring, which they, by turns working two shovels, dug out, making a capital waterhole, which Jemmy Cargara and I in the meanwhile fenced in. We stopped till 8.30, watering the horses one by one, and then Mr Haughton with Paddy and Coreen Jemmy relieved us, and every horse was satisfied, and with abundance to return to during the night; luckily there was very good burnt grass here. (Camp N° 34) but I am too tired to mark it) Is not this a tributary of the Flinders? Ground very heavy all day. Aneroid 29.25.

Saturday, 9 November 1861. The horses were soon collected, and we started early; nevertheless, so great was the heat and so heavy the ground, that the horses were much distressed, and it was a great comfort to find some bulrushes, good springs of water, and grass, at the end of ten miles. Our course has been, on an average, 32° N of W and we had crossed over to a large creek still running WNW. This camp will be an important one to us on our return and will probably be the place where I shall stop to spell the horses, especially as this morning (Sunday); Coreen Jemmy has discovered a better spring and first-rate grass. (Camp 35)

Sunday, 10 November 1861. Great delay in collecting the horses, and we did not start until 10; the consequence was that the heat and heavy ground, the latter worse than ever, nearly brought us to a standstill with the horses. My course for the first six miles and a half was NW by compass. I then turned 32° N of W for four miles, when I pulled up a large river, with a fine pool of water six feet in depth. This must be the Flinders River. Of course, short as the day's stage was, we were obliged to camp. (N° 36)

Monday, 11 November 1861. We got an eight o'clock start and did our 12 miles down the river to another fine pool 14 feet deep, before the heat of the day. The ground is also harder. An anabranch turned me NW by compass, one mile and a half, then 10° N of W seven miles and a half, where we hit the river again one mile and a half WNW, and one mile and a half NW to Camp N° 37. One horse stopped about 1 mile above the camp. I intend leaving him and 7 more at the 40 Camp and push on with the remainder. If the ground opens, instead of being the brushy sandy country we have encountered hitherto in these waters, I intend taking advantage of the moonlight nights. There is no doubt now of this being the Flinders. Lost my opera glass out of the case to-day.

Tuesday, 12 November 1861. Many of the horses were astray this morning, but I started Mr Haughton with 28 packs at 8.30. It was near 1 before the others were found, in ones and twos; and two horses were completely knocked up searching for them. I waited until half past three, to get over the heat of the day, but the two knocked up horses I was obliged to leave with two more I had previously determined upon leaving here until my return. The ground was dreadfully heavy, and before we reached the camp, about 15 miles W by S from Camp No. 37, five more horses and two packs had to be left. We passed also a mare of Mr Haughton's party knocked up. We got to Camp 38 at 8.15. This day, I find from Mr Haughton's report, as well as my own experience, has knocked our horses out of time altogether, so I must spell here a couple of days, and then push on the best way we can. I fear much that the steamer will have left; however, I have enough to carry us home with care.

Wednesday, 13 November 1861. Spell, but sent back for the packs and missing horses. The thermometer at 109° at 5 pm in the shade. I repaired the case of the aneroid, which is as high as 29.51.

Thursday, 14 November 1861. Spell. Upon looking at the horses no one would suppose they were so completely done up, for none are in bad condition, but the dreadfully heavy ground, with the heat, brings them to a standstill at the end of eight miles. This is a melancholy good-for-nothing country. Aneroid 29.59. What does this mean, for the sky is very clear, and there is a cool breeze? The nights are still delightfully cool. Thermometer at 3 pm 103° in the shade. Aneroid fell again to 29.51. There are flocks of bronze-winged pigeons at this hole, and thus we have a supply of fresh meat, some being shot, others being knocked down by the men with sticks. They came at sundown every evening. Thermometer at sundown 91°. Friday morning at daybreak 61°.

Friday, 15 November 1861. Did not collect all the horses until near sundown, as I waited until they by twos and threes came to water, instead of knocking up more horses looking after them. We started at 5.30 and had a pleasant ride for seven miles; the first four over hard ground W by S 10° and the other three WNW; this brought me to a pool of water, and I camped, for although we have a splendid moon the bush is too thick to travel by night. All the horses appear to be recovered, but I left one at the last camp. Hot wind all night from the east, but towards morning it got quite cool.

Saturday, 16 November 1861. As we had hobbled nearly all the horses we got a 7.30 start; the first two miles I went W, then three miles W by N, when we pulled up the real river, the last two camps having been, as I suspected, on an ana-branch. The river turned us 32° N of W by compass, for two miles, when another mile WSW brought us to a pool, where it was deemed prudent to Camp, as the heavy ground was showing its damaging effects on the horses. This is very tantalising, but I must have patience. Aneroid 29.64; thermometer at 2 pm 105° in shade. Marked a tree on one side FW/40 and on the other RSV/16 Nov/1861. I hoped this tree would be on Gregory's track, where he crossed the Flinders, but in this I have been disappointed.

Sunday, 17 November 1861. To-day has been more encouraging, we got an 8 o'clock start, and went nine miles W by N by compass, over ground which was rapidly improving and getting more sound. I now turned W by S for two miles and was delighted to see some box trees. The ground now is quite hard along what I take to be an ana-branch; this turned us WNW for 1 mile, and then 6° S of W for 4 miles, when the watercourse was no longer visible; still keeping the same course for one mile, we crossed over to another branch. This is still too small for the main river, but my men are inclined to think it is so notwithstanding. If so, this is not the Flinders, but merely a tributary; it now turned WNW for 1½ miles, and then NNW for 1½ miles, which brought us to a small pool of temporary water, at which we camped. We had to change four of the riding horses, otherwise the horses have stood twenty-mile stage well; as we had a gentle breeze blowing from the gulf, the day was not unpleasantly hot. At this camp, marked FW/41 is a remarkable oval ring, planted all round with tall thin saplings, placed about a foot apart; none of my men understand the meaning of it. It is a great relief to feel that the machine is moving again.

Monday, 18 November 1861. Having started at 7.30, we managed to make twelve miles before the heat of the day, when we found a pool of water, and as Jingle could find none within two or three miles lower down, camped. The morning was made pleasant by the cool breeze from NW. The river to-day has averaged a course 48° W of N by compass; it has a better-defined channel, and we passed one lagoon only just dried up; after all it is a mere apology for a river. The ground still continues hard and is nearly all closed with spinifex; Jingle saw large plains when looking for water lower down; thermometer at 3 pm 104°; aneroid, 29.82. The pigeons, both at the last camp and at this, have been in large flocks; I was unwilling to expend powder, of which I have only three canisters left, but as I thought a change of diet beneficial, I allowed the men to shoot at this camp, and the result was we had twenty-seven pigeons.

Tuesday, 19 November 1861. Started at 6.45; at the end of 8 miles pulled up a good pool of water, at which the horses all drank; we passed another 2 miles further down, and probably another at the end of 14 miles, for we saw and heard many cockatoos in a bend on our right; 5 and a half miles further down we came to an excellent pool with fish in it, and with good burnt feed around it; horses looking quite fresh, for we did this distance before the heat of the day, and the breeze was cool from NW. Near this camp we found some gins; their men were hunting, so they said, and Jemmy Cargara could understand one of them pretty well; they had heard of no white men lower down; I thought they might have heard of the Queensland party; they told us one piece of good news, which was that henceforth there was plenty of water. Our course to-day has been by compass 30° N of W five miles, NW by N 3 miles, NW by W 5 miles. 20° N of W 1 mile, 5° N of W 2 miles, W 3 miles, and half a mile NW to Camp N° 43. The country to-day is much more open, but there were no plains; Jingle has had so much brush of late, that he is inclined to term open forest plains. Aneroid 29.83; thermometer at 3 pm, 103° in shade. The river is more respectable; it was joined by a creek from SE 4 miles below Camp 42.

Wednesday, 20 November 1861. Started at 7.15, and for the first 6 miles travelled 30° W and N by compass; then NNW for 2 miles, when we crossed the river, having to-day been on the right bank. It now for 1 mile kept the same course, NNW, and a plain extended along the south bank; but now it turned N by E for 3 miles, and then NNE for 1 mile, when we came to a deep permanent waterhole and five blacks with gins and children at it. A friendly intercourse was established, and I gave them some tomahawks. They were subsequently joined by ten or twelve more men. We camped here; the blacks on one side of the water, we on the other. As this NE turn of the river was perplexing, an endeavour was made to ascertain which way it now went. The blacks made us understand clearly enough that this river now ran NW by N by compass; we understood, but not so clearly, that it joined another running more to the westward. They told us to follow this water-course and we should at short intervals find plenty of holes like this one. Large plains lay to the NW and strange to say, they used for this the word "coonical," the same as Weerageree and Coreen Jemmy's language. They said we must avoid going to the west, as the country was no good, like what we had seen if we came down this river. They had heard of no white fellows being to the NW or WNW. I have all along stated to my party that what Mr Gregory called the eastern end of the Gilbert; I believed to be tributary of this river. I now suspect it is the real Flinders; and this I believe to be the tributary (rivers noureron). The country is now good, but a large proportion is subject to inundation. It is a great relief to be done with the heavy sandy country-with spinifex and brush of melaleuca, and other rubbish. Aneroid, 29.85; thermometer at 2.30, 108° in the shade. The NW breeze was cool this morning, but after twelve it now and then brought a hot blast from off the plains, which are visible from the back of this camp (N° 44).

Thursday Morning. The blacks appear to have acted upon the mutual confidence principle, for they slept as quietly at their camp all night as if they had not been under the muzzle of our guns. We, however, on our side, kept a strict watch all night. There was no probability of an attack, considering the brilliancy of the moonlight; and, moreover, ten times the number of blacks ought to have been defeated in an attempt on a camp so well situated as ours was, protected by overhanging trees, with an open slope to a plain at our back.

Thursday, 21 November 1861. Four of the horses, although not far from camp, were not found until 9.20; they were camping under a large tree. The day's work was in consequence spoiled. The first three and half miles I went the course directed by the blacks, NW by N, but as this brought me, after passing the flooded plains, to heavy sand, I turned N for 2 miles, then NNW 1 mile, when I had again to go N for 2 miles. The day was oppressively hot, so I now turned N by E for 1 mile, to a chain of good waterholes in the river, with good grass, and there camped. My men got a few fish here, about a pound weight each. Thermometer in shade 108° at 3 pm; aneroid 29.84.

Friday, 22 November 1861. To-day I followed the course of this river, merely cutting off the bends. Great doubts are entertained as to what river this is, for if it is the Flinders, I am 20 miles out of my longitude, and the way the blacks point, it ought to take me by my map to the camp of 11th of September of Gregory; but how this can be, is a puzzle considering the width of the inundation and the abundance of permanent water. How does this correspond with Gregory's dry irregular channels? Our course was by compass 5° W of N 2 miles, NW by N 2 miles, NNW 1 mile, NW 5 and a half miles. NW by N 1 and a half mile, NNW 3 miles, WNW 1 mile, and another mile NW by W brought us to camp at one of the finest sheets of water I have seen for many a day. Our latitude, both by observation and dead reckoning, is 18°18', and this corresponds with Gregory's 11th September camp, and so does my longitude.

Saturday, 23 November 1861. We went at first 3 miles NW, and then 1 mile 15° N of W brought us round the end of a magnificent reach of water. Here some blacks, alarmed at our approach, swam across the river to avoid us. It took us another mile W by N to get quite round the bend, and then it extended N one and a half miles, and N by W two and a half miles; here it ended, and we went WNW to some small pools to camp. In the afternoon, Jingle, Coreen Jemmy, and I rode out to reconnoitre. I saw the river was now going a little E of N and was again in long reaches. I struck out to the W, and came on some box flats, and on my return to camp passed a lagoon, which I had no doubt was that which Gregory passed on his way from 10th September camp to that of 11th September. My map is right after all, and this I suppose is the river marked on the maps as Bynoe - what the devil is Bynoe?

Sunday, 24 November 1861. I just went out 5 miles, a little to the N of W by N, and camped on the creek on which Gregory camped 10th September.

Monday, 25 November 1861. An eventful day, sixteen miles W by S 5° by compass, brought us to the Flinders River. We found it a beautiful large river, with high banks, and a delicious cool breeze blowing up it. We got a good many ducks, which were very acceptable, for our meat was finished yesterday. At this camp, lat. 18° 7', were found by Jingle the well-defined trail of either three or four camels and one horse. They had come down the Flinders. This evening we supposed Burke had gone down on Leichhardt's track, intending, probably, to follow Gregory's up the Gilbert. This night we had a tremendous thunderstorm - the first heavy rain we have had since starting from Bauhinia Downs (Mr Dutton's station).

Tuesday, 26 November 1861. I had to go up the river eight miles before I could get a crossing-place, and last night's rain had made the ground so heavy that the horses were much distressed. I therefore camped as soon as we had crossed. I here marked one tree FW/50 and another RSV/20 Nov/1861. This morning Jemmy Cargara, in collecting the horses, found Burke's trail returning across the plain, and going SSE. He has, therefore, I conclude, made back, after having seen the Gulf of Carpentaria, towards the south again. It is to be hoped Mr Howitt has pushed far enough to meet him with supplies. I hope to get rations from Captain Norman to enable me to run his trail now I have found it. I shall be dreadfully disappointed if the steamer has left, for I have barely enough to carry me back, and it would be madness to follow Burke south without an ample supply. Grateful Creek, and the three large creeks crossed upon leaving it, are evidently the heads of the Flinders, but the southerly trend which the main one took caused me to cross it. The tableland is therefore the dividing range. I suppose that Burke followed up the Barkly and the Stawell, and then cut across to the Flinders, not more than twenty or thirty miles to the west of my course.

Wednesday, 27 November 1861. We went 18 miles W by compass, crossing Gregory's 8th September creek in nine miles. We have had plains all day, but I can see low sandstone ranges not far on our left. At a black man's camp, from which he had just fled, we found two blank leaves out of a book. A mare got bogged last night, and she was so weak when we pulled her out this morning, that I was obliged to leave her. The ground is drying up fast indeed. I think but little rain fell at this creek; nevertheless, two horses had to be left betwixt the two creeks, knocked up. (N° 51) Night oppressive. Aneroid rose to 29.96 from 29.84.

Thursday, 28 November 1861. Started at 7.45, and steered W by N by compass. The first miles we passed over plains so full of holes as to be distressing to the horses, who were constantly stumbling. We now crossed a creek with deep holes, but now dry. Higher up where I saw many calares and a clump of trees, I think there is water. We now began to rise and crossed over a spur of red sandstone ranges. At the end of four miles we began to descend. Crossed two dry channels, then ridge of good downs, and at the end of fifteen miles from Camp 51 reached one head of Morning Inlet and camped on some lagoons. This is very good pastoral country, but I fear too hot for sheep. There is much thunder hanging about, and some storms appear to have again fallen on the Flinders, but none have reached us. A cool NNW breeze rendered the afternoon very pleasant, but the forenoon was very oppressive. The immense plains which stretch away to the N and NW, I suppose are the same mentioned by Captain Stokes (Camp N° 52) Sent a rocket up at night.

Friday, 29 November 1861. Heavy clouds, and the great rise in the barometer caused us at daylight to make all snug for a storm, but it passed over with a smart squall; there was, however, evidently rain not far from us. We now saddled up, and by eleven had reached the main head of Morning Inlet, on nine miles W by N by compass. After rising from the creek at No 52, we rode over red sandstone all day until we descended on to the box flats, within one mile of the main creek; the first part box trees, broad-leaved and good grass; and the latter portion melaleuca, nearly no grass, and with innumerable cones, some six feet high, made by the ants. On the banks of Morning Inlet was again, where the sandstone abutted on the creek, the hateful spinifex grass. The plains are visible north of our Camp N° 53. Cool breeze from NW. Night very oppressive and sultry. Mosquitoes triumphant. Thermometer 86° at sundown.

Saturday, 30 November 1861. I started Mr Macalister with all the horses which were ready, at 7.45. I was delayed until 9, waiting for two missing ones, which were, after all, within gunshot of the camp. A thunderstorm threatened as I was saddling the last two, and a few drops of rain fell. The day has been delightful with a cool breeze from NW. I crossed three creeks, or branches of a creek, within three miles W by N of the camp. We now cleared the sandstone and rode across a fine plain for three miles more. We crossed a small creek in the centre of the plain, and on the west side found a large creek, with two anabranches and a fine lagoon. Is this the creek of Gregory's camp of the 5th of September, or is it the first one? In one of his maps there is a second creek, which would correspond with the latter. We now crossed a sandstone ridge, with good grass and box trees, and reached a plain in three and a half miles. Six and a half miles more over downs and stony plains, of an excellent description for pasture purposes, brought me to a hole in a good downs creek. I was very glad to water the horses. Another mile brought me to where Mr Macalister had judiciously decided on camping, as he had come W by N 17 miles, quite enough for our horses. This creek is evidently flowing into the Leichhardt, which cannot he much more than two miles a-head of us; indeed, I think I can see the trees of it. We are now fast approaching the climax, and the anxiety of my party is intense lest the Victoria should have left. Is it not strange we see no traces of the Queensland party? I have sent up rockets the last two nights, in hopes of attracting their attention. To-night a rocket might be seen from the Albert which at one place is only 26 miles from here, and that is probably as far as the boat would come up. The camp of Gregory is 31 miles.

Sunday, 1 December 1861. To-day has been an annoying day. I first went W by N to some sandstone cliffs, descended from them WSW. to a saltwater creek, which we had to run up ESE for nearly 4 miles, and the last corner took us east to complete the 4 miles, so that we have come back parallel to our course. We now found some small holes of fresh water; having crossed this, we went W by N and WNW, when we at last got to the Leichhardt River--the water as salt as brine. We ran it up SSE by compass for 8 miles, passed by a black fishing at what looked like a ford, just above the junction with a creek, which I take to be that of Gregory's camp, 3rd September. The black never saw us. There was now a good crossing place, but as Jingle signalized there was fresh water in a creek at the back of a plain close at hand, I went to it and camped. My men shot two ducks in the river, and a couple of blacks were watching them a little lower down the river. After dinner, or a make-shift for one, my men went over towards the river in hopes of getting some ducks; but as they were crossing the plain they saw two mobs of blacks approaching. As their appearance looked hostile, they returned to camp. Presently it was reported that they were stretching out in a half moon, in three parties. This move, which my men term "stock-yarding," is peculiar to blacks throwing spears with a woomera, the object being to concentrate a shower of spears. It was one long familiar to me, and I charged their left wing. The result was that the circular line doubled up, the blacks turned and fled. Their right wing, which was the strongest, got over the river and were off; but the centre and left wing suffered a heavy loss.

Monday, 2 December 1861. Rodney found in a black's camp a sailor's jumper and an empty cognac bottle. The men (black) have all gone to the river to shoot ducks, for I cannot cross over until low water, which will be about 2 pm After crossing I made for Gregory's Creek, of 3rd September, and there camped, reaching it in four hours.

Tuesday, 3 December 1861. Went WNW twenty-two miles to the Albert River; found plenty of grass and the water fresh, but with a suspicion of salt; more decided when the tide rose. We had crossed an alternate succession of plains and flooded box-flats with small watercourses. This morning was very sultry but the last eight miles was pleasant, a thunder-storm having crossed a little to the north and cooled the air. I left six horses here to spell. We had some trouble in finding a suitable place to water the horses and that which we did find was by no means good. One horse got bogged and would make no effort to relieve himself. We had to pull him out by main strength; marked a tree FW/57. Gun heard down the river at 8 pm.

Wednesday 4 December 1861. Some trees marked Victoria and VQNE were seen this morning. I directed Mr Macalister to proceed higher up and pick a camp with a good watering place; Jingle and I proceeded down the river to reconnoitre; five miles below our camp I found a tree marked with a chisel Victoria/Dep/8 miles. Four miles lower down I saw some trees outside of a saltwater inlet, one marked V and the others merely common marked trees; about four miles further I saw a smoke but failed in reaching it on account of the tide waters. I went round them and upon higher ground found some pools of fresh water; about four miles further I reached a saltwater inlet and here I saw some blacks. We now moved towards the camp but had not got more than two miles when we found the blacks were cutting us off from the river; unluckily Jingle's horse gave in and we were in a dangerous predicament, the more so as Jingle now told me he had only two cartridges. I thought we were lost; but we managed to reach a belt of timber and there, Jingle abandoned his horse and proceeded on foot at a great rate for two hours; I had to put my horse to a canter every now and then to pull him up; got up a tree and could see no more signs of our enemy whom I had last seen giving chase across the plains. We had been thrown out of our course a great deal and I relieved Jingle every now and then by walking and letting him ride my horse and the noble animal although evidently distressed brought us about 8.30 to the river or rather creek, for river it was no more. I saw now we must be above our camp and had come seventeen or eighteen miles since we saw the blacks trying to cut us off. We were now however safe for the creek was as good to us as a rifle pit and my revolver would have disposed of some besides out two guns. I turned my faithful horse out and we descended into the bed of the creek which was dry and followed it down climbing and tumbling over numerous fallen trees until we reached a pool of water. Here, having refreshed ourselves we lay down and were soon fast asleep; but the cold night awoke us frequently; we were both completely knocked up but I was very grateful for our providential escape.

Thursday, 5 December 1861. Mr Macalister had found Gregory's marked tree, and also a bottle underground, near a tree, marked by Captain Norman, with directions to dig. The bottle contained a note, stating the Depot of the *Victoria* was about 12 miles lower down on the left bank. We now having saddled up went up the creek until we could cross it, just above where I had slept last night. We then went NW by W to Beame's Brook. Some delay took place, owing to the creek being boggy, and I was glad to camp as soon as we had crossed, for I was unwell from yesterday's anxiety and fatigue; and as Captain Norman's note is dated 29th November, there is now good hope of our meeting to-morrow.

Friday, 6 December 1861. Proceeded ENE, about sixteen miles but had to camp, in order to make all safe for a storm. Night dismal, but the sound of a cannon within 2 or 3 miles was a comfort, and produced loud cheers.

Saturday, 7 December 1861. In 2 miles, through a pelting hurricane of rain, reached the Depot, and I had the pleasure of shaking hands with Captain Norman. (sgn) Frederick Walker, Leader of the Expedition.

I hereby certify that I have been in the constant habit of reading the above journal; that it was frequently referred to me, in order that I might supply any omissions; and that it is correct in every respect. Daniel Macalister, Second in Command.

ROCKHAMPTON PARTY FREDERICK WALKER, LEADER, CORRESPONDENCE

Frederick Walker to Com. Norman, 10 December 1861

In handing over to you a copy of my journal, and a tracing of my map, I have deemed it advisable to supply you with a few notes relative to what had been my original plan and the course I wish now to follow out, with your approbation.

In the first place, if Mr Burke had attempted to make east, the more west my party went the greater was the probability of my crossing his tracks. From my journal and map, you will perceive that I went as much west as was consistent with the safety of my party, and as soon as I became aware of the system of the Barkly River watershed, I went a whole degree more west than I had intended when I wrote to Captain Mayne; and also to you, in a letter left by me with our mutual friend Captain Hunter, of Rockhampton, but which you, of course, did not receive.

In my journal, I at once came to the conclusion that Eyre's Creek is a tributary of my Barkly River, and that Burke consequently would hit that fine river, and probably run it and its great feeder, the Stawell, until he got to a latitude which would enable him, with some prospect of success, to hit a watershed flowing into the Gulf of Carpentaria, which probably would be that of the Flinders.

That he did so there is now little doubt, as I found his well-defined trail running down the Flinders; and at present my belief is that he has returned up that river, but of his certain course I shall inform you when I meet your boats on that river, according to the arrangement I made in our consultation.

It was a matter of great satisfaction to me that I found that, without any hesitation, you cordially approved of my proposal to follow out these tracks wherever they may go; and the zeal which my aboriginal comrades evinced when they assured you, in my presence, that they would not abandon these tracks, was as gratifying to me as it was to you.

There are some arrangements necessary to make relative to this expedition, but I propose making that the subject of a separate letter.

Frederick Walker to Com. Norman, 10 December 1861

I do myself the honour to state that the report of your surgeon, Dr Patterson, has confirmed my fears that my storekeeper, John Horsfeldt, has a fistula, which would render him incapable of assisting me in future.

I therefore shall have to avail myself of your offer to convey him to Rockhampton and have to request you will give him a certificate that he had satisfactorily fulfilled his agreement, which commenced on the 15th August, and for which he was, by the authority of Captain Mayne, to be remunerated at the rate of three pounds (£3) a week.

Captain Hunter, of Rockhampton, holds an authority signed by Horsfeldt, and witnessed by Mr Dutton, to receive all pay due to him, and through that gentleman it will be therefore advisable that Horsfeldt be settled with.

P.S. As I shall be one man short, it may perhaps be convenient for you to supply me with a man, in Horsfeldt's room; but, at the same time, I would draw your attention to the fact that, unless such a man was prepared to carry out my wishes without demur or grumbling, my party would be better without him.

Frederick Walker to Com. Norman, 10 December 1861

I explained to you that out of the pay, at the rate of £1 per week, to my aboriginal explorers engaged by me for the Government of Victoria, I have since had to provide the means of supporting their families during their absence, and of paying one of their comrades who remains at Bauhinia Downs to look after and protect their families. The consequence is that these men, who have so faithfully served the Government of Victoria in this matter of the Expedition for the relief of Mr Burke, had, upon reaching your depot on the Albert River, but a few shillings over £2 each due to them.

I therefore have considered it but just to guarantee them 10s. per week additional, commencing from the 15th of this month; and have to request you will authorise Captain Hunter, of Rockhampton (who holds an authority to act as agent for these men), to continue to supply their families with rations according to the rate of which he has a memorandum, until at least my return to Rockhampton, or his receipt of a letter of advice from me. In the meanwhile, you will understand that the families are already supplied in full for six months from the 1st of September last.

I have also guaranteed to these men that the Government of Victoria would, upon their arrival in Melbourne, either provide them with a passage to Rockhampton, or give their families the means of re-joining them in Victoria. As a matter of course, until you have submitted this guarantee of mine for the consideration of His Excellency the Governor of Victoria, you cannot give me any positive assurance that his Government will relieve me of it, but, should it meet with disapproval, you will be so kind as to request that any remuneration which might be intended to be made for my own services should be appropriated to carry out my guarantee, as my men have, for so many years, considered my promise as sacred. P.S. It is necessary that you should bear in mind that these men would not have come on the expedition at all, if I had not, in the presence of Mr Jardine, police magistrate of Rockhampton, engaged them as servants of Her Majesty's Government for the colony of Victoria. This was comprehended by them, whereas the Royal Society was to them an enigma.

Com. Norman to F. Walker, 11 December 1861

I do myself the honour to acknowledge the receipt of your letter of the 10th instant, also copy of journal and tracing of route from Rockhampton to the Albert River, and to state that I consider you have taken the likeliest route to fall in with the tracks of the missing explorers, which you at last discovered on the Flinders River, and were unable to follow up until a supply of provisions was obtained from me at the depot on the Albert River.

I much regret to find by your journal that, in defence of your party, you were compelled to fire upon and kill a number of hostile natives in several instances, but the well-known feeling of humanity which you have for so many years exhibited towards the natives, assures me that no alternative was left you to protect the lives of your party when they were surrounding you in such numbers.

Coinciding as we do in our opinions as to your future movements, it is my direction that you proceed to the Flinders River so soon as possible, find Mr Burke's camp and any documents he may have left there; I will join you by boat to receive them for the Government and Royal Society of Victoria, and you will then, in all probability, be the better prepared for following up the tracks to wherever they may lead to. It will be as gratifying to the Government and Royal Society as it was to me to hear it from your officers and comrades their determination of following up, under your command, the tracks they had found to wherever they might lead them, and that no exertions on their part would be spared to assist you in finding the missing party.

Be so good as to inform your officers, comrades, and natives I shall not fail to represent their conduct to the Governor and Government of Victoria.

Frederick Walker to Com. Norman, 12 December 1861

With reference to the letter of instructions which I have received from you, I do myself the honour to state, that it will be necessary that the attention of the Government and of the Royal Society of Victoria should be drawn to one matter which has formed a serious point in our consultations.

As it is nearly certain that Mr Burke followed down the Eyre's Creek of Sturt to the Barkly River, it is probable that he will

> return by the same route. It is probable that as Mr Howitt would be in these latitudes about September and October, he would have the short rainy season in his favour, and may have reached the Barkly River, and supplied Mr Burke with provisions. Now, if I follow out Mr Burke's return tracks I shall just reach that part of the Barkly where those tracks leave it to go south, at a season in which my long experience would make me expect a drought in that latitude. If so, I may find that I cannot pursue the tracks further without endangering the lives of my party and, at the same time, if Mr Burke had got this far on his homeward route, I shall be pretty easy as to his safety, as he would be able to reach Cooper's Creek with his camels. Therefore, if after having from a temporary stockade tried, by means of my water-bags, if I had a chance of water in Eyre's Creek, and finding my route barred for want of water, I should make round by the Carragaree of the natives, and this large sheet of water I have no doubt has a communication with Stuart's great lake, thus giving me a safe retreat into Adelaide. You will observe that I place great confidence in the statement of the friendly Aborigines on the Barkly River; but that I am justified in doing, for my journal shows how minutely correct was their information whenever I had the means of verifying it.[284]

Sunday, 8 December 1861 [Albert River Depot]. The night after my arrival, it was blowing very hard from NE, and a great quantity of rain fell.

Monday, 9 December 1861. The wind abated the next day, and the rain cleared off through the day. I now accompanied Captain Norman in his boat to the *Victoria*, and that vessel upon our arrival moved over to the anchorage at Sweer's Island. Here, as it was smooth water, I was enabled to make a tracing of my map, which Captain Norman takes charge of, together with my journal, which he had copied by his clerk, and both will be given to the Royal Society of Victoria. Having completed all the

---

284 *Argus* 16 April 1862 p 7.

supplies that Captain Norman could muster, in order to fit me out for my search for the traces of Burke, we returned to the depot.

On Monday, 16 December, we crossed over the horses to the right bank of the river, having had the assistance of two of Captain Norman's boats. Several of his men now worked at making me some new saddle bags, my former ones being most of them useless.

On Wednesday, the 18th, Mr Houghton, with three men, succeeded in getting the horse abandoned by Jingle on the 4th, but the saddle they could not find. I marked one tree FW/60 and on another limb RSV/7 Dec/1861.

On the 20th, everything being packed, the saddles, rations, tents, and all were moved to the other side of the river, and the tents being pitched, my party all camped there the night.

As Jack Horsfeldt has been compelled to return to Rockhampton by the *Victoria*, on the report from Dr Campbell that he was quite unfit for a land expedition. I was much pleased when Captain Norman obtained for me the services of Mr Moore in his stead. Mr Moore's duties especially are to have the sole charge of all the stores. On this subject, I may as well mention that Captain Norman was much pleased to find that my experience corroborated the opinion he had given Mr Landsborough upon the necessity of a land party having one person answerable for the stores. It is impossible to avoid waste where every person is at liberty to help himself.

As we left the Albert River the next day, I may now mention how gratified my men were, especially the natives, at his approbation of their good conduct, and the zeal they expressed in their determination to follow Burke's tracks; and too much cannot be said by me to express my thanks for the kindness shown me by Captain Norman, and of his endeavours to fit me out as completely as possible. I now start with 130 days' rations of flour, tea, and sugar, and 50 lbs. rice, 50 lbs. peas, to assist. Unfortunately, we have but 30 days' meat. This would be of little consequence, as we have lots of powder and shot, but, unluckily, very few caps for the fowling-pieces, I trust, however, that when I meet Captain Norman upon the Flinders, he will be able to supply this awkward deficiency. It has been a source of great satisfaction to me that Captain Norman has coincided in opinion with me as to my future movements.

I was also glad to find that, from his observations of the soundings in the gulf, he had come to the same conclusion as I had from what I obtained on land. Mr Gregory says that the plains which he makes to stretch across the whole width of the bottom of the gulf were formed by the retiring of the sea. Now, in the first place, the sandstone ridges which Mr Gregory crossed continue much further to the north, making the division of the different watersheds. These ridges in many places are very fine downs, and on the Flinders, there are traces of basalt and trap. The country, therefore, is a succession of plains, hills, and downs; and as Captain Stokes places on his chart three hummocks on the very verge of the water of the Gulf of Carpentaria, I have no doubt these are the terminations of three of the low ranges crossed by me. The plains are formed by the crumbling down of these ranges, and this process is still going on. The land is gaining on the sea, not the sea retiring from it; and this, as I have stated above, was the opinion already arrived at by Captain Norman.

I have been led in my journal to fall into an error, through Mr Gregory having called the running rivulet of the Albert 'Beame's Brook.' Mr Woods, first lieutenant of the *Victoria*, showed me, by Leichhardt's map, that 'Beame's Brook' was not anywhere near it.

The Plains of Promise, as marked by Mr Gregory on his map, I found to be a succession of small plains, intersected by flooded box; and Captain Norman showed me Captain Stoke's map and his track up the salt-water inlet, where he went on foot over the very ground crossed both by me and Mr Gregory. He there places no Plains of Promise but does mention the flooded box. The Plains of Promise were not seen by Mr Gregory at all, for he crossed to the north of them.

****

Started on the 21st December 1861. Captain Norman came over the river to take leave of us. First went 1-mile SE to get off the bend, but a salt water creek made me turn E by S ½ a mile. I now recognised the ground Jingle and I had been over on the 4th December. Now turned south-½-west for 5 miles to clear the salt water arm. Crossed a salt water creek which I mistook for the arm and in 1½ miles SE by E went to camp near a pool of water on some high land. The reason why I camped so early was that I was doubtful whether I had crossed the salt water arm or not. Mosquitoes terrible.

Sunday, 22 December 1861. Jemmy Cargara having seen the arm this morning when collecting the horses. I started SW by S and at the end of 2 miles over fine plains crossed the salt water arm. I now turned ESE as I wished by hitting the Leichhardt lower down to ascertain whether it was not the river Captain Norman had come up in his boat, supposing it to be a branch of the Albert and the same as Landsborough's Creek, a salt water arm issuing from that river. In 2 miles over high plains, crossed one creek, another 2 miles was flooded box and another mile brought us to a salt water creek which I could not cross, but which I think from the high banks must be flowing into the Leichhardt. By turning S by W for ½ mile we cleared the salt water and crossing the creek went ESE 3 miles to another creek which at first, I thought was our creek of December 2nd. Ran this creek up S by E for 4 miles and then crossed it on our old tracks. In 4 miles, we pulled up the 2nd December creek, but Coreen Jemmy who was leading, would persist in going E instead of E by S and this brought us nearly 2 miles below our old camp. Mosquitoes very troublesome.

Monday, 23 December 1861. Men looking for horses all day. Found five out of the six, but the black horse could not be seen. The two saddles left at the camp were recovered all right. The blacks had walked round and round the tree upon which they were left but had not molested them probably taking them for some infernal machine.

Tuesday, 24 December 1861. Again, in vain searching for black horse.

Wednesday, 25 December 1861. Went 30° north of east to Leichhardt. Crossed it in three miles, the ford seen by Jingle and Coreen Jemmy yesterday was a little too deep. However, all was got over without accident. We now went east by south in order to clear the head of the salt water inlet, but a sharp thunderstorm compelled us to camp in about 2½ miles. I had delayed already so much looking for the black horse that I would not stop to look for that which was left near here.

Thursday, 26 December 1861. Went on a course parallel to our former one. Crossed one branch of salt water inlet, of course here fresh and ran up the other mistaking it for the creek we had camped on the night of 30th November for they are so exactly similar. We now crossed over the downs and sandstone ridges and descended to camp in the most westerly of the branches of the creek stated on 30th November to run in three channels. The country here is very good downs, the hills mostly ironstone, lightly timbered on summit. Some of the stones appeared like pure iron. The horses by going at night to the top of one of the high ridges got at last, a night pretty clear of mosquitoes. As for us an atmosphere of smoke is our only chance.

Friday, 27 December 1861. Still parallel to our old course. We went and camped at the creek two miles to the west of what I previously called the second branch of Morning Inlet. A fine permanent lagoon and many ducks was too tempting to pass. The reason I called this the second branch of Morning Inlet is that Mr Gregory supposed the two to join, but this I now doubt, for I observe that all these creeks have a tendency to keep an independent course, or as Jingle says, to go 'myself, myself,' and moreover I believe that the high sandstone ridge dividing these two has its terminus in one of the hummocks laid down by Stokes on the verge of the Gulf.

Saturday, 28 December 1861. Still same parallel course. Crossed the creek of Camp 53 about ½ mile above that Camp. An annoying occurrence now destroyed our day's work, for after having passed through the sandstone and melaleuca ground and come out on the first plain, Jingle who was leading the pack horses, instead of following my tracks unaccountably struck considerably to the south of east. I waited under a tree for half an hour and then thinking they might have passed me I went on to the first creek flowing into that of Camp 52, no great distance on our left, thinking they must have struck for it, but on consideration determined to follow my own tracks back. On the top of the ridge I set fire to the grass as a signal well known to my men. When I got back half way across the plain, I met Jemmy Cargara looking for my tracks and soon after saw Jingle. Having now after some delay found the main party, we went to camp at the creek where I had waited so long.

Sunday, 29 December 1861. By leaving our Camp of Number 52 to our left, I had an opportunity of seeing how much the Downs extended in the direction I was now on. They are very fine and I observed some acacias. Captain Stokes says he saw some on the Albert. I had no doubt been too anxious to look after them but at all events I told Captain Norman I had none. On all these waters, there is an abundance of small sized trees with small leaves out of which a milky fluid exudes when the wood is cut, which if not "gutta percha" is uncommonly like it. After having crossed over the high sandstone ridge, we descended on to a plain and I now turned more to the north to a clump of trees under which my horse had rested until the party came up on our outward route. Five miles across the plain on our old course brought us to the Camp of number 51, at which we had lost three saddles, one of which having tumbled off its branch had been torn to pieces by native dogs. In crossing this last plain may be seen to the north the hills rising again, although in the intervening space they have crumbled away, leaving merely the plain.

Monday, 30 December 1861. Started Coreen Jemmy, Patrick and Jemmy Cargara to look for the two horses left behind betwixt this and the Flinders. The main part of packs proceeded with me accompanied by Mr Macalister and Mr Moore. Mr Houghton, Rodney and Jingle had to stop behind on account of four horses not having been found. Upon approaching the Flinders, I observed Mr Houghton's party to our left and both parties reached the river at the same time. In the afternoon, the other three came in with one of the horses but could see nothing of the tracks of the other since the rain. They had seen large mobs of blacks who had chased them. They could not get off to get a drink at the creek, so close were they pushed. Knowing how reluctant I was that unnecessary slaughter of these people should take place, they had refrained from firing although the blacks all had their spears. Had they liked they might with their Terry's rifles and fresh horses have played with the enemy on these large plains. It shows that a small party runs considerable risk as the blacks here, however civil they may be to a strong one, would destroy a small party had they a chance. That chance is at night or in wet weather when the horses on this heavy ground are rendered useless. Here at our old Camp [Camp 50 on the Flinders?] we had again the cool breeze which generally blows up the Flinders and as we were on high ground we were comparatively free from mosquitoes. I cannot conceive how Mr Gregory could come to the conclusion that a river like the Flinders with a bed 100 yards in width and with flood marks 80 feet above the present level when the river is upwards of 300 yards wide, could flow only 100 or at the utmost 150 miles. Double that distance is the real course of that river. Why I followed its dry irregular channels upwards of 150 miles from the rise where I first struck it, on the river which I have now called the Norman after Captain Norman, it must have come some 60 or 70 miles more. Moreover, there is a contradiction in Mr Gregory's statements, for in another place he correctly judges that the Flinders and Leichhardt come from the ranges either south east or south west. Now how they could do that in 150 miles is a mystery. I say correctly as regards the Flinders, as I am by no means satisfied that the Leichhardt takes its rise south west. South east I know it does not. Its course is from south-southeast and it must take a peculiar turn if its sources are to the southwest. The tableland which is the continuation of the great Cordillera south of the Gulf of Carpentaria is, I believe, 1,600 feet high where I crossed it and my belief is that further to the west it rises to a much greater height and that there the Leichhardt takes its rise. The slope on the south side has in many places basalt rocks and the downs are formed of decomposed basalt. There is therefore every possibility that these basalt rocks in some places still exist at a great height. The great desert of the interior has been a great bugbear. If the discoveries made by Burke are preserved, it will be reduced to a small extent and my Barkly River I believe to flow through good country, at least on its north bank. Mr Gregory is quite correct in his observations about the small slip of available country in the Gulf of Carpentaria. I told Captain Norman that I did not think it was more than 45 miles in depth and that only on the Flinders and Leichhardt Rivers. As regards the latter I may be wrong as I only go from surmise, but on the Flinders, I have seen with my glass the red sandstone spinifex country approaching the river to the south of the 50 tree. I regret I do not know something of geology, for it is evident that the soil forming the plains and downs is not sandstone, but some other stone which lay on the red sandstone and has crumbled away. Were it more black I would say basalt but it is a light brown, sometimes grey.

Tuesday, 31 December 1861. Coreen Jemmy, Paddy, Jemmy Cargara and I proceeded down the river. When we came to where [blank] had seen the camel tracks going SSE. We searched about for some time before it was evident Burke's party had camped thereabouts [C118?] but we could see no sign of a camp. About seven miles further we came to where the sandstone range [Reaphook Range], here about 300 feet high, abuts on the river. So far, the tracks of Burke's outward route were plainly visible, but beyond that range no further tracks were visible. We went and camped at a lagoon about 21 miles from our Camp number 50. A mob of blacks were discovered to be camped on the river just below us but just before sundown the disagreeable news was announced to me that another party were watching us from the creek we had lately crossed. With my glass, I observed several up the trees; there was probably another party on the river abreast of us, but them we could not see.

Marginal note: 'What we took for the river abreast of us turned out to be a branch of fresh water. Tracks of many blacks were found there by Rodney and Jingle. It will be remembered that no rain fell here on 1st January.

Our position was critical and I caused four horses to be caught and we rode at the creek mob which broke up and fled across the plains. It was necessary they should know our strength and I allowed two long shots to be fired, both of which took effect. As my object was attained, I stopped further firing and we got back to camp at dusk. As I supposed I was about seven miles from the spot where I had agreed to meet Captain Norman I sent up a rocket at 8pm.

Wednesday, 1 January 1862. A very dark cloud extended nearly over the sky this morning and I feared we could not move. However, it went off more north of us and we proceeded on down the river passing by a bend of the river on the opposite bank of which were the blacks. We called to them, but could get no answer comprehensible, but when we pointed down the river they did so too. The river, whose general course has been N by E now tended more to the E and at the end of 6 miles from our camp an old black called out to us. Paddy went to meet him but could make nothing out of his signs. In another mile leaving the bank of what I then thought was the river to my left, we came upon a fresh water creek. The thunder cloud had burst here and the ground was very boggy, the water running strong off the plains into the creek. We had to go two miles SSE before we could cross it and now, in attempting to make NW again we had awful work, the ground being all under water and we having to cross what were now large running creeks. At the end of 4 miles, which took two hours to travel, we stopped to rest the horses for a couple of hours under another sandstone ridge. When we went on we found the sandstone more boggy than the plains and we had to lead our horses to the edge of a salt water inlet, now however fresh, where the sand gave the horses' good footing. Our old black was here again, two or three gins, some children and a cripple who had lost the use of his legs and travelled on his hands and feet. They took to the water, being afraid of the horses. We now ran up on good hard sandstone and from the summit saw the salt water inlet, with numerous branches running under the foot of the range and the river a great way from us to the west. I now was very ill and vomiting, so I determined to return. At the end of 4 miles wading we reached a dry ridge upon the top of which we camped. The mosquitoes were intolerable at night and the poor horses kept under the smoke which we kept up all night.

Thursday, 2 January 1862. Started at 6 and after passing over the ground deluged yesterday we got on very well. We saw a small party of blacks on one plain, but did not stop to have a parley, which after all was not comprehensible. Passed by the lagoon and the range. This range is another instance of what I have mentioned, the plain which divided the watershed of the Norman from that of the Flinders without any perceptible elevation, here rises to the height of 300 feet and forms a deep, sharp point round which the river runs. When we got to the place where the camel tracks were first seen, Jemmy Cargara tried to run the course further SSE. He overtook me before I reached the camp and told me he had to give it up as one camel was going to the right, another to the left, and no distinct track was made. This was alarming, for it was at once surmised that there was no one with the camels, moreover, the horse track was not seen. Mr Macalister had according to my instructions removed the camp to the east bank, but I regretted to hear, that although the tracks had been seen, the mare we had left had not been found.

Friday, 3 January 1862. Moved the whole party 13 miles down the river. Jingle found a camp fire of Burke's, but no marked trees. In the evening Jingle and Coreen Jemmy set out to examine tracks. They returned and reported that the camels had gone right into the point at the range down to the water's edge and they thought had crossed over. This is very perplexing. The camels had, I saw, frequently turned up large clods of mud.

Saturday, 4 January 1862. I started Mr Houghton, Coreen Jemmy, Jingle and Rodney first thing with instructions to search for Captain Norman's marked tree inside of the salt water inlet. With the remainder of the party I moved down to what on the first tour I had taken for the river but now turned out to be a magnificent reach of fresh water, 100 yards if not more wide, and two miles in length. At the north end I camped, according to the preconcerted arrangement, and I saw that Mr Houghton's tracks had passed this way. Shortly after camping, I saw them riding over the plains betwixt us and the river and they soon came into camp. Mr Houghton reported that there were no signs of Captain Norman. He had seen the tracks of a horse!!

Marginal note: Jemmy Cargara and I today saw under the range the tracks of three camels, but no horse, going ESE, but each at a short distance from the other.

Sunday, 5 January 1862. By observation last night, taking the moon from Aldebaran and Capella, we are in lat. 17°48' [C119 was at 17°53'] and the place I had appointed to meet Captain Norman is 17°47'. Mr Macalister, Mr Moore, Paddy and Jemmy Cargara today made another attempt over the sandstone range from which I turned back on the 1st, but the salt water arms were so intricate that it was impossible to approach the river.

Monday, 6 January 1862. Today Coreen Jemmy is looking for the horses; found again the track of the horse and with it the tracks of four men on foot, two of whom only had boots. As these tracks were close to our camp, we all went to examine them and nothing was now more evident than that Burke had unaccountably abandoned the camels and the party was making its way on foot. At first the tracks were going NW, for what reason I cannot make out, but the salt water arm having pulled them up, they turned E by N, their proper course if they wished to hit the Gilbert. Jingle and Jemmy followed the tracks on foot to where they saw the horse had bogged in a creek and they had been compelled to drag him out. Mr Macalister and Rodney went with us to the river and on the bank, I marked a tree visible right down the reach.

FW/6 Jan/1862/DIG/N 6ft. Here I buried a bottle with all the information I could remember and took the precaution of making a small fire over the hole to obliterate all signs of digging. I stated that on Thursday, I must cut and run on Burke's tracks.

Tuesday, 7 January 1862. Mr Macalister, Paddy, Coreen Jemmy and Jingle taking a day's ration with them, started to track Burke definitively for at least 10 miles. Rodney today looking for horses saw some blacks cross the river. He made them understand we were tracking four men and one horse and that the men wore hats like him. They immediately pointed E by S then W by SE.

Wednesday, 8 January 1862. This evening Mr Macalister and his party returned. They had tracked the party on foot on a most circuitous route. The men (natives) frequently having to turn down the grass to find the tracks. At last the trail turned up the river again, went into one point and out of it again and into another where was found a tree marked: B/ CXIX and another: SEE/14.

Here they had evidently returned to the camels, the tracks and dung of which were all around. It is now supposed two of the party had remained in camp and that the naked footsteps were blacks following them. Moreover, Mr Macalister's party had further out seen the tracks of large numbers of blacks, following their trail. They tried digging 14 feet from the tree south east by east, but the ground had evidently never been opened and would require a pickaxe to make much way into it.

Thursday, 9 January 1862. Whilst the men were packing, Jemmy Cargara and I proceeded to the river as low down as the salt water creeks would allow and there I marked a tree: DIG/6ft E and buried another bottle with the latest information also desired whoever found it to get the other bottle in the bend above. Having returned to camp and all being ready, the whole party moved up the river to within ¾ of a mile of Burke's tree. I examined it the same evening and tried digging at 14 inches and 14 yards, but with no success.

Friday, 10 January 1862. Patrick, Rodney and Jemmy Cargara went with me in a direction SE by E, diverging at various points to our left in hopes of meeting with Burke's track. We crossed over the range and went about 12 miles but we travelled 17. Having seen no signs of a track we returned on the upper side of the mountain and arrived after dusk at the camp. We saw the tracks of a large number of blacks quite fresh and on our return fell in with a boy of about fourteen years of age. He was awfully frightened and of course nothing could be got out of him. I have never seen a country so thickly populated with blacks.

Saturday, 11 January 1862. Mr Moore and party went out today to see what they could do, but although as usual the tracks of camels feeding could be seen, no track out of this could be seen. They, according to instructions, crossed the river on their return but no camels had been over. The river could not have been fordable when Burke was here for he had fresh water from the river at his camp and he had to head two fresh water creeks. Mr Houghton and Coreen Jemmy went down to my marked tree but no one had been there.

Sunday, 12 January 1862. Mr Macalister and one party went ESE to examine some tracks seen there, but beyond a short distance none could be seen. I went with another to examine the tracks seen by Jemmy Cargara and I under the range on the 4th. These, we found, were Burke's downward track going ESE to head the fresh water creek then turning WNW to round the range on the opposite side. Thus we can track every inch of his route from above our 50 tree to his CXIX Camp and beyond that, all our efforts are in vain. A surmise is now gaining strength that Burke's party never left the camp and that the camels have strayed back singly leaving no definite trail. Why he left the camp at all on the mad foot expedition is astonishing, the two men left behind may have been killed in his absence and he have shared their fate on his return. There is still one chance which is that the tracks went through the long grass on the plains ESE from his camp and that although we have seen on these plains the tracks of single camels going in every direction yet we may have missed the trail. Unluckily the grass is green and I cannot burn it. Marked a tree: FW/12 Jan/1862

Monday, 13 January 1862. Proceeded with the whole party to opposite the 50 Tree but Mr Houghton, Patrick, Jingle and Coreen Jemmy went up on the left bank in hopes of falling in with two of the missing horses but they met no success. My plan now is to run up the Flinders to opposite where I left the horses on the Norman, send over for these and then if we have not cut the trail of Burke on the red sandstone where it would be like print, I must steer E by N to the Gilbert. This will be very disappointing to me, but my first object is to find the trail again if I can. Marked a tree here: 1 FW. Turkeys and ducks, the latter abundant. Thermometer, 7 am, 81°; aneroid, 7 am, 29.8.

Tuesday, 14 January 1862. Went 25° S of E 1¼ miles, 20° E of S 2 miles, E 1 mile, 30° S of E 1 mile, SE 4 miles, 15° E of S 3 miles, 12° W of S 3 miles, 40° W of S half a mile, 15° E of S 1 mile, (the last three and a half miles down a creek), and then turned 60° W of S to the river, which was only ½ mile on our right. Mr Houghton, Mr Moore, Rodney and Jemmy Cargara had gone on the left bank looking for horses, still, however, in vain. They joined us after we had camped at a deep hole in the river, which is here a sandy dry river in two branches, with water at long intervals. Marked a tree: 2 FW. Jingle to-day saw Burke's downward trail. The spinifex I had seen south of the 50 tree is only a spur coming into the river. I was astonished to find the country so good, being on both sides splendid plains.

Wednesday, 15 January 1862. Had a very bad start, and as the day was oppressively hot, I only went a short distance, 30° S of E ½ mile, S 1½ mile. Now, to my annoyance, 40° W of S 1 mile, and then 2 miles 35° E of S, brought us to a good pool of water, where we camped. We had barely got everything snug when a thunderstorm from the NW, which had been threatening all day, came down with tropical violence, making the waterhole flow over, and the river run enough to fill another large reach below us. The rain caused me to omit marking the tree. I here pointed out to Mr Moore that there were specimens of black basalt quartz and slate, besides the grey stone mentioned before.

Thursday, 16 January 1862. Coreen Jemmy luckily shot a turkey. Everything that spares our meat is valuable. The river to-day has trended more E; had it not done so, I must have abandoned it. 30° S of E ½ mile, S ½ mile, SE 1 mile, 10° S of E ½ mile, 30° E of S 2 miles, E ½ mile, 30° S of E ½ mile, 43° S of E to camp. Marked a tree: 4 FW Here we had just got the tents pitched in time, when down came another thunderstorm, this one from the SSE. The country still beautiful. Water doubtful.

Friday, 17 January 1862. This morning, Coreen Jemmy having mistaken the trees of a creek for these of the river, I was led too far to the east, and had to turn south to hit the river again. The ground from the rain has become very heavy, and the horses were greatly distressed. As it is necessary that at the start I should not impair the fine condition they are in, I made only a short journey, camping 10 miles above the 4 tree, in a direction 30° E of S by compass. The plains to-day have been flooded from the river, which in consequence has now but a small channel, and this also accounts for our seeing nothing of Burke's downward trail. Blacks' tracks quite fresh were seen at Camp No 5. A net and a bundle were found, and in the latter a small plait of fine auburn hair, certainly not that of a black. Rain at night. Mosquitoes kept every one awake all night.

Saturday, 18 January 1862. Just after daylight the blacks were seen close to our camp. As they had some children with them, it was evident their intentions were friendly. A parley ensued. We showed them the picture of a camel, and tried without effect to discover where such animals, if they had seen them, had gone. I doubt whether they understood the meaning of the picture. The Flinders, they explained readily enough, came from ESE - they pointed direct for Grateful Creek. It is as well to mention here that this young black was trying to make us understand something relative to the four white men we inquired about, but was stopped by the sinister looking men, much to the indignation of Jingle, Paddy, Coreen Jemmy, Rodney and Jemmy Cargara. Thermometer at 3 pm, 102°; aneroid, 29.63. One of them brought to my camel-boy a seed necklace; and I gave them in return a couple of Dover knives. Mr Moore and Mr Houghton gave them also a couple of shirts. The young men were good-looking lads, and the boys also of a pleasing appearance. The men, with the exception of a good-humoured ugly old fellow, kept aloof, and some of them had very sinister looking countenances. My course to-day was 25° E of S 3½ miles, 30° E of S ½ mile, SE 1 mile, 20° S of E 1 mile, and 35° E of S 2 miles, to a fine water hole where we camped. The plains still flooded; the river on two occasions so insignificant that I doubted whether we had not left it, but immediately above were, on both occasions, pools of water, rather low now, but with evidently last year's water in them. Above our Camp No 6 are several fine pools of water; one certainly, if not more, permanent.

Sunday, 19 January 1862. Went SE 2 miles, 25° E of S 2 miles, 5° E of S 2 miles; we now had to turn 35° W of S, as the river was a long way on our left, and 42° W of S, which brought us in 3 miles to a lagoon in an ana-branch of great size, but now dry; 25° W of S brought us in another mile to the river, and by following it SE 1 mile we came to camp at a good waterhole, evidently permanent. The strange course to-day has been owing to Coreen Jemmy having led, as I remained behind with Mr Moore, Patrick and Jingle being delayed by four horses not being found. The country is still flooded plains, but now quite destitute of vegetation, as it has been burnt, leaving only the stumps of long water-grasses, and a long drought has evidently been experienced here. The river where we first hit it was an insignificant channel, but at our camp was again a broad river. The mosquitoes are to-night reasonable. Thermometer at four pm, 91°; aneroid, 29.60.

Monday, 20 January 1862. Went 15° E of S 2 miles and a half, and 25° E of S 1 mile and a half, when a dark cloud coming from the NW caused us to pitch our tents in all haste. I regretted having done so subsequently, for a NW squall ought not to have stopped us, and it now cleared off, leaving a fine day. Above this camp is a long reach, 3 miles in length, and of great width; at it were some gins and children. One of them spoke a language a little of which Jemmy Cargara understood. She asked if we were the party that had gone down the Norman. Having been informed that we were, she said that nearly all the blacks had gone over to meet us, as we had said we would return that way. She said Burke had gone down the plains on the left bank, and repeatedly answered he had never returned that way. Aneroid, at day-break, 29.01; at half-past six, 29.70. Thermometer, half-past six, 81°. A shirt that was in the camp, she said, had been received from the blacks down the river, her own men were up the river fishing. Mosquitoes again manageable. Ana-branch seen a long way on our left.

Tuesday, 21 January 1862. We had barely got half the horses saddled, when the rain came down from the NE. I still persisted in pushing on, for we must not be caught by a flood in a country like this, where we might find ourselves out off from the sandstone country by large ana-branches. We went S half E 1 mile, then 20° S of E 1 mile. We now crossed the ana-branch, and went on 40° E of S 2 miles, having had the long reach nearly all the way in view. We passed by the blacks' camp, but they had left it. 20° E of S 1 mile, then SE 4 miles, the river now running in two or three narrow channels. Here we camped, and the horses had had enough of the boggy ground. The men and boys of the gins below are camped at some large pools above this camp; they were friendly, and gave us some fish, but nothing new as to intelligence was gained from them. Heavy storm of tropical rain from SW at night.

Wednesday, 22 January 1862. As the blacks, here had confirmed the story told by the gins of Burke having gone down the left bank, and that he had not returned by the Flinders; and as this was evidently what the blacks at Camp N° 5 had tried to make us comprehend, I saw no use in following up the river. Moreover, the continued heavy rains had made the plains very boggy, and I was apprehensive that the wet season had set in three weeks earlier than usual. I therefore determined upon striking across the country for the Norman; a course 25° N of E by compass, ought to take us in three days to a spot 6 miles below my 41st tree. We started at 2 pm and, after dreadful work for the horses across the plains, and passing over two ana-branches, we reached the sandstone country, which the blacks here call 'Mangolas,' in six miles and a half. We camped ½ mile further, near a good-sized creek, which no doubt joins the ana-branch with the big lagoon. The night was fine until an hour before day-light, when a NW storm of rain burst over us, again deluging the country.

Thursday, 23 January 1862. The state of the ground prevented us starting until half-past two, but we found the ground better than we expected after the first 2 miles, the country was more undulating, and the further E we went the less were the symptoms of rain having fallen; at last I began to fear we would have no water for our camp. This would have been the more awkward, for the heavy rains had caused us not to fill any of our water-bags. Luckily, at the end of 12 miles we found sufficient in a small swamp for our purpose, and we camped. At the end of the first 6½ miles, we fell in with five blacks, but there were tracks of many more. From them we got the old story about the four white men having gone down the Flinders, but, as usual, no information as to whether they had gone from there. At this camp, at half-past one pm, another tropical storm visited us, lasting until near daylight. It came first from the SSW, went round by the NE, and returned to us with a second edition from the SSE.

Friday, 24 January 1862. This morning heavy rain caused us to delay starting until 1 pm. In the interval we were visited by nine blacks, out of whom no intelligence could be got. Two of them received a shirt each, but subsequently one of them was detected stealing an American tomahawk. We have given so many away, and so many have been lost, that tomahawks are now with us precious articles. Rodney, whose tomahawk it was, called to the fellow to drop it, and snapped his gun in the air. They all now made off; but Paddy, willing to hasten their movements, fired his breech-loader over their heads. This I was very angry at, as it was done without my orders; nevertheless, it had the good effect of showing them what they, I surmise, were utterly ignorant of the immense range of Terry's carbines. I heard them scream when the conical ball struck a tree some distance ahead of them. We reached the Norman in 11 miles. We did not find the ground at all heavy; in fact, the very heavy sands which caused us so much vexation on our outward route were in the wet season very acceptable to us, as we had good travelling ground.

Saturday, 25 January 1862. As my horse and another were late coming into camp, I started Mr Macalister on at half-past eight; for, as we had had a fine clear night, and the morning was splendid, it was necessary to take advantage of it. At nine I started after him; passed the 41 tree in 6 miles, and overtook Mr Macalister in 5 more, at some pools of water with ducks on them, and, as we were out of meat, we camped in hopes of getting some. We found here that the bag containing the tobacco had opened, losing one half (all one side). Three men must, in consequence, return to-morrow, as this is a loss of too serious a nature for Australian bushmen.[285]

Sunday, 26 January 1862. I had intended giving the horses a day's spell, whilst Mr Houghton and two men went back for the tobacco, but they found it within a short distance. We now received an unexpected notice to quit, as the late rains had caused the river and an ana-branch to run, and we happened to be camped on the box flats, into which the

285 *Argus* 6 June 1862 p 7.

latter merges. We had just time to get the packs on the saddles, and I have not yet seen it done so quickly. We now moved up to the 40th tree and found the Norman River nearly bank and bank. We had made a timely escape from the inundated plains on the Flinders. I have marked no trees since we left that river, but here, where a tree is marked as observed formerly, RSV/16 Nov/186, I added on the next tree the date, 26 Jan 1862.

Monday, 27 January 1862. Moved up to 39th tree; I had intended going as far as the 38th tree, but a very late start frustrated that purpose. I hobbled many of the horses here. The ground in many places is boggy; but in general, it is much firmer from the rains, than when we came down.

Tuesday, 28 January 1862. Went to 38th tree, and immediately upon our arrival there saw the fresh tracks of a horse. Two men went, after dinner, to look for him; but although the fresh tracks of to-day were seen, the horse was not seen. During the night, I heard a great noise among the horses, which I believed to be caused by the advent of the missing one.

Wednesday, 29 January 1862. The horses were much scattered this morning and were not all found until near 11 am; but among one mob was, to our joy, the horse we had left here on the 15th of November. After dinner, we moved on to about 8 miles higher up the river or (ana-branch). Some soup which we made with the sausages cut up fine on Monday - and this was the only way we could soften them at all - made many of us sick, me especially, and they were all thrown away. We had previously been obliged to throw away all the dried turtle, as it was damaged.

Thursday, 30 January 1862. We got an excellent start and arrived at the 37th tree at 10 am. Within 2 miles of it we saw the tracks of the horses left here, and Mr Houghton and Jemmy Cargara turned off to look for them, but shortly after our arrival Coreen Jemmy and Jingle, who had gone up the other side, fetched two of them into camp. Rodney, to my great joy, found my favourite compass, which had been forgotten here. After dinner Coreen Jemmy and Jingle went out again to look after the other two horses. They returned at 4 pm and reported they had tracked them up the river on our old track. The tracks appeared to have been made just after the rain which fell on the morning of the 24th of January. I will follow them as far as the Springs, although I wished to leave this river here, and start for Mr Gregory's 4th October camp. Should we not fall in with Burke's tracks betwixt the Springs and Gregory's 4th October camp, I must try for the Lynd. If we fail there, I do not know what more can be done.

Friday, 31 January 1862. Moved up to the 36th camp, Jingle and Coreen Jemmy, who went on in front to track the two missing horses, found that the tracks that they had seen yesterday must have been those of the two already recovered, for they now saw on their way from this camp to the Springs the tracks of the other two, of so old a date as to lead them to think they were made when we had the great storm of the 6th and 7th December on the Albert River. They noticed that the horses were travelling side by side. They are probably at the stations ere this and may possibly pick up the mare at Grateful Creek, and likewise Nanny, on their road. I expect them to go straight on to Albinia Downs. I now, therefore, resolved to leave this for Gregory's 4th October camp. I have marked a tree here with the date upon which we arrived first viz., 10th November 1861, and the day we leave it, 1st February 1862.

Saturday, 1 February 1862. Course 33° E of N. Went 12 miles over gradually rising sandstone country, the ground sometimes boggy, but we in general managed to evade the bad places. We camped on a very large creek, but I afterwards found that it and another branch joined a much larger one a few hundred yards lower down, forming a bed upwards of 100 yards in width, and now with a running stream fifty yards in width. This is much larger than the Norman. Is this Gregory's Creek, of the 13th and 14th September? These rivers all in places run out to small channels as they get lower down into the *mangoola* ground, but then there are box flats all subject to floods. One would not fancy so to see them in dry seasons, but on the Norman, I have seen them in dry and wet weather. Called this river the Jardine after the police magistrate at Rockhampton. A small dry creek was passed two miles back. Marked a tree: 20‿FW and RSV/2 Feb/1862.

Sunday, 2 February 1862. Went on for eleven miles, same course, 33° E of N, crossed an ana-branch of the river, a small tributary in 6 miles, another in 7 miles from camp. Then over a ridge. Within 2 miles came to a creek running SE, and from the next ridge we got a clear view of the Gilbert River Range. They had been seen from the top of a tree at the last camp, likewise the tableland at the head of the Flinders. We are now, no doubt, at some height, but the many thunder squalls render the aneroid all but useless for this purpose of finding the approximate height. At 12 (meridian) it was 29.12; at 3 pm 29.9; and at daylight, after a fine clear night, on the morning of the 3rd, 29.20. Marked a tree: 21 FW

Monday, 3 February 1862. This morning ten of the horses were missing. Mr Macalister, Mr Moore, Jingle and Coreen Jemmy stopped for them whilst the remainder of the party pushed on with me. We kept rising all the morning for the first six miles, passing over two diminutive creeks running NW. We now reached the top of a considerable range; the summit was formed of the grey stone spoken of formerly as having been seen in the Flinders. I now suppose this to be porphyry, from Gregory's mentioning hills of that stone: but, as on the next hills or ridges, I observed the conical hills or summits of these rocks, just similar to the ends of basalt columns, I should have supposed them to be basalt, notwithstanding their light colour. We went over fine pastoral country, almost downs, so thinly timbered were the ridges with small box trees. The ground, however, is trying for horses, being much like a newly macadamised road. At the end of three miles we camped on a small creek anxiously, but in vain, looking for the missing party all evening. Just ahead of us is a beautiful valley, into which I can see that three large creeks are flowing. Beyond it are the high Gilbert Ranges; and to the north-west a splendid country can be seen as far as the glass can be brought to bear from the top of a high ridge at the back of the camp. The aneroid here was 29.14 when we arrived: it fell to 29.9 before the arrival of a thunderstorm, and after it passed away rose again to 29.12, and there remained till three pm next day. Marked a tree: 22 FW

Tuesday, 4 February 1862. The men found the horses at the first creek in the next valley. They say it is a fine country, and the creek has large reaches of water in it. Waited anxiously until now, quarter to four, for the missing party. If not here to-night, I go back to-morrow. Aneroid at three pm fell to 29.6. Thunder heavy to the south and west, only a few drops of rain here. The last three nights have been cool, and the mosquitos not troublesome. The thermometer, at daylight yesterday, was 67°; this morning 77°. At 12 pm, it was at 97°; at 3 pm, 95°; at 5 pm, 87°. Party arrived, to my great relief, a little before sundown. Our last tin of bouillie, which had been kept for an emergency, was made into soup, with the addition of rice. Aneroid during the night rose again to 29.16, but afterwards settled at 29.13 until two pm next day. Blacks had followed Coreen Jemmy, who, when looking for the lost horses, had been obliged to drive before him his own, knocked up. He had to fire once or twice to keep them off, but without knowing whether he hit anyone. They also followed Jingle.

Wednesday, 5 February 1862. As the party, yesterday evening had arrived without two of the horses, Mr Macalister, Mr Houghton, Patrick, and Jemmy Cargara went back, each with two horses, and they had with them also a packhorse. Four of the horses cannot be found again this evening. An old grey horse, I notice, is always the ringleader. The party are well armed which started this morning and have strict orders not to separate. Two of the horses, including the grey, were found at four pm, but the other two are yet missing. Mr Moore and I took all the horses we have found, twenty-seven in number, over to the next creek, and left them. On our return from the top of the high ridge before mentioned as being at the back of our camp, I took the bearings of the following mountains: A very high tableland, the northern end of which bore, by compass, 15° E of S, I or rather Mr Moore, called it Mount Barry, after Sir Redmond Barry of Victoria. Two remarkable peaks, one bearing 62° E of N, Mount Orestis, the other bearing 52° E of N, Mount Pylades. A queer looking range, which we accordingly named Mount Queer, bore 65° E of N. A range in the middle of the valley, 36° E of N. A remarkable peak in the distance, we called Mount Picken, after my old friend Captain Picken, now, I believe, marine surveyor at Williamstown. This bore 3° E of N. Thunder to the S, and clouds passed over from SE to NE, but no rain fell here.

Thursday, 6 February 1862. Horses all mustered, including the two missing yesterday. Horse flies very troublesome.

Friday, 7 February 1862. Fish for dinner, which is acceptable. Horses all mustered. At three pm, 102, saddled up now, and shifted our camp one and a half. 15° N of E. A little before sundown, Mr Macalister's party returned with both horses; they had to go for one to the Norman, but the other, as I expected, was close to our twenty-first camp. I expected a thunderstorm, but it passed over, with strong squalls from ENE, which, however, had the effect of giving us a cool night.

Saturday, 8 February 1862. The horses, which have been to the Norman require a spell, and I intend giving them to-day and to-morrow. It looks very much like thunder. There are very heavy clouds gathering in the east. Marked a tree: 23 FW. After sundown, very heavy clouds gathering to the NE.

Sunday, 9 February 1862. Rain heavy at times and continued all last night: notwithstanding the aneroid kept rising until it reached 29.11, where it stood until twelve to-day. Sun came out about ten am, but occasional showers continued coming up from NE. I do not like the look of it, for it is from that quarter I expect the rainy season to set in, and this is the time of the year for it. After twelve the aneroid kept falling, and at half-past two it is 29.8; at five pm, aneroid 29.0. A heavy thunderstorm now burst over us, and lasted till sundown, when it cleared up, and the aneroid rose to 29.10.

Monday, 10 February 1862. Clouds are now moving from the NNW, and the night has been fine; there is a prospect of fine weather. I find I am camped between two branches of a river, both now running; but last night's rain has made the water rise very much and caused a third branch to run. I observe that during the night a fourth was also running. I conclude that this is the 'Carin' of Leichhardt. Jingle having told me that a considerable creek joined that at our camp above it, I first went 67° E of N two miles, and found myself under Mount Omer. Jingle's creek was a humbug; but I followed it up 27° E of N for one mile, and then crossed over 55° E of N in one and a half miles to another, which for the first three quarters of a mile took me 19° W of N, and then 14° E of N for one and a half miles, passing at the back of Mount Pylades. We were now pulled up by a wall of rock, and turned round WNW, betwixt Mount Orestes and a cliff of red rock, or rather a series of terraces, one over the other, until we found what Patrick calls a chimney, and close to the top of Mount Barry, at south-west end of it. We now went 25° east of north for about two and a half miles, and camped. From the top of Mount Barry, we had a fine and very extensive view. We could see the valley of what I suppose to be the Cairns, stretching a long way to the WNW, and as far as we could see it was good pastoral country. At an immense distance 32° east of south, were very high mountains; probably the main head of the Flinders comes from them. This corroborates the opinion before stated by me that the tableland I crossed betwixt the waters of the interior and those of the Gulf of Carpentaria, rose to a great height further to the west, and probably from these mountains were washed the specimens of basalt and slate picked up by me on the left bank of the Flinders, on the 15th January.

Tuesday, 11 February 1862. This morning I first went six miles 52° E of N, and then, as far as I could manage to keep the course, about eight miles N of E, but the many deep ravines, in an excessively broken country, have made my route so tortuous that I wish much we could have an observation, and that cannot be on account of a haze which overhangs the whole atmosphere.

Wednesday, 12 February 1862. At first starting we had to go a little to S of E, and to wind for two miles down a circuitous broken gully, but then we came out on a fine sloping green valley, and next onto a creek, which, as we got lower down, was running. The rock here appeared to me to be sandstone, but of a strange appearance, in layers, and full of quartz pebbles, In the valley itself, were detached masses of all shapes and sizes, giving the place a fantastic appearance. The course of the creek was a little north of east until it entered, for a few yards, into a gorge so narrow that we travelled in the bed of the creek. At the end of about seven miles from our camp of last night, we emerged from the gorge, and our eyes were delighted by the sight of the most pleasant looking green ridges, all of basalt, and covered with the best possible grasses. Two miles brought us to a large river, now running too high for us to cross. This, I, suppose, is the large sandy creek crossed by Gregory before he reached the Lynd. I am again disappointed by a cloudy, night from having an observation taken here. Marked a tree: 26 FW

Thursday, 13 February 1862. This morning the river had so much fallen that we were able to cross; but one packhorse had a narrow escape. Luckily nothing was damaged. I now found that the river, instead of rounding a range, as appeared from the opposite bank of the river, ran so close to it, in a westerly direction, that there was no room for a horse, so I had to strike over the range, but much time had been lost. The result was that I had to camp nearly on the top, where I luckily found sufficient water for the horses. An observation was taken tonight, but with great difficulty. I ordered the trees to be cleared off a round knob at the back of the camp. In the meanwhile, I went to the top of the range on foot. I now saw that I had a clear road for the next day. I was, however, much puzzled, for the country appeared to me to resemble Gregory's description of the Gilbert. Camp 27, not marked.

Friday, 14 February 1862. [Camp 28U]. This morning I had an early start; some trouble was encountered owing to the sharpness of the quartz reefs, which here are all extending from east to west; a great part of the way we had to walk; however, we reached another river about one pm, and got a good camp, marked by me: 28 FW. I am now satisfied that this is the Gilbert; but I differ a great deal both in latitude and longitude from Gregory. An observation got this night makes our latitude 18° 46'. I am therefore, as near as can be calculated, fourteen miles above the 19th parallel. This also tallies with the observation taken at Camp 27.

Saturday, 15 February 1862. Got a good start. I proceeded up a creek which joins the river just below our camp. For the first three miles my course was 17° N of E, but as the valley of this creek trended too much from the north, I took advantage of a gap here. I halted the party, because a peak to my left would give me a good opportunity to examine the country before me. (That must be the granite range which is before us.) I now went nine miles east by compass and fixed my camp on a large stream, which is either the river we camped on at No 8 or a tributary of it. The county to-day has been alternately slate, porphyry, and granite, with many quartz reefs, all, with the exception of two, bending west by compass. The two exceptions trended very nearly WNW. There can now be no doubt that this is the Gilbert country of Gregory. On my map, which as usual I make up every night, I have named a peak Mount Mica; and a remarkable mountain, round which this river winds, Mount Granite. My track left the former on my left, the latter on my right. The slate has inured the horses' feet very much. I must make only a short stage to-morrow to the foot of the range. Marked a tree: 29 FW

Sunday, 16 February 1862. To-day my course has been again east by compass, and the distance ridden six miles. I saw in one of my walks yesterday evening that a peak, about two miles from Camp 29, would give me an opportunity of having a good sight of the granite range.

With the help of the opera-glass I received from Captain Norman, I was able to discern a spur, by which we could ascend the range. This peak was called by Patrick Mount Byrjuenee, which means in his language to climb a steep ridge, or anything else, or to spring up. (The same word is also used to express to jump down). Marked a tree: 30 FW and another: RSV/16 Feb/ 1862.

Monday, 17 February 1862. East by compass 4 miles to gap on range. A different track about ENE brought us to the top of range in about five miles. In a straight line this cannot be more than six miles from Camp 30, but the ascent has been very tedious. Whilst the men were getting the camp fixed, Mr Moore and I took a walk after dinner, such as it was, to see which way we had to go the next day. In my opinion, this granite range is the Great Dividing Range, an extension of what the Rev WB Clarke calls the cordillera, and which terminates at Cape York. I observe a valley to the north. Is not that the valley of the Lind? I am getting much alarmed about the horses. What we are to do for boots I do not know. Not one of us has got a sound one. The best I have now is an old pair given to me by Captain Norman. Camp 31 not marked.

Tuesday, 18 February 1862. Our course to-day has been about 27° S of E, and the distance, as near as I can make it, 8 miles. I have had to abandon ten horses, they can travel no further. Camp 32 not marked.

Wednesday, 19 February 1862. Travelled with difficulty five miles, 7° S of E by compass. The actual distance ridden was nine miles. From the top of a remarkable sandstone ridge, surmounted by large boulders of granite, I got a view of a very high mountain, distant, I suppose, about thirty-five miles, and the bearings due north from this camp. There is a remarkable peak at the eastern end, which appears to be detached from the mountain. Marked a tree, by mistake 32 FW, but the camp is No 33.

Thursday, 20 February 1862. I steered as I could 45° E of S, my object being to get to a river which must run under a range in that direction. The actual distance ridden this day was 8 miles. In a straight line, I made it 6½. What is this river? It is evidently the Lind of Gregory; but I believe it to join the Burdekin. Two very good observations were got during the ensuing night. The latitude here, taking the mean of the two observations, is 18° 57', which places me about 1¾ of a mile above the 19th parallel.

Friday, 21 February 1862. At 8 am three of our best horses are incapable of moving; the horse carrying the instruments is this morning the most incapable. They must be left here at Camp 34, 21st February. All this trouble is occasioned by the want of horses' shoe nails. There were plenty of shoes at the Albert, but no nails. Had I continued up the Flinders, and either went home by my outward route, or tried for Adelaide, the shoeing of the horses would have been a matter of no consequence, and so I told Captain Norman. For example, the horse which led the party out, and which was my own private property, was not shod when I started on the outward route.

I had determined to strike 45° N of E as the ranges to the SE seemed to be too stony, and I was in hopes of reaching better ground. As I neared the valley of the Burdekin, in 1¾, we reached a tributary of the Copperfield, which I called the Quartz Mis, on account of the enormous reefs of quartz. Before reaching our camp, we had some trouble in descending a gully; but at last it opened into a good plain of decomposed basalt, with a river which I called the Moore running through it. I think to the north this valley must open onto a good sheep country; that is, if the climate is suitable. Luckily, Jingle got three ducks, the first meat we have had, except two opossums, since leaving Camp 24. I marked a tree: 35 FW

Saturday, 22 February 1862. This morning I found that two more horses, one belonging to the Royal Society and one my own property, were incapable of proceeding further. They had to be left, as well as a bag of dried apples and one of peas. I may here mention that the dried apples which I brought with me from Rockhampton have, in my opinion, been the cause, of none of my party having hitherto suffered with scurvy. I have still one small bag left. Macalister, however, is now showing symptoms, which, I think, are scorbutic. In about 9 miles we reached a sandy creek, where we camped. The course still the same, and our route over a succession of ridges, all of which I have placed on my map. The rain came down during the night in torrents.

Sunday, 23 February 1862. I wished now to go SE, being tired of looking for the Burdekin Valley, but Jingle, who had been out reconnoitring, caused me at first to proceed a little north of east. The appearance of the slope soon struck me with surprise, and I could not help thinking that it was lava; but in about three and a half miles we reached the edge of a cliff, which we descended with great difficulty, and found ourselves in an oval basin about a mile and a half in length and about 500 yards in width, the northern end full of water and bulrushes. The opposite side was not a cliff, and the ridge or side of the basin not so high as that by which we had descended, here were some blacks. A parley was held with some gins, but nothing comprehensible elicited from them. A ride of four miles down the eastern slope of the lava brought us to a granite creek, where we camped. To the south I observed, at a distance of about one mile, another basin, and I think there are more still further south. These, I suppose, are extinct craters of volcanoes. At this camp, just at the bend of the creek below my tent, I observed a peculiar rock. Mr Moore and I examined it. It was in layers, the lowest about three feet in depth, was similar in colour to the granite in the creek, and was full of mica, but it crumbled under my fingers. Next there was a layer of ashes about one foot in depth, but running into a point, and this point was filled up with a mass of quartz; next, another layer of granite looking stone, and then another layer of ashes, then more granite and a third layer of ashes about two feet in depth, and on this the black soil of the plains. Camp 37‿FW. These slopes of lava are good pastoral country.

Monday, 24 February 1862. I now turned about ESE. In about six miles and a half we crossed a river called by my men Yananoa; its course was NE. We attempted to cross the dividing range betwixt it and a valley to the east, but failed, and had to camp in a narrow gully where to our great relief, Coreen Jemmy shot a kangaroo. In the evening, with much trouble owing to the dilapidated state of my boots, I reached the summit of the range, and determined upon my route for the next day. Camp 38‿FW

Tuesday, 25 February 1862. Started a little south of east. In about three miles and a half we reached the edge of a red sandstone cliff, and under it an extensive valley was seen stretching to the north of east. Descended the cliff with some trouble, and after a ride of five miles camped on a creek. The rain came down in earnest, and we were delayed here until 3rd March. The country has become very boggy. Luckily, Coreen Jemmy shot another kangaroo and three opossums were got by Jemmy Cargara and him. I marked a tree on one side 39‿FW; on the other side RSV/25th Feb to 3rd March. The wet ground improved the horses, and by the evening of 2nd March were all fit to go on again.

Monday, 3 March 1862. Course about 30° south of east over undulating sandstone country. In about nine miles we camped on a small creek.

Tuesday, 4 March 1862. Same course, over undulating and rather broken country, brought us in eight miles to a pretty valley near some peaks, basalt and porphyry. Macalister walked over to a river about a mile and a half from our camp. Is this the Clarke? 41 FW

Wednesday, 5 March 1862. Crossed the river. I cannot believe this to be the Clarke. In three miles more crossed another river, after having ridden over some very boggy ridges. The last I have called the Belmenoa, and the other the Porphyry, there being large rocks of it in this river. We went and camped under the foot of the range, as I wished to walk to the top to reconnoitre, which I accordingly did in the evening. This night a good observation makes our latitude 19° 20'. This would make the Belmenoa correspond with the Clarke, according to Gregory's map, 42 FW

Thursday, 6 March 1862. Three more horses have to be abandoned. Course about 10° south of west. At the end of seven miles camped in a narrow gully, or rather ravine. 43 FW

Friday, 7 March 1862. A hard day's work, nearly all done on foot, on account of the roughness and steepness of the ranges. We did not make more than four miles due east in a straight line. From the top of a remarkable red sandstone cliff near our camp we had a magnificent view, and the valley before us must at last be that of the Burdekin. 44 FW

Saturday, 8 March 1862. In about four miles east, crossed a gap of some sandstone ridges, descended to a creek, and in three miles more east reached the Burdekin River, here running from north to south. On the opposite side, distant about five miles, is a range which I have called Mount Welcome. We went down the river about a mile, to the junction of the creek with the Burdekin. 45 FW. By observation this night our latitude is 19° 20'.

Sunday, 9 March 1862. Soon after crossing the creek the river was found to flow ESE, and at the end of six and a half miles we camped on a small basalt creek. 40 FW

Monday, 10 March 1862. In about two and a half miles ESE we came to the junction of a river from SW. This river is as big as the Burdekin.

As the river was rather high, we had some trouble in crossing it; the difficulty being occasioned by the horses stumbling over the basalt and porphyry rocks: however, everything was got over safe. Two miles ENE brought us to a small river full of slate, and which I have named Slate River, here we camped. 47 FW. One horse completely knocked up. In the evening, I went to the top of a high range. On the opposite side of the river under Mount Welcome, I observed some good little plains, but on the Burdekin, I noticed a very bad description of grass growing wherever the slate is. It reached a height of from six to nine feet and is surmounted by the worst grass-seed I have ever seen. The pain caused from a wound by this grass-seed in exactly like that from a bite of a soldier ant.

Tuesday, 11 March 1862. An attempt made to-day to go under a sugar-loaf hill, close to the bank of the river, failed. Macalister succeeded, but immediately sent back Coreen Jemmy to warn me that the pack-horses could not pass. A detour over the porphyry and slate ranges had to be made, and when we re-joined Macalister we were glad to camp, having only made about five miles NE. The track could be followed by the drops of blood from the poor horse's feet. The view here down the river is very fine. My party, although still in good health, are getting weak from want of meat. The only way in which we can use the damaged flour we received at the Albert is to sift it through a veil, and we lose one pint in every four. Macalister has still slight symptoms of scurvy, kept under by dried apples and the native cucumbers, which, luckily, are abundant.

Wednesday, 12 March 1862. Our course to-day was about east on the average, but at first, we had to go north-east to clear the ranges of the porphyry. A dense thicket stopped us for some time, but when we got through it, we found some basaltic open ironbark county, with some small waterholes, at which we camped, much tired. 49 FW

Thursday, 13 March 1862. Our course to-day was ESE, but the slate was so bad that we were obliged to camp at the end of three miles, on a small creek. 50 FW

Friday, 14 March 1862. The ground to-day was much better, a great part near the creek being sand; still the porphyry and slate rocks at times caused great suffering to some of the horses. We made about seven and a half miles ESE and camped at a bend of the river near a high peak, which Moore and I ascended in the afternoon. Numerous blacks are all round us at this camp; a vain attempt was made to get a parley with them. 51 FW

Saturday, 15 March 1862. To-day, with great trouble, we succeeded in passing under the ranges which here shut in the river; and, having found a creek with water at the end of five miles, a little E of S, we were obliged to camp one half of the horses being completely done up.

Sunday, 16 March 1862. I made up my mind to divide the party. Our sugar was nearly out. The peas which we roasted for coffee were finished, and I saw no prospect of getting meat. I therefore to-day started Macalister, Richard Houghton, Coreen Jemmy and Jingle, with the seven best horses, and instructions to procure food for us wherever they could get it. The remainder of the party moved over to a better camp one mile and a half off. 52 FW

Sunday 16 to Wednesday 19 March 1862. We stopped, spelling our poor horses. The men got us two opossums during this time; but, on the morning of the 20th, as they were going out to make another attempt at hunting, we discovered that the blacks were around us in too large numbers to admit of dividing our party. Moore and I had been to the top of a peak at the rear of our camp, and I find now no difficulty in coming to a conclusion that the river we had crossed on the 10th was the Clarke. I could see the sandstone ridge crossed by Gregory.

Thursday, 20 March 1862. Started on the tracks of Macalister. Made ten miles; luckily, Rodney got a young emu. 53 FW

Friday, 21 March 1862. To-day we made a long push of about eleven miles, and camped at the junction of a large creek (or small river). To-day, I saw a patch of good sheep country. One of the horses completely done. We, luckily, got abundance of fish. 54 FW

Saturday, 22 March 1862. To-day we made another long push, having abandoned the knocked-up horse. Our journey was about thirteen and a half miles, and we camped at Macalister's second camp. Abundance of fish and some figs. 55 FW

Sunday, 23 March 1862. To-day we crossed a strong running rivulet, and two miles below it Macalister had crossed the river. The crossing place was good, but the descent to it very rugged. We encamped on the left bank, at a bend of the river. 56 FW

Monday 24 to Wednesday 26 March 1862. Still following the tracks. I took down carefully every mile of the route, and made my map, as usual, every night. From several points I got cross bearings of different high mountains. On the 26th I saw a camp and made-up tree of Dalrymple's. Houghton ought now, therefore, to know where he is. The river crossed to-day must be the Fanning. The trees marked B are, no doubt, Blacks, and, consequently, the high range before us must be Roley's Range. If so, why is Macalister still following the river, instead of striking direct for Port Denison, or rather M'Donald and Collyns's station, at Mount Abbott? 59 FW. Plenty of fish and figs.

Thursday 27 to Monday 31 March 1862. Still winding down all the bends of the river; very much puzzled as to what Macalister's party was about. No improvement in the country. It may do for cattle, but I fear heavy losses will be incurred by those who attempt depasturing sheep in the valley of the Burdekin. At Camp 60, I had to leave another horse, and at this camp I must leave two more, as their feet cannot stand any more slate or granite. Abundance of fish and figs. 64 FW.

Tuesday, 1 April 1862. To-day we tracked Macalister down the river, and to our surprise saw the tracks returning up the river. After some delay we discovered that, having tied their horses to a tree, his party have gone to the top of an isolated peak. We did likewise, not without damage to our feet. From here I saw a mountain nearly south, which I at once came to the conclusion was Mount M'Connell. Macalister had evidently arrived at the same. We now turned north and camped at a small water-hole under the range. Rodney, luckily, got another young emu. 65 FW

Wednesday 2, and Thursday 3 April 1862. Winding up a different pass on one side of the range, and, down a ravine on the other. Another day will bring us to a stand-still; so much have the horses suffered.

Friday, 4 April 1862. Yesterday evening, Moore, with Jemmy and Rodney, went out to reconnoitre, a mob of blacks being near, but from them they could get no information. They reported the country as opening out, and that fresh tracks were here seen as if some one or two horsemen had been back on Macalister's track to fetch a horse which had evidently been left here. To-day we got on pretty well over the sandy soil, and at the end of about seven miles E by S camped on a creek, into which the ravine of yesterday emptied its waters. 68 FW. We had been two hours in camp when the cheers of a party on horseback made us aware that relief was approaching. It turned out to be Macalister, and he reported we were only four miles from Strathalbyn, the station of Messrs Woods and Robinson, on the Burdekin. I now got the news of the sad fate of Burke and Wills.

Saturday, 5 April 1862. Reached the station. I here marked a tree: 69 FW border round, and on the other: RSV/5 April/1862 border round. All the trees marked by me have part of the bark taken off.

Tuesday 29 April 1862. Having gone for supplies to Port Denison, on my return to Strathalbyn I started Mr Houghton, Mr Curr, Patrick, Coreen Jemmy and Jingle to collect the horses, twenty-two in number, which had been abandoned. To enable them to do so I gave them the best six horses I had, and purchased six fresh horses, for I was aware that any delay in collecting those horses might be the cause of their being lost. Macalister and Moore, I sent on with the despatches to Rockhampton, but to enable Moore to proceed I had to lend him my own horse. I followed slowly behind with the remainder of the party and reached Rockhampton on the 5th June. Frederick Walker, Leader Albert River Expedition.[286]

Frederick Walker to Secretary Royal Society, 29 April 1862

I do myself the honour to inform you that the party under my command reached this place distant about seventy miles from Port Denison, on the 5th instant. I enclose so much of my journal as will explain the reason of my having come in this way, and also a portion of my map, showing the Flinders River and Burke's track to his CXIX tree. You will observe that I have been much misled by Burke's having marked a tree SEE/14. Has the Royal Society any information as to the meaning of this mark? We have had a tedious and unpleasant journey since leaving the Norman River. The want of shoes soon lamed the horses when we had to cross the porphyry and slate of the Gilbert River; and when we had crossed the

286 *Argus* 11 November 1862 p 7.

great granite range I found myself compelled to leave thirteen horses on a river I have called the Copperfield, and one of those called the Lynd by Mr Gregory. Since then I have been obliged to abandon nine more horses. Had we any meat we might have camped and allowed the horses to recover, but the want of animal food was tolling upon my party, and I was anxious to push on, hoping to fall in with some station on the Burdekin, but in this I was disappointed, for no settler had come out, except Mr Black, and he was some fifteen miles up the Fanning, and I missed him. Since I have come here five parties have gone out, and had they been earlier I would have found a station at the Clarke. Had the act of the legislature been carried out in its integrity these runs ought to have been occupied three months ago, and that was what I was depending on. The great incorrectness of Mr Gregory's map has also hindered me much and I wish I had not had it with me. I make difference of twenty miles in longitude on the Burdekin, but as mine is dead reckoning this I would not mention were it not that Mr Gregory's is also more dead reckoning, and that, moreover, to suit his map, he has shifted the Belyando twenty-six miles more to the west than Sir T. Mitchell has placed it. I well remember Sir T. Mitchell's saying how careful he was of his chronometers. If I remember right, his instruments were carried slung on pole by two men, who walked after the drays. You will observe when you receive my map, which I will forward as soon as I reach Rockhampton that Sir Thomas Mitchell's longitude will tally with mine.

But Mr Gregory is not a bit more particular in latitude; as, for instance, he places the latitude of the junction of the Clarke 19.12 degrees, whereas we found it by observations, repeated on account of this difference on several nights, of the stars Pollux and Arcturus, to be in 19 degrees 27 minutes 25 seconds. Luckily, we had enough flour, otherwise my party might have been wrecked through such a blunder, for we thought we had crossed the Clarke long before. The flour I got from Captain Norman made all my party ill, until one of the men hit upon the expedient of sifting it through a veil; however, by this process we lost one pint out of every four, in all, 250 lbs. flour. I have written to Captain Mayne relative to some rations obtained by me with great difficulty in that miserable hole called Port Denison. I wanted to get some boots and other clothes for my party, to be hereafter deducted from their pay; but not having brought any cash from the Gulf of Carpentaria, I would have had to come back to my camp without any had not Mr Gordon, the collector of customs, kindly come forward and made himself responsible. This the police magistrate refused to do, although in your letter to me you state that I would receive all assistance from the Queensland Government. I know them too well to believe in it. I have started Mr Houghton, accompanied by a Mr Curr, with Jingle, Coreen Jemmy, and Patrick, to collect the horses left behind; but as many of the expedition horses were yet too weak, and any delay would be fatal, besides the cost of keeping the party, I purchased six; fresh horses, five for £25 each from Mr O'Connell, and one for £25 from Mr Powell. I had intended buying these horses on my own account, but for the reason mentioned before, viz., the want of a bank at the Albert River, I was obliged to give vouchers for them; but I am quite willing to take them off your hands when they reach Rockhampton. I now broke up the expedition, and my pay, Rodney's and Jemmy Cargara's cease from this day. Mr Macalister and Mr Moore claimed to be paid until they reached Rockhampton, and this I could not object to; but I have given them the best horses and sent them on with despatches, and they ought to be in Rockhampton on the 5th May. I will feel obliged if you will be so kind as to have the money due to Mr Moore placed at his disposal without delay, as he is anxious to join his friends in Melbourne.

I expect Mr Houghton to be in Rockhampton with the horses in nine weeks, and I have promised to meet him on the road or send to meet him as soon as I receive your instructions.

The rations I got at Port Denison were obtained from a Mr Williams, with the exception of meat and 100 lb. flour, which I procured here. For the former, I gave a voucher; and for the latter, I gave my promissory note. The accounts I have forwarded to Captain Mayne, with the exception of Williams', which I have lost.

I shall do myself the honour to address you again from Rockhampton, which I hope to reach in about three weeks, and will enclose maps and journal. In the meanwhile, I remain your obedient servant. Frederick Walker, Commander Victorian Expedition. Mr Moore joined on the 15th December, and his pay is £3 per week. Of course, I do not give up the command until all have reached Rockhampton.

Frederick Walker to Secretary Royal Society, 29 April 1862

Sir, I do not know whether the Royal Society have entertained any wish to have the Barkly River traced to the Carygaree of the blacks. The Burke River I believe to be the Stawell. Should, however, such an expedition be resolved on, I think I have the first claim to command it, and I would willingly give my services gratis, if required. In fact, so anxious am I about it, that, independent of the use of six of my own horses, I will subscribe all I can spare towards the outfit. I know not how much that may be until I see my agent in Rockhampton. I have written thus early in hopes that the horses of our present expedition might he sold in Adelaide, in lieu of Rockhampton.

WC Mayne to Secretary Exploration Committee, 30 May 1862

I have the honour to forward the enclosed letter, journal, and map of route, received from Mr Frederick Walker on the 28th instant.

The letter addressed to you reached me in the state in which I forward it, Mr Walker, in one addressed to myself, stating I have left my letter to secretary of Royal Society open for your perusal. The letter to myself, I may mention, reached me open, like that to you.

Having, in accordance with Mr Walker's wish become possessed of the contents of his letter to you, I must express my regret that he should have adopted the tone he has with reference to

Mr Gregory and to the Queensland Government, who were, I am well assured, sincere in their desire, and their instructions for aid being afforded to the expedition. In writing to Mr Walker, I have conveyed to him what I have here expressed.

I have requested Mr Walker to prepare and transmit to me a separate account (Dr and Cr) for each member of the expedition up to the date of their ceasing to be in the service of the committee; with a written authority from each, specifying the person or bank appointed by him to receive the balance that may be due. On receipt of these, I shall at once draw on the committee, through the Bank of New South Wales, to the amount required to liquidate the sums due. I have apprized Mr, Walker that the final disposal of the horses and equipment of the expedition must wait the instructions of the committee. These, when communicated to me, I shall give my best exertions to have carried into effect.

Frederick Walker to John Macadam, 21 October 1862

Sir, I do myself the honour to forward to you the conclusion of my journal, also the specimens of metal found at Camp 26, on one head of the Gilbert River, and the hair found in a black's dilly at Camp 5, on the Flinders River.

You will observe, with respect to the latter that a dark coloured plait, which might belong to a black, has been interlaced with that of the lighter colour, and which certainly belongs to no tribe ever seen by me during twenty-two years spent nearly all on the frontier: nor have any of my men (Aboriginal) ever heard or known of any of the Aboriginal having similar hair. I would recommend that this hair should not be examined by candle or gas light. I have the honour to remain, sir, Your obedient servant, Frederick Walker.

9

Telegraph Line

On 6 June 1859, Queen Victoria signed Letters Patent erecting Moreton Bay into a colony called Queensland. Brisbane was appointed the capital city. On 10 December 1859, a proclamation was read by Sir George Ferguson Bowen, whereby Queensland was formally separated from the colony of New South Wales. As a result, Bowen became the first Governor of Queensland. On 22 May 1860, the first Queensland election was held and Robert Herbert, Bowen's private secretary, was appointed as the first Premier of Queensland.

On or about 23 June 1860, the Colonial Treasurer in the Council proposed the sum of £10,000 for the purpose of carrying an electric telegraph to the frontier near Warwick.[287] The Governor writing to the Duke of Newcastle[288] on 30 September 1860 regarding the western boundary of Queensland which was set by Letters Patent at the 141st meridian of east longitude[289] sought to extend the boundary further west so, among other proposals and projects, that a settlement at the head of the Gulf of Carpentaria could be under-taken of paramount importance, not to this colony only, but also to the whole of Australia, and to the Empire at large. For this was the point at which it was proposed to connect Australia with India and Europe by means of an extension of the telegraphic line from Singapore, passing by the Dutch possessions in Java and Timor.[290]

Consequent on the retirement of Captain Martindale in January 1861

287 *MBC* 23 June 1860 p 2.

288 From 18 June 1859 to April 1864, he served as Secretary of State for the Colonies.

289 It is now 143°E.

290 *MBC* 20 May 1861 p 2. Note, the line eventually ran from Adelaide to Darwin and Java in 1872, OTL.

from the several offices held by him, considerable changes took place in the departments over which he lately presided; Mr Rae was appointed Under-Secretary for Public Works, and Commissioner for Railways. The Telegraph department was placed under the separate charge of Mr Cracknell, as Superintendent.[291] Then in June of 1861, the Colonial Treasurer proposed the following item in connection with the Telegraphic Department: "from Toowoomba to Gayndah, via Dalby with a branch line to Maryborough; and from Gayndah to Rockhampton, via Gladstone £22000." It was thought fair to give the northern districts the benefit of telegraphic extension. In extending the telegraphic lines, it was intended as the commencement of a further extension to the Gulf of Carpentaria.[292] Finally in November of 1861, Brisbane was connected to Sydney by electric telegraph.

With the opening of parliament on 2 May 1865, His Excellency Governor Bowen said "the colony would have a telegraphic line to India, via the Dutch settlements. A reserve of ten miles square, on a convenient locality at the head of the navigable portion of the Albert River, which flows into the Gulf of Carpentaria, was declared." The government appointed an expedition to examine and report upon the country between the Gulf and the eastern ports, with a view to the extension of the telegraph wires to the Gulf coast, and also to obtain up to date information about the country in the northern parts of the colony. To attain the information required, Mr F. Walker was to lead the expedition. A delay had, however, taken place, in consequence of nothing having been heard of the Jardines, absent above nine months, who had taken a party and their cattle overland to Somerset.[293]

On 7 March 1866 Mr Cracknell, the Superintendent of the Telegraph Department, left Brisbane for Rockhampton, for the purpose of meeting Mr Frederick Walker, the well-known explorer, who was about to select a suitable route for laying down a line of telegraph to the Gulf of Carpentaria. Mr Walker had now under his command a lightly-equipped flying party, together with an experienced line-repairer; and he will start

291 *MBC* 22 January 1861 p 4.

292 *Ipswich Herald and General Advertiser* 21 June 1861 p 2.

293 *The Brisbane Courier* 22 May 1865 p 2.

from Cleveland Bay. Rockingham Bay was at first selected as the point of departure, but it was found that many very heavy ranges could be avoided by the change which has been made.[294]

Mr Walker and party arrived in Townsville, Cleveland Bay on 17 May 1866 from Bowen, for the purpose of marking the line for the telegraph from Bowen to the Gulf. Mr H E Young, second in command of Mr Walker's survey party recorded in his diary as follows:

> May 17th. Shifted on seven miles and camped close to the sea beach within half a mile of Townsville.
>
> May 18th to June 5th. Camped at Townsville, Cleveland Bay. Mr Walker had horses shod and got supply of rations. About seven miles from our camp there was a camp of about thirty black gins, the most decrepit and miserable looking objects I had ever seen. Two of the youngest and best looking of these gins took a great fancy to two of our black boys, who requested that they might be allowed to accompany us to the Gulf. This request Mr Walker would not accede to, much to the disappointment of the parties concerned; so much so that one of the boys eloped with the lady of his choice who unfortunately possessed only one eye but was recaptured after a short time. This affair gave rise to an unfounded rumour and an article appeared in the Cleveland Bay Express stating that the blacks had been bold enough to come into our camp and steal one our blackboys.[295]

The *Brisbane Courier* of 18 June 1866 retold the incident as follows:

> THE BLACKS. We are informed that the blacks paid a visit to Mr Walker's camp on Thursday morning, and took one of his native boys with them. A party, well-armed, started in pursuit, immediately the discovery was made. The party returned in the afternoon, having been successful in finding the missing lad.[296]

Mr Walker and his party arrived in Burke Town at the end of October 1866 from Townsville. Mr Walker did not speak favourably of the road and stated that there was no timber along it fit for telegraph posts. His

---

294 *Sydney Mail* 17 March 1866 p 10.

295 Report from the Superintendent of Electric Telegraphs on the condition of his department/Department of Electric Telegraph, Brisbane: Govt. Printer, 1867, Appendix C No 2.

296 *The Queenslander* 23 June 1866 p 8; *The Brisbane Courier* 18 June 1866 p 4.

party suffered severely from sickness.[297] Frederick Walker died in camp at Floraville, Leichhardt River, on 19 November 1866. The following is a great obituary of Frederick Walker:

> We subjoin a short biography of one who, in many respects, was a man of great intellect, if not a genius. His father was an officer in the English army and occupied a good position as a landed proprietor it one of the counties of England.
>
> Frederick Walker came to the colony of New South Wales many years ago and began his career as a "colonial experience youth" with Mr Wentworth, the well-known old colonist of New South Wales. Mr Walker is described by those who knew him then, as a tall, handsome, yellow-haired, blue-eyed Saxon, the beau ideal of a pure Anglo-Saxons. He was after-ways and for some years, engaged as Clerk of Petty Sessions at a township on the Murray, and subsequently organised the Native Mounted Police Force. He selected his boys from the Murray tribe, and trained them to become expert horsemen, smart soldiers, and intelligent members of a most, efficient and serviceable force. These boys remained true to their leader from first to last, through good report and bad report. This was owing to the fact that Mr Walker had the rare gift of managing in a complete manner the aboriginal population. His slightest nod was a command which none ever dreamt of disregarding. There is no doubt, however, that he ruled his black boys more through love than fear. Much has been written and spoken about Mr Walker's harsh dealing with the blacks, but we know from actual experience that the aboriginal race ever found in him an indulgent rather than a discriminating or just master. So far as respects the half-dozen of Murray boys who remained with him throughout his chequered career, it may be truly remarked that they belonged to him. It has been said that the only secure method of dealing with the native population of this country is to place implicit confidence in them. This was the plan Mr Walker invariably adopted, but if his confidence was betrayed, the constant state of armed peace, which was his normal condition in the bush, enabled him to teach his assailants a lesson which was leant in one sitting. Mr Walker's career as commandant of the Native Police force was everything that could be wished. His was a nature and intellect beyond the average of humanity. His intellect was keen, his brain capacious, but, like many others similarly gifted, he was in-

297 *The Queenslander*, 17 November 1866, p 6.

capable of descending into minute details of schemes which, in the gross, he sketched with great power of mind. He had every sense but common sense. His enthusiasm in the planning and carrying out his schemes of exploration was combined with a wonderful energy; and although a want of business arrangement in the police accounts terminated in Mr Walker resigning his appointment as commandant of the force, still all who knew him at that time assert that the corps was in a better state of discipline and efficiency then ever it has been since. After resigning his connection with the force, he had created a number of the boys who had come to Moreton Bey with him accompanied him to the station of Serocold and Mackenzie, on the Cockatoo Creek, on the Dawson River. There, with a kind friend of a congenial taste, Mr Serocold and the ex-commandant drew up a plan of exploration, in which it was proposed to examine the heads of the Comet River described by Leichhardt; but at that time known only to a few men, such as Landsborough, Gregory, and others of like tastes. Mr Walker, accompanied by Mr Wiggins and three black boys, one of whom was named Peabody, succeeded in discovering large tracts of good pastoral country lying on the slope of the Main Range and Carnarvon Range; and after two months' exploration in these parts turned homewards towards Cockatoo. During his homeward journey, as he was in camp one night near Aldis' Peak, in the Zamia Valley, he was attacked by the blacks of the country through which he was travelling and received two severe spear wounds. His description of the attack, from his own lips, divested of irrelevant matter, may not be out of place in this notice; it was given to the writer on the spot where the occurrence happened. Mr Walker and party were in camp all day, chiefly for giving the explorers, or as they were called at this period, "run-hunters", leisure to work up their route and trace their maps. While Walker and his companions were thus engaged, the blackboy, Peabody, asked Mr Walker for his guns to go and shoot kangaroo, and the request was granted. Sundown came, and the boy did not return, and some uneasiness was felt thereat; but Walker's disposition could not allow him to feel uneasy in his mind for any lengthened period, consequently he fell asleep, and towards midnight he was awakened with a shower of spears and nulla nullas falling in his tent. He arose on his elbow, and saw his black boy Jamie Sandeman, who had been asleep in front of the tent, grappling with another blackfellow, with all the fierceness of murderous hate. Jamie succeeded in throwing his foe on the fire. Mr Walker by this time had fired a shot at another blackfellow, and this was a signal for a hasty retreat. Mr Walker, however, was badly wounded, and his journey from this spot to Scott and Thompson's station, at Palm Tree Creek, was slow and painful. Shortly after Mr Walker recovered of his wounds. What is known as the Hornet Bank massacre occurred, and he, at the request of Mr Andrew Scott, along with his boys, Coreen, Jamie, Rodney, &c., took up his abode on Hornet Bank, and lent his powerful aid in preventing outrages by the blacks during these troublous (sic) times in that locality. Subsequently Mr Walker by arrangement with Mr Daniel Cameron, of Planet Downs, Comet River, undertook to settle the station known by the name of the Planet Downs. His faithful boys still went with him, and while at Planet Downs Mr Walker received a commission from a company in Sydney to find a tract of country capable of depasturing 100,000 sheep. This he found on the Barcoo waters, which, if he was not the first to ride over, was by his description and exploration opened up for occupation. Up to this period his claims as a bushman were well known and recognised on every side, and the occasion arose when his qualifications as an explorer of the pathless woods were to be tested. He received instructions from the Victorian Government to start out in search of the ever to be lamented Burke. It is not necessary to go fully into the circumstances of this journey. The narrative written by himself has been extensively perused, and those who studied the subject most, grieved very deeply that Walker, misled by a marked tree, and altered his course and that of his party, so as to preclude the possibility of following up the tracks he crossed. His services on this occasion were fully recognised by the Victorian Government, and the Royal Geographical Society of London; what before had only been known to a few intimate friends then became patent to the whole world, viz., that Mr Walker was not simply a bushman, but a man gifted with every qualification to enable him to become a great practical explorer. Our readers will remember that some months ago, Mr Walker was appointed by the Government of Queensland, to find out and mark a route for the erection of a telegraph line between Port Denison and Burketown. In the accomplishment of this commission poor Walker has died, we have not heard under what circumstances, but we may surmise that he died in his tent, surrounded by some of the boys he brought from the Murray River; those boys who had known him in his days of social exaltation and humiliation. Of this, one thing, however, we are well assured that in whatever circumstances Frederick Walker died he resigned his latest breath with that fortitude and heroism which have characterised every incident of his chequered career. (Contributed to the Guardian)[298]

Further and better particulars surrounding the death of Frederick Walker was obtained from the *Northern Argus*:

Our respected townsman, David Perrier, Esq., has kindly placed at our disposal some very interesting particulars connected with the death of Mr Frederick Walker, the explorer, and leader of the expedition which it will be remembered, was started under his auspices to mark a telegraph line from Cardwell to the Gulf. The communications referring to this subject are from the pen of Master William Henry Perrier, who is attached to the expedition, and to whom we are indebted for very interesting details very well told. In writing to his father, he says:

Burke Town, November 2, 1866.

We arrived at this place about three weeks ago, and on the second day of our arrival Willie Ewan was taken ill with the Gulf fever and had to be taken into town to the hotel, where he was laid up for ten days. For the first two or three days, I kept all right, and then got the fever. I had it frightfully bad. I was obliged to stop at the camp for the first five days, during which time I lost my speech, and I had also a sort of lockjaw. I had to live on port wine and eggs, and the only way I could get it into my mouth was by forcing a knife between my teeth and forcing my mouth open, but I managed to get into the public-house and am a great deal better in consequence of the care I received. At one time, I thought I should never see home again. Mr Walker has been very ill also with diarrhoea, which reduced him so much, that he was unable to rise without assistance, but he is now getting much better. The whole of the camp have been ill with the exception of Mr Herbert Young. Mr Walker has been very kind to us, only for him I should have been compelled to have drawn more money than I have done. I drew a £9 order, which went in about five minutes. We have had a very easy trip out, plenty of water the whole way; lost two horses on the journey, one bogged the other we could not find a trace of. Mr Walker and I go out to the camp this evening and make a start for home to tomorrow.

298 *Queensland Times, Ipswich Herald and General Advertiser* 22 December 1866 p 4.

We have had some good fishing with the net I made, and as for shooting it is superb-I've knocked over eighteen flocks of pigeons in two shots, &c., &c.

The second letter is dated some eighteen days later, November 20 which makes the date of Walker's death, as telegraphed from Bowen on the 16th incorrect. The letter contains the following:

Leichhardt River, 20 November 1866

It is with extreme grief that I have to inform you of the death of our dear friend Mr Walker, which sad event took place yesterday morning about 1 o'clock, from extreme weakness caused by repeated attacks of diarrhoea. He was for some time suffering in town but got so much better that he wished to start on the homeward trip. We had proceeded about thirty miles on the road when he was taken ill again. We were a week making sixteen miles to Mr McDonald's station. He was seriously ill when brought to the camp, the doctor from the Leichhardt Search Expedition came to see him and did not think there was any danger; he prescribed for him, but his stomach was too weak to retain anything. He lingered on three days at the camp, and on the morning of the fourth day Miller and I were going for the doctor, when one of the men asked us to see him before we went, as he thought he was dying. When I got to the tent door I remarked his strange colour, and upon kneeling down by his side found he was quite dead. We believe that he was unconscious for an hour before he died. He seemed to pass away calmly, and he looked as though he was sleeping. We had to bury him the same afternoon, Mr Young reading the burial service over him. We fenced in his grave today and intend placing a rude tablet at the head to mark the spot, with the words, *Sacred to the memory of Fred. Walker, explorer.* It is a most sad event, and we feel it deeply. It is only a week ago, that Mr Sloman, the leader of the Leichhardt Expedition, died within six miles of our camp. This is a frightfully unhealthy place. I shall rejoice when I see the last of it. Mr Young now takes command of the expedition and intends taking the party to Rockingham Bay by the road which from the reports we have of it, seems to be the most practicable route, as there is good timber and plenty of water. Our outward route has proved a failure, there being no timber for telegraph or general purposes. We are at present delayed here, most of the horses being lost, but as soon as we recover them we will show the place our backs. We expect to be in Rockingham Bay within two

> months from this date, so you may expect to see us about the latter end of February, 1867.
>
> Game is also plentiful here, Alligators ditto. Some fine specimens came up and looked at us from the depth of the waterhole where we were camped. I remain, W. H. Perrier. I have taken a sketch of Burke Town, which I propose having lithographed.[299]

The *Rockhampton Bulletin* was able to obtain further correspondence relating to the Walker expedition which was published as follows:

> WE (*Rockhampton Bulletin*) have been favoured with a perusal of a letter received last week by our respected townsman, Mr David Perrier, from his son William, the youthful companion of the late Mr Walker. The letter is dated Rockingham Bay, February 10th. The writer says: "We had a fair trip from the Leichhardt River here. We had to camp at the Flinders for a week, in consequence of heavy floods in it. Mr Young and I had a good deal of swimming to find a crossing. I lost my mare Traviata and left two black boys behind to pick her up, but they didn't succeed. One of the boys got ill and has since died. He might have recovered, but in crossing the Norman, which was also flooded, he kept too low down, and he, with his horse, went over a precipice into deep water, and got a thorough wetting.
>
> He remained in his wet clothes until he got into camp, and the result was an attack of fever, to which he succumbed. We spent a miserable Christmas; it was very wet; we had neither currants nor raisins and had to celebrate it on very hard salt meat, but we hope to do so when we get to Rockhampton, in a month or two.
>
> Mr Young has received a telegram, directing us to go on to Port Denison without delay. We passed through the Valley of Lagoons country on our way here. The head station is very pretty, with fine buildings like Gracemere. The Coast Range is frightfully steep, but the views from different points of it are extremely beautiful.
>
> The scrub is very thick and quite dark inside, in consequence of beautiful palms, which tower up for a hundred feet without a branch or leaf, and then burst out at the top in one large cluster, and so close together that they form one large canopy. What between mountain rivulets tumbling down and the odour of different flowers, the place

---

299 *Northern Argus* 16 January 1867 p 3.

seems a paradise. Then there are some things disagreeable about it also; among the plants that are most disagreeable is the 'stinging tree,' which sometimes kills horses. The Native Police lost four horses from this cause. Poor Rocky, a pet horse, got stung and went nearly mad. I was obliged to walk to camp leading him; the poor brute plunged and kicked the whole way. There are also small vines called 'lawyers' and well they deserve the name, for when they once get hold you are fast, and it is no use trying to get away by main force as all your clothes are sure to be torn off. We intend to start from here in a couple of days for Port Denison. This is a small place, only about a dozen houses and very few people. The harbour is very pretty and well sheltered; it reminded one of Cleveland, near Brisbane. P.S. I nearly forgot to tell you how close I was to have been choked. Whilst running up the Gilbert we saw two blacks digging for roots, who, when they sighted us, bolted at once leaving everything behind them. When we got up to the place, I picked up one of the roots and tasted it, when my mouth and throat swelled to such a degree that I was nearly choked and did not get over it for a week. We saw a large mob of blacks on the Lynd, but they were very harmless.[300]

Mr William Perrier has furnished a Rockhampton paper with further material concluding the narrative of the proceedings of the exploring party sent out by the Government under the leadership of the late Mr Walker to discover a practical route for the Queensland electric telegraph from the east coast to the Gulf of Carpentaria: "On the 7th or 8th of February the party, consisting of four white men, under the leadership of Mr Young, who took the command after the death of Mr Walker, and three black boys, all in very good health, started from Rockingham Bay on their return to Port Denison. They had twenty-seven horses and plenty rations. About ten o'clock on the evening of the 2nd March 1867, whilst camped on some low flat ground, about thirty miles on this side of Cleveland Bay, they felt the first shock of the cyclone which broke over that district. The gale increased during the night, and during Sunday their tents were all blown away, and they were obliged to put up gunyahs to break the force of the wind. The waters of the lagoon near which they were camped rose rapidly and swamped the camp, destroying the entire stock of tea and sugar. The map of the route out was also, unfortunately, thoroughly soaked and completely destroyed.

300 *The Brisbane Courier* 25 March 1867 p 3.

> This was a great loss; it was carefully prepared by young Perrier and showed minutely the different features of the entire route outward to Burketown. He afterwards prepared a plan of the inward route, which, being made on dead reckoning, though sufficiently close for all ordinary purposes, cannot be compared to the other plan in accurate details. The party shifted to higher ground on the Sunday evening, when the storm had somewhat abated, and the next morning moved to the foot of a neighbouring range, each man humping a bag of flour. Though great trees were blown down, and branches were flying in showers, no accident occurred to any of the party. Starting from this point they arrived at the Burdekin, which they found running bank high, and were obliged to camp there for a fortnight before it was safe to cross. Even then they had to swim the horses over. At the end of four days they got into Bowen all safe, where Mr Young discharged the party. The leader left Bowen for Gladstone by the Boomerang, en route for Brisbane, to report the result of the expedition, taking with him the journals and papers of the late Mr Walker. Mr Perrier came down with the three black boys and Mr Ewan in the same steamer to Gladstone, and arrived there in an open boat, the Darling, on Tuesday, looking none the worse for the hardships he has endured."[301]

In some quarters, it has been suggested that Gulf fever may have been typhus. However, Mr Walker's symptoms don't reconcile with typhus. From Walker's log, it is painfully apparent that Walker was seriously ill when he started the survey. On 2 August, he reported: "I was very bad with diarrhoea all day; 9 August: My complaint is getting worse again; 15 August: To-day's work has been too much for me, and I am both sick and weak; and then he said on 23 August: Last night first one since 15th that I took no medicine." This suggests to me that Walker had a pre-existing medical condition which he was treating. Given his major symptoms were very ill with diarrhoea and his strange colour, together with Herbert Young's log as follows:

> November 19. On reaching the camp I received with great surprise intimation of the death of our leader, Mr Walker. When leaving the camp on the previous morning I went to see him and thought he was improving. He requested me to give him a glass of spirits before I started, which I desired Perrier to do, after assuring myself that

301 *Queensland Times, Ipswich Herald and General Advertiser* 21 May 1867 p 6.

> he had only taken one glass that morning. I was allowing him four glasses a day with some port wine in food by the Doctor's advice. Garling who attended on Mr Walker that day informed me that towards evening he appeared to get much weaker and during the night was talking in a delirious manner in his sleep but towards morning became quiet. It was then that Garling became alarmed and called Perrier and Ewan who thinking he was faint for want of nourishment (for he would take nothing but a little arrowroot or corn flour) fed him some stewed quail. About dinner time observing a great change for the worse they gave him a few drops of sal volatile and a gentleman was requested to come from the station and see him. This gentleman came but stated that he did not think Mr Walker would live through the day. As soon as the horses were brought up and a couple saddled Perrier and Ewan were starting for the Doctor of the Leichhardt Search Expedition which was camped about six miles off but he died before they mounted. He died at noon and was buried on the evening of the same day. I read the burial service over his remains. The funeral was attended by nine persons, besides those belonging to the camp.[302]

I am of the view that Walker was suffering from cirrhosis of the liver and died of complications arising from that condition.

***

[302] Report from the Superintendent of Electric Telegraphs on the condition of his department / Department of Electric Telegraph, Brisbane: Govt. Printer, 1867, Appendix C No 2.

JOURNAL OF F. WALKER, ESQUIRE, LEADER OF EXPEDITION SENT TO EXPLORE SUITABLE ROUTE FOR ELECTRIC TELEGRAPH LINE FROM CARDWELL TO THE ALBERT RIVER.

June 20 – This day we left Dalrymple. We made a very bad start, owing to four of the horses not being found until two o'clock in the afternoon; this is invariably the case when we camp near a township. My first object was to get over a piece of country, either basalt or lava. We first had to go one mile and a half west-north-west by compass, to clear a bend in Fletcher's Creek; but first I marked a tree FW Tel 20 June. (I think it would be best not to follow my marked lines for this first mile, but to take the telegraph lines from that tree under the foot of the basalt ridge.) We now went three and a half miles west-south-west, crossing several small anabranches; one-mile south-west brought us across Fletcher's Creek to camp, and I caused a tree to be marked Tel 1. The trees are well blazed all along the line. I had instructed Merrywether to report every evening as to the timber, and he has been of much use to me, as my attention is too much taken up by keeping the proper course, and I cannot attend as much to the timber as I would wish. His report to-day is that there is sufficient good timber; but the hardness of the basalt and lava will cause the digging of the holes to be an arduous task.

June 21 – A good start; at the end of half a mile, 30 degrees south of west by compass, we crossed McLellan's road; one mile more brought us to a long dry swamp; two miles more across it (a slight detour of a few hundred yards would clear this swamp, if deemed advisable); two and a half miles more, crossed a gully running to the left; one mile more, crossed a dry creek; half a mile over basalt ridge; three miles skirting another dry creek; and one and a half miles more to the end of to-day's work. I marked a tree Tel 2; in al, thirteen miles 30 degrees south of west. Merrywether's report very favourable as to timber; the ground easy to dig; the line well blazed. I now went five miles south to a creek, to camp; the Commissioner and I have agreed to call this Dillon's Creek.

June 22 – Got an early start; I sent Mr Young, with the packhorses, up the creek, with instructions to proceed ten miles and camp; I resumed the line from the tree Tel 2, proceeded six miles 30 degrees south of west, and crossed a dry creek; thence five miles more, and marked a tree Tel 3. Merrywether, who of course accompanied me, reported again very favourably as to timber; the ground still very good. I now went three miles south to Dillon's Creek, but, to my disgust, had to go two miles down the creek to camp, as Mr Young had only come eight miles. This camp is 36 degrees east of south from the tree marked Tel 3 four miles. We had a heavy shower of rain on leaving that tree.

June 23 – I only marked six miles to-day, 30 degrees south of west, owing to having had a late start; at the end of one and a half miles we came to the head of a gully which, I think, must empty itself in a lagoon, as we shortly after crossed a small tract of ground occasionally slightly flooded; I marked a tree Tel 4. I now went three miles south, to Dillon's Creek and camped; we had to dig for water, of which we got ample, my shovels and spade are now appreciated. Merrywether's report highly favourable.

June 24 (Sunday) – We camped to-day half a mile below our camp; found two waterholes which we had not noticed in our search yesterday; they are just below the junction of a gully, and I think are springs. This camp lies one point east of south from the tree Tel 4, three miles.

June 25 – Same course; at the end of two and a half miles, having crossed over a basalt ridge, we skirted a dry swamp, which we left on our right; four and a half miles more brought us to a sand-hill, where I marked a tree Tel 5. This has been another short day, owing to some of the horses not being found until nearly two pm; good timber; I went two miles south, when, observing the creek on my left, I turned half a mile east, and camped.

June 26 – Another bad start; I could, in consequence, not proceed further than five miles same course, when, seeing a beautiful lagoon, which we have called Charley's Lagoon, after one of our blacks, I turned to it, and camped. I carried the line on to the south end of the lagoon and marked a tree Tel 6. This lagoon is covered with wildfowl; timber not quite so plentiful, but abundant at the lagoon; sharp frost at night.

June 27 – I now turned my course west-south-west; at the end of three and a half miles crossed a creek, which I was not sure was the main one; at the end of two and a half miles more camped on a gully where I had found some water; marked a tree Tel 7; in the afternoon proceeded two miles to the top of a peak (still west-south-west); I called this Mount Tommy, and another adjacent hill Mount Paul, after two of my blacks; I had a good view from here; I crossed a marked tree line running nearly east and west; good timber throughout the day; thermometer at 30.

June 28 – Proceeded 10 degrees south of west, passing under north end of Mount Tommy; crossed the main creek twice; here the marked tree line seen yesterday ends abruptly; to distinguish it from ours a larger T is marked on our line where they join; three miles more same course crossed the creek again; had to go for one mile west-north-west to clear a bend of the creek, then west-south-west one mile, and 40 degrees south of west another mile, when I turned off to our camp; I feared when I saw it that we would have a bad start next day; timber good all day; marked a tree Tel 8.

June 29 – We were so late to-day in starting, owing to many horses being missing, that I sent on Mr Young with those that were packed to a more suitable camp, and followed with the others when they were found; I carried the line on two miles 10 degrees south of west, and marked a tree Tel 9; timber very good; sharp frost at night.

June 30 – I first went one mile 10 degrees south of west to clear a bend of the river, and then six miles 30 degrees south of west; I here had to make a slight detour of about two-thirds of a mile; crossing a deep and wide gully, one mile 25 degrees south of west, brought me to Dillon's station, where I marked a tree Tel 10.

July 1 – Sunday, and rest.

July 2 – Stopped to-day, shod many of the horses, went to top of rocks opposite Dillon's to take bearings, made up maps, and wrote letters.

July 3 – Not a good start; went first one mile 10 degrees south of west; crossed a gully at its junction with Dillon's Creek; three miles more to edge of dry swamp; one mile more crossed creek having Hand's station in sight; on our right also a sugar-loaf hill, of which I had yesterday taken the bearings; one mile 12 degrees south of west, crossed road; one mile crossed creek twice, and then the road again one and a half mile, having again crossed creek to top of basalt ridge; one mile top of high ridge, having for the last time crossed Dillon's creek; two miles more to top of hill of which I had taken the bearings yesterday; 12 degrees south of west two miles, over gullies and a dividing ridge; south-west by west two miles, over hill and gully, to large creek; 10 degrees south of west, four miles down creek, crossing it repeatedly; barked a tree ready for marking; left the line and went down creek, looking for water, three and a half miles; at sundown found none; turned the horses without hobbles down creek, and camped; I had four water-bags at starting and twenty gallons of water, so that the party were well supplied; timber excellent all day.

July 4 – The horses had luckily found water during the night but were not all collected until near sundown; moved the camp one mile to water.

July 5 – Mr Young ill with ague; I went to top of high hill or mountain to see the country, thence returned with Merrywether and three blacks to take up the line where I had left it; brought it three and a half miles 10 degrees south of west, under foot of the mountain, which I have named Mount Lookout, leaving in on our left; thence half a mile 40 degrees south of west to a permanent water-hole; marked a tree Tel 12; I also marked one Tel 11 where line on the 3rd; returned to camp (sharp frost); shod horses.

July 6 – I only carried the line one mile over a large creek at the junction of that which we had come down; I wanted to get as near to the foot of the Basalt Table as possible, before attempting it. Mr Young went three miles down the big creek, and reports that its course is southerly. (Is this the head of the Cape River?) Marked a tree Tel 13.

July 7–Went 25 degrees south of west one and a half miles up hills and over gullies; turned a little north-west to get on to leading spur; then 10 degrees south of west over table land and down into a ravine one mile (turn north-west a few yards); west two miles over table land to a very open gully; west one mile cross another gully; I now turned 5 degrees north of west to avoid a deep gully on our left, and proceeded four and a half miles, where we lunched; the last mile over a lovely plain. The table-top mountain which bore from last night's camp west-north-west now bears north-east. Turned now again west four miles over the tableland in to open downs, where we saw numerous tracks of sheep;

two miles more down open slopes to big creek; marked a tree Tel 14. Timber very scarce; the last six miles there is hardly any – I only saw one suitable tree, in the ravine above mentioned there is a large supply of good trees; but I believe that so long as a line has to be taken over the basalt, recourse must be had to the river oak, so plentiful in all the rivers and creeks. The objection is that they open by exposure to the sun. It would be cheaper to have them ringed with iron then to draw timber from a long distance. They are as straight as an arrow and will last any time. These must not be confounded with the forest oak, which is not a good timber.

July 8 (Sunday) – To-day Mr Young rode up the creek to the station of Messrs Muirson and Co; Mr Muirson and Mr Thompson returned with him; they told me that this creek, which they called Porcupine Creek, ran south into the Flinders, and that the other at Tel 13 joined this. I can hardly credit this, as I saw no such creek joining the Flinders. I saw to-day a considerable number of suitable trees for telegraph posts on both sides of the creek.

July 9 – Proceeded west for two miles; at the end of first two miles crossed new Flinders Road; the next two miles a plain was on our right; the next one and a half across a plain one mile more, another plain on our right; next one mile plain on our left, extending to foot of Mount Emu south-south-west two and a half miles more; crossed Flinders old road, and lunched. After lunch went eight miles 5 degrees south of west and turned off to camp on a creek.

July 10 – A half mile to top of downs (Mount Emu, 8 degrees south of east) one and a half over downs; were pulled up by a terrific gorge; tried for miles up it to cross, and at last made up my mind to find Anning Station, which I reached that evening; it is situated near the head of the gorge, at some springs.

July 11 – I had now lost one day and one half of the work done on the 9th; I to-day returned to where we lunched on the 9th; I here marked a tree Turn WNW, and blazed a new line five miles on that course, the last one and a half mile a little more northerly to clear a gorge, a tributary of that before mentioned; the line thence follows Anning's road three miles, a very little south of west to Anning's Station, where I marked a tree Tel

15; good timber very scarce, but plenty said to be four miles to the north-west; ample at Anning's Station. Mr Anning told me he believed that Porcupine Creek and the creek across at Tel 13 ran east of south passing near two mountains, which I had on my previous route called Mount Mayne and Mount Ward; if so, one is the head of the river called by me the Macadam, and that at Tel 13, the head of the Flinders (or Barkly, as it was called by me). His own station is without doubt at the head of my Dutton River. He mentioned two large creeks, one eight miles west-north-west, and the other twenty; one of these must be the Stawell.

July 12 – I went, accompanied by Mr Anning, eight and a half miles 30 degrees north of west to avoid gorges running into the Dutton, when we came to the first, where I marked a tree Tel 16; good available timber all day. As soon as I saw the creek, I had very little doubt that it was the head of the Stawell; the other creek, mentioned by Mr Anning as being twelve miles further, I have no doubt is a tributary of the Stawell, named by me the Weelgar Creek. I was confirmed in this opinion by Mr Young having after dinner, ridden three miles down the creek, and upon his return reporting that on an average its course was west-south-west (my 30 tree lies thirty-two miles' south-west); dreadfully cold night; ice in all the tin cans.

July 13 – I had intended to-day going ten miles down this creek to re-connoitre, leaving the pack horses in camp; but in this I was frustrated, as six of the horses were not found until 3 pm; Mr Anning returned home; to-morrow I intend following this creek as long as it continues south-west or west of that; if it runs too much south, I must strike off for the other creek; I shall fill all four water bags in case of my not hitting water.

July 14 – I first went one mile west, thence two miles south-west to the junction of a tributary, which we crossed; thence one mile west-south-west, crossing three gullies; south-west one mile; south one mile over spinifex; crossed another tributary at its junction west-south-west one mile; south west one mile to top of a hill; thence 15 degrees west of south to camp. Timber to-day good, principally yellow blood wood Tel 17.

July 15 (Sunday) – Rested; rode out a few miles to a hill under a mountain called by me after one of the blacks, Mount Alfred; Mount

Emu bears five degrees south of east.

July 16 – South by west 5 degrees one and a half miles, 30 degrees south of west half a mile, and south-west half a mile to the hill I had come to yesterday; after leaving this we made a vain attempt at first to reach the end of a spur I had seen yesterday; in the meanwhile, Paul found a route down a spur, which a little clearing, and the removal of a few large stones or rocks (sandstone), could be made passable for drays; 10 degrees west of south one mile to waterhole in gully; one mile same course to main river; one mile same course to camp. Timber can be got on the banks sufficient for this day Tel 18.

July 17 – Cleared point of range half a mile 15 degrees west of south; mountain called by settlers Mount Welcome and by me Mount Casinner, bears south-east; south-west one mile to rather an abrupt descent; west-south-west one mile down gully, and south-south-west mile to rather an abrupt descent; west-south-west one mile down gully, and south-south-west one mile to a rock basin in gully full of water; west by south down Bason Creek two miles; south-west by west two miles down same passing by a large waterhole; west-south-west one mile to junction with main creek; west-south-west one mile to Tel 19. It will be advisable to bring the line down the main creek, because the timber is ample on it, and not elsewhere.

July 18 – South-west half a mile; south-west by west one mile; south-west one mile; south-west two miles to N° 20. I have been anxious, because the creek has made so much southing that it cannot be my Stawell. I went out in the evening three miles north-west to range but am not satisfied.

July 19 – Went out reconnoitring and was satisfied; I must be on the Dutton.

July 20 – 5 degrees south of west five and a half miles to edge of a gorge; having crossed two creeks with available timber; thence half a mile north-west to a point from which I had a fine view; Mount Emu bears ten miles north by east; Mount Casinner east two miles north-west by north on to tableland three miles more north-west to a higher plateau, and two miles to what I believe to be the Stawell; unluckily, the last seven miles there is not a tree suited for our purpose.

July 21 – Rode down creek to examine; at the end of five miles crossed a large tributary; went two miles more and returned to camp.

July 22 (Sunday) – Mr Young, Charley, and I, went ten miles more and struck the tributary I had seen yesterday; I have since called it Deception Creek.

July 23 – 10 degrees south of west; crossed tributary three and a half miles; cleared swampy ground three miles south-west to a fine sandy creek joining main creek on left bank; timber on banks ample. Mr Young and William Ewan went out reconnoitring.

July 24 – 9 degrees south of west sixteen miles to a small lagoon; at the end of the first nine miles crossed a tributary, and another one and a half miles before reaching camp. I have been expecting to find my tree marked FW˯30 & RSV over 31 Oct over 1861.

July 25 – In twelve miles about west-south-west reached Henry's station, and found I was on the Stawell; my tree I had passed to-day. The questions now were what to do; on this river I have ample timber, but it is not connected with No 16; I have enough rations to carry me by rapid stages to the Albert, but I want to try back.

July 26 – Mr Young went to Macdonald's.

July 27 – Mr Young returned with intelligence that Macdonald could supply me.

July 28 – Stockman proposed to go to tree, and take me to it on Monday, I accepted.

July 29 – Sunday.

July 30 – Monday. Went with stockman, accompanied by Merrywether, John Paul, and Charley, 6 degrees north of east north-east three miles to waterhole on plain, 16 degrees north of east two miles to Wombat holes, 12 degrees north of east three miles to main creek, and one and a half miles north-north-east to junction of anabranch, where I found my 30 tree. Two miles more brought me to camp of 25th. I have been feverish the last few days. I attribute it to water at Henry's. Mr Smith, overseer, with (missing words) joined us.

July 31 – Went and dined at Reedy Camp and camped one mile above the tributary called Deception Creek.

August 1 – I am afraid of the Stawell, and therefore went eight miles north-east by east dividing the waters of the river and Deception Creek, but after that we met with awful gorges and rocks; found it impossible to lay the course down, and at last having had to cut through one mile of scrub had to camp in another without water. Horses tied up. My water bags came in well to-day. Mr Smith and overseer left us this morning.

August 2 – Got to a waterhole and having failed in getting down to the valley returned to it and breakfasted. After we had headed several awful gorges we found a gully, which led us in three miles to the Stawell; from the top, I had a view of Mount Emu, the bearings of which told me my position. This route is, therefore, a failure. I know that to attempt a line betwixt the Stawell and the Dutton is hopeless, and my remaining hope is the valley of the Stawell itself. I was very bad with diarrhoea all day.

August 3 – Went over the table land to the Dutton in twenty-two miles and found my 16 tree. Cut down this tree and marked a new one same number.

August 4 – Marked the line north one mile cross two gullies, one mile more to tributary north-north-west one and third miles to top of gullies (Mount Emu bears thirty-five degrees south of east), north-north-west one mile to open ground, two miles west-north-west by ten, one mile to head a gully, west two miles, north-west by west one and a half miles to head another gully, west-north-west two miles. Turned now south-west by west one mile, west one mile, south-west by west half a mile to top of falls, 10 degrees south, one and a half along top, south-west by west half a mile down falls, 15 degrees south of west down gully three miles to Basalt Creek, and south-south-west one mile to camp on Stawell. Marked a tree Tel 17. Still unwell, but a little better. Timber good all day.

August 5 (Sunday) – To-day was awful weak. I was disappointed, for after the first three miles the valley was impassable for drays, in fact, I could not have brought all my packhorses down it. It is a wonder how our party escaped without some accident. The river is nearly all basalt, and where it is not the rocks are pouring perpendicularly on both sides over the gorge. I was glad when at least we came out on to more open ground, not far, I thought, above where we had struck the Stawell first; below is the copy of my note book. There was no water all the way after the first two miles; this is very discouraging. I am still unwell and getting weak. South-south-east two miles, south-south-west one mile to top of gap, south-south-west one mile down gully and over cliff, south one-mile bed of river, south-west one-mile bed of river, west-south-west two miles partly on left bank, west two miles, cattle tracks, west by south four miles, better ground but very heavy. 12 degrees south of west four miles ditto, west-south-west one mile, camp nineteen miles. Tracks of blacks very numerous. We passed by a large camp seemingly of last night's; a party is ahead of us but turned off to the right. Horses to-day much fatigued.

August 6 – Three miles 15 degrees south of west brought us to our old camp. I went on to the Reedy Creek and camped.

August 7 – Went to Lagoon and stopped three hours to rest the horses, and went on to Henry's, which we reached at sundown, but one of the horses knocked up, the others were nearly so, found Mr Henry and Mr Quiny at station.

August 8 – The horses I had left behind were much improved, and most of their backs recovered. I am much better.

August 9 – I made up my maps; the latitude of the 30 tree agrees to a hair's breadth with my former map, but in the longitude, there is some difference. I know, however, that on my former route I had allowed two miles too much easterly variation, and when I worked up this difference, it brought the longitude of the 30 tree exactly the same as on my present map. My only plan now is to bring the line down the Dutton from the 20 tree and I intended sending Mr Young to-day, but the horses were not mustered until sundown. My complaint is getting worse again.

August 10 – Mr Young started to-day with Fred, Garling, Alfred, and Tommy.

August 11 – I started with main body down Stawell and went and camped at an abandoned sheep station. Course to-day, 16 degrees south of west one mile; 6 degrees south of west three and a half miles; crossed a creek west two miles, 5 degrees north of west three miles; camp one mile above junction of Weelgar Creek. I am still bad.

August 12 (Sunday) – A little better.

August 13 – Went down to Macdonald's. I am very bad to-day, but better at night. Course to-day south one mile, west-south-west one mile, south-west three miles, south one mile; west-south-west one mile, south-south-west one mile; south two miles, 30 degrees west of south one mile, 40 degrees west of south one mile, south-west two miles.

August 14 – Rested and got better. Took in 200 lbs. flour, 70 lbs. sugar, some tins of jam.

August 15 – To-day the route has been tortuous, as there were so many roads. I followed the creek and reached the junction of the Flinders in eighteen miles. Met Mr Young and his party. Marked a tree Tel 23 (all the other lines are now trial lines except the Dutton line). To-day's work has been too much for me, and I am both sick and weak. Course to-day, south four miles, 6 degrees east of south one mile, south by west one mile, south-west one mile, south-south-west one mile, south-west one mile, south-south-west two miles, east-south-east one mile, south-east by south one mile, south-south-east two miles, south-west one mile, south two miles. Mr Young had proceeded according to my directions south-east and struck the Dutton in twenty-five miles; he there marked a tree Tel 21. He next followed the Dutton to its junction with the Flinders, about nineteen miles. He here marked a tree Tel 22. This is opposite, or nearly so, to the post office at Richmond Downs. Timber ample on the Dutton. Below is the course down the Flinders to Tel 23, at the junction of the Stawell. Timber sufficient.

10 degrees west of north	1 mile	20 degrees north of west	1½ miles
20 " north of west	1 mile	North-west	1 "
North	0½ "	West	5 "
20 degrees north of west	2 "	10 degrees south of west	2 "
30 " west of north	2 "		9½ miles.
	6½ miles		

August 16 – Made rather a late start. The river here runs south of west. I went west for six miles, when I came to the top of a box-tree creek. Followed it down west-south-west two miles and passed opposite a sheep station west-south-west one mile, and went back a few miles to see the timber, which is sufficient. I am still very weak.

August 17– Merrywether and Willy Perrier kept the river to-day to look for timber, of which they reported sufficient. I first cleared a point of the river in one mile north-west by north; then along river one mile west-north-west; next west, one mile, passing by a sheep-yard; same course eight miles to camp near Pigott's camp, having crossed anabranches four times. Bad feed this camp Tel 25.

August 18 – did not get the horses until too late to start. Hobbled all we could.

August 19 – Move four miles downriver. Timber sufficient.

August 20 – Merrywether and Fred followed the river. I went 25 degrees north of west to a clump of trees, which I mistook for the river. I saw there a dry waterhole and sheep-tracks; 15 degrees north of west cross plain, passing by a dry lagoon, one and a half miles, same course; one and half miles to a small branch of a creek, which I sent Mr Young to look at; 5 degrees north of west, one mile to corner of branch creek; west, two miles; 5 degrees south of west five and a half miles to camp, on a very large anabranch of the Flinders. Mr Young reports that there was no timber on the creek he had examined. Merrywether came to camp late. For nine miles, he had found an ample supply of suitable timber, but the next six miles there was none. Marked tree Tel 26.

August 21 – Merrywether and Willy Ewan followed the river; I went west-north-west 25 degrees two miles, west by north four and a half miles, and lunched on anabranch, which we crossed; then west-north-west one mile; crossed a smaller branch west by north one mile; crossed another branch close to its junction with the large anabranch, which we left on our right; then west four miles to river; and north-west by north two miles to camp. Merrywether's report very bad, not more timber than might do one half of the way. Tel 27.

August 22 – North-west one mile, west by north four and a half miles; crossed the river by mistake and west north-west by west two miles to camp, at a splendid chain of lagoons abounding with clouds of corellas and flock pigeons. Merrywether's report as bad as yesterday's Tel 28. Chestnut pony, Lion, very lame on off hind leg.

August 23 – Last night first one since 15th that I took no medicine; Merrywether and Willy Ewan again followed river; I went 40 degrees north of west four miles; north-north-west three miles, north one mile, north-north-west one mile, and north-west one mile; horses, some showing marks of fatigue; the holes here very boggy, one mare we had great trouble in extricating. Merrywether reports no timber of any sort Tel 29.

August 24 – I intended only going a short distance down river, on account of Lion and the grey mare Daylight, but the river turning at the end of three miles abruptly to the west, I did not reach the lagoon at which I camped, under eight miles; Lion dropped behind on the route; Willy Perrier, with Paul and Alfred, who had followed the river looking for a sound waterhole, joined us two hours later; and Merrywether and Willy Ewan still later. Merrywether still reports no timber. Daylight had again to be drawn out of the mud on the bank of the lagoon; course, north one mile, north-west two miles, north-west one mile, west-north-west two miles, west two miles – eight.

August 25 – Poor Daylight had, during the night, got into the lagoon again, and was found, to my sorrow, dead; this morning some of the horses not found until near sundown as we had hobbled only a very few; I shifted the camp by two instalments, five and a half miles down the river, but four horses were still missing besides Lion. No timber. Course, west-north-west two miles, 40 degrees north of west one mile, west-north-west one mile, and 15 degrees north of west one and half miles Tel 30.

August 26 – Mr Young returned from Anderson's station, three and a half miles below our camp; he reports singular boulders of soda springs on the plains near here. I am getting strong. Three of the missing horses found this morning; Lion and grey horse called Marlborough are still missing; the four blacks went back in search; showers at dark.

August 27 – Mr Young and Fred went to station to look for a small supply of rations; Willy Perrier and Ewan mustering horses; blacks returned with Lion, who is still lame, they did not find Marlborough; Mr Young and Fred returned to camp. Heavy rain at night.

August 28 – Paul and Alfred started again in search of Marlborough; W. Ewan went to look after three missing horses; very heavy rain at night.

August 29 – Still showery; lots of fish.

August 30 – Paul and Alfred returned this evening; Mr Young and Fred went and got another sheep; Marlborough not found.

August 31 – Late start; went to Andersons and settled with him; course to-day north-west by north three miles and crossed anabranch north-west by west half mile to station, north-north-west one mile, north-west one mile, north-north-west one mile, and crossed anabranch north-west two miles, west by north one mile, west-north-west one mile, passed old sheep yards, and one mile west by north to camp Tel 31. Fine feed here for horses.

September 1 – Best start made yet – 5 minutes past 8 am; went fifteen miles to tent on anabranch; some of the ground very heavy sand; three and a half miles more to camp on anabranch near river; chestnut mare "Sundown" gave in last two miles. Course to-day north-west by north one mile, 40 degrees west of north one mile, north-west four miles, north-west by north one mile, north-west five miles, west-north-west one mile, and 5 degrees north of west to tent, west by north two miles, west one and a half miles to camp; marked a tree on the river Tel 32.

September 2 – Rest.

September 3 – North-north-west two miles outside the anabranch to river two miles more, leaving river from half a mile to one mile on our left. Mr Young had gone on ahead with the packhorses, and I here lost his tracks; I turned north by west, and at the end of two miles I overtook him, where I turned the party north-west to a small range I had seen; we reached the summit in two miles, having passed by a hot spring; I followed the foot of the range north-west by west two miles to another hot spring, and camped opposite a station belonging to Mr Gibson. The river is here about two miles off, and to the north-east; the Saxby is about the same. The water here is strongly impregnated with soda, lime juice causing it to effervesce. I saw some sandstone on the ridge, but it appears to have been heaved up by other rocks – some, I think, granite. I have taken a bottle of the water from the hot springs, in order to have it analysed Tel 33.

September 4 – Mr Young and F Garling ill with fever. Having been told there was suitable timber within seven miles to north-north-east, I went, accompanied by Mr Beardmore and Merrywether, but it proved totally unfit; we crossed the Saxby where the timber was useless.

September 5 – Horses very late mustering; we did not get away until the afternoon, went two and a half miles west to the Flinders, and followed it down one and a half miles north-west by north, and one mile west by north, until we found water. Tel 34.

September 6 – Some of the horses went back to the springs; I therefore sent Mr Young and Garling on with the first lot packed, before the heat of the day could come on, for the heat yesterday had caused with Garling a bad relapse; the next lot I stated with William Ewan, John Price, Paul, and Charley; Willy Perrier, Merrywether, Tommy, and I, followed, when Alfred had returned with the stragglers; we went nine miles west to a chain of lagoons, since ascertained to be the Gideon Creek or Cartive Creek.

September 7 – Four miles west brought us to the Cloncurry; I crossed, and W. Ewan marked a tree Tel 35; the brilliant reports relative to timber on the Cloncurry proved to be delusive; I followed it down five miles north-west, and had to camp, because a chestnut mare called "Sundown" showed symptoms of distress Tel 36.

September 8 – This morning it was found that "Sundown" had, during the night, given us a colt foal. Had this been the only instance, I would have killed the foal, but I knew that in a few days I should have two more. I therefore determined to rest to-day, and to put into execution a plan I had some time before thought of, which was to push on with a light, party, leaving Mr Young to follow leisurely with the remainder. This, however, I deferred until I should reach Palmer's station. During the day, in walking about, I observed several long tea-tree saplings, and also a few sound box-trees which would answer.

September 9 – Delay again in mustering horses; sent Mr Young on ahead, and also Merrywether, to examine the tea trees in the river; I followed late in the afternoon. Alfred told me that up the river from whence he had fetched the missing horses, he had seen several groups of tea tree saplings similar to those I had seen. On my way down on Mr Young's tracks, I found that at the end of the mile he had been obliged to abandon Sundown, as the foal would not travel; I observed several clumps of suitable tea tree saplings, and also several box trees, which would answer. The course to-day has been about north-west by north four miles to where I found Mr Young camped, Tel 37. Upon my arrival, I asked Merrywether what luck he had had, and was surprised when he told me that the tea trees were too crooked, for I have seen many on *established telegraph lines not near so straight.* He does not appear to have taken any notice of the box trees, thinking probably that they were not sound; in this he is mistaken, for my long experience in this kind of box tree enables me at once to distinguish the sound from the unsound.

September 10 – This morning I again started Mr Young ahead and followed when I had found the three horses which were missing. We reached Palmer's Station in fourteen miles north-west, having crossed a large sandy creek under a sandstone ridge, two miles before we came to camp; of this creek I had great hopes, as I had been informed I would find an ample supply of suitable timber, and I accordingly saw some very fine saplings of the size required. Merrywether, who had followed the river, gave a better account of his success to-day, but still says there was about only half the required quantity, Tel 38.

September 11 – Mr Young went to Campbell's Station to get some tea and sugar, of which we are totally deficient. Merrywether went to examine the sandy creek, and he reports good timber, but not plentiful. I was not very well to-day.

September 12 – Mr Young returned; Willy Perrier and I made up our maps.

September 13 – This morning the black mare June had foaled. I sent Charley and Tommy back for Sundown, with three day's rations; Willy Perrier, WG Ewan, Paul, Alfred, and I, started with three pack horses; I left instructions for Mr Young and the remainder to follow leisurely. Merrywether objected to my arrangements; stating that he had Mr Cracknell's orders, and that I was interfering with them. I told him, in reply, that I should do as I please, and not as he chose. I had been told he had said something of the sort previously, but I chose to take no notice of what I heard. My object is to travel as light as I can; and as the two boys share my tent, I only require one; besides that, Merrywether is the hardest man on a horse in the camp; however, by following me slowly, he can more leisurely examine the neighbourhood as to timber. On passing Mr Palmer's hut, he told me that on the river one and half miles at the back of the hut there was a dray road to it. We followed down the anabranch on which Palmer's hut is situated, and at the end of twelve miles, about north-west by west, reached the station of Seward and Marsh, at which place I was kindly received by their superintendent, and an old acquaintance, Mr Atticus Tooth; I saw not a trace of suitable timber, Tel 39.

September 14 – Followed the dray road to Campbell's Station, which we reached in seventeen miles, but we went and camped at a lagoon one mile higher up; here I met with another very old acquaintance in Mr Campbell, whom I had known in 1849 and 1850, on the Darling River. No timber Tel 40.

September 15 – Again followed the road for ten miles, when I turned off at a place I had been previously informed of, to a good waterhole with excellent feed; still no timber Tel 31. Made up my map.

September 16 – Rested, but Willy Perrier and I rode out three miles west to a sandstone ridge covered with spinifex grass, and saw what had been a large black's camp; from here, bearing by compass 15 degrees north of east, saw a range with two humps – one, the northern one, higher than the other; we found no timber notwithstanding we had been told that we would; marked a tree Dig, and under it buried an empty jam pot, enclosing a note for Mr Young; Paul marked the trees from this to the turn off at the road, and I marked a tree at that turn off, Water.[303]

[303] Report from the Superintendent of Electric Telegraphs on the condition of his department/Department of Electric Telegraph, Brisbane: Govt. Printer, 1867, Appendix C No 1.

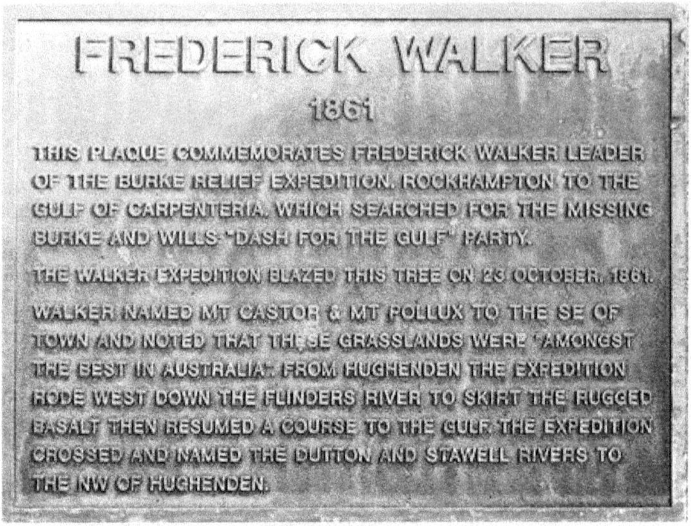

Memorials to Frederick Walker, Hughenden

10

Letters to the Press

To the Editor of the Moreton Bay Courier

Sir, Perceiving that in one of your recent leading articles on the subject of the native police, you state that you have heard from time to time of the services rendered by Mr Marshall and his party in the district of Maranoa, I think it right to inform you that neither Mr Marshall nor any of the police under his command have at any time been seen within the limits of this district, although their services have been and are urgently required, no less than nine men having been murdered, and thousands of cattle and sheep destroyed by the blacks. And further, although it appears from Mr Walker's letter to the Colonial Secretary, of date 31st December last, and published in your paper of the 29th June last, that "In the meantime (that is, during Mr Walker's absence in the south country) the original force of fourteen men will proceed under the command of Lieut. Marshall to the Maranoa district," you will probably be surprised to learn that when an official communication was made to Mr Marshall by the Bench of Magistrates of the district, requesting the prompt assistance of himself and party, his reply was that he had received instructions from his commanding officer to confine himself to the Macintyre and Condamine districts. I have merely troubled you with these remarks to show that this district is guiltless of having monopolised the services of the native police, which you and our fellow-sufferers at Wide Bay would appear to think has been the case, and remain, Sir, Your most obedient servant, W. Johnson, Bolloon River, Maranoa, 25 Aug 1850.[304]

---

[304] *MBC* 5 October 1850 p 2.

To the Editor of the Moreton Bay Courier

Sir, I shall feel obliged by your publishing the following correspondence that has recently taken place between the Colonial Secretary and myself. It may be interesting to the residents in the northern districts, and particularly in those more recently formed. Your obedient servant. Richard Jones. Brisbane, 5 December, 1850.

Richard Jones to Col. Sec. 5 October 1850

I do myself the honour to bring under your notice, for the information of his Excellency the Governor, the very unprotected state in which the Graziers occupying the northern districts have lived since their first settlement in them, and as a consequence, aggressions on the part of the black population are of constant occurrence, and fearful losses of life and property on the part of the settlers and their servants have already taken place. To convince you of some of their doings recently, I copy extracts from two letters, written in last month, and recently received here: "You will doubtless have heard of the murders perpetrated around me by the blacks; one employer and three men at different stations have fallen within a fortnight, and more than 2,000 sheep have been destroyed. Our curses rest upon the Government for so neglecting us, and at their door does the guilt of these murders lie."

The writer is known to me I put in the latter part of his paragraph, not in an offensive sense, but to let the Executive know somewhat of the feeling that prevails in connexion with these tragedies. "The blacks with us (near Maryborough) have not been more troublesome of late than usual, but up the country (full particulars of which I wrote you in my last; they have been carrying on fearfully. Corfield will, I think, be ruined by them."

The above paragraph is from a letter addressed to myself, but thanks for the want of postal communication, I have not yet received the letter said to contain particulars, although it must have been written six weeks ago. What is meant by the blacks being not worse than usual, is that whenever opportunity presents itself, they are sure to plunder, and if in their power, they will commit murder at the same time; I had a shepherd in charge of a flock murdered about fourteen months ago, and since then I have been plundered several times by the savages; in fact, the rapine is general. It was stated months ago, that two divisions of Native Police were to be stationed in the Burnett and Wide Bay districts, and when I visited those places in May last, the blacks were aware of it, and that they were soon expected, and became very jeering, but in consequence of the delay, they now think it is all gammon, and are become more daring in consequence. The Petty Sessions police is utterly useless, as regards the black population; in fact, nothing but a strong body of Native Police will restore and keep order in the frontier districts, and as the squatters are taxed for the purpose of such protection, I trust the Governor will immediately cause orders to be issued for this police to proceed to these districts, so that the lives and property of the residents therein shall have the necessary protection.

Richard Jones to Col. Sec. 21 October 1850

I did myself the honour, about, a fortnight ago, to address a letter to you, or the information of His Excellency the Governor, detailing a series of murders and robberies committed by the blacks in the Burnett and Wide Bay districts. I received on the afternoon of the 19th instant, a letter dated Maryborough the 1st instant, from which I take the liberty of sending you an extract. "Mr Murray has just had another man speared by the blacks, who have taken 300 of the sheep in his charge, and although the shepherd was on horseback he was completely surrounded by them, although well-armed. Three days since they murdered a shepherd of G. Scott, and took away 2,000 sheep, none of which have yet been found. Mr Bidwell has started in pursuit. There seems no doubt that all the present settlers in this district will be ruined. The murders and depredations committed by the savages are terrible."

I would renew my request for you to urge that his Excellency will be pleased forthwith to order detachments of the Native Police to the disturbed districts, it being the only corps useful for such a purpose; otherwise the residents will be obliged to take the matter into their own hands.

Col Sec to Richard Jones, 29 October 1850
I do myself the honour to acknowledge the receipt of your letter of the 5th instant, bringing under notice the unprotected state of the Wide Bay and Burnett districts, and the consequent commission of outrages by the aboriginal inhabitants thereof; and requesting that immediate instructions may be issued to the Native Police to proceed at once to the above districts.

2. In reply, I am desired by his Excellency the Governor to acquaint you, that the Commandant of the Native Police had, in a communication received from him on the 16th instant, reported his intention of proceeding from Callandoon on the 4th proximo, with the whole of the corps, through the Condamine and Dawson country and the districts of the Burnett and Wide Bay, for the purpose of stationing at the places most suitable for the public convenience, the detachments allotted for the protection of those districts.

3. I am, however, instructed to remind you, that in some of the instances of outrages committed by the Aborigines (that of Mr Blaxland for example), however much to be deplored, the parties who have suffered had located themselves beyond the protection and control of the Government; and his Excellency can by no means admit that the Government has in any case been guilty of neglecting to afford such protection and assistance as the means at its disposal admitted of.

4. Neither can his Excellency, I am further to add, pass over the offensive manner (although you deny quoting your correspondent's words "in an offensive sense") in which you have thought proper to put forward the coarse and undeserved reflections of your correspondent upon the conduct of the

Government, and which his Excellency must request, if you expect your communications to be attended to, may not be repeated.

Col. Sec. to Richard Jones, 8 November 1850

In acknowledging the receipt of your further letter of the 21st ultimo, on the subject of the outrages committed by the Aborigines in the district of Wide Bay, I am directed by his Excellency the Governor to refer you to my letter of the 29th ultimo, in answer to your previous communication on the same subject, dated 5th ultimo.[305]

To the Editor of the Moreton Bay Courier.

Sir, I forward you an extract of a letter from my superintendent and feel assured you will cause it to be inserted. I remain your obedient servant, John Stephen Ferriter, Kangaroo Point, 22 Dec. 1850.

Extract

Toomcul, Burnett District, 19 December 1850

No doubt you have received my letter of the 24th November, with the unpleasant news it contained, and you will have seen what steps I have taken respecting that calamity. On December 2, Mr Marshall, with ten of the black police, arrived here and one hour after his arrival an express arrived from Mr Bertelson's, with news that part of a flock had been taken by the blacks from that establishment. However, Mr Marshall informed me that he should first go in search of my sheep, and that I must accompany him if I wanted the sheep back. We started on the 3rd and, following the track about thirty miles that day, camped. On the 4th, about six o'clock at night, after having cut through four scrubs, and having made a distance of about fifteen miles, we came in sight of the blacks' camp unperceived. We immediately dismounted and rushed the camp; (the camp was surrounded with scrub). The blacks dispersed with an awful howling into the scrub, pursued by the police. When the camp was cleared, I gathered five lots of sheep, all, it seems,

305 *MBC* 14 December 1850 p 2.

parcelled off to the different families. The poor sheep were in a wretched condition. The following morning, we visited the camp again, and set fire to all their traps. We found some handsome maritime specimens, and plenty of nets and fishing-hooks! On the 5th, we returned and reached home on the 8th, with 256 sheep; nine I was obliged to drop on the road from wounds and injuries they had received. In all, I have got back 818 sheep out of 943. Since then eleven have died from injuries received while with the blacks. The unfortunate man, Dixon, I buried on the 25th November, when we found that besides the severe blows on the head, he had five small wounds. His carbine I have also recovered from the blacks.[306]

To the Editor of the Sydney Morning Herald

Gentlemen, with reference to a statement made in the Legislative Council by R. Jones Esq., on the 19th November, and reported in your paper of the 20th respecting the inefficiency of the Native Police, in the above district: We, as stockholders, feel anxious to bear testimony to their great efficiency.

The year previous to their arrival, the number of murders were four, and flocks were repeatedly carried off by the blacks; but, since their arrival here, there has been only one case of loss of life, and one instance of a flock having been taken, which was speedily recovered, at once establishing the fact that the Native Police are of the greatest service, and that the officers of the corps never shrink from doing their duty.

We trust that whatever unsupported statements may be made; the Government may not deem it necessary to withdraw a force which we consider so essential to the protection of life and property. We are Gentlemen, your most obedient servants. James and Norman Leith Hay, Gigoomgan, Wide Bay, 15th December 1851.[307]

306 *MBC* 23 December 1850 p 1.

307 *SMH* 24 January 1852 p 2.

To the Editor of the Moreton Bay Courier.

Sir, Are you aware that the Native Police were ordered into these parts, about two years ago, for our protection; immediately on arrival received such instructions as made the officers declare "they would not and could not act;" left soon after to go into Callandoon and winter quarters; remained until our annual disasters were over and nine or ten lives sacrificed; denied, upon their return that they ever said, "they were going away for clothing;" have the power of apprehending a native upon warrant, establishing an alibi and dismissing him, consider the whites (their employers) invariably the aggressors and to blame, and the blacks a very mild people; imagine themselves just the men for the "Kaffir war," "escorting the gold to Sydney," or finding Leichhardt;" cannot boast of what they have done, but what they mean to do; secure the peace of an establishment, generally for twelve hours after they leave it, but not always; find it quite as difficult to keep a prisoner when caught as to catch him; model their accounts of battles after the style of Napoleon's veracious bulletins. And are you aware, Sir that these are the men sent to obtain satisfaction for upwards of fifty Britons' lives, and to guard the remainder. I remain, Sir, in despair, your obedient servant, Melancholy, Mount Misfortune, March 24. [Of many of the circumstances mentioned we are not aware. Others have been before brought under notice in this journal. Our correspondent should furnish facts, dates, and particulars, on a subject of such consequence to the frontier settlers. Ed. *MBC*][308]

To the Editor of the Sydney Morning Herald.

Gentlemen, the Districts of Wide Bay and the Burnett are much indebted to the Messrs Leith Hay for the valuable information they have furnished regarding the efficiency of the native police. On all such doubtful points the testimony of an honest witness is beyond all price, and no doubt some future historian will find a word of praise for the faithful chroniclers

[308] *MBC* 10 April 1852 p 2.

who rescued the actions of this valiant corps from unmerited obscurity.

That the native police have been efficient in the Messrs Leith Hay's neighbourhood, I am not disposed to deny; I only wish some of their efficiency could have been spared for mine. It must be acknowledged, I think, that I have had some claim upon the sympathy and protection of the Government. My station is about sixty miles from the township of Gayndah, about eighty from that of Maryborough. The melancholy fate of my near relative and partner, Mr Gregory Blaxland, who rather more than twelve months since was murdered by the natives, not above a quarter of a mile from my present residence, must be yet fresh in public recollection. About a year before that lamentable occurrence, I had buried the bodies of two boys, the eldest fourteen years of age, who had likewise been slaughtered by these savages hard by the very spot where my late partner fell. On twelve different occasions have the shepherds on this establishment been attacked and their lives endangered by tribes of armed and ferocious savages, and their sheep taken from them by fraud or violence. On one occasion a hutkeeper was left for dead on the ground, and the hut, of course, plundered of its contents. The sheep lost by these incursions may be safely estimated in round numbers at more than a thousand, not to mention the destruction of other property and the many incidental losses and injuries inseparable from attacks by blacks, the nature of which every settler will understand, but which I need not endeavour to particularise. I cannot, however, suffer this opportunity to pass without most solemnly protesting, whatever may have been reported to the contrary, that the hostility of the natives was in the first instance entirely unprovoked, nay, more that the greatest pains were taken during our early intercourse with them to conciliate their favour and attachment.

Would you not imagine, Gentlemen, as this station is remote from and beyond all others and consequently, as experience has shown too well, more than all others liable to suffer from aboriginal depredations, that the most vigorous endeavours would have been directed by the authorities towards the coercion of the marauding tribes in its vicinity? Would not the security and welfare of this and the adjacent district seem to be involved in the pursuit and punishment of the leaders of those acts of murder and of pillage to which I have called your attention above? And, seeing that warrants have actually been granted by the Gayndah magistrates against seven or eight, if not more, individuals, how could the efficiency of the native police be better exhibited than in strenuous and persevering efforts for their apprehension? I am bound to acknowledge, gentlemen, that the native police have visited this station twice. The first was merely a visit of inspection, and the warrants remained unexecuted.

The second was made with a view to recover some sheep taken by the blacks from one of my shepherds. The greater part of the sheep having been found before the arrival of the police, for the natives only helped themselves to a few, no pursuit was attempted; and still the warrants remained unexecuted. On another occasion, at Maryborough, an attempt was made to apprehend two blacks, charged with participation in the offences committed on this station; shots were even fired, but the guilty parties escaped, and the pursuit was not continued for more than a few minutes. And this is all the protection and assistance I have had from the native police. It is quite true, as the Messrs Leith Hay have told you, that since the arrival of this force depredations by the blacks have not been so frequent as before. It is true that for ten months the blacks have not molested me and that I have lived so long, if not in security, at least without injury from their incursions. But I cannot in my own case allow the native police the credit of this. The aggressions of the blacks were checked before their appearance in this district, and I rejoice to be able thus publicly to express my thanks to my very good neighbours, without whose assistance I must inevitably have abandoned this station.

But, Gentlemen, I do not deny the efficiency of the native

police. There is no doubt they can be very efficient in certain quarters. Nor would I reflect with any severity on the conduct of the officers in command, for I am aware they are subject to the caprices of an ill-informed and prejudiced central authority, which seldom influences but to perplex and paralyse their activity. A despatch from Sydney, rashly administered, is said to be more potent in its effects than the stroke of a torpedo. I only wish the Government would distribute some of their despatches among the blacks.

The general impression here is, I believe, that good management is alone necessary to render the native police a creditable and useful body. The first lieutenant, who is on all sides well-spoken of, would, it is thought, make an excellent commandant and the present commandant a very good commissioner of Crown lands. In all cases of colonial mal-administration, the difficulty is to discover on whom to fix the charge of mismanagement. Wherever aboriginal aggressions remain unnoticed by the authorities, the Attorney-General is loaded by the settlers with a large share of the blame. Rather more than his fair share, I cannot but think, since it is obvious that not even the highest legal opinion ought to deter an intelligent and conscientious officer from a plain and simple duty. It certainly was not the Attorney-General's fault that last winter, when the two districts were tormented by the assemblage of large tribes of blacks, who did not disperse without mischief, the Native Police were engaged in an overland trip to Callandoon, to be provided with uniform, it was said. For this piece of folly, the Commandant was censured, how justly I cannot say; but it is evident his having taken such a step with or without instruction argues some deep-seated defect in the organization of the corps, which the Government is bound to remedy.

For my own case, I have not submitted to be neglected without having addressed some complaints on the subject to head-quarters and have been favoured in reply with a liberal amount of stilted civility and superfluous prevarication. To my last letter, putting a direct question, whether the warrants I have alluded to above would be put in force, the answer was, that "the matter was in the hands of the ordinary authorities." They do their work it seems, in what soldier's call "ordinary time." I am, Gentlemen, Your most obedient servant, William Forster, Gingin, Wide Bay, March 2.[309]

To the Editor of the Moreton Bay Courier.

Sir, Another tragedy testifies to the uselessness of the native police. More victims are offered up at the shrine of Government remissness! Possibly you may hear of the catastrophe I now allude to; but I do not suppose you are aware that the station where Mr Trevethan and his men have been murdered had for months and months been almost in a state of siege; and indeed, only a few days before this last case occurred, afforded shelter to that inert, inexplicable, and inferior "force," before alluded to; and consequently the painful inference must be drawn, how annoyingly inadequate, destructively inadequate, is this body of black men to prevent and punish crime, or preserve life. The awful sacrifice of our fellow creatures hitherto, and especially last winter, the woeful commencement of this, the impunity with which crime was committed, and the few, though sad, attempts ever made to bring the blood-thirsty wretches to an account, all too plainly fore-signified what a price we should have to pay in consequence. Within these few days no less than five or six stations have been robbed; at two, lives have been taken or attempted, and until we get some protection, some real and rational protection, these terrible times will continue. The infatuated Government, "Northern Members," and even the recipients of their liberality, will one day be ashamed of our past. And, pray, don't imagine because you seldom hear of our troubles that they are few: but be assured that we have long found it an aggravation of our losses to report them; and, therefore, our lives and actions are the

309 *SMH* 2 April 1852 p 3.

very converse of the fable of the "wolf and the shepherd." Mr Gregory Blaxland in 1850, Mr Ross and Mr Street in 1851, and Mr Trevethan already in 1852, ought to satisfy even the enemies of the "pioneers of the wilderness;" and those who are determined to persevere still in a black police experiment, should bear in mind that they have done so, and will do it, at the expense of men, women, and children, as well as much money. These be indeed sad times, when the Press, as well as the Government, slumber over their sadness. Yours unfortunately, Burnett River, April 5th, A Squatter. [Our correspondent is scarcely consistent in first confessing that the squatters find it to their interest to conceal these disasters from the Press, and then complaining that the Press slumbers over the events so kept secret. So far as the local Press is concerned, we have always observed the strongest possible advocacy of protection for the settlers. Ed. *MBC*][310]

To the Editor of the Moreton Bay Courier

Sir, Only a few days ago I wrote of some of the fruits of the mismanagement of the Native Police, and now I have the humiliating opportunity of adding further proof of the unhappy fact. A Mr Clarke is the victim this time, having been murdered at Mr Roache's station, only two days after the Police had left. How many of our fellow-creatures are to be slaughtered before you and the country will understand that in no instance have the perpetrators received a deterring punishment from those who ought to bestow it? In too many cases, the feeble acts and strange opinions of the black troops, have aggravated our disasters, and emboldened the causers of them; and it is expensively curious to know that where ever this "Little Band" moves to and from, there crimes are more frequent, and deeds the darker; and it is indisputable that since its arrival in our districts, murders, and robberies, have steadily increased in size and quantity. Five years' residence in the Northern Districts has taught me how easily these Aborigines are kept in

[310] *MBC* 24 April 1852 p 2.

awe—how little will keep them quiet. Two years' observation of the Black Police has demonstrated how incapable is that force to do this "little,"—nay, how mischievous, apparently, is their presence. A request from a suffering neighbour, to an "officer of a section," for assistance, is met by the (correct in practice) answer, "I can do nothing." An appeal to Government against the conduct of these men, brings back "the hope that the zeal of these officers in the discharge of their duties, will atone for any mistakes they make," or "offence may give." Whether we survive the coming winter or not, there can only be this opinion remaining, that in the northern part of this colony an Englishman's life is not worth guarding. As objects of experiment the Native Police answered very well, to see if savages with swords in their hands could save their lives: or perhaps they are to come out as the instruments with which the Attorney-General will work, in some ensuing session, for his darling project—the Aborigines Evidence Bill.

If you, Mr Editor, cannot assist us in getting adequate protection, or rid us of this "Force" (which should be spelt with an "A"), may we not induce you to agitate for our having a share of immigration? So that these districts may not be entirely left to the blacks and the black police. If the past month is to be taken as an index of the coming winter, our portion and proportion of souls to come will be about equal with those to go; and, even if they are not quite so many, will be acceptable. I need scarcely add that some of Mr Roache's men were severely handled by the natives. I am, Sir, your obedient servant, Burnett River, April 18, A Squatter. [While giving insertion to the above and declaring our continued anxiety to ascertain and give publicity to the truth on the highly important question alluded to, we deem it but an act of justice to repeat that merely general complaints are insufficient to sustain a case against any man, or body of men; and that particular facts, with dates, should be supplied, before a verdict of condemnation should be given by the public. Ed. *MBC*][311]

[311] *MBC* 1 May 1852 p 2.

To the Editor of the Moreton Bay Courier

Sir, I thank you for publishing my letter bearing upon the murders of Mr Trevethan and men and will further thank you to afford me an opportunity for making known that, that "inert, inexplicable, and inferior force" the black police, has totally failed in capturing, the perpetrators, nay given up all notion of doing so. The slaughter of Mr Clarke is evidently beneath their notice. And so, the last four murders, like the previous forty, are to pass entirely unavenged.

The "active zealous officer" (of your correspondent), with a degree of appreciable delicacy, has very properly retreated back to the locality where his conduct will be applauded, and his presence allowed. And yet, Sir, the diabolical committers of these late crimes upon the Dawson, are in undisturbed possession of sheep, the living residents and sufferers are not relieved, nor their dangers less imminent. This "active zealous officer" indeed, has well displayed THOSE virtues by his rapid march from the dangerous neighbourhood into the Wide Bay district. We ask, Sir, is this "Black Farce" to be put up with any longer? Ask your fellow townsman Mr Tooth if the police have ever been useful in protecting his station, and he will tell you "that so long as the natives can be persuaded to confine their peculations to his cattle, and their attempts upon life to his men, so long may his neighbours, the Messrs Hay, startle us all by their *Sydney Morning Herald* announcements."

I need not omit to say the police affirm that they came up with and shot the leader in the "Trevethan tragedy;" nor need I add that they are unbelieved. In a flight decrepid (sic, decrepit) old men and women invariably bring up the rear-the guilty and strong go before.

If a commission were appointed to enquire into the merits and demerits of this sadly managed corps, strange things might transpire; reasons would be ascertained why "Neddy" the assassin of Mr Blaxland was not apprehended, when pointed out to that "zealous active officer" by a magistrate? or from whence these melon stealing, garden robbing troopers, obtain their authority or orders to attack, and violently beat, our servants for approaching too near their encampment? If the same regulations require them to take possession of all the "gins" on the establishment, where they may happen to be for the night? Whether such acts are likely to promote morality, health, or quietness in our tribes, and particularly what promise, or return, do they make the husbands, in this unrestrained intercourse with their wives? These few are trifling matters to what might be elicited by such a commission; but I trust, Sir, sufficient to induce you to join in the feelings of three-fourths of our thinking community, that of all colonial jobs the black police is the greatest, and no one can deny the darkest. I am, Sir, Your obedient servant, A Squatter, Burnett River, May 11.[312]

To the Editor of the Moreton Bay Courier

Sir, Through my interpreter, I learn, with satisfaction, that I have still some white friends in this district, and considering the annoyance my tribe has been put to by those rascals my own countrymen, called by the whites Native Police, I have ordered a letter to be written for the purpose of expressing my warm thanks to "Squatter," "Melancholy," and others, who I hope will not rest till they get those blackfellows that carry the "delumpy," and wear the red cap, sent back to their own land. Not being able to speak English, I have ordered the interpreter to put down on paper what I say, so that the white fellows may understand me.

Now, Sir, what right have the Black Police (as they are called in the last letter interpreted to me) to come to my territory, and stop or try to stop, my tribe from eating a few monkies when we feel hungry? Is not all the country ours, having descended from generation to generation, before we knew such an animal as a white man? And I am sure you will agree with

[312] *MBC* 29 May 1852 p 2.

me in thinking that the least thing the white-fellows can do, is to let us take sheep for the use of the grass. Squatter, in his letter, talks of crimes being more frequent and deeds darker. He also talks of fellow-creatures being slaughtered. No doubt he alludes to us, who have suffered severely from the Black Police. We have not half a chance to knock a croppy on the head and get off safe with a flock of sheep. If we try it, down come these savage police, and take the property, which is as much ours as the kangaroo is the white man's, and they always drop a few of us, only just because we try to defend ourselves or run away.

Pray, Sir, try all you can to get the Police disbanded. We long for the good old times again. The white fellows can't track, and we know some snug places, where we could kill and eat a few thousand sheep at our leisure, if it were not for these devils of Police. I am Sir, your obedient servant, Wangallibee, Chief of Wide Bar Camp, Burnett Range, 10 June 1852.[313]

To the Editor of the Moreton Bay Courier

Sir, Referring to a letter published in your issue of 29th ult., signed "A Squatter," on the subject of the Native Police, perhaps a few remarks may not be out of place, from one who has had as good an opportunity of judging and comparing the state of the northern districts as your correspondent, both before and since the appointment of that force, which has lately been so bitterly attacked in your Journal. Squatter sneers at the Police, in the first instance, because they go to the district of Wide Bay for the purpose of protecting a station which in another part of his letter he accuses them of neglecting. He refers you to your townsman, Mr Tooth, for the truth of some of his statements, but I would recommend you to apply to Mr Tooth's superintendent, who I should think the better judge and he will tell you that this despised force has been the means of saving the lives of his men and preventing the destruction of his master's property.

---

313 *MBC* 10 July 1852 p 2.

Your correspondent seems to think that Wide Bay is not entitled to protection; and because the officer appointed for that district, after a two months' absence in the Burnett, thought it his duty to return; another officer in the meantime remaining in the neighbourhood where the late outrages complained of were perpetrated, his conduct is sneeringly animadverted on.

Again, he states that the Police are not believed in saying that the leader in the "Trevethan" tragedy was shot, when it is a well-known fact that Mr W. Trevethan, who accompanied the Police, deposed that the black shot was Jacky, the ringleader in the attack on the station in February last, and he was sworn to by a servant on the establishment, as the leading man in the murder of Mr Trevethan. He was known to Mr W Trevethan for three years; therefore, he could not be mistaken as to his identity. With regard to "Neddy," the assassin of Mr Blaxland, he never was pointed out by a magistrate, as described by "Squatter," but the magistrate told one of the officers that a blackfellow, answering to the size of Neddy, was on his station, and the answer given was that if any person could be brought forward to identify him, an attempt would be made for his apprehension.

The report published in the Courier of the 5th instant, mentioning the natives having taken 270 sheep, together with pipes, knives, and tobacco from the Messrs Hay's men, is without the slightest foundation, and proves that your Burnett correspondent is hard up for news, when he has recourse to fiction. In conclusion, I may remark, that the police have a frontier of 700 miles to protect, with a force of only 40 men, and they deserve great credit for what they have done, considering their strength. I am, Sir, Your obedient servant, Fiat Justitia. Burnett District June 10.[314]

[314] *MBC* 17 July 1852 p 2.

THE NATIVE POLICE

Editorial: About two years ago, we noticed the experiment, which had then been recently commenced in the Middle District, of employing the Aborigines in the public service as mounted policemen. We had the pleasure of congratulating our readers on the very encouraging success with which the model attempt had so far been attended. The Commandant of the sable corps, Mr Walker, had found no difficulty whatever in raising recruits; on the contrary, so eager were the blacks to enlist, that he could with ease have obtained ten times the number he was authorised to employ. Nor did he find half the difficulty that might have been expected, in training them to habits of regularity and obedience. Contrary to all the received opinions as to their indolence, fickleness, and stupidity, they turned out to be commendably industrious, persevering, and intelligent in the discharge of their duties. Military occupation proved to be just the thing best suited to their natural prepossessions, and for which they had a sort of instinctive aptitude. They soon became expert horsemen, and in several desperate collisions with marauding tribes of their own countrymen, acquitted themselves in a soldier-like style, and came off with flying colours. We are glad to find that those hopeful beginnings have not been discredited by subsequent experience. The Commandant's report for the present year, recently printed by order of the Council, and published in our columns of last week, confirms the favourable representations to which we have been referring. It is now four years since that officer began the organization of his corps, and he reports that during this period, he has never witnessed one instance of insubordination, nor one of intoxication, or one quarrel amongst themselves of a serious nature. No bad language has ever been heard from them; they have been remarkable for their orderly and good conduct; and Mr Walker's attentions to their improvement have been rewarded by tokens of gratitude which, he says, far surpassed even his own sanguine expectations.

Now, one would have thought that this useful officer and his faithful troopers, maintained by the Government for the express purpose of protecting the lives and property of the settlers in the outlying districts, would have received from those settlers every possible encouragement and support. This, we should hope, has in general been the case; but we learn from his report that some of the northern settlers have given the Commandant much reason to complain. They are, it seems, dissatisfied with him because in his proceedings against the turbulent blacks he is not sufficiently sanguinary. His rule of action has uniformly been to proceed according to law. Before resorting to extreme measures, he deems it requisite that he should know a felony has been committed and have reasonable grounds of suspecting the offenders. And in every instance in which, through his endeavours to put a stop to hostilities, a death occurs, he deems it his duty to report the circumstances to the Attorney-General, and to forward depositions setting out the facts.

Every right-minded man will admit that in thus acting, Mr Walker takes the only course which, as a British officer, he could either consistently or safely pursue. Some of the "northern settlers" think otherwise. They have got into their heads that the Government, although they will not allow the squatters to shoot the blacks, have sent up the Native Police for the express purpose of shooting them. They are of opinion, moreover, that as the Government have taken the business into their own hands, they are bound to carry it, on without scruple, and even to evince "a certain amount of vindictiveness against the blacks." In short, their policy would be for nothing less than extermination; and because Mr Walker's policy stops far short of that root and branch extremity, they will have it that he neither performs his duty to the Government, nor affords to the squatters the protection they are entitled to demand. How any man of ordinary intelligence can be so perverse as thus to misjudge the intentions of the Government is really inconceivable. Nothing, surely, is more notorious than the fact, that "vindictiveness against the blacks" is as repugnant to the spirit of the Executive as vindictiveness against the whites. The Government, it is true, hold the blacks amenable to the law, and do not hesitate to punish them for its infraction; but they also hold that the blacks are entitled to the protection of the law, and that the murder of a black is not less a capital felony than the murder of a white. These "northern settlers" would do well to set themselves right on this point; and to understand clearly that if Mr Walker were to cause a single native to be put to death in an unlawful manner, he would to a certainty, on conviction, be hanged by the neck. Instead of finding fault with him because he will not thus trample on the laws of his country, and hazard his own life, the settlers ought to co-operate with him in every practicable way in seeking to put down violence, and to maintain order by lawful means. They must be blind, indeed, if they cannot see that by so doing they would promote their own interests, and that any other course can only serve to increase their troubles and their dangers.

We gather from the Commandant's report, that one fertile cause of turbulence amongst the blacks in the interior is the refusal of the settlers to allow them to come on their stations. Were they allowed to do so, they would, it appears, be separated into small groups, and be comparatively powerless; but being driven off, they herd together in large tribes, and are emboldened to rob and plunder for their common maintenance. On this head Mr Walker, says: "When the experimental force was raised, it was first sent to the Macintyre. With the exception of three stations, the blacks in that portion of the Darling Downs district were in a manner outlawed in their own country, being hunted from the river and creek frontages, and thus deprived of means of lawfully obtaining food. Driven to desperation, they carried on a constant war of retaliation with the whites and lived solely on cattle. So, accustomed were they become to this life, that force had to be resorted to, to make the ringleaders submit. The Native Police arrived in

May, 1849; in October, the settlers laid aside their weapons; the blacks were admitted everywhere at the stations; and a run which would not have fetched £100 in May, 1849, was disposed of in January, 1850, for £500, so much had property risen in value by the increased security of life and property. One settler told me, that for eight years he had expended £150 per annum on his cattle station, and now, for the first time, had a return from it in the shape of fat stock." So much for the advantage of a mild and rational procedure over rage and cruelty.[315]

To the Editor of the Moreton Bay Courier

Sir, Seeing so many efforts at wit and sarcasm published weekly in your paper, emanating, from the Wide Hay and Burnett districts, relative to the Native Police; I deem it but a matter of justice, as an exparte (sic expat), to say a few words on that head, and state, as far as my observations go the *Causa Belli.*

The squatters here appear to look upon the Native Police as a body of men sent to these districts for their special use, to be at their call at any time, and that the duty of the officers consists in seeing their views carried out, without any reference to their own opinion in the matter. I do not say that this is the expressed opinion, but still the feeling does exist.

When the police first arrived here they were warmly received, and actively cooperated with, and appear to have used their utmost endeavour to forward the wishes of the squatters as far as they legally could; but this was the point upon which the first misunderstanding arose. As far as I can gather, Mr Walker took the advice of the Attorney-General upon the matter and acted up to it. This did not please the settlers, nor did the arrangements made for carrying on the duties of the force, each considering that he had a right to the constant protection of the Police, which a little consideration would have shewn, was at the time impossible with but forty-five or fifty men, no

315 *SMH* 23 June 1852 p 2.

spare horses, and so large an extent of country as the districts of Wide Bay and Burnett. Finding, I presume, that it was useless attempting to give satisfaction to all, Mr Walker appears to have pursued an independent line of conduct, such as he considered best adapted to carry out the duties in the most efficient way. This gave still less satisfaction and several declined either receiving or rationing the police at their stations. An animus arose against them, and I must add that I think a personal dislike created a prejudice, in more than one instance, against the whole force. Their movements were criticised, and few endeavoured to cooperate with them, or promote their views in any way.

This is, as far as I know, a plain unvarnished sketch of the actual facts of the case between the squatters and the native police; about which I see so much sparkling wit from the pens of "Melancholy," (who, by the bye in not a bad fellow if he were not so prejudiced) "Squatter," and others. I remain, Sir, Your obedient servant, Glee. July 25th, 1852.[316]

To the Editor of the Moreton Bay Courier

Sir, For several weeks I have been most anxiously examining your papers, hoping to find that our fearfully increasing woes, our perhaps irreparable injuries, would receive notice from your Editorial pen; but alas! even your issue of the 10th inst. is at hand, and still no sympathy expressed, no word of consolation sent for our miserable positions. I suppose however, you have conned over Mr Commandant Walker's barefaced, ungrammatical, egotistical epistle, and admired his distant manner, and trust if you have that, it has convinced you how sad are our prospects of relief from the Aborigines, while such a man is at the head of a force, supposed to be employed in warding them off. As true as I am writing this our prospects are becoming desperate. I assure you they are, for Mr Herbert and Mr Landsborough have been "victimised" of sheep; Mr

316 *MBC* 7 August 1852 p 4.

Tooth and Mr Brown of cattle; three Wide Bay townspeople are found tomahawked into insensibility (left for dead) in their houses; and, worse than all, another man murdered at Mr M'Kay's station, and all within these few weeks. Ah, well do I remember that when we relied on our own efforts for saving life, property, &c., our losses were far, far less; but I am desponding, Mr Editor, for, in the words of a Poet:

I could have borne the slave's rude scorn, the wreck of all I cherished

Had one, but one been left to mourn o'er me when I too perished.

Persecuted by the natives; by the Government, by the letters and orders of Mr Commandant Walker, by the "active zealous officer's" joyful obedience of those orders: forsaken, nay attacked by the *Sydney Morning Herald* (vide their leader for June 22nd)[317], I feel we are now at the very last extremity, and though our remonstrances are going down to the Government and their toadies, and our properties to destruction, I fear all is too late. The sweeping charges (in peculiar English) made by Mr Walker against a body of colonists, in every respect his superiors, the adoption of those charges by our Government; the reception and retailing of them by the *Herald*, are all awful evidences of the necessity for "separation" at once, from their iniquitous part of this continent; and forgive me, Mr Editor, for complaining that yon have not done your duty to us. In your mind's eye yon know the bush, and the habits of its wild inhabitants. You are aware that the smallest amount of judicious and judicial acting, from any police, would stay the attacks of our tormentors. You have heard that we have a "Police Farce," and you must have heard that our disasters are increasing, then why did you not come to our assistance. Surely, "when all the world and our wives" (the Government old women) were against us, it would have been more noble (like the good sister Augusta) for you to have stood up in our defence, and stood by to beat off, at any rate one enemy, even if he were the "zealous active officer." Without labour, or the remotest prospects of any; without justice, or the recollection

317 This appears a typo by the author and should read 23.

of having any; without a single characteristic of happy old England, save perhaps of her workhouses, where the harder an inmate works the poorer he becomes, I close this dirge, and that I may be recognised, from all my fellow sufferers, beg to subscribe myself as the "individual" pointed out by the "Commandant" as the 10th "cause of difference between me and some of the northern settlers," and unfortunately A Squatter. Burnett River, July 22.[318]

THE NATIVE POLICE

Editorial: It would be difficult to exhibit a more convincing proof of the difficulties which beset the conductors of the public press in arriving at satisfactory conclusions on matters occurring at a distance, than is shown by two letters published in our fourth page. Both are from gentlemen known to us, and whose words, in all the ordinary transaction of life, would be considered sufficient guarantees; yet one reproaches us for not strongly condemning the proceedings of the Native Police, whilst the other contends that the charges brought against that force are wholly unfounded. The difficulty is increased by the fact that there appears no reason to suspect any personal ill feeling or hostility between the two writers. For our part, we can only repeat what we have before advocated. It is plain that some grounds of complaint must exist, or that some misunderstanding has arisen, which, for the sake of the efficiency of the Native Police, should be promptly and searchingly investigated by the Government.

The appointment of a Commission of Inquiry, on the spot, could not, under the circumstances imply any affront to the officers of the force, who might be glad of an opportunity to exculpate themselves from the charges brought against them; and on the other hand, such an inquiry would convince the settlers of the willingness of the government to redress any grievances that exist. This, then, is the course most likely to

318 *MBC* 7 August 1852 p 4.

have a beneficial effect, and the one which all who are most interested should urge upon the Executive. Another barbarous murder by the natives is recorded in our pages this day, and it is of the utmost consequence that those whose duty it is to prevent these occurrences, or, at least, to apprehend the murderers, should be established in the confidence of these whom they are employed to protect.[319]

To the Editor of the Moreton Bay Courier

Sir, Several letters from "A Squatter," on the subject of the Native Police, condemning in unmeasured terms the conduct of the force and its officers, have lately appeared in your columns. In this district, the writer is pretty generally known, as is also his aversion to public officers and those of the Native Police in particular. It is amusing to observe the facility with which your correspondent allows his feelings to blind his understanding, and how eager he is to gratify the former at the expense of the latter. This obliquity of mental vision enables him to distort facts into any shape most gratifying to his resentments, and, thus perverted, he presents them through your columns to the public. Here, where the writer's motives and peculiar bias of mind are well known, the letters are taken for what they are worth, and no more; but as you, Sir, and your subscribers generally, might give some credence to the statements of your correspondent, I shall take the liberty of answering his letter of 11th May.

1st. That inert, inexplicable, and inferior force, although it has not succeeded in capturing the perpetrators (upwards of 100 blacks) of the murders at Mr Trevethan's station, has not given up all hope of doing so; on the contrary, every exertion is still being made for their apprehension, and the surviving Mr Trevethan states, that had it not been for this inert, inexplicable, and inferior force, he would neither have been able to keep the blacks off, nor the whites upon his station.

319 *MBC* 7 August 1852 p 2.

2nd. Mr Marshall's (the active zealous officer) section of police is stationed in the Wide Bay District. Upon his own responsibility, he marched his section to "Rawbelle," Mr Trevethan's station where he remained until relieved by the section especially appointed for this district. What would the Wide Bay stockholder have said, had any outrage been committed by the blacks during his absent, had that been protracted to a longer time than the circumstances rendered absolutely necessary?

3rd. The Police do not affirm that they came up with and shot the leader in the Trevethan tragedy; but Mr Trevethan states upon oath that they did so. He saw the body and knew the man.

4th. A magistrate did not point out "Neddy" as the murderer of Mr Blaxland. The magistrate merely surmised that an ill-looking blackfellow, in a camp among other blacks, might be Neddy, and the officer in charge of the Native Police Force made every enquiry, but neither he nor the magistrate could learn that he was the man. This I had from the magistrate.

Of the other charges made by the Squatter, who, by the way, is a squatter without stock or station, I know nothing, but it is only fair to infer that they also are unfounded.

That the Native Police force is not as efficient as it might be and, I hope will be, cannot be denied. It is unreasonable to expect that either the officers or men, in a newly raised corps, should, in difficult circumstances, upon all occasions, hit upon the best course to be pursued. A knowledge of the service is only to be acquired by experience. As far as my own observations have gone, the officers have shown no ordinary seal in the discharge of their "duty". Every man is liable to err in judgment, particularly when cases without precedent spring up in all directions. Your correspondent, A Squatter, has stated in conversation, that with half a dozen white men he could keep all the blacks in the country quiet, yet I will safely assert that not only three-quarters but the whole of our thinking community is very sure that he errs, and that the inordinate self-esteem has, in this instance, capsized his judgment. Most reasonable men in this concur in the opinion that considering the limited number of troopers (ten) the extent of the district and the harassing nature of the country for horses, the Native Police have done as much as could well be expected from them and that the officer in command has shown very considerable ability in the discharge of his duty. Acknowledged that he has obtained a wonderful influence over the men and it is impossible to be in his company for many minutes with perceiving that the whole mind of a man of more than average talent and energy is beat upon the one object of rendering the corps efficient.

The object of A Squatter is to annoy the officers by disparaging the force. For this purpose, he has put forward surmises as facts, and, to gratify a paltry resentment, he would doubtless be glad to see the force disbanded to the great injury of all the stockholders in this district. I am, Sir, Your obedient servant, WHW Burnett River, June 24. [The publication of this letter was delayed for the real name of the writer, since received. Ed. *MBC*][320]

To the Editor of the Sydney Morning Herald

Gentlemen, In your supplement for the 16th June, appears a copy of a letter from the "Commandant of The Native Police to the Colonial Secretary," which contains accusations against settlers in these districts, of so unmerited, untrue, and yet of so grave a nature, as will induce you in common fairness, I hope, to publish the following refutation by one of the accused, and I will premise the remarks by saying it is hard to comprehend how the Government and yourselves can tolerate, much more be deceived into believing such representations against a body of men, who are quite the equal of their accuser in the ordinary walks of life, and his superiors in its ennobling characteristics. This (Mr Walker's) shameful letter is the unjust return for the unbounded liberality and hospitality my neighbours have shown

320 *MBC* 14 August 1852 p 2.

to the Native Police officers; a hospitality extending even to the winking at most glaring faults! —the sad consequences of which we have daily evidences.

N° 1 and 2 "Causes of a difference between me (Mr Walker) and some of the northern settlers!" should have been rendered intelligible by naming the latter.

N° 4 states that we do not try to procure evidence upon which the police can act and is untrue, because there are scores, and perhaps hundreds of warrants out from our two benches and must have been all issued from depositions made before Magistrates.

N° 5 is too coarse to require, (I hope) answering. 6, 7, and 8, are very well; but N° 9 ambiguous, for I cannot see, "because it was resolved to try the experiment of a Native Police force on a small scale, and the forming of such a corps was entrusted to me, (Mr Walker) that it should be one of the causes of differences between me and some of the northern settlers."

N° 10 is "Exeter Hall," like and met by my request to know from Mr Walker whether troopers sent out to find stray horses—themselves straying 50 miles to, and getting drunk at Maryborough, returning from there disunited and disgraced, is not a direct contradiction to it.

N° 11 is also incorrect; unless sending the troopers without an officer, to apprehend a man for breach of the Masters and Servant's Act, is felony; moreover, "the Attorney-General is (not) the best judge whether I, (Mr Walker) have acted legally or not," for he does not know all.

N° 12 is answered by my statement, which I defy the officers to contradict, that the most clamorous persons we have had in these districts against the Government, are the officers themselves, which their conversations have shown—And their writings can!

N° 14 must apply in all its meaning, to Mr Walker's coterie on the Macintyre, and does not in the least allude to these parts.

N° 15 is deserving of more notice, because so very far opposed to all our views, on a subject gathered by years of experience; however, I admit, "it is impossible to persuade," Mr Walker, for often I have wasted hours in foolishly trying to do so, but when he says "on the contrary when they are seen, (meaning the natives,) it is known where some are, and it can generally be learned from them where the others are and what their doings are," he is manifestly wrong. Blacks are frequently known to be sent by their tribe into stations for the sole purpose of misleading the whites as to their whereabouts, are proverbial for lying, being clever at deception, and invariably deceiving as to where their offending kinsmen are located; and which is somewhat natural. Again, Mr Walker says, "if every settler were to allow only ten Aborigines on his station, there would be such a small number of them in the bush that they would be hardly dangerous," all of which needs mending, — for instance, in these two districts I am prepared to prove that more than ten Blacks, on an average, are allowed in at the stations, and during the time this, Walker panacea, has been administered, even within the last twelve months, we have lost three times the number of lives, and as much property, as in any former corresponding period. Take Maryborough for example, where the Blacks are allowed in *ad libitum*, three men were left for dead about a month ago. Houses are daily being robbed, working bullocks speared, and all perhaps from the magistrate's fruitless requests sent to the adjacent section of idle police for assistance.

N° 16 Gentlemen applies in particular to the writer, and although I do allow ten blacks into the station, still I keep others out, because the tribe belonging to the place abounds with individuals charged upon oath with murder, &c., and did so ere the country was taken up, and at the time of conversation with Mr Walker I gave such also as my reason for keeping the strong tribe away, and I repeat to you, what I have again and again told him, that I have a pleasurable retrospection in remembering my system has been attended with the uncommon advantages of having escaped from losing a single man's life, or as many as half a dozen sheep, and yet enjoyed the benefit of having always two or three thousand sheep tended by the Aborigines.

N° 17 must be interpreted exactly opposite to the way it is written, and only then can be "cause for a disagreement between me (Mr Walker) and some" (most) "of the Northern settlers." The fact is, I tell you, gentlemen, and I tell the Government too, that there never was such a force turned into such a farce, or a body of men so cruelly mismanaged as these Native Police. They came into these districts inspiring joy and hope in all; they continue in it to the great disgust of most of us. Often and often have I heard these "misinterpreting despatch readers" excuse their do-nothing existence, by railing against and abusing the Attorney-General for his interfering with them. When this flimsy pretext for idleness was cast aside by the language of the Colonial Secretary to a deputation, they held a council of war, and resolved, though winter was coming on, to go to "Callandoon" for the summer clothing; and upon their telling me of their intention, I expostulated with, as well as wrote them, against their insane project, but to no effect, except that Mr Walker promised to leave one officer behind, which he failed to do. I had previously pointed out to him, in conversation and by letter, that so many months of useless inactivity, followed by the departure of the force altogether, would produce dire results in these districts; which, alas, became painfully true, in the murders of ten men and women, while they (the police) were at Callandoon. The officers have been over and over again told that it is no use shooting promiscuously six, nine, or nineteen blacks in one tribe, but far better to hunt down the actual criminals it may harbour, let these bands once know that so long as they conceal a murderer, they will be pursued until he is caught, harassed until he is given up, and readily, to prevent these annoyances, they will succumb. Why do the blacks continue the fearful depredations in these quarters? Merely because the police have never properly followed up the truly guilty ones. The loss of a companion or two is nothing in their eyes to the deprivation of a night's fire or a night's rest and let the police therefore, pursue a harassing instead of a destructive course, and soon the results will be beneficial for our own and humanity's sake. Take, for example, a severe and useless act enacted only a short time ago at Mr Tooth's station. The natives for months had been killing cattle, and occasionally attacking his men. Warrants for the known and worst characters were in existence (and had even been trifled with), something, however, induced a "section of the police," accompanied by a neighbouring squatter to visit that station, and the blacks of course were found at no great distance from the cattle, a charge was made upon them and some six, eight, or twelve shot. The Police committed their old fault by immediately returning to that Squatter's place, about twenty miles off, and there idling away nearly a month. Now witness what are the results of this fearful slaughter, the blacks at Mr Tooth's station are again killing cattle, and must be again checked, and all because this force is too inert to properly do its duty. If the warrants for the murders and felonious doers in that tribe were executed, if Mr Walker would order his officers to pursue the guilty and spare the unknown, to convince the blacks of that which it is well known they so much dread, viz., that they will be caught whatever they do or wherever they go, then this useless expenditure of blacks' blood might be avoided nor their accidental onslaughts be heard of. There can be no falser statements made against settlers, than to say "they are anxious for the government to carry on warfare against the blacks." Too many of us have derived the greatest advantages from their assistance, to harbour such ideas, and too many of us look mainly at these poor but useful creatures for help in the present trying times; and, above all, there are few, I hope, amongst us who have so far forgotten the feelings and the actions of a Christian, or that we are occasionally reminded by the Government of having such a one.

In conclusion, gentlemen, let me urge upon yourselves and the Government to know more of this "Force," see if there is something objectionable in the officers making a profit out of the rations supplied their men; whether such gain are not likely to induce them to stay for long periods (months) at one or two stations, and to neglect all the rest of a district. If the horses purchased for Government are properly bought, properly managed and properly accounted for; why crime has increased ever since the police first came amongst us, and continues to do so whether a young good looking gin in each section is not an objectionable adjunct to it; and whether it would not have been as well in your responsible position as important journalists, before condemning a host of respectable fellow countrymen, to ascertain for certainty whether they have merited such repeated charges at your hands, and if the accusations upon which those condemnations are poured out, have not emanated from an officer as fit to be one as the Hermit of Darlinghurst was? I am, Gentleman, One of the Slandered. Burnett River, July 19, 1852. PS.—Intelligence has just reached us of another murder having been committed at Dalgingal, (Mr M'Kay's station) and is additional and painful evidence of the incorrectness of one of Mr Walker's statements; and is further sad proof of the uselessness of shooting numbers of blacks in any, or one tribe, while the warrants are unexecuted and considered of "no value."[321]

To the Editor of the Moreton Bay Courier

Sir, Mr Commandant Walker of the above force, the Colonial Government, and the *Sydney Morning Herald*, seem to have organized a sort of triple alliance against the northern settlers, whose situation may be compared to that of the Romans, when in the last days of their falling republic, those two combined tyrants, Antony and Octavius, admitted the dull brute Lepidus, as a species of make weight, into their confederacy, and thus completed the fatal Triumvirate, which rendered itself so infamous by its proscriptions.

You are of course aware, of what is unfortunately too notorious, that since the Native Police were sent to protect the settlers in the Northern Districts, some, of which had acquired a most unenviable notoriety, in the frequent murders

[321] *SMH* 14 August 1852 p 2.

of white men and children by the Aborigines not only has the annual rate of those and other atrocities considerably increased, but scarce any attempt has been made to apprehend or punish the individuals guilty of them. The settlers, naturally enough growing tired of this novel method of protection, in their simplicity address repeated and urgent complaints, both to the Government and the press, of the gross inefficiency and mismanagement of the Native Police, and of the mischievous eccentricities of their commandant, who really appears to have been amusing himself with an experiment of the degree of uselessness to which his troopers might be brought. But Mr Frederick Walker, either in reply to or in anticipation of these complaints, comes out with a report, wherein the blackest calumnies against the characters of the northern settlers, are set forth, not in the best English, and in gloomy contrast to the judgment, foresight, and humanity of the aforesaid Mr Frederick Walker, who treats the latter portion of his subject quite in the style of a master, and lays a thick coat of varnish over it to the best of his ability. It is not easy, in raking though such a mass of slander, egotism, and bad grammar as the remarkable document exhibits, to discriminate insinuation from broad accusation, and for this very simple reason, that its author himself is not sensible of their difference; but the upshot of all is that the northern settlers are painted as little better than a horde of blood-thirsty ruffians, while Mr Frederick Walker, very much to his own satisfaction, stands magnificently forth, covered with glory and honour. Hereupon, what does the government do? It very complacently stuffs its ears with the report, quietly lays on the shelf the complaints and counter-charges of a large body of settlers and affects to regard the matter as settled. You may remember, too, how in the last session of Council our polite friend the Col. Secretary took upon himself to fear that the settlers wished something or others — I forget the exact words — to be done "which no Christian government could sanction." It is evident from this that Mr Walker had been previously firing small shot at the same mark at which his great gun of the 1st March was discharged, for I am persuaded so painfully courteous and discreet an officer as Mr Thomson, would never have given utterance to that atrocious calumny, had he not taken care to fortify himself with a dram of Mr Walker's oil of vitriol.

After this little is left for the *Herald*, but what little it can it accomplishes in the manner and fashion of the *Herald.* It swallows the report and disgorges it in the shape of a leading article, not improved as to cleanliness by the filthy process. Mr Walker's egotism and calumnies are paraded on the second page of that amusing journal, decorated with the tinsel and glass beads for which they have taken out a patent. And the Commandant of the Native Police is besmeared with the slime, and the northern settlers are buffeted by the wind bags of the *Sydney Morning Herald.* Had such an article appeared in any other paper it must have seriously damaged its reputation for impartiality. But in this respect, I fancy the *Herald* is pretty much in the condition of the traveller, indicated in that celebrated line. *Cantabit vacuus coram latrone viator*

In what a singular, nay in what a sad state of society are we placed, where a government officer can dare to publish so many slanderous misrepresentations in the shape of an official report; when the government to whom they are addressed can receive them without further enquiry and without discouragement, and upon their sole authority can refuse to entertain the complaints of its injured subjects against the man who has neglected and insulted them; and when the leader of the local press can echo his insults with declamatory approbation. I cannot descend to argue with Mr Frederick Walker. His statements and insinuations can be met only by denial. It is not true that in general the northern settlers consider it "necessary and the duty of government to evince a certain amount of vindictiveness against the blacks." It is not true that "they still fancy that a system of warfare ought to be authorized by government, and do not try to produce evidence upon which the police can legally act;" and it is evident from the tone of Mr

Walker's report that he makes these charges against the generality of the settlers, though not so expressly stated. The fact is that innumerable warrants have been placed in the hands of the officers of Native Police, which they have neglected and even refused to put in force. It is not true that "many settlers" have any such object as Mr Walker's vulgar language attributes to them in clause 5, of his report. The settlers are not afraid of enquiry. They court it. Only let the conduct of the Native Police officers be also enquired into. And the sooner the better. And now, Sir, can I not prevail on you to offer a word in behalf of outraged justice? Have you forsaken us altogether? Your judgment on this matter is anxiously desired. The press, we must all gratefully acknowledge, has not yet learned to play at "follow my leader." Otherwise I had not addressed you on this subject, nor appealed as I now do, from the *Sydney Morning Herald* to the *Moreton Bay Courier*. I remain, Sir, your obedient servant, Shadow, Burnett River, July 24, 1852.[322]

To the Editor of the Sydney Morning Herald

Gentlemen, I have read your article of June 23, on the above subject, with somewhat of a feeling of compassion. How blind you must have been to your own obvious interests, how deplorable, insensible to the high duties which are the privilege of your profession, when you could thus descend from the position of a judge, to that of a special pleader, when on the interested and *ex parte* statements of Mr Frederick Walker, and in direct opposition to the reiterated complaints of a large body of respectable colonists, you could suffer yourselves to become the prejudiced advocates of a system pregnant with corruption and abuse, and the champions of a man who seeks to perpetuate that system by unfair means, and for the most selfish purposes!

Why must you echo his egotistical self-glorifications, or retail the gross and unfounded calumnies by which, under the mask of an official report, he has dared to assail the characters of

322 *MBC* 21 August 1852 p 2.

a class of persons, to say the least, in no respect his inferiors? Can you not perceive that, from the moment your readers have reason to doubt your thorough impartiality, your influence over public opinion must begin to decline, and that your wide circulation, of which you are continually reminded, can only serve to extend your disgrace and deepen your humiliation? Why not, before you hastened so rashly to pronounce a judgment, which promises to be far more fatal to your own reputation than injurious to those against whom it is directed, why not have taken some little pains to ascertain whether Mr Walker might not have had a motive for exercising his ingenuity in the invention of malignant accusations against the "northern settlers"—whether it might not have been necessary to shelter from their inconvenient clamour the tender ears of the Executive, or to secure against impertinent truths, the vested interests of inefficient and overpaid officials. Are the charms of Mr Walker's peculiar style so magnetic as to have lulled your judgment into complete forgetfulness of the many previous communications admitted into your columns, by which his slanderous assertions had been anticipated and contradicted. Surely it would not have been unworthy of a journal that places all its glory in moderation, before it gave so decided a preference to Mr Walker's statements, to have compared them with other testimony than his own, and to inquire what credit they might derive from his general character. Yet as your error in this matter has in all probability arisen rather from an unfortunate propensity to exaggerate the authority of official misrepresentations, than from any deliberate disregard of justice, and as you have already given extensive publicity to Mr Walker's report, nay even honoured it with more than ordinary notice, I am persuaded that you will not now refuse insertion to my denial of the accuracy and correctness of many of the assertions contained in that report. And although the Government may affect to believe that veracity is a quality monopolized by their own officers, I have no fear but that all persons acquainted with Mr Walker and myself will at least allow my word equal weight with his.

I challenge Mr Walker to produce the names of those settlers who have given utterance to or have adopted the sanguinary sentiments charged against them in his 1st and 2nd clauses. If he is unable to do so, I can scarcely conceive by what means either himself or his assertions can be rendered more contemptible. At the same time, I must protest against the highly disingenuous assumption he so strenuously labours to draw, that a feeling of virulent vindictiveness against the Aborigines is entertained by the generality of the northern settlers. It really would be an amusing, were it not also a melancholy proof of the avidity with which the Government would swallow such abominable charges, however weakly substantiated, that Mr Walker has dared to found so black and sweeping an accusation on a few idle words picked up in a conversation with three settlers, and "a Mr Cowper." The evident aim of his report is to exhibit himself as a high-principled protector of the blacks against the blood-thirsty propensities of the settlers. But I pronounce all such insinuations to be as false as they are treacherous. I call on Mr Walker to prove our treatment of the Aborigines, from actual facts. I require him to particularise instances of the operation of those sentiments of which he so magnanimously disapproves. And I beg your reflecting readers to consider what a deep interest, both personal and pecuniary, the settlers, particularly in these times, have in conciliating the goodwill of the wild tribes around them; and whether it is reasonable to suppose that the blacks would not be welcomed wherever it can be none [sic] with safety. The fact is, that in too many cases conciliatory measures have been carried to so dangerous an excess as to have encouraged the natives to those depths of pillage and murder so frequently recorded in your columns, and which I regret to say have, at least in this and the neighbouring districts, been seldom followed by the punishment of the perpetrators. It is necessary, gentlemen, to refer you to New Zealand and the Cape for examples of the folly and even wickedness of attempting to conciliate barbarous tribes, without accompanying demonstrations of superior force, and without making the subjects of such attempts fully understand that their aggressions will be visited with retribution? Is it to be supposed that the admission of known murderers to a station can be agreeable to those residents upon it, or that their vicinity can increase the security of the solitary shepherd, when it has become notorious that the chance of obtaining assistance in cases of depredation is dependent upon such casualties as the humour of a petty officer, the prices of rations in certain localities, or the good or bad cheer furnished in this or that neighbourhood? Are the evil inclinations of other blacks likely to be discouraged by an open exhibition of the impunity with which murder and outrage can be effected? I appeal to all acquainted with the melancholy history of the last three years in these districts, whether those friends and servants whose violent deaths by the spear or waddy of the savage we have had such frequent reason to deplore, have not been in general sacrificed on stations where the natives were admitted to friendly intercourse.

If Mr Walker is really sincere in wsihing [sic] the blacks to be on familiar terms with the settlers, let him and his officers take a little more pain to do their duty, and satisfy the latter that all aggressions upon their lives and properties will be promptly and severely noticed. Let them visit the dangerous localities as often as they do the quiet and peaceful stations; let them execute only a fourth of the warrants placed in their hands, instead of endeavouring to screen their indolence or incapacity under a hypocritical show of solicitude for the safety the natives. Nothing can be more audacious than the assertion in Mr Walker's 4th clause that the settlers "do not try to produce evidence upon which the police can legally act." Let Mr Walker name, if he can, a single case of murder having occurred within his recollection for which warrants, if procurable, have not been granted by the local magistracy. Let them particularize those instances of which he complains of his having been prevented by the settlers from procuring evidence, and I pledge myself to point out twice as many instances of warrants having been placed in the hands of the native police which to this hour remain unexecuted. What has Mr Walker or his officers done with the numerous warrants issued against the parties concerned in the murders of Messrs Blaxland, Trevethan, Clarke, Ross, of Mr Wilkins' two servants (father and daughter), of Messrs M'Kay's, Coutts's, and Corfield's shepherds, and of so many other victims of aboriginal violence. The evidence we have produced has hitherto demonstrated only the uselessness of the force sent to protect us. The local magistracy are absolutely tired of issuing warrants, and no wonder. Why, gentlemen, it is not long since a notorious murderer, for whom a warrant was actually extant, was pointed out by a magistrate to one of the lieutenants, who, nevertheless, refused to arrest him.

In reply to Mr Walker's 5th clause, I solicit the Government to institute a formal enquiry into the proceedings of the Native Police in these districts, and I venture to predict its result would be most effectually to deprive Mr Walker of the opportunity of writing any such despatches as the one under consideration.

The encomiums passed by Mr Walker upon the general conduct of his troopers, upon himself for his skill and judgment in training them, are unfortunately not quite in unison with facts that have occurred since their arrival among us. If no cases of intoxication, or of the use of obscene language had been chargeable against any of them, I should rejoice to find they were capable of setting so good an example to others who have enjoyed superior opportunities; but as there is evidence to the contrary, I can but regard this as another instance of Mr Walker's unscrupulous distortion of facts, or melancholy defect of memory.

Can Mr Walker explain how far the constant attendance of a number of native women, selected from the various local tribes, by whose agency the inevitable consequences of illicit intercourse has been introduced among his troopers, and have notoriously impaired their health and efficiency, is consistent with that moral training of which he boasts? And as Mr Walker has taken upon himself to set forth the causes of difference between him and the northern settlers, I wonder he has not enlightened us as to the reasons which have induced so many of the latter to decline that familiar acquaintance with which he has shown himself disposed to honour them—why some are shy of admitting him into their houses—and why one Commissioner of Crown Lands thought proper unceremoniously to eject him from his premises?

In conclusion, let me assure you, neither I nor any of the northern settlers would advocate the entire abolition of this force. With others, I am of opinion it might be made useful, but cannot agree with its commandant that it is so now. Its institution in the first instance was doubtless well intended, and its failure may in the main be attributed to the almost irresponsible power entrusted by the credulity or apathy of the executive to the abovementioned officer, whose caprices and eccentricities are daily growing more and more intolerable. The publication of his report is but an additional proof of his unfitness for the post to which he has been appointed. The man who could dare to promulgate such statements ought never to have filled an office of high trust and authority. But as no complaint against him has hitherto availed to produce any effect on the dignified indifference of the Government, as he is most jealously protected from the trouble-some interference of all local authority or control, as, in appointing his lieutenants, he is in fact allowed to nominate four magistrates, he has been led naturally enough to form rather extravagant notions of his own importance.

He appears to reserve the services of the police for his friends and favourites, or otherwise to dispense them with a view to his personal convenience or advantage. No greater mistake has been committed than the placing of Mr Walker and his officers in the commission of the peace. Their ministerial and executive functions are thus confounded to the injury of both. Another fruitful source of mismanagement may be found in the method by which the troopers are victualled and clothed.

I have no space to dwell at length on this topic, but shall only express my wish that some sharp-eyed member of Council may cast his eye on this abuse, which seems to me to measure the protection afforded the settler by his readiness or ability to furnish cheap rations; and has already had the effect of nearly excluding the police from some stations, and inducing them to spend months in idleness at others. William Forster.[323]

To the Editor of the Moreton Bay Courier

Sir, Amongst other doubtful statements put forth in a letter signed "WHW" and published in your journal of the 14th inst., appeared the following assertion. "The police do not affirm that they came up with and shot the leader in the Trevethan tragedy." Now as I was present with Mr Marshall in the Public Inn at Gayndah when he did repeat so, I feel it my duty to vindicate so far, the Squatter's statements. I send you my name. I am, Sir, your obedient servant. Truth, Burnett River, 21 August 1852.[324]

To the Editor of the Moreton Bay Courier

Sir, Observing a letter in your paper of the 14th inst., speaking in favourable terms of the Native police, and disparagingly of one of your correspondents, and which letter bears my initials for a signature, I beg you will allow me to make known that I am neither the author of it, nor could be; unless I notoriously perverted truth, or miserably erred in judgment. I am, Sir, your obedient servant. Wm. Henry Walsh, Degilbo, August 25th, 1852.[325]

To the Editor of the Moreton Bay Courier

Sir, The long threatened letter, I see, has appeared at last, and is signed WHW, and, like all documents embodying the wishes, words, and antipathies of several men, bears a very laboured appearance: but as this family of composers-or

323 *SMH* 21 August 1852 p 3.

324 *MBC* 11 September 1852 p 4.

325 *MBC* 11 September 1852 p 4.

maybe the principal one, has chosen to defend the police by throwing out insinuations against a private individual; has vindicated the corruption of that force by conjoining up obliquities of my mental vision; has denied truths which he cannot confute, for the sake of exhibiting that he knows how to utter mere contradictions, and indeed has pursued a very singular course for the purpose of proving that which is now past believing, I feel it my duty to ask you to allow me opportunity for reiterating all my previous complaints against the "inert, inexplicable, and very inferior force", and, in a measure, explaining the cause of them.

With your leave, I will follow WHW through his defences, and hope the result will bring conviction to all disinterested parties that truth, at any rate, is on our side. To No 1, I have to say that when the police returned from the disastrous attempt to overtake Mr Trevethan's murderers, the officer in command, in answer to the reproach of a gentleman, replied "that he must confess the force was of no use, and that if he were a squatter up here he would grumble as loud as any of us? With what Mr Trevethan has sworn to I have nothing to say, beyond recommending those who are so fond of quoting his "depositions" to be more consistent in their relationship as neighbours.

In reply to No 2, I have to relate that during the absence of the Police upon that deplored expedition, outrages were committed by the blacks in the Wide Bay district and the inhabitants did not, could not consistently complain, because matters were no worse then, than while the Police were present.

To the assertion of No 3, I give a most unqualified denial, and reassert that the officer alluded to told several persons of my acquaintance that the Police had shot the leader in the Trevethan tragedy &c. As this fact is so notorious it is difficult to understand how more than one individual can lend assistance towards denying it and it does seem strange that WHW takes upon himself to contradict so much, unless he has never been absent from attendance on, or beyond the hearing of, the said officer, since the supposed occurrence.

I also again repeat, in answer to N° 4, that I have heard "the magistrate" say that he pointed out to Mr Marshall the supposed murderer of Mr Blaxland, and that the officer refused to apprehend him, because there was no person on the ground who could swear positively to the man. He also said that his own blacks first came and told him that "Neddy" was in the camp and wished him either apprehended or killed. Although the natives cannot-very properly-give evidence on oath, still one would think that when they go to some trouble in acquainting us with the intrusion of, and pointing out, the person charged as a murderer it would not be too great a stretch of the law, nor too severe a performance of public duty, if they were to secure such a possibly dangerous character, for the purpose of identification.

I have thus far noticed the paragraphically portions of WHW's letter, and it is very consoling that he knew nothing more of the charges made by "Squatter" against the police, or maybe they too would have been denied by an appeal to personalities; but I must ask his pardon for correcting one mistake of that sort which he makes, by announcing to him that "Squatter" is not "a squatter without stock or station," but, unfortunately, they do not belong to a brother; and though, apparently, the very supposition that any of your correspondents are without stock and stations would be an insurmountable objection to their having, or expressing, an opinion, I think, Sir, that you will never join him in such an idea, especially when we are battling for the security of our lives. Time and circumstances reveal most things, and when the motives of the writer of this can be compared with the extraordinary conduct of others on the question of Native Police, the former will be amply rewarded, and yet not by (what has been facetiously termed) a rational way. Thanks to you, Sir, for taking a step in the right path. Your recommendation for appointing a Commission to inquire into the charges made against the Native Police is very satisfactory, and I am sure you will more and more see the necessity for it when I tell you that since I last wrote, the Messrs Hay, J. D M'Taggart, Esq., J. B. Reid, Esq., and Messrs Lawless, have been robbed of sheep, and in one or two instances, to a serious amount; while Mr Reid's hut at the head station has been forcibly entered by the Native Police, for a most illegal purpose, and it is even said a disgusting one. Surely these atrocities cannot be tolerated much longer, although we see the Colonial Secretary evidently intends to try and prolong them. We have lost 15 lives in as many months, and the extract read from Mr Commandant Walker's letter, in the Council, the other day informed that body that since the formation of the force only one life had been lost in the Wide Bay and Burnett districts which is a pretty good index of the means the employees and favourers of the police adopt to carry out their views. I am, Sir, your obedient servant, Squatter Burnett River, August 22nd, 1852.[326]

To the Editor of the Sydney Morning Herald

Gentlemen, in consequence of the publicity given through your columns and remarks to Mr Commandant Walker's charges against some of the northern settlers, they have felt it their duty to address the accompanying letter to the Government, and to request your publishing a copy of it in your journal. I remain your most obedient servant, William Henry Walsh.

P.S. – I may add that, doubtless, many more signatures from the Burnett would have been added if circumstances warranted our waiting for them; and that all the resident Wide Bay squatters have signed it with the exception of two — one of whom I know has not had the opportunity. WHW, Burnett River, July 29th, 1852.

(Copy)

To the Honourable the Colonial Secretary.

Burnett River, 24 July 1852

Sir, A document, signed by Mr Frederick Walker, purporting to be

326 *MBC* 11 September 1852 p 4.

a report on the causes of difference, presumed by the writer to exist between himself and some of the Northern settlers, having appeared in the *Sydney Morning Herald* of June 16th, 1852, we desire to place on record our dissent from the conclusions at which it points, and our disbelief of the statements in which they are founded. We have the honour, therefore, to request that you will convey to his Excellency the Governor-General the following results of our experience on the subject referred to. If it should be found somewhat awkwardly to clash with that of Mr Walker, we trust that he will be called on to explain the incongruity. We think it scarcely necessary to vouch for the accuracy of our statements of facts, which are unfortunately too notorious to all residents in the two adjacent districts of Wide Bay and Burnett River.

In the first two clauses of his report Mr Walker attributes certain very extraordinary sentiments to three settlers, whose places of residence are not indicated. We confidently challenge Mr Walker to produce the names of these individuals, without which we must express our doubts of the accuracy of his interpretation of their opinions. At the same time, we must indignantly protest against the inference at which Mr Walker's despatch seems to aim, that such sanguinary views are generally entertained by the northern settlers. We do not consider "it necessary, and the duty of the Government, to evince a certain amount of vindictiveness against the blacks," and we deny that such an opinion is at all common among us.

2. Clause 4 requires no comment beyond the mention of the disgraceful and notorious fact that innumerable warrants on capital charges, granted by the local magistracy, have been repeatedly placed in the hands of the officers of the native police, who have so generally failed to execute or even to attempt enforcing them, that it is by no means wonderful if complainants should have grown tired of "trying to produce evidence upon which the police can legally act." We again challenge Mr Walker to particularise the cases in which he or his subalterns have been prevented from obtaining evidence.

3. To the insidious calumny conveyed in clause 5 we can give no better answer than by soliciting the Government to institute an enquiry into the proceedings of the native police and the settlers towards

the Aborigines. In such case, we pledge ourselves to produce more evidence than will be agreeable to the officers of this corps, and which we anticipate will convince the Government of the imperative necessity of reforming its organization.

4. With regard to the system adopted by many settlers of not allowing the natives access to their stations, Mr Walker's opinion that it is a principal cause of the outrages of the natives is not borne out by facts, inasmuch as it is too well known that most of the murders and outrages perpetrated by these savages have taken place on stations to which they were admitted, and where they were supposed to be on friendly terms with the residents. We need only allude to the murders of Mr Blaxland and his two shepherd boys, of Mr Trevethan, of Mr Wilkins' two servants, of Messrs Humphreys and Herbert's, Mr Corfield's, and Mr Murray's shepherds, as a few out of many instances contradictory of Mr Walker's observations on this point. We would most respectfully represent that this system is not general, prevailing only in the most dangerous localities, and has been in a manner forced upon its favourers by their repeated experience of the danger and ruin resulting from a contrary course. We must impress upon the Government that it is no less our interest than our desire to be on friendly terms with the native tribes, but that, as with most other barbarous people, attempts at conciliating their favour, however desirable, cannot always be safely made, until they become thorougly [sic] convinced of our superiority in strength. We are not insensible of the advantage to be derived, and which might accrue to these districts from the presence of a well-managed native police force, and are of opinion that had the present corps done its duty, by the capture or punishment of well-known and easily recognised offenders, we should have found the task of conciliation much easier; but we must confess we have little hope that the force will ever be useful without a complete reform of its present defective management, which seems to us to be in a great degree owing to that unlimited confidence reposed in the Commandant by his Excellency the Governor-General, spoken of with such complacency in clause 17.

In conclusion, without affecting to be surprised at any of Mr Walker's statements, we cannot avoid the respectful expression of our regret that the Government should adopt, without discouragement, the calumnious misrepresentations of an individual against a respectable community. We have the honour &c., Signed. Wm. Humphreys, J.P. – Arch. Thomson, J.P.; Henry Herbert, J. P. – Jno. Landsborough; J. O. Mactaggart – Thos. Herbert; James M'Laren – Robert Wilkie, J.P.; Wm. Henry Walsh – H. C. Corfield; Joshua Sewell – A. Mactavish; Wm. Richardson – George Herbert; Wm. Forster.[327]

To the Editor of the Moreton Bay Courier

Sir, With extreme pleasure have "I read the long letter published in our local contemporary, and signed "Anti-Humbug". Our thanks are due that writer for removing the little doubt which may have existed in our minds of the thorough uselessness of the Native Police, even on the Macintyre River. I never could conceive how so intelligent a body of squatters as are known to live in that quarter, could have been ever brought to their wits' end on the subject of managing blacks, or that they were only saved by the arrival of the Police. Moreover, it did seem strange that a force which has been so proverbially useless here, had done so much good there; and stranger that Mr Walker had ever induced the settler to cooperate with him, an act we hold to be impossible. Thanks, then, for "Anti-Humbug's" information; but not for his suggestion that the Commandant should leave off parading, &c, the men at Callandoon, to come out this way. The blacks at Maryborough have crowned their eight or ten months of unrestricted crimes by "finishing" a man at last. A Chinaman, while on his way down to that place, was met by some savages, and cruelly killed. His body, I hear, was found mangled by men and dogs. The poor fellow had absconded from Mr Walsh's, and it is supposed that his blankets, &c, excited the cupidity of his murderers, to do the deed. You may remember that in December last the whole of the black police were taken down to Frazer's Island; and, as a writer in the *Herald* facetiously said, "great preparations

327 *SMH* 11 September 1852 p 3.

were made for the jaunt; squatters and storekeepers swelled the party; moist and dry provisions were abundantly laid in, &c., &c., &c." You may likewise recollect that frequent allusions have been made to the extraordinary secrecy of the result of that jaunt, and much surprise expressed at the profound silence maintained concerning their exploits by this most heterogeneous body of black hunters. True, now and then we receive little bits of information from Sydney, (of all places in the world), that rumours are afloat that the natives were driven into the sea, and there kept as long as daylight or life lasted; but even this we need not believe, although it would in some measure account for the unusual barbarity displayed by the inhabitants on that part of the coast towards the passengers and crew of the *Thomas King*, and verify the prophecies made by many Maryborough people, when they saw the police going down there. Again, the conduct of the natives before the jaunt, to the wrecked crews of the *Countess of Minto* and *Rokeby Castle*, was so kind, so opposite to their behaviour since that it is difficult to find reasons for the change, except from a spirit of revenge. The jaunt might also account for the numerous and enormous crimes which the blacks have of late so indulged in. It will be a matter of nice investigation, however, whether some of the worst of these atrocities might not have been prevented if the police had listened to the repeated applications from the local magistracy for assistance. I know it is said that had Mr Marshall attended to the first request of the Bench. I allude to the time when our boiling-down sheep were being stolen, the fearful maltreatment of the two Chinese would, in all probability, never have occurred. I know too it is affirmed that if this zealous, active officer had gone down even after this bloody attack upon the Chinese, when he was again particularly urged to by the Bench, this last shocking murder would never have happened; and it is painful to hear that threatening weather and soft roads are some of the soft reasons given for the absence of the police from the wretched settlement, since the too memorable jaunt, notwithstanding the frequent calls made for protections. Picture to yourself, Sir, the feelings of our few townspeople, when they reflect that for months and months, a section of police has been hanging about, within a few miles of all their disasters: during which time their children, their houses, milking herds, and even horses, have been attacked by insolent and over whelming numbers of naked savages. Then try and picture to yourself, Sir, the sensations caused in the minds of such people when they are occasionally told by their respected Resident Magistrate "that he has made another ineffectual attempt to bring the Native Police down to their assistance, nay, that his leaders on their behalf, to the officer in command, are not even acknowledged."

You must allow that it is harrowing enough to be constantly living in an unprotected state, amongst numbers of unclad and hideous savages; but say, what amount of anguish and disgust do we feel, when we find that all our prayers for help are treated with contumely, by the very men from whom we have a right to expect so much. If ever there existed a class of suffering Englishmen, here they are to be found. Having once enjoyed the blessings of dwelling under a watchful government, we feel, of course, the more bitterly our present unhappy positions; and were it not for the annual demand made through the Commissioners, by some Sydney powers, for a tax which we receive no return for, and now and then an official insinuation against our characters, we might be killed-die-or live on, in perfect ignorance of having a very bad government at all. I am, Sir, your obedient servant, A Squatter, Burnett River, August 31, 1852.[328]

To the Editor of the Moreton Bay Courier

Sir, In your issue of 11 September, I perceive "Squatter" is once more in the field. In my opinion his letter is unworthy of an answer, but your readers in this neighbourhood appear to think differently. Before entering upon the only topic that can have any interest for the community generally, I will make a few remarks upon "Squatter's" observations upon my last letter. His sneer at its laboured appearance is unworthy of no-

328 *MBC* 18 September 1852 p 2.

tice. There is no pretension to elegance of style, but my meaning appears to have been clearly conveyed to your readers, and the statements contained in my letter have met with very general approbation. A graver charge made by "Squatter" is, that instead of producing proofs, I have met his charges with mere contradictions and personalities. But where are the proofs of "Squatter's" charges against the Native Police? I have always understood that the onus of proof lay with the accuser; and as to personalities, I think "Squatter" ought to thank me for my forbearance. The only, charge of any real importance made by "Squatter" referred to "Neddy," the supposed murderer of Mr Blaxland and the true circumstances are so very far different from those set forth in his letter, that any one unacquainted with the writer and his unfortunate prejudices, would have looked upon them as wilful misstatements. I knew your correspondent better. His mind greedily swallowed that portion of the statement which fed his dislike to and rejected whatever was in favour of the Native Police; a force which he has expressed his determination to write down at all hazards. Actuated by such feelings, he could hardly be expected to use his judgment; he gradually persuaded himself that what he wished to be true was true; and deceived himself before he deceived others. That such is the constitution of your correspondent's mind is generally admitted in this district, and generally regretted by his acquaintances, as a failing which goes far to neutralize many good qualities which he undoubtedly possesses. These are statements that can have little interest for the public, but I am tender of your correspondent's reputation. I do not believe him capable of deliberate misrepresentation, where his judgement is free to act; but on the subject of the Native Police he is a perfect lunatic and ought not to be held responsible for what he either writes or says.

I shall not follow "Squatter" paragraphically through his letter but dispose of that charge which I take to be the most important first-viz: the refusal of the officer in command of the Native Police to capture a black who was pointed out to him as the supposed murderer of Mr Blaxland. I have since made further enquiry into this matter and find that I was substantially correct in the statement given in my former letter. "The magistrate" further told me that his own blacks did not tell him that "Neddy was in the camp, and wished him either apprehended or killed," as stated, in your correspondent's last letter, and at the same time expressed great surprise that "Squatter" never had asked him the real truth of this much-vexed question, although he had had frequent opportunities of doing so. "The magistrate" has no doubt in his own mind that the black was "Neddy," but agrees with everyone who has any knowledge of the character of the blacks, that to have apprehended him would have been most injudicious, as no proof could possibly have been procured against him, and he must necessarily have been liberated after a few days' confinement, carrying with him a thorough contempt for a warrant, and a strong impression that he had received a tacit permission to commit other murders. With all the confidence inspired by the unusual circumstance of "Truth" being at his side, "Squatter" gives a most unqualified denial to my assertion "that the Native Police do not affirm that they came up with and shot the leader in the Trevethan tragedy," &c, &c. Unfortunately, I have no copy of my former letter, nor the number of your paper containing that from "Squatter," to which it was an answer; but I will venture to say that any candid reader, with both before him, will understand my assertion to be that the Native Police did not, upon their own knowledge of the fact, state that the black shot was the leader in the Trevethan tragedy, but made the assertion relying upon the truth of Mr Trevethan's oath. But "Squatter" is determined not to believe anything that might redound to the credit of the Native Police, even when supported by the oath of a disinterested party. He refuses to have anything to do with Mr Trevethan's oath, except recommending those who believe in it to be more consistent in their relationship as neighbours. This is certainly treating that gentleman's deposition in a most extraordinary way.

After reiterating his former charges, "Squatter" proceeds to inform us that certain parties, whom he names, have been robbed of sheep. One of these I have had an opportunity of seeing, but neither he nor the gentleman superintending his station are aware of any sheep having been stolen. Upon what authority did your correspondent make this statement? My own impression is that he dreamt it, and afterwards persuaded himself that it was no dream. But even supposing it true, does "Squatter" argue from this that the Native Police force ought to be disbanded?

Shall our Police establishments and Criminal Courts be abolished because some offenders escape unpunished? If "Squatter" is actuated by anxiety for the public good, why does he not suggest some improvement in the management or composition of the force, by which he considers it would be rendered more efficient? Is he aware that his exaggerated statements have a most injurious effect upon the labour market in these districts, and even give some colour of truth to a statement said to have been made, on board an immigrant ship, by Mr---, of Brisbane, "that it was better for the immigrant to take £20 from him than £60 to go to the Burnett or Wide Bay districts?"

"Squatter" will, I dare say, agree with me that this is a most impertinent piece of misrepresentation. But looking at the columns of the *Moreton Bay Courier* devoted to Original Correspondence, one is almost inclined to excuse the man. From these it would appear that we are kept in a constant state of excitement, "battling for our lives," (as "Squatter" has it), in daily dread of robbery and murder; while the truth is that on most stations on the Burnett, where the blacks have been allowed up, they have been most useful auxiliaries during the lambing season, and upon some establishments, hutkeepers have in a great measure been dispensed with, and the huts left, with the greatest safety, to take care of themselves.

Your correspondent corrects a mistake I appear to have made and tells us that he is not a squatter without stock or station. I can only say that I was not singular in this supposition, and the fact that he had both, until it received publicity through your columns, was not generally known. My object in making that statement was not to throw any slight upon " Squatter's" social position, but merely to point out the man, whose personal antipathy to the officers of the Native Police is well known, and whose assertions regarding that force would thus be received with considerable abatement, if his conjecture that I have no station of my own be correct, how could I possibly have any insurmountable objection to others in my own position "having or expressing an opinion." It is not what a man is that makes him ridiculous, but assuming to be that which he is not. I will not insult "Squatter" by attributing a letter which appeared in your issue of 4th September, under the signature of "A Squatter" to his pen. The writer, with many touches of the true pathetic, would fain awaken our compassion. But as his principal fear appears to be that not one will be left to mourn for him when his time to die comes, I think, Mr Editor, we may be excused if we reserve our sympathies for the really unfortunate, and do not waste them upon the imaginary grievances of a dreamer. He, who is unhappy because he fears he will be the Last Man, must have a vivid imagination, and a lot singularly devoid of real troubles. On the whole, his letter is about the most amusingly absurd production that ever figured in the columns of a newspaper. It is unfortunate that the Commandant of the Native Police is personally obnoxious to many in this district. Had he been a popular man this correspondence would, probably, never have come before the public. Had "Squatter" gratified his personal feelings without injury to the interests of others, he would certainly have met with no interruption from me. The public, who reads the letters of "Squatter" and others, does not take the trouble to reflect that it has before heard the blacks' outrages detailed therein. Every reiteration is looked upon, by it, as a fresh outrage, and not the carefully scraped up and exaggeratedly stated misfortunes of a series of years. If your correspondents have not succeeded in writing down the Native Police, they have certainly managed to inspire the working classes with a most unfounded dread of seeking employment in these districts. It is to be regretted that, if "Squatter's" mind is of such an unusually active stamp that it cannot find full employment in his own avocations but impels him to mix himself up in public matters, he has not chosen a subject in the treatment of which he would do less injury to his fellow-squatters.

My object is not to write a panegyric upon the Native Police, nor to represent it as thoroughly disciplined, or, in its present imperfect state, efficient for the purpose for which it was raised. In my former letter, I pointed out that it was unreasonable to expect that a corps, in which both officers and men had to learn their duty from experience, should at once start up perfect. I will again state that, as far as my own observation has gone, the officers have shown considerable zeal in the discharge of their duty, and with the limited force at their command, have done much to repress aboriginal outrages. The corps is too weak in numbers for the duty required from it: there appears to me to be a great want of petty officers: and by giving each trooper two horses, nearly double the amount of duty might be performed. Measures are, I believe, being taken to supply some of these deficiencies, and if, in its perfect state, the force does not fulfil the expectations of reasonable men, I shall join in raising my voice against it. If, in the meantime, this letter should have the effect of persuading you and your readers to receive "Squatter's" statements, regarding that force, with extreme scepticism, my object will be attained. I am, Sir, your obedient servant. WHW, Burnett, 8th October 1852. [Our readers must have observed, with regret, that correspondents on both sides of this question have indulged far too freely in the introduction of extraneous and purely personal matter. If any further communications on the subject are to appear, it must be on the distinct understanding that personalities are to be avoided. The public does not care for them, and they are only calculated to produce ill feeling. Ed. *MBC*][329]

---

[329] *MBC* 23 October 1852 p 4.

To the Editor of the Moreton Bay Courier

Sir I am sorry the vituperative animosity of your correspondent signing- himself, WHW, compels me, by his letter of the 8th ultimo, again to take up my pen about the Native Police: for I participated in the hope that, as this mismanaged body of men had been of late somewhat more active, and, consequently, more useful, than at any previous period, t'would be as well to leave it alone for a while nay, if possible, afford it praise for these quieter moments. But their champion will not suffer this; and as my previous letter affected him exactly where I most wanted it to, he has invoked lunacy, want of veracity, &c, in me, this time, on their behalf: and after most effectually giving reasons for the public to disbelieve every statement I make, he tells me his motive for doing so is because he is tender of my reputation. I thank him. Now Sir, there is nothing I would regret more than finding fault with individuals without occasion. The moral guilt of such conduct I hold to be very great, and as WHW will have that I have done so, you must suffer me to lay a synoptically account of the Police before your readers, so that they may think for themselves, and therefore dispense with WHW's arbitrary wish, and if the Police don't cry out, save us from our friends, when I have finished, they may perhaps at a future time. Nearly two years ago, then, the three sections arrived simultaneously by the Burnett, the Mary, and unfortunately the Brisbane. Mr Fulford with the first, Mr Marshall the second, and Mr Walker the third. At that time, there was a fearful debt for rapine and murder due by the savage to our laws; and few there are but think that if it had then been energetically wiped off, the bloodier and darker history of the last two years would never have been written. On the arrival of the Police, two or three murders at once greeted them; but as they were evidently intent upon obtaining satisfaction for the older ones, it remained for us to wonder at, and pass over the strange disregard for the new. Mr Marshall commenced operations at "Toomcul" and Mr Murray's; Mr Fulford in earnest at Mr Corfield's. Numbers of warrants had been previously granted for blacks at all these stations, and anxiously we waited for their execution. During this time, Mr Walker was supposed to be reducing the Upper Brisbane to order; and as his force contained as, many men as both his Lieutenants had, it was thought he would have easy work. Well do I remember the disgust felt then, when Mr Walker suddenly crossed over the range, and under the plea that his force was not strong enough to attack the blacks at the "Bunya," took away those sections which had begun so promisingly here. And as he did not attack the Bunya blacks after all, I believe, from that day to this, neither his officers nor the public have ever discovered the real motive for the whim. But the cloud of our misfortunes was only then gathering, and but dimly seen. Our blacks for some time had been awed into quietness by the constant reminding that a force was coming out specially to watch and punish them; and many of us then foresaw that if the well-known murderers were let alone, our future must be worse than the past. Judge our horror, then, when on the return of the Police from this sad journey, we heard the officers say that their recent instructions from the Attorney-General prevented their acting; that positively they would do nothing. "It is no use your talking" (was their language), "we will not run our necks in a noose for any man; and if the Government have not the courage to openly countenance our punishing blacks, &c., &c., we will not please them by doing so without express orders." Painful as these resolutions were to us, still they seemed fair enough from men in such positions; and consequently, we set to work imploring government to grant Mr Walker more latitude in acting more chance of removing our perilous times. You will hardly credit, Sir, the treatment we now experienced. When one of our deputation repeated to Mr Thomson some of the Commandant's own words as to the conflicting orders he had received, the Colonial Secretary told him "that he did not believe Mr Walker ever made use of such sentiments, but if he had, why then the Government had formed a wrong estimate of his character."

It is an old saying that "idleness begets mischief;" and, as, at this period of my narrative, the police were most religiously observing their vow "to do nothing," they had well verified the proverb. The natives, who from first to last should have been kept in constant dread of the force, we noticed had opened a family intercourse with it; and, finding that the Black Police were essentially black men, our former warnings and their own fears were alike forgotten, nay the murderers and less guilty found themselves admitted to their friendship on precisely the same terms.

The officers, too, from their abundant leisure, had made many discoveries concerning our treatment of the natives, and the conclusions they drew from them you may have gleaned from Mr Walker's manifesto of the causes of difference between him and some of the northern settlers. News, however, reached the officers that they had wholly misinterpreted their instructions, and so, instead of setting to work and retrieving their lost time by much activity for at this period, bear in mind, no murderers had been apprehended; they announced their intention of one and all going off to Callandoon. Our prayers and remonstrances were alike unavailing. Winter was coming on, "and they must have their summer clothing." Besides there was a probability of the Colonial Secretary visiting Callandoon, and he must see the troops go through their exercise. These, I positively assure you, were reasons given for their going, and though their presence, so far, among us had been injurious, in that it dispelled the dread we had inspired in our natives of them, still it would be hard to portray the fear most of us have at the bare idea of once more being totally abandoned. Two sections had already left; the third was on the eve of starting when a message was sent from Mr Forster's overseer, that the blacks had taken a flock of sheep. Much praise was awarded the remaining officer for his alacrity in at once going down to the station, and much commiseration expressed by the good people about Gayndah when they heard that he had been led a wild goose chase, or, in other words, that the blacks had not taken the sheep; and only for his having told Mr Forster's immediate neighbour that the blacks had taken some, the overseer to this day might have been wrongfully blamed, nor the wet weather received its due. Away, however, they all went to Callandoon, and then commenced such a scene of bloodshed and woe, as few districts have ever endured. Neither age nor sex was spared, and stations which had hitherto escaped scatheless from the bloody hands at the savage, now suffered most. I need not recapitulate all the murders which then took place: the recollection of them, much more recital, is still sickening; and so, let us turn to a more amusing theme, viz., the doings of our Burnett Savans (sic, Savants) at this time. It became evident to them that something must be done about the police. When, according to their own statements, they could not act, they were with us; and when, according to Government they could act, they went away: and so "petition-petition" was the cry. And petition on petition was the result; but here was a dilemma. Those manufactured up the river could not be signed by the orthographical race around Gayndah, while the Gayndah concoctions were utterly beneath adoption by the syntactically correct who illuminate and enchant the higher regions of the Burnett.

Time flew on, months passed away. Little or nothing was done, save by the natives; and the police returned. But matters were growing positively worst, as not only the blacks but even the police were at last against us. Some were dubbed "Burnett Legislators;" others had to try and live without the Commandant's smiles; and more were charged with assassin like conduct. Severe as these were, still we comforted ourselves with the idea that at any rate, the latest murderers would be pursued. But vain hope! A suggestion had been thrown out in Sydney that the natives at Frazer's Island wanted, I don't know what! and could anything be more delightful than a trip there to give it them? Besides, see the opportunity it afforded of injuring the "Burnett Legislators," by deferring the execution of the warrants they had caused to be issued: and so down the troops marched to Maryborough, which when they reached they soon astonished by the following acts: the town was full of blacks; a vessel lay at the boiling place, and which had been piloted up from the bay as usual by the natives. Three was the number, and these three Mr Walker resolved to catch. The vessel was accordingly surrounded by the police, and two out of the three poor creatures caught; and, Sir, if ever under the disguise of law, an atrocious act was done, this is it. Without rhyme or reason, these men were dragged to the lock-up, and thereupon an order of Mr Walker's, confined to the 27th of the month, rather more than a week. No charge was preferred against them, nor any crime suspected, and if his object were to prevent them from returning to the Island before the Police could get there, he had stultified this scheme by not capturing the third. Moreover, the troopers were night and day mixing with all the other blacks while the incarcerated pair had confided themselves to a sailor's generosity; had most assiduously piloted and worked his vessel up from the bay; and, at the very time they were thus molested, were heaving away at the anchor. A more disgraceful act was never perpetrated in the British name. But their freaks did not stop here. The resident Magistrate next fell under their displeasure and was most grossly insulted in his own house. The jaunt was performed; the picnic came off: the result, or known result, the capture of two or three blacks, and a small dingy, the former it is said were enticed on board the vessel; the latter was found moored in a creek. But the farce was not complete. The entrapped had to be committed by hook or by crook; the court house was not the place to do this. Besides, the insulted Magistrate had right of access there, and consequently a private dwelling was preferred; and to convince you of the regularity of the proceedings, I will merely say that on the face of one of the depositions against one of the accused blacks, he was described as having been captured at the "Great Sandy Island" and that I have been assured by the resident Maryborough magistrate that he was taken from his boiling down establishment. The Magistrate, Clerk of the Court, and Chief-Constable all told me of the deposition which was intended thus to pacify the Government for the trip; and if by any chance, they should overlook the important fact that men had been captured while on it, Mr Walker remedied such a piece of neglect by forwarding to Sydney, for their inspection, the Maryborough dingy; notwithstanding the remonstrances of the owner! It may look childish to you, and the expense of sending the boat both ways may appear useless to others; but pray don't overlook the fact that many view its capture as the most useful act the whole force have yet performed. Their next step, sir, was notorious likewise. Mr Tooth's station and men had endured an unusually severe siege by the natives: shots were fired, and spears thrown; and as soon as some of the men could get away, they posted off to Maryborough for help. One black fellow, a most unmitigated scoundrel, was particularly sworn to as the leader of the besiegers, and a warrant sent to the police for his apprehension. And now mark what the officer in command did towards executing it. Before ever he saw the accused, before ever he saw the accuser, he provided himself with the written and oral testimony of two or three very distant settlers that the black fellow charged upon oath could not have been at Mr Tooth's station on the day named in the deposition; and so conflicting were these alibis, or mere statements, that unless the fellow were ubiquitous, they must have been one and all wrong. But granting they were all right; that the villain is gifted with the power of omnipresence, is this the way to treat an Englishman's solemn oath? Is his deposition to be thus cast aside or his character for perjury to be thus lightly established, merely because he unfortunately made his complaint to the insulted magistrate, or for some other unEnglish reason? Is it the practice to apprehend men charged with felony, and, without confronting them with the accusers or defenders, acquit them on the spot?[330] To us it seems monstrous. And then, again, with Mr Blaxland's murderer "Neddy," can any reasoning be more humiliating than that adopted by WHW in defence of the officer for dereliction of duty. Hear what he says, the magistrate had no doubt in his own mind that the black was Neddy but agrees with everyone who has any knowledge of blacks that to have apprehended him would

330 See F Walker's letter Maryborough, 31/12/1851 to Hon CS, para 16 Re: Ball.

have been most injudicious. I repeat, sir, can anything be more humiliating than such a reason for a Police officer neglecting his duty. A suspected murderer was before him, but anyone who has a knowledge of blacks knows 'twould be injudicious to secure him! *O tempora, O mores*. And once more let me tell WHW that the magistrate did say, almost word for word, what I wrote, and which I can remind him of by time and place. To proceed with my history, I am afraid would weary you; though I could relate the failings of the Police in numbers of places besides, and perhaps could astonish WHW by shewing that if one officer only had conducted that disastrous expedition after Mr Trevethan's murderer, the result might have been more satisfactory. I could explain why the most dangerous stations in the districts, have not been visited by the Police for months, and the most settled had their constant attendance; of the warrants against the blacks treated as so much waste paper; and of those apprehended who have escaped. I might enlighten you why the barracks had been built in their present position, and why they were not situated about here. But I am sure you will have heard sufficient to convince the disinterested that the whole management of the police has been very bad and therefore I will say in conclusion, with your permission, a few words to WHW. My expression "battling for our lives" was justified by the fact that just after that time one of the Messrs Elliot had every reason to suppose that he narrowly escaped assassination from a well-known murderer named Jupiter; and that the fellow had been watching an opportunity for days. And the writer of this, too just then, was cautioned and almost guarded by his own blacks, who apprehended something of the sort menacing him. The imputation that I dreamt of sheep being stolen at a certain place is without cause, for the robbery occurred, and can be proved: and to the charge that I have injured the district by keeping labour away, I can only say it appears at the least ungracious. Finally, may I enquire of WHW in which school did he beget the logic, "that it is not what a man is that makes him ridiculous, but assuming to be what he is not." Now who has not seen a bad rider look ridiculous on horseback, or a drunken man look very ridiculous in any position: and yet it would be hard to say one was not a bad rider, and the other was not drunk; and therefore, we must allow that it's what they were that made them ridiculous. And again, who has not heard of very charitable men, men who give large alms and yet do not wish to be thought charitable. Surely these men are not ridiculous for assuming to be that which they are not: at least if they are (their) scripture commends them. And if WHW is satisfied that the settlers around him are amply protected, it is no reason we should be that we are. I hope that his conscience approves of his endeavour to prevent our getting what mine assures me I have been justified in endeavouring to obtain. Your obedient servant, Squatter, Burnett District.[331]

To the Editor of the Moreton Bay Courier

Sir, Thinking we had already heard both sides of the question, at any rate "Squatter's," in common with many of your subscribers, who have grown really tired of his weakness for seeing himself in print (as of course he is perfectly aware that his name is as well-known as though he signed it), would beg to suggest that, as he can make no reasonable complaint against the space which has been devoted to him in your paper, he should either change the so often repeated and tiresome subject, or that you will step in with your editorial power and save us. There are others besides "Squatter" who are equally aware of the management of the Native Police; and, admitting that, like most other men, they are not faultless, still the good they have done far more than balances any individual faults of either commanders or men. It is too plain that more than the reformation of the force is sought by "Squatter." There is evidently a vindictive feeling, towards the head of that force, to be gratified; and it seems quite clear that for Mr Walker to do right would be utterly impossible, and even annoying to "Squatter." I would ask not, for goodness sake, to be answered how he reconciles his high indignation at the fact

331 *MBC* 20 November 1852 p 4.

of Neddy not being dragged to the lock-up when no person would identity him, with his complaint of the atrocious act committed on the three poor creatures who have so enlisted his sympathy for the very same cause? Again, with very bad taste but overcharged with bile, he says the blacks wanted something at Fraser's Island, and innocently knows not what; and that the police were sent to give it to them. Now what does "Squatter" want of the Police if it is not to give it them when they deserve it? Or if not, what is all his writing for?

At this moment, a gentleman has called from the lower Condamine, who tells me the Police on the Dawson are "giving it to them," and that for three hours the blacks fought the troopers almost hand to hand, and that, after the most determined resistance, many were killed and several captured. Surely one act of disciplined courage such as this, although of seldom occurrence, should veil many faults in men who are only from discipline above the bloodthirsty savages against whom "Squatter" asks them to protect him. I further put the question to the person giving the above information, whether he considered the Police of any value in his district; and the answer was we are as quiet now as you are here. Hoping this will not induce "Squatter" to inflict on us two more columns in your valuable journal, which might be more amusingly filled. I am, Sir, your obedient servant, November 25th 1852. Subscriber. [We agree with our correspondent that this subject has already occupied enough of our space, and further communications must be declined, unless they can throw some additional light, upon the question. Ed. *MBC*][332]

To the Editor of the Moreton Bay Courier

Sir, A circumstance tending to show the management and state of discipline of the Native Police force on the Upper Dawson, deserves to be made public, and may not prove uninteresting to your readers. For the accuracy of the following narrative I enclosed my name as a guarantee. About three months ago,

332 *MBC* 11 December 1852 p 2.

Lieutenant Bligh and a party of Native Police, travelling past the sheep station of a gentleman on the Dawson, dismounted, and two of the troopers set out in quest of adventures. They descried a shepherd's hut, the only occupant of which was a woman, the wife of one of the shepherds, whose husband was of course out with the sheep. They entered the hut and attempted to take indecent liberties with the woman; and only for the timely arrival of assistance, would no doubt have succeeded in their designs.

This circumstance was reported to Lieutenant Bligh by the owner of the station, and he promised to inquire into the matter, and have the men punished. Sometime after this the same officer again passed the same station, and as its owner had some reason to suppose that he had not fulfilled his former promise, he inquired again whether he had punished the two troopers, as, if not, he would represent the matter in another quarter. The only reply he received was that he "might go and do his best." This was all the satisfaction that he was able to obtain for a most indecent outrage attempted to be perpetrated upon one of his servants.[333]

It is important to squatters living so far out that matters of this kind should not be permitted to occur, or that if they do, the parties implicated should be severely punished. Newly arrived immigrants are sufficiently terrified from proceeding into the interior already, without the additional fear of being molested and maltreated by those who are paid to protect them. I am, Sir, your obedient servant, A Squatter, December 13, 1853. [If it be true that conduct such as this has been passed over in the manner mentioned, the whole affair is one of the most disgraceful that has for a long time come under our notice, and all the culpable parties should be forthwith brought to account, if there be even a shadow of good Government in this part of the colony. Ed. *MBC*][334]

---

333 See Chapter 11, F Walker's letter Traylan, 31/12/1853 to Hon CS Re: incident.

334 *MBC* 17 December 1853 p 2.

11

Native Police Operational Correspondence

SIR CHARLES FITZROY TO EARL GREY, 12 August 1848 (Despatch N° 180, per ship Robert Syers)

My Lord, I have the honour to transmit the usual copies of the Financial Papers, submitted to the Leg. Council during its recent Session, for the years 1848 and 1849.

At page 81 of this Book, your Lordship will find a copy of the explanatory Message with which I submitted to the Council the Estimates of Expenditure for the year 1849; and at page 85 a copy of a Message transmitting to the Council an Estimate amounting to £1,000, for the formation of a small Corps of Native Police beyond the Settled Districts. I have reason to believe that the establishment of this force will not only have the effect of checking the collisions between the white Inhabitants and the Aborigines, referred to in the Message, and which in some instances have had very deplorable results; but I am also sanguine in the hope that it may prove one of the most efficient means of attempting to introduce more civilized habits among the native tribes. I have, &c, CHS. A. FITZROY.[335]

Message N° 26.

CHARLES A. FITZROY, Governor: Circumstances having been recently brought under the Governor's notice, in respect to certain collisions which have taken place, in parts beyond the settled districts, between the white inhabitants and the Aborigines, which appear to him to require that immediate steps should be taken for their suppression, he transmits to the Council an estimate for the formation of a small corps of native police, to be employed on this service, amounting to £1000. It has not been possible to prepare on estimate in detail; but the Council may rely that, if the money be voted, it will be expended for the purpose with

335 HRA 1 xxvi p 559.

every regard to economy. The amount will be chargeable on the assessment raised beyond the settled districts. Government House, Sydney, 8 June 1848.

(Enclosure to Message)

Additional Supplementary Estimate for the year 1848. For the formation of a small corps of native police, to be employed beyond the boundaries of location in the Sydney district £1000. E. Deas Thomson, Colonial Secretary. Colonial Secretary's Office, Sydney, 8th June 1848.

The Colonial Secretary in moving the sum of £1000 for this purpose stated that he had been long of opinion that the establishment of a corps of native police would be most beneficial as the means of preventing those collisions between the natives and the Europeans which unfortunately in some districts of the colony were of frequent occurrence. The localities where it was intended this force should be principally employed were the Clarence River, Darling Downs, and beyond the district of Wellington. The estimate was then put and passed, and the House resumed.[336]

Colonial Secretary's Office, Sydney, 4 August 1848

HIS Excellency the Governor has been pleased to appoint Frederick Walker, Esquire, of the Native Police, to be a Magistrate of the Territory and its Dependencies. By His Excellency's Command, E. DEAS THOMSON

Colonial Secretary's Office, Sydney, 17 August 1848

HIS Excellency the Governor has been pleased to appoint Frederick Walker, Esquire, to be Commandant of the Corps of Native Police, to be employed beyond the Settled Districts in the Sydney District. By His Excellences Command, E. DEAS THOMSON

Col. Sec. to Frederick Walker, 21 August 1848

I do myself the honour to acknowledge the receipt of your letter of the 18th instant and to state to you in reply that his Excellency the Governor approves of you having purchased sixteen horses for the use of

---

336 *SMH* 13 June 1848 p 2.

the Native Police of the Sydney District at an expense in all of £146 5s. (SRNSW 4-3860 Reel2818 p 271)

Col. Sec. to Frederick Walker, 21 August 1848

In acknowledging the receipt of your letter of the 18th instant. I am directed by his Excellency the Governor to inform you that your pay as Commandant of the Native Police in the Sydney District will commence from the time you cease to draw salary as Clerk of the Bench at Wagga Wagga.

In compliance with your request, the Auditor General has been authorised to prepare a warrant for advancing to you, three months' salary and a sufficient sum to enable you to provide forage for sixteen horses for fourteen days at the rate of 2s 6d per ration. In respect to the remuneration to be allowed to the men to be appointed to take charge of the horses as far as Mr Boyd's Station, I am directed to request that you will propose a rate to which you can obtain a suitable man for the duty. (SRNSW 4-3860 Reel 2818 p 272)

Col. Sec. to Frederick Walker, 21 August 1848

With reference to your letter of the 18th instant representing the difficulty in procuring a suitable person to appoint to as sergeant of the Native Police, I have the honour to inform you that his Excellency the Governor approves of a compliance with your recommendation that no sergeant should be appointed for the present. His Excellency direct me to add that when the time arrives for the appointment of a sergeant the question of increasing the pay attached to that situation shall receive due consideration. (SRNSW 4-3860 Reel 2818 p 273)

Col. Sec. to Frederick Walker, 26 August 1848

In reply to your letter of this date, I do myself the honour to inform you that his Excellency the Governor approves of the man employed by you to assist in taking the horses for the Native Police as far as Mr Boyd's Station being allowed 10s a week and a ration in remuneration for his services for a period of about three weeks. (SRNSW 4-3860 Reel 2818 p 275)

Col. Sec. to Frederick Walker, 4 October 1848

Certain murders having been recently perpetrated by the whites on the Aborigines at the Macintyre River and the latter having in retaliation murdered a white person, I am instructed by His Excellency the Governor to request that you will expedite as much as possible the formation of the party of Native Police to be sent to the Gwydir District. I am at the same time to state that in the meantime the Bench of Magistrates, Warialda have been authorised to engage three more additional constables for the purpose of checking these proceedings on both sides. (SRNSW 4-3860 Reel 2818 p 286)

Col. Sec. to Frederick Walker, 14 October 1848

I do myself the honour to acknowledge the receipt of your letter of the 28th ultimo reporting the death of a man who has been employed by you to assist in driving the horses of the Native Police and that expenses to the amount of £340 had been incurred in taking charge of the horses during the illness of this man and for his internment for the payment of which I have to convey to you the sanction of the Governor.

You also report the death of one of the horses of the corps and in compliance with the request contained in your further letter of the 30th of that month. His Excellency directs me to authorise the purchase of a horse in his place at an expense not exceeding £15. (SRNSW 43860 Reel2818 p 294)

Col. Sec. to Frederick Walker, 24 November 1848

I do myself the honour to acknowledge the receipt of your letter of the 13th ultimo reporting you having enlisted ten troopers for the corps under your command and stating your intention of proceeding to Warialda and requesting authority for obtaining rations for the men at nine pence per ration and I am directed to inform you that his Excellency the Governor approves of the application made by you being complied with. (SRNSW 43860 Reel2818 p 306)

Col. Sec. to Frederick Walker, 30 November 1848

In transmitting the accompanying letter from Mr JB Nixon preferring complaint against yourself and Mr John Peter JP, Gumly Gumly, Murrumbidgee, I am instructed by his Excellency the Governor to request the favour of any explanation or observation you may wish to offer on the subject. (SRNSW 4-3860 Reel2818 p 308)

Frederick Walker to Col. Sec. 30 November 1848

I have the honour to acknowledge the receipt of your letter of 11th October informing of certain murders committed on the Macintyre River and requesting me to expedite the formation of the Police party under my command. I have to report that ten of the police horses have been lost and from the fact of their having travelled 60 miles the first night I have no doubt they were driven away. However, after a search of 450 miles, I succeeded in recovering them all and have just returned with them. I was delighted to find my ten recruits still in the Police camp and have today completed the whole fourteen by enlisting 4 more.

I regret to report that Sergeant James has been obliged to resign his appointment from a recurrence of ill health. I have to express my satisfaction with his care of the police during my absence. I fear that I cannot replace him in that part of the colony which will throw a great increase of duty and anxiety on myself. I do myself the honour to annex a list of the party and to state that I expect to start about the 6th December. (QSL Reel A2.19 p 364)

Corporal Logan formerly Border Police Yabala Yabala
Corporal Jack formerly Border Police Wirri garow
Simon cook engaged and rationed by Police
Edgar engaged and rationed by Mr Walker
Sims (white) cart driver and rationed by Mr Walker
Trooper Henry Wirri garow
Trooper Jacky Jacky Yabala Yabala
Trooper Wyjatta Yabala Yabala
Trooper Geegwaw ≈
Trooper Edward ≈
Trooper Aladdin Buraba Buraba
Trooper Paddy ≈
Trooper Larry ≈
Trooper Jonny Hindmarsh ≈
Trooper Willy ≈
Trooper Walter ≈
Trooper Yorky Iota Iota

Frederick Walker, Wampa 115 miles up the Darling to Col. Sec. 15 February 1849

I do myself the honour to inform you that after a journey rendered tedious by the illness of the horses belonging to the Police, I have reached the last station up the Darling. Four days after I had left Deniliquin six of the horses (had) sickness and I was obliged in consequence to wait at Mr Boyd's Lower Edward station where unfortunately one of the best of the horses died, the other five recovered but were so sick as to prevent me travelling more than 8 miles a day. In escaping the Moulamein another horse was in an un-mountable manner although he was pulled out of the water immediately by the police who all plunged into his assistance.

In crossing from the Edward to the Murrumbidgee, I had great trouble in preserving the sick horses having been obliged to carry water to them in a keg and the skin of a kangaroo. At Mr Wentworth's station, I stopped five days and the horses all improved. The months of December and January are generally the best for grass on the Edward and Murrumbidgee but this year the flood being six weeks later than usual the good grass was all under water and the plains eaten base by sheep. If I had not had two reaping hooks, the sick horses would have perished but with them I procured a sufficient quantity of seeds not only to preserve their lives but even to improve their condition before I reached the Darling.

When I arrived at Mr Fletcher's the first station on the Darling finding plenty of grass I stopped fifteen days and now the horses are in fair condition. I proceed up the Darling tomorrow and hope to average 15 miles per diem. I have to observe that in consequence of the death of two horses, the police make use of two of mine I have now no spare horses. I have therefore the honour to request his Excellency will be pleased to sanction the purchase of two new horses upon my arrival in Warialda. Margin note: Approved at an expense not exceeding £12 per horse. 17th March. (QSL Reel A2.19 p 358)

Frederick Walker, Moanna to Col. Sec. 23 March 1849

In my last letter dated 15th February I have etc. of informing you that I was on the point of leaving the uppermost stations on the Lower Darling, I now have to report that I have reached the lowest station on the upper Darling with my party all in safety. On the 26th February, I fell in with a very large tribe of natives, the Bargunda tribe and was received with great kindness by them.

On the 4th March, a few more belonging to another tribe accompanied me throughout the day and on the 6th, I fell in with a large number fishing and I gave them some empty bags and two tomahawks in exchange for abundance of fish. On the 7th, a few more came to my camp after dark and accompanied us the next day to where the tribe was camped in large numbers, to these I gave a native dog a very acceptable present; at one o'clock in the morning of the 9th I was awakened by Corporal Logan who informed me that the blacks were coming up in great numbers to the camp and to my astonishment I saw them by clear moonlight evidently following on the tracks of my cart but not yet seen my encampment.

The natives had been so friendly the day before that I could not allow my men to fire but cooed to them when they immediately fled in great terror. The discovery when the sun rose of several nulla nullas or clubs cut and hardened that very night and thrown away in their flight shewed however what their intentions were. On the 10th, Trooper Geegwaw arrived with his carbine and Larry unarmed were encountered by several blacks who at first were friendly but in a short time a strong native spired Geegwaw's carbine and attempted to take it from him when Larry catching with great activity the jarred spear thrown at him extricated his comrade by spearing his adversary killing him on the spot, five more natives came up and luckily myself and my men firing as they came up killed four more natives and the remainder escaped although Corporal Logan and three troopers swam the Darling with their carbines and ammunition in pursuit while I however immediately recalled.

On the 13th, I was obliged to abandon one of my own horses knocked up and on the 17th, I reached Fort Bourke which I found burned to the ground. I then crossed the Darling for fear of missing the Lawson's station which I reached on the 21st having travelled by my computation 462 miles from station to station or 577 miles from the Murray. The whole of the much-abused Lower Darling is well adapted for depasturing cattle or sheep being equal or superior to similar country on the Lachlan where such stock have answered so well; but I am satisfied that unless a strong police force is at hand to restrain both parties great loss of life either whites or blacks must attend the forming of stations on that river.

On the 26th, I intend returning to where I left my horse in hopes of recovering him and several more whose fresh tracks I saw and suspect belong to the Crown, having been I am told abandoned by Mr Kennedy the surveyor. This will occupy me 8 days and about the 4th April I shall leave this when the horses having had nearly 14 days' rest will be able to go to Warialda in 14 more. At all events, you may depend upon my reaching that place on or before the 20th April of course I leave the cart behind. Margin Note: Was Mr Walker on appointment informed of the instructions from home respecting the necessity of taking depositions in all cases of collisions with the Blacks? Apparently not. This should now be done, and he should be instructed to do so in this case, have reports and to transmit the depositions to the Attorney-General, Charles Arthur FitzRoy (CAF). (QSL Reel A2.19 p 355)

Mr Goggs, Chinchilla to Col. Sec. 9 April 1849

Since my interview with you in Sydney in the month of February last respecting being afforded to this district on account of the hostilities of the natives, I beg leave to report that no more men have been murdered belonging to a M. Edwards that many of the natives were recognised by one man that escaped, William Adeg the names of some of the natives Adeg knew viz, Jacky, Bungaree, Billy, Mr Dennis, Jacky Jacky, Bucksmall. I wish to call your attention to the conversation between us respecting the sending of the Native Police from the Macintyre River to this place. I fully understand they were to be sent here immediately and I again urge the great necessity of their assistance for if they do not come quickly every squatter will be compelled to abandon their stations as the lives and of all are now at stake. Ten men up to this time have been murdered and we have fearful anticipations of many more if prompt protection is not sent. Goggs supported by Chauvel, Blyth & Ewer & C Mackenzie and Mr Edwards.

Frederick Walker to Col. Sec. 1 May 1849

I etc. that the party of police under my command has arrived here safe. Having been informed at Moanna that the country up the Darling was in a fearful state for want of grass and daily getting worse, I started at once instead of attempting to recover my horse. I was soon compelled to dismount all my men and to cause them to drive their horses, all of which are safe and sound. I had the misfortune to lose another horse of my own.

I have received only one letter from your office. The rest having been sent to the Macintyre. I know not therefore whether his Excellency has been pleased to sanction two new horses or not. I have the honour to request his Excellency the Governor will be pleased to sanction the purchase of four additional horses to be used as packhorses as I have no means of carrying rations and arms, often not able to procure any at some stations and am unable to replace my own two horses which have carried them hitherto. The expense will be twelve pounds each which I hope will be allowed as the expense of a sergeant has been same since December and had better perhaps not be incurred until next year.

I have sent in a requisition for the second suit of clothing for the police which is more than due as they have worn their first, seven months and it is getting rather shabby. I propose the next suit to last until January 1849 (sic, 1850) in order to get the supply for that year at the proper season. I proceed to the Macintyre on the 3rd and upon my arrival there intend to turn out the police horses for six weeks. I have received several warrants to execute on that river and intend doing all the duty on foot until the horses are in good condition. My men are in good health and great spirits and have behaved much to my satisfaction. The saddles furnished to me have caused me a great deal of annoyance as they hurt the horses' backs and I cannot prevent it. I have had them all new stuffed under my own inspection and all the accoutrements mended where required at an expense of 5s each amounting in all to £4 which I hope his Excellency will sanction. I am glad to (be) able to make a good report of all the force except two. They are indeed excellent. (QSL Reel A2.19 p 350)

Frederick Walker to Col. Sec. 1 May 1849

In reply to your letter of the 18th ulto. requesting me to hold an inquiry into the late collision between the Native Police and the natives of the Darling, I etc. to inform you that I have requested Mr Commissioner Bligh to hold that inquiry as I myself am the principle witness. I take this opportunity of pointing out the inconvenience arising from the evidence of the native troopers not being admissible. This is very annoying as I cannot send my men on escort duty for fear of an attempt at rescue which might cause great trouble to my men if they used their arms which they certainly would. Margin notes: This may be laid before the Executive Council when the Bill is introduced by the Attorney-General for admitting the evidence of the aboriginal natives before the courts. CAF 12th. (QSL Reel A2.19 p 346)

Frederick Walker to Col. Sec. 26 May 1849

I do myself the honour to report that the Native Police force under my command reached the Macintyre River on the 10th inst. On my arrival, I found the river had not been fordable for several days and then the natives taking advantage of the height of the flood which prevented the stockmen from looking after the cattle were spearing them to a great extent on the runs of Messrs Dight and How, also that the murderers of Mr Perrier's shepherds were in the marauding party.

I in consequence caused my police to cut a bark canoe and my party having crossed the river in safety. I proceeded on foot in search of the hostile blacks, guided by a friendly native called Tandy on the 13th we unexpectedly encountered them in the midst of a dense Brigalow scrub when they fled, leaving their tomahawks, spears and boomerangs and also the carcase of a newly killed steer in our possession, my men were so much fatigued by their long journey and the day's march in a heavy rain that they were unable to overtake the fugitives which I regretted much as the murderers were pointed out by Tandy. The stations of Messrs Dight and How are however for the present safe.

The next day having learned from a carrier called George Smith that was unable to proceed with his load of supplies for Augustus Morris on account of his having been informed that the blacks intended robbing his dray, the Native Police escorted him when we were all but surprised by a party of 20 to 30 natives who came suddenly on us when the police were assisting the carrier in extracting his dray from a bog. The police fired on them and one man named Cockatoo was shot through the leg, the remainder escaped over the river. Cockatoo confessed to me that their intention was to rob the dray. His leg was banged by Corporal Logan and I left him two days' provisions.[337]

[337] See QSL, 5823 John Watts Typescript 1901 John Watts 1901 p 39, for a civilian description of this incident.

On my return to the station of Mr Yeomans where I had left the horses I met Mr Morris, who informed me that the blacks who have rendered themselves so notorious by murder and slaughtering cattle were in the vicinity of the station of Mr Jonathan Young where they were killing his cattle. I immediately proceeded in pursuit with the Police accompanied by Messrs Morris JP, Marshall, and Rennes, guided by their friendly blacks. We followed them for six days and in three different camps found the remains of four head of cattle newly killed. We however failed in our attempt at capturing the criminals principally through the treachery of the guides and partly through our being encumbered with the horses. During this expedition, the whole party were without food for 48 hours excepting a few pieces of bullock's hide. The police neither complained of their fatigue or their hunger and yet this is their first day's rest since our arrival.

On our return, we fell in with a man who had been lost for four days and took him in safety to the station of Mr Jonathan Young. I intend starting again on foot in a few days in pursuit of the same party who have been the perpetrators of nearly all the murders in this district and have been rendered audacious by long impunity. I believe for 8 years. I intend never leaving their tracks until I overtake them, each man will take 7 days provisions. I have thus given the details of my proceedings because I consider it necessary that his Excellency the Governor should be made aware of the real state of affairs and of the obstacles which the Police force under my command have to surmount. Margin notes: This Report of the conduct of the Native Police is very satisfactory. 2. The Cmd[t] should be informed of the approbation of the government of the zeal and activity he has displayed in effecting so much with so small a force. CAF 15th. (QSL Reel A2.19 p 325)

Frederick Walker to Col. Sec. 26 May 1849

In my letter this date N° 49/8, I stated my intention of attempting the dispersion and subjugation of the hostile tribes in the neighbourhood of the Macintyre, I have the honour call your attention to the iniquitous practice carried on at some stations which is to drive off all blacks from them. This system they call keeping them at a distance.

As every black has his own hunting ground from which he is thus expelled and he is not allowed to trespass for any length of time on the others he is compelled for his own subsistence to kill cattle. It is my wish that the marauding parties which now infest the brigalows should be broken up which can only be done by allowing each native to return to his own ground. I have also the honour to point out the great injustice done to those few settlers who have been so kind to the natives and where stations are considered by many of the blacks as a place of refuge when expelled from their own homes. These settlers therefore have to support a large number of blacks who otherwise would be among the marauding parties.

I therefore have the honour to request his Excellency the Governor will be pleased to sanction my refusing assistance to all parties who contrary to my request refuse to admit the natives on their runs. Margin notes: The practice referred to in the 2nd paragraph is much to be regretted and is certainly not creditable of the parties referred to. The Cmd^{t} should use his utmost influences to discourage it and induce a better state of feeling but I cannot authorise assistance being withheld as suggested in the last paragraph from those parties who refuse to admit the natives on their runs. CAF 15th (QSL Reel A2.19 p 332)

Frederick Walker to Col. Sec. 26 May 1849

In answer to your letter of the 1st March 1849, N° 49/52 relative to the outrages on the Condamine I do myself the honour to state that I will proceed to that part of the Colony as soon as I have dispersed and subdued the tribes that are now desolating this district. I hope to start in three weeks from this date. Margin note: Read. CAF 15th. (QSL Reel A2.19 p 338)

Frederick Walker to Col. Sec. 28 May 1849

I do myself the honour to inform you that I have just received a letter from Mr Commissioner Rolleston reporting the state of affairs on the Condamine to be so desperate that it is imperative for the Native Police to start without delay for that run. I accordingly start with ten troopers as soon as the next post arrives. I am delayed until then for want of percussion caps for which I have written to the Colonial Storekeeper desiring him to forward them by post.

Four troopers will be left under the command of the only resident magistrate Mr Augustus Morris and he has besides my two-native orderly Edgar and Simon who are clothed and armed the same as the Native Police. I have also desired him to call in the assistance of several settlers of respectability to enforce the peace during my absence. Several murders have been committed on the Condamine and Mr Dangar's stations burned to the ground. Margin note: Approve of the proposal proceeding reported herein. CAF 15th (QSL Reel A2.19 p 335)

Frederick Walker to Col. Sec. 12 July 1849

I do myself the honour to inform you that on the 1st Inst, I had made every preparation for starting the next morning for the Condamine. During the day, I had been informed by friendly natives that Pantaloon one of the ringleaders had come to the camp the proceeding night with proposals for peace. I had previously told them I would make no terms with the murderers but was willing to forgive and forget all the depredations of the remainder if they were not repeated.

At nine o'clock at night however I received information that Pantaloon and his brother Bobby had on their way stolen two sheep and that Darby's lot joined to a strong reinforcement of Moonie blacks, (who) were camped at a place called Cumba. I saw at once that there was some concealed design and that the proposals for peace were intended to mislead.

I therefore resolved on an immediate pursuit and at eleven o'clock, at night we were already two miles on the way. We followed the lead from camp to camp finding at every one the remains of slaughtered cattle and at last late in the evening of Monday the 9th July, we fell in with the hostile blacks near Carbucky on the Macintyre River; in the act of cutting up a cow the property of Mr R Pringle.

The blacks at first took into the scrub but it being of small extent one party attempting to escape across the plain where they were immediately driven back by a detachment of the Police under Corporal Logan at the same instant on the other side two troopers drove back a large body who were attempting to escape on the side nearest the river. Unfortunately, at this critical moment I was cut off from the main body of men by a party of 30 or more blacks who threw themselves into a thick bush and set up loud shouts of defiance and made a great din by striking their spears and boomerangs together.

It was now near dark, my men without a leader were hesitating, I determined therefore with the small party near me, consisting of Messrs Morris, Marshall, Rens and four troopers to drive the blacks from their position. My party accordingly rushed in on foot and delivering their fire at twelve paces, at first staggered the insurgent blacks and at last drove them from their cover, my orderly Edgar was speared through the leg but he immediately drew the spear out and drove it several inches into the body of his adversary. Mr Rens was also wounded by a boomerang in the face.

I now joined the main body of my men but the blacks escaped in the dark. On visiting the scene of action, the next morning, we found one black dead and saw that several had been badly wounded having crawled off on their hands and knees leaving a trail of blood. I would call your attention to the fact that this affair took place near Carbucky, a place where five men are buried who were killed by the blacks.

On my return last night to Cunongermoro (sic), I understand what the design of the blacks was. The Boobera mob having returned strengthened by a party of Severn blacks; and they would have been united with Darby's lot the next day if we had not defeated it. I much regretted not having one hour more daylight as I would have annihilated that lot, among which were six murderers and all the rest living solely on cattle. Since I have been here, this lot have killed at the rate of upwards of 300 head of cattle per annum.

I leave tomorrow morning for the Condamine leaving six men with Mr Morris. I do myself the honour again to press upon your attention the necessity for a very large increase of the force under my command. The blacks have established a regular system, attacking at the same time stock and station on the Severn, Macintyre, Wootu creek, Moonie and Condamine and are consequently more than a match for my small party. I have to express my thanks for the assistance I have constantly received from Messrs Augustus Morris, R. Purvis Marshall, and Rens and especially the last affair. Margin notes: With every disposition to award the praise that is due to Mr Walker for the zeal he has displayed in the organisation and management of the Native Police under his orders, it is evidently necessary that he should again be cautioned to be careful not to permit his zeal to excite him to acts of aggressive warfare against the Natives with which he may come in contact. The command of this admirable force has been intrusted to him in the confidence that he will use it for the maintenance of order and peace and not for the purpose of carrying war into an enemy's country. CAF 3rd (QSL Reel A2.19 p 316)

Simpson & Diamond, Solicitors, London to Frederick Walker, 16 July 1849

By direction of Mrs Walker, the Administratrix of your late brother Reginald John Walker Esquire, deceased has the pleasure to send you a letter of credit on the Commercial Banking Company at Sydney for £26 2s 5d being the amount of your 1/7th share of the net proceeds of your late brother's estate and we should feel obliged by you acknowledging its safe arrival by the return mail. (QSA Series ID14733/86134)

Francis Gwynne, Barralta[338] to Frederick Walker, 16 August 1849

You promised to write to me when you left this, how you got on, but alas for human frailty you have never done so. I certainly have seen an article or two in the Sydney papers relative to your proceedings but after all such information is anything but satisfactory. I am afraid I cannot take the credit of writing to you from disinterested motives. For I am afraid, this is a very selfish letter. The truth is our case with Boyd comes on very soon before the Arbitration Commissioners and we wish to get all the evidence we can relative to the justice of our claims; and as your evidence will have great weight, we are anxious to have it in as legal a form as possible. I enclose you a map, copied from Parkinson's survey, which I wish you would look at and if you believe the boundaries laid down on it are correct, you would do us a very great favour. If you would make a solemn declaration before a magistrate to that effect and also your being

[338] Sometimes spelt Barratta, Messrs Gwynne (brothers Thomas, Henry, Richard, & Francis) owned and operated Barratta Station on the Edward River, next-door to Ben Boyd's Deniliquin.

present when Morris and my brother and my brother Richard agreed about them and in fact anything that you can recollect about the affair. A few words on the map countersigned by a JP, especially, if you can recollect about the date would also assist us very materially. By the bye I wrote Boyd about the case and in his letter, he said that he was willing to refer the affair to you, now that was false for he told Henry that it was Morris that he wished to arbitrate the matter and as Morris had so many things on his mind in those days Henry refused to agree to that to that except in conjunction with you. And now with the full belief that you will oblige us if you can, I will drop the shop.

Henry has been gone some time to California, heartily sick of this horrible hole. If there is a place in this world where an enterprising fellow like you would get rapidly on I believe California above all others would be the place and I am surprised that you have not turned your attention to it. By Heavens Dear Walker, if you'll go there I'll go with you, for this country after all is "weary, stale, flat and unprofitable". Think on it. Old Lewis is in status quo, grumbling as usual. Daniels has taken unto himself an illegitimate rib that is to say he keeps a woman who was servant at the Woolshed, to the extreme disgust of old Hindmarsh and the rest of that creditable establishment, who would have thought D would have been so foolish. E Bloxham I believe intends getting spliced sometime next month and he has rented Phillipe's house for six months to spend the honeymoon in. A miss Kenny is the happy intended. I dare say you saw her at Carnes when you went down. The Bloxham's lost their case with Boyd and I am afraid will lose another. Their affair I am sorry to say are not at present in the most flourishing state. Phillips, I believe is rather in a mess as in fact are a great many in this quarter. Old Bill Peters is as jolly and fatter than ever. So much so that he is in great danger of dropping off from apoplexy or by Woodford who has a boiling down establishment at Maidera who looks upon him as a little fortune if he could only get him once into his pots. Tibb is lately married and of course is doing his best to multiply images of his own beautiful self. The Moulamein certainly is a successful place for breeding and matrimony. P Brougham is engaged to Miss Kennedy. ... *page damaged* ... There won't be a single man on the river. The rage for marriage. Our last race meeting went very well off and I had the melancholy satisfaction of having the swiftest horse on the course and seeing it beat through bad riding. I must leave off the postman has been at me twice. With kindest regard from Dick. I remain Dear Walker yours very sincerely, Francis Gwynne Write me as soon as you can!!! (QSA Series ID14733/86134)

John Strachan, Tumut to Frederick Walker, 28 September 1849

It is now a long time since I heard from you and I thought after you had made your appearance among the whites again that you would have found time to have written a few lines to me. I have sold the Tumut Store to Sydney G Watson and the Laradisle (sic) to the church's so I am now completely on my oars and I am now staying at Tumut for short time to wind up all my accounts. I have never received one farthing from Bloxham on your account and I have only received two amounts from the Treasury on your account one on 27 June last £41 5s and the other one of 27 July for £30 15s. In the last letter, you wrote to me you mentioned that you have no salary abstract but that you would send one. Have you attended to this? I am very anxious to have all my accounts settled as soon as I can and I feel convinced that you will do what you can to assist me in this respect. I send you your account to date which I think you will find correct. The last quarter salary has not been paid and consequently I have not given you credit for the amount of it. You will observe that there will be a large sum due by you even after giving credit for the quarter salary ending in June '49. I shall expect to hear from you shortly after you having got this and I am in haste. (QSA Series ID14733/86134.)

Frederick Walker to Col. Sec. 16 October 1849

I do myself the honour to acknowledge the receipt of your letter of the 8th August, in which I am cautioned not to commit acts of aggressive warfare against the Aboriginal Natives and that the command of the Native Police has been intrusted to me for the maintenance of peace and order and not for the purpose of carrying war into an enemy's country.

In answer, I have the honour to declare that in no case whatsoever have I acted beyond what I deemed was my duty. In the case immediately referred to, I held warrants for the apprehension of sundry blacks accused on oath of a most atrocious murder, and followed them in the same manner as I would any body of white murderers until I overtook them, when I found them in the act of committing felony; the circumstances attending my attempt at capturing them it is needless to recapitulate, you know that they the murderers were aided and abetted by a large number of blacks, and I was obliged to engage them or retire, what the consequences would have been if I had retired it is impossible to foresee, for the result of my proceedings I refer you to the enclosed report from Mr A Morris JP and I have also to state that the number of blacks anxious to show themselves to be friendly is three times the number that it was previously.

2 In reading over my letter I feel that his Excellency may have thought that the using the term annihilate shewed I was too much excited, but in explanation I have to state that if it had been a number of armed white men, I should have considered it my duty to make use of my arms against everyone who did not lay down his (weapon), which not a single black did. I have also the honour to observe that if I had retreated or even shewn any hesitation you would not have been troubled with any more reports of the duty of the Native Police, for these same blacks had before beaten and chased large parties of settlers and stockmen, who escaped only by the freshness of their horses, and mine were all but knocked up from a long day's march, and it soon could have been dark.

3 I would call your attention to the fact that I have never received any instructions as to what my particular duties were to be, nor did I consider such instruction necessary, as I well knew that I was to try and maintain peace and order by carrying the law into effect both against white and black, without distinction, and that I conceive I have done, I have considered the hostile blacks as British subjects who like armed bushrangers were defying the law and were committing murder and felony so as to make roads unsafe and render it dangerous for anyone to go a few yards from his house without firearms. I tried to apprehend these blacks and they resisted me and never yet has a Native Policeman under my orders fired a shot unless it was under such circumstances, since I reached the Macintyre. I would now however beg you would be so kind as to inform me what course I am in future to pursue under similar circumstances.

4 I have thought it requisite in order that his Excellency might have implicit confidence in me, never to disguise either the real facts of the case

or ever my feelings and intentions, and I think my reports and the affidavits I have always sent into the Honourable Attorney-General will fully convince you that I have never done so.

5 I feel grateful that his Excellency the Governor has been pleased to appreciate the value of the Native Police and of my exertions in organising and managing that force. Margin notes, page 1: It is impossible at this distance to issue particular instructions as to the course Mr Walker is to follow in the performance of his duties beyond those he has already received in the letter of the 8th of August now acknowledged. He must be guided by his own discretion and I have no doubting that the zeal and ability which he has undoubtedly displayed in the management of the Native Police will be so transformed by that much reported quality as to need no further cautioning on any ground. Page 2: He should clearly understand that the Col Secy's letter of the 8th of August was intended solely as a caution for the future and not in any way as a reprimand for the past. 1st Nov CAF. Mr Morris's letter is very satisfactory and shows the value of the Native Police Force, CAF. (QSL Reel A2.19 p 306)

A Morris JP to Frederick Walker, 18 October 1849

I have the honour to report to you that, that part of the Native Police which you left under my orders has during your absence conducted itself in a highly satisfactory manner.

Immediately after your departure, I went in company with the Native Police to meet and assist the carrier drays on which were the police clothing and ammunition, this was safely done and I am happy to say that the road down the Severn is not now looked upon with the dread it was previous to the arrival of the Native Police. The Police have visited nearly all the Stations within fifty or sixty miles of this and have rendered considerable service to many of the settlers during the floods. They have also been employed in assisting to build a Barracks for themselves.

I have also great pleasure in reporting to you that a very favourable change has come over the hither to hostile Aborigines. Since the engagement near Carbucky they appear to think that they cannot carry on their former depredations with impunity.

Many more of the blacks than formerly came into the Station and although not a few of them have been wounded in their encounter with your men; they feel confident that as long as they conduct themselves peaceably no injury will be done to them.

I have also been informed by them that Darby the most notorious of all the ringleaders has died from his wounds to which circumstances we may no doubt attribute much of the present quiet. There have however been a few cattle speared by those blacks who still hold by the murderers, but the force left with me was too small to permit of my attempting their capture.

I cannot conclude this report without contrasting the present peaceable and orderly state of the neighbourhood with the lawless and disturbed condition in which it was last year. Twelve months ago, few could leave their abodes without being fully armed but since the arrival of the Native Police our arms are totally neglected and the enforcement of the peace and order is altogether left to you and your force. (QSL Reel A2.19 p 312)

Col. Sec. to Frederick Walker, 17 December 1849

I have laid before the Governor your letter of the 14th instant reporting your arrival in Sydney in pursuance of the instructions contained in my letter of the 31st October last N° 346.

2. His Excellency is desirous that you should be prepared by Tuesday next if in your power with some proposal for the augmentation of the Native Police so as to expend the sum voted for the corps during the ensuring year to the best advantage with reference to those parts of the country where its services are most required.

3. The Governor will be in Sydney on that day (tomorrow) when you will have the goodness to wait upon his Excellency. (SRNSW 4-3860 Reel2818 p 034)

Frederick Walker to Col. Sec. 17 December 1849

In another letter of this date I did myself the honour to lay before you an estimate of the probable expenditure of the Sydney Native Police for the year 1850. I now have the honour to submit, for your approval, what I consider the most efficient mode of making use of that force.

1. I propose that Callandoon, with which place there is now postal com-

munication, shall be the headquarters of the Native Police; and as that place is in the Macintyre portion of the Darling Downs District, in which peace and order has already been established by the means of the police force, it will be sufficient to leave a sergeant and ten men to act under the direction of the local magistrates during my absence.

2. One officer, with twelve troopers, will establish himself on the border of the Wide Bay and Burnett Districts.

3. The other officer, with ten troopers, will take charge of the Lower Condamine and the Maranoa Districts. Those two forces will occasionally meet on the Dawson.

4. Twelve troopers under my own charge will form an available force, which you will be able to send to any part of the colony where they may be most wanted. Three divisions will be constantly on patrol, and the men will exchange places as they meet, it being necessary, for the sake of maintaining discipline and health among the men, that each party of police should have an equal amount of work.

5. I do myself the honour to state that, with this force, I should be able to maintain peace and order in the Darling Downs District, and bring the districts of Wide Bay, Burnett, und Maranoa, to the same state. The police will also en route visit the whole western bounds of the occupied part of the colony, and thereby be of great benefit to the settlers: and the party immediately under my control will be able to afford their assistance at some future time; but you will easily see that the force even now would be unable to give permanent protection beyond that portion of the colony which I have described above.

6. Especially I entreat that, for the present, at all events, no portion of my force may be sent to the Macleay, Richmond, or Clarence River Districts, for though the police may be wanted there, yet the emergency is much greater in the distant out-settlements; and if so small a force attempts too much it will do nothing.

7. In time, as the country gets quiet, the Native Police can be moved to other parts, and the great advantage of the force in future will be that they will accompany the settlers as they move out, and thus prevent those lamentable collisions between the settlers and the aboriginal natives which have invariably occurred when a new portion of this colony

has been at first occupied.

8. On my arrival at the Macintyre, I propose taking the whole force through the disturbed district, as the display of so strong a party will tend greatly to quieting the country. I would then leave the detachments, as before mentioned, and then return to headquarters to be ready to receive instructions from you. (SMH 15 Jun 1850 p 3.) (QSL Reel A52 p865) Margin notes: The arrangement for stationing the Division of the Force, particularly as proposed by Mr Walker appear to be very judicious and he may be authorized to carry them into effect whensoever he may be prepared to do so. 19th CAF. Forwarded to H.M. Secretary of State by despatch N° 197 of 26 October 1850.

Frederick Walker to Col. Sec. 31 December 1849

I do myself the honour to furnish you with a report of the proceedings of the Native Police under my command from the period when I first raised the force up to this date.

1. I have the honour to inform you that I had no difficulty in getting volunteers for the police; on the contrary, I could have obtained ten times the number, the pick out of eight tribes. In the present force of fourteen, there are men from four tribes, each speaking a different language.

2. Owing to various causes, among others that of ten horses having been driven away, I did not complete my arrangements until the 6th December 1848. On that day, I started for the Macintyre, where I arrived in safety with the Native Police Force on the 10th May 1849.

3. I have already reported to you that on my journey I visited all the out-stations, i.e., squatting stations, on the Lower Murray, Darling, and Barwan rivers, and owing to the great drought the horses were much distressed, having scarcely any grass. The police and myself had to walk 300 miles, and for seventeen days had no rations of any kind, living solely on game and fish.

4. From the 18th May to the 14th June, the Native troopers were entirely employed checking the aggressions of the aboriginal natives; and I have reported, that owing to the resistance made by them to me when I was attempting the apprehension of six blacks, charged, on oath, with a most atrocious murder, there had been some lives lost, and that two of my

party were wounded. During a great portion of this period the duty was done by the police on foot, frequently walking from 20 to 30 miles a day, and being many days without food.

5. On the 24th of June I arrived, with ten troopers, on the Condamine, leaving four, and my two orderlies, at the Macintyre, under the charge of Mr A. Morris, J.P., who reports that in my absence this small party behaved much to his satisfaction, had visited all the stations within 50 or 60 miles of Callandoon, and had given great assistance to the settlers during the floods.

6. I found the Condamine country in a most disturbed state, several of the stations had been abandoned, twelve white men had been murdered, and the loss in cattle and sheep was immense. The greatest danger existed at the station of the late Mr John Dangar, where the store had been robbed and burnt, and damage done to the amount of £250; the hut-keeper was killed.

7. An attempt made by the combined FitzRoy Downs, Dawson, and Condamine blacks, about 150 men in number, to repeat their attack on this station, brought on two collisions with the Native Police. On the first occasion, the FitzRoy Downs blacks, the same who had killed seven men of Mr Macpherson's, and Mr Blythe's shepherd, besides spearing himself, and also murdering two of Mr Hughes' men, suffered so severely, that they returned to their own country, a distance of 80 miles. On the second occasion, having been informed that some blacks were on the Tannin, near Mr Dangar's, among whom were some who had been sworn to by the survivor of Mr Edwards' three men as the murderers of the other two, I proceeded in pursuit. The Native Police tracked them for eight days: and at sundown, on the eighth day, I found that we were within one mile of their camp, but the Condamine much flooded between us; at 12 o'clock at night we swam the river, each man carrying his carbine and ammunition; the water was so cold that two of the settlers who accompanied us were nearly drowned; they were pulled out by my men. At daybreak, we approached the camp, when we were perceived by the blacks; they seized their spears, and an engagement ensued; but they were soon compelled to fly, leaving us the camp, spears, &c., and a great deal of damaged property identified as belonging to Mr Dangar.

8. Having replaced Messrs Blyth and Chauvel, and also Mr Ewer, in their

stations, and re-established confidence among the other settlers, I returned to the Macintyre, where I was much pleased to find peace had not been broken in my absence, that the blacks were flocking in to the stations, and that the settlers would all have large quantities of fat stock, which was unprecedented on this river.

9. Since then the police have visited the Severn, the Macintyre Brook, and the Wootu Creek, and peace seems likely to become permanent in that part of the colony.

10. I may observe, that in the different encounters with hostile blacks, the Native Police have frequently shown great personal courage, and it is not easy to determine which is the best when all have behaved so well; but I do think that the two corporals are the pride of my little band; their cleanliness, obedience, and steadiness, has been a good example to the remainder, and has done a great deal towards establishing the esprit de corps which now exists in the Native Police Force.

11. I am convinced that, if properly officered by white persons, the natives of this colony would make as good troops as the natives of India. I know that as long as their officer stood none of the Native Police would stir.

12. On the only occasion on which I had to act upon a case of felony being committed by a white man, the offender was tracked and captured within two hours after I had received the information and within four after he had committed the crime.

13. One great advantage in employing aboriginal natives of this colony as police is that it is impossible to tamper with them.

14. I have now come to Sydney for the purpose of carrying out the increase of the force under my command. It will consist of a commandant, two lieutenants, and a sergeant-major, three native sergeants, six corporals, and thirty-five troopers. The headquarters will be at Callandoon, on the Macintyre River, and, in general, there will be a force stationed there, consisting of the sergeant-major and ten men, to act under the direction of the local Magistrates during my absence. A lieutenant and twelve men will be stationed on the border of the Burnett and Wide Bay districts; a lieutenant and ten men will take charge of the Lower Condamine and the Maranoa district; and the remaining twelve will be an available force

to act under me wherever they may be most required.

15. I intend raising the increased force in the Murrumbidgee district, and on my return to Callandoon I shall visit all the out-stations on the Lower Murray and Darling, and also the Barwan country. In the meantime, the original force of fourteen men will proceed, under the command of Lieutenant Marshall, to the Maranoa district, taking the Condamine and Dawson on their way.

16. In conclusion I have the honour to inform you that at any time the headquarters, or any of the police stations, can be moved without any extra expense to the government.[339]

Frederick Walker, Deniliquin to Col. Sec. 3 March 1850

I do myself the honour to inform you that I have reached the Edward River and that I have already got 15 recruits for the additional Force under my command. I have the honour to pint out to you that I should be prepared to start down the Murray tomorrow, only that the arms, clothing and saddlery have not yet arrived and I have received no information of their having been forwarded. I greatly fear that this delay will cause me a great deal of trouble and annoyance, and instead of reaching the Macintyre in the beginning of June, I fear that my arrival there will be in July and in the meanwhile a great deal of damage will probably be done to settlers in the Wide Bay and Burnett District. Margin Notes: Lengthy comments were made which are summarised in Col Sec's letter of 5 April 1850 to F Walker, see below. (QSL Reel A2.52 p 863)

Colonial Secretary to Frederick Walker, 5 April 1850

I do myself the honour to acknowledge the receipt of your letter of the 3rd ultimo reporting your arrival at Deniliquin and the enlistment of fifteen recruits for the Force under your command.

2. Having referred your letter to the Colonial Storekeeper with respect to that portion relating to the non-arrival of the stores and saddlery that officer reports that the articles in question were forwarded to Melbourne by the Brig *Dart* on the 12th of March adding that the saddles were only

339 *MBC* 29 June 1850 p 4.

obtained from the contractor a few days previous to the departure of that vessel.

3. In apprising you as above of the cause of the delay alluded to in your communication I am directed by his Excellency the Governor to remind you that in making your arrangements you must always calculate upon some delay or uncertainty in the transmission of stores to distant and out of the way places. (SRNSW 4-3860 Reel2818 p 110)

Frederick Walker, Deniliquin to Col. Sec. 4 April 1850

I do myself the honour to inform you that having found it impossible to manage 12 police horses without assistance, I have hired a man at 10s each horse to back[340] them before the Native Police mount. I therefore request his Excellency the Governor will be pleased to authorise the sum of six pounds (£6) for that purpose out of the sum included in the estimates as contingencies.

2. I also have the honour to state that owing to the delay in the arrival of the police accoutrements and especially the want of saddles I have had much trouble with the horses. Three of which were missing, the whole lot has frequently broken out of the yard and I have considered it necessary to keep on the two men who accompanied me from Sydney to look after the horses. I have in consequence to request that his Excellency the Governor will be pleased to allow the payment of 10/- per week to the two men (10/- per week two men say for 4 weeks) and the usual ration until I am ready to start for Callandoon.

3. I have to call your attention to the fact that there has been no delay on my part, the whole of the rations for the road have been ready for 4 weeks and the men are enlisted with the exception of ten, which I take up on the way and thus save the cost of rationing them for the present. I have as yet heard nothing of the arms, saddlery etc.

4. I have been also hitherto deprived of the assistance of Lieutenant Fulford, he not having yet joined me. He had to come 900 miles and his horses got tired. He has now reached within 80 miles of this place.

5. One man and a trooper are looking for the three stray horses and two troopers have just returned from an ineffectual search for them. You will

340 To train a horse to be ridden.

be pleased to hear that I have obtained free of expense the use of a very well grassed paddock where the horses are now getting into good condition. They are looked after daily but cannot be exercised as I have only six saddles all of which are in use. Margin note: Have payments necessary be authorized. 24th CAF. (QSL Reel A2.52 p 860)

Frederick Walker, Murray River to Col. Sec. 15 June 1850

I do myself the honour to inform you that I received the accoutrements and clothing for the Native Police Force on 6th May and I started then on the 13th under the command of Lieutenant Fulford. I have to go back some distance to search of the stray horses all of which I accounted except some which were found by a person engaged by me to search for them.

I have had much trouble in accustoming so many horses to stand fire and carry their accoutrements but have happily succeed. The new recruits are all in great spirits and I have left hundreds of Abl Natives much vexed that they were not enlisted. The roads are very heavy but I expect to average 10 miles a day and hope to reach Callandoon on about 15th of September. I have the honour to point out that had there not been so much delay in forwarding the accoutrements I ought to have been there now. Margin notes: Some enquiry appears necessary as to the cause of this delay — 12. I think Col Storekeeper has already accounted for it in a satisfactory manner. 13th CAF. The cause of delay is explained in the Colonial Storekeeper's report of 27 March in 50/3041 herewith. Read. 13th CAF. 15 July. Mr Walker I presume has been informed. (QSL Reel A2.52 p 858)

Frederick Walker, Darling River to Col. Sec. 15 July 1850

I do myself the honour to inform you that the newly raised Force under my command has reached this place Laidley's Ponds in safety.

2. There has been some delay owing to 10 horses having strayed near the junction of the Darling and Murray, but they have been recovered.

3. As the horses are daily improving, I intend should there be sufficient grass after I reach the stations above Fort Bourke to push on with the police and leave the dray to follow. I still hope to reach Callandoon about the 10th September.

4. The A^{bl} Natives on the Murray still continue peaceable, but those on the Darling have been committing great depredations, one case of assault on a shepherd is I believe unprecedented and at first I could not believe it, but Frederick Gardiner JP having in conjunction with me held an enquiry, we have found that a large number of A^{bl} Natives surrounded the man named in the margin (Theophilus Jones) tied him down, gagged him, blindfolded and bled him in the neck, and then sucked his blood to such an extent that the man was senseless for a considerable time.

5. Being anxious to reach my destination and not liking to fatigue the horses, I could not spare time on attempting the capture of many of the guilty parties, but I succeeded in apprehending four all accused of sheep stealing and assaulting and severely beating another shepherd. I found the charge not sufficiently borne out against two and released them. One a great ruffian named in the margin (Larry) escaped by slipping the handcuffs at light, off his ankles which I did not think possible, and the other I shall take up with me, although I do not think any good will arise from putting the colony to the expense of prosecuting him; but he is too mischievous to leave behind. Several Natives I believe were wounded in the attempt at capturing these individuals and the prisoner states they were all guilty of stealing sheep from the settlers and especially from Mr Macmillan.

6. I have information that the principal ringleader concerned in the assault named in the 4th paragraph is at a station higher up the river. I therefore hope to apprehend him. Margin notes: I should wish to have copies of this and 49/11968[341] being transcription to the Sec of State. 2nd Sept, CAF. Forwarded to H.M. Secretary of State by despatch N° 197 of 26 October 1850. (QSL Reel A2.52 p 855)

Col. Sec. to Frederick Walker, 22 October 1850

I beg to acknowledge the receipt of your letter of the 6th instant reporting on the state of the discipline of the Native Police and the efficiency of the Sergeant Major.

2. In reply I am instructed to acquaint you that your report appears to his Excellency the Governor to be upon the whole satisfactory and that it is

[341] F Walker's letter of 17 December 1849, see above.

gratifying to learn that Sergeant Major Whitmill has proved so zealous and efficient.

3. With respect to the discipline of the corps much must be left to your own discretion and his Excellency feels assured that the Government can rely upon your not misusing the confidence placed in you. (SRNSW 4-3860 Reel2818 p 200)

Frederick Walker to Col. Sec. 7 November 1850

I etc. that Lieutenant RP Marshall started with the 1st section of the Native Police on the 14th inst. for Gayndah and Wide Bay.

2 On Monday next, the 11th, Lieutenant Fulford starts with the third section for the Condamine where he will only delay a short time and then proceed to join Lieutenant Marshall on the Burnett.

3 Both these sections are in admirable order and their horses in splendid condition. It will give you some idea of the 1st section when I state that they average 5 feet 10 inches in height and 11st 5lb in weight. I have not hitherto been able to turn any party out in such a good state of discipline.

4 The second and fourth sections will accompany me on a short tour in the Wootu and perhaps the Moonie and will return here to start again in the first week in December for Wide Bay.

5 I regret to state that there has been a great deal of sickness in these two sections from influenza and that I have lost another of my faithful companions by death. Several of the others were in a dangerous state but have all recovered. (QSL reel A2.19 p 300)

Frederick Walker to Col. Sec. 7 November 1850

I do myself the honour to inform you that the Instructions the adoption of which has been approved of by the His Excellency the Governor have been issued to the officers of the Native Police together with the opinion on them of the Hon Attorney-General.

2. I have the honour to state that I thought it better to omit the 9th paragraph rather than amend it, because I found the two Lieutenants had from their own experience arrived at the same conclusion as myself and there is consequently no necessity for it.

3. On the subject of the third paragraph I wish to draw your attention to the opinion of the Hon Attorney-General and I would feel obliged if you could procure from the gentleman an opinion as to what he considers the duty of a Police force would be under the circumstances alluded to which are in fact one of the greatest difficulties I have to contend with.

4. The case is simply this, a large number of blacks are assembled together armed, cattle are killed and the remains found in all their camps; although the ownership cannot be sworn to positively. Sheep are stolen in large numbers and men are callously murdered. No man is identified as one of the murderers or thieves. The only evidence which can be obtained is that which my men and I can generally (almost always) track the aggressive party; but if it implicates anybody would it implicate any blacks who may have joined the party since the offence?

5. It is in such a case (a case which now exists at Wide Bay and the Burnett) that I would wish to know from the Law Officers of the Crown how the police force under my command can act legally in order to put a stop to such outrages.

6. His Excellency the Governor has hitherto left it to my own discretion which although flattering to me, involves a great responsibility on the officers which I would like to see diminished. I in my turn am obliged to leave a great deal to the discretion of my officers and as I stated in conversation with you in Sydney their ideas of discretion might possibly differ from mine.

7. In the Macintyre country, I used my own discretion and altho the Hon Attorney-General told me that he feared I had not acted legally throughout yet the results shews I was morally right for I affirm that the country of Cumberland is not more secure from the aggressions of the aboriginal natives.[342]

342 On 7 March 1856, F Walker asked Hon CS for the return of letters or copies of letters of his still held by the Native Police. This copy was found among others and returned to him. QSL Reel A2.37.

Frederick Walker to Col. Sec. 9 November 1850[343]

It is with feelings of great regret that I perceive that his Excellency the Governor has taken such an unfavourable view of the report of Lieutenant Marshall.

In the third paragraph, you observe that no less than seven times the blacks have been fired on but these collisions lamented as they may be, it must be remembered, have not taken place in a period of nine months, not in the one tribe nor at in one District but with six different tribes and at distances of from 50 to 200 miles apart. When Mr Marshall was on the Condamine, he was not sworn in as a magistrate and could take no depositions, when he could procure a magistrate to do so he did.

I now send copies of every document and affidavits in my possession which can explain Mr Marshall's conduct. You will observe that in respect to the collision in the Condamine that two warrants were issued for the apprehension of nameless blacks, you will see from Mr Ferret's letter which I have mentioned etc., that the guilty parties were in his neighbourhood and from his letters etc., and that of Mr Blyth an immediate attack was reported. Mr Bennett's affidavit goes to show that these hostile blacks resisted the Police and I consequently do not know how they could avoid using their arms.

This took place 200 miles from here and I am at a loss to understand by what means I am to arrive at what number were wounded on the 29th July except from the blacks and they say nine. ~~Mr Bennett thinks nine were slain but Mr Marshall himself doubts that~~. You must remember such collisions invariably take place in dense scrubs.

With respect to the death of Nobody, I have the honour to inform you that he was accused on oath of being one of the murderers of Edward Bradly that he was taken prisoner and twice attempted to escape from his escort; the third time as Corporal Logan states ~~that~~ when he found

343 Frederick Walker's reply to Colonial Secretary's letter 26 October 1850, N° 302, on the report of Lt R.P. Marshall. I have tried to reproduce this letter as accurately as I can. The above document is unsigned. Furthermore, it shows strikeout alterations which suggests to me the letter is a draft. I have reproduced it here as certain commentators have sought to rely on it as proof of Native Police unlawful killings. The Legal Opinion following it suggests the matters at issue were satisfactorily resolved.

he must have escaped into ~~an~~ a scrub impenetrable (for horses) ~~scrub~~ he fired. I enclose a copy of Mr Young's affidavit[344] and in addition I have to state that I place implicit confidence in Young's report as I have known him for six years *letter damaged* to tell a falsehood *letter damaged.*

By Mr Ferret's letter you will perceive that all the ringleaders were again collected together and he seems to think that the apprehension of these parties, who I may mention had murdered 12 men within 11 months would put a stop to all aggressions forever. I am not astonished that these men who knew themselves guilty and who were backed by all the Fitzroy Downs blacks should prefer the chance of resisting to surrendering. I observe from Mr Bennett's affidavit that two of these murderers lost their lives in the affray of which was ~~fortunate~~ is not to be regretted, as these men generally make off as soon as they can get their companions into an affray.

His Excellency the Governor thinks Mr Marshall has been too warlike but as I had several letters from you calling my attention to the very numerous murders on British subjects and the extraordinary damage done to property by the blacks on the Macintyre, the Condamine, the Burnett and the Districts of Maranoa and Wide Bay I had come to the conclusion that these blacks were belligerent parties and that the Native Police had been formed for the purpose of putting a stop to these outrages and you have conveyed to me his Excellency's ~~cors~~ orders to use my own discretion in doing so.

I am fully aware of the difficulty attending the issuing of measures necessary for such a step without acting illegally and have more than once called your attention to it. I have been so much troubled by the receipt of your letter that I really do not know how I am to act in future especially at Wide Bay and the Fitzroy Downs and I hope his Excellency will promise an immediate answer to my letter of —.

The settlers who have suffered so much loss and have witnessed the murder of so many of their friends and servants and have to pay for the suppression *damaged letter* conscience strong enough for the emergency naturally expect that the outrages of hostile blacks will be put a stop to at once and it is no satisfaction to them if I tell them I have no legal

344 See Nobody, Chapter 7.

power to act. They state with justice that an armed body of white men would never be allowed by a strong government to commit such fearful depredations and cruelties unpunished and if the law is defective it requires alteration to meet such an emergency of which this circumstance is no doubt.

I am of opinion that whatever measures may be decided upon to put a stop to these outrages must be put into force at once and with energy as the result must I know be the same as has been in the Macintyre viz: put a stop to bloodshed, introduce a better class of white servants into the Districts which are now filled with the most desperate of the population diminish the rouges and be of the same service to the blacks as it has been here by gaining their admission into the stations where they could be kindly treated under the protection of the Native Police have a large increase to their means of obtaining food and ~~find them~~ be provided in sundries such as tobacco, pipes and blankets and other clothing of which I never find the settlers niggardly when a District is peaceable.

In conclusion, I repeat what I stated in my report … that in no place did so much danger exist as at Mr Dangar's station, a danger much increased by the threatening retiring of his neighbours from such a scene of misery, ~~with the exception of Mr Goggs a gentleman whom you know I would not consider a very desirable neighbour under such circumstances~~. (QSA Series ID14725/86134, part 2 pdf p 121)

James Bennett's deposition, 14 March 1850

Before me Roderick Mitchell Esq JP for the Colony aforesaid, cities of Sydney and Melbourne excepted:

Appeared Mr James Bennett of Wallann, Darling Downs who being duly sworn deposes: Since the month of December (1849) up to the 1st instant the blacks around this station have been constantly spearing cattle and driving them from the Run as fast as we would bring them back. Mr Marshall commanding the Native Police arrived here about the beginning of the month, and I called upon him for assistance, he went out; that is to say, John Ferret of Wallann and myself accompanied by Mr Marshall and the Native Police on the tracks of the blacks and in three days came up with them. Some of the blacks ran away and a portion remained and resisted Mr Marshall's endeavours to apprehend them. It was therefore deemed necessary to fire upon them and an affray took place in which some of the natives fell. Having dispersed the natives he examined their camp and found several articles which have been taken from this station when it was burnt down by the natives in April last. He also recognised amongst the blacks who had fallen two natives who were present on the occasion referred to when I may add the Hutkeeper was murdered. I did not count the number of natives slain. James Bennett. Taken before me at Wallann, Darling Downs this fourteenth day of March 1850. Roderick Mitchell JP

Att.–Gen. and Sol. Gen. to Col. Sec. Legal Opinion

The Honourable Attorney–General and the Solicitor General to the Honourable the Colonial Secretary reporting on letter of Commandant, Native Police to the report of Lieut. Marshall.

We have gone carefully through Mr Marshall's report and Mr Walker's explanatory letter with its summonses and are of the opinion that the explanations now given are so far satisfactory that no further notice need be taken of the subject.

2. For the future it will be proper that the officers of the Native Police should be strictly enjoined to cause enquires to be held touching the death of every aboriginal native who may be killed by themselves on any of the men under their orders. So soon as circumstances will permit. The duty thus imposed will probably operate as a sufficient check upon the corps.

We are aware that in many cases much difficulty will arise from the circumstances that the witnesses to the transactions to be enquired of will for the most part be incompetent to make oath. The troopers as well as the tribes and men with whom they come in collision being all Aborigines possessing no knowledge of or belief in a future state of reward and punishment; but in cases where no legal evidence can be obtained the officers should take and forthwith report the unsworn statements of the witnesses and should themselves state on oath as soon as conveniently may be what they themselves know or have reason to believe to be the facts.

The Reports should enter into details as that e.g. in place of a mere statement of resistance by the blacks such as we find in Mr Walker's and Mr Marshall's letters. The government should be informed of the acts done or demonstrations of forcible resistance made by them. We presume that the Reports should be forwarded to the Attorney-General as in the case of Coroners Inquests. JH Plunkett Attorney-General, MM Manning Solicitor General, 3rd December 1850 (QSA Series ID14733/86134)

Frederick Walker to Col. Sec. 18 February 1851

I do myself the honour to enclose you the accompanying resolutions of the Magistrates relative to the necessity of apprehending several aboriginal natives accused on oath of murder.

2. I do myself the honour to state that I have no means at my command by which I can reach Fraser's island.

3. That the settlers have failed in procuring the boats which they wished to supply and that it is impossible to find any men who will pull (row) except at an exorbitant rate of wages.

4. The Native Police have never yet seen the sea and cannot pull.

5. I do myself the honour to suggest that either a vessel belonging to the government be sent to Wide Bay to assist in this matter or that an arrangement be made in Sydney for a coaster to land the Native Police on the island and wait for their return.

6. Either of the plans would be preferable to procuring the assistance of settlers in any way as I would have no control over their proceedings and moreover their views differ from mine.

7. I am satisfied that unless the Native Police do go to Fraser's Island that as soon as three sections leave the District and the fourth goes to a distance from Maryborough the natives of Fraser's Island will recommence their outrages and probably again induce the well-disposed to join them.

8. I am going with some men into the Burnett District but will return in three weeks to this plan where I shall await your answer.

9. I have also included copies of affidavits for your perusal the originals of which are forwarded to the Attorney-General. These will show you that the disturbance in the Wide Bay District was very serious. I am glad to be able today that a large number of naturally well-disposed blacks

have abandoned the murderers and are shewing a wish to live peaceably with the whites.

10. I am therefore very anxious that the natives on Fraser's Island should learn that they cannot place the law at defiance by retreating to that place.

11. I do myself the honour to state that should His Excellency the Governor determine upon putting it into my power to proceed to Fraser's Island requests that there may be little delay in communicating with me as it will be imperative on me to go next month to the Maranoa and anything short of three sections thirty-six would be useless on Fraser's Island. Margin Notes: Refer this letter to the Attorney-General and request his opinion whether the statements contained in the depositions will justify the Govt in acting according to Mr Walker's suggestions. 15th CAF. Request an answer as soon as possible. To Mr Plunkett, 15 March 1851.

Resolved, at a Meeting of Magistrates, JG Bidwell JP, Edmund B Uhr JP, Frederick Walker JP, RP Marshall JP, and George Fulford JP held at Maryborough, 19 February 1851:

1st That it is expedient that some measures should be immediately taken to put into force the warrants issued against: Neddy, Jacky Jacky, Tourning, Nosy, Boomer, Mr Bunce, Tuenay, Grassoom, Bobby, Tangera, Ben Bullen, Jimmy, Pepo, Coola, Wananinga, Perika, Charlie, Bungalee, Tom, Old Athlone, Old Diamond, Peter, Puckemall, Toby, Tiear, Boney, Paddy, Tommy, Doughboy, Lawley, Big Diamond, Peter with one eye, Athlone, Woolge, and Diamond aboriginal natives accused of murder & felony.

2nd That it is now understood that the majority of the accused are on Fraser's Island.

3rd That on previous occasions the aboriginal natives of Wide Bay District always retire to Fraser's Island after committing murders.

4th That the aboriginal natives consider that place as a stronghold from which they can issue at any time to commit fresh crimes.

5th That the lives and property of the inhabitants of Wide Bay District will not be safe until the aboriginal natives understand they will not be able to continue the above system.

6th That hitherto there has not been a police force that could be of any material use in checking the outrages of aboriginal natives.

7th That it is necessary now that the Native Police force is at Maryborough that the warrants issued should be put into force at Fraser's Island.

8th That we are satisfied that such a proceeding will finally put a stop to collisions between whites and blacks. (QSL A2.23 p 842.)

Frederick Walker to Col. Sec. 5 March 1851

I etc. to refer to a letter by you from the Bench at Surat, Maranoa District.

2. I observe that you have informed that bench that two Sections were to start for the Maranoa in December; but I do myself the honour to remind you that I was unable to proceed by that route on account of the non-arrival of the police clothing and that I was forced in consequence to go round by Ipswich.

2. I have to state this there has been only one letter received by any officer of the Native Police from the Bench at Surat and that in answer to that letter Mr Marshall stated he had not received instructions from me to go the Maranoa. I do not understand what is meant by that District being especially excluded from participation in the benefit which might be derived from the Native Police. The Native Police cannot be everywhere at the same time and the Bench at first must like every other party wait with patience until I can send them the assistance required.

3. His Excellency the Governor has not ordered me to go to the Maranoa at any time; but has left me untrammelled in carrying out the places proposed by me in my letter and report of January 1st and would suggest that should any letters similar to that from the Bench at Surat be address to your office, the writer should be referred to that report and be informed that the plans proposed will be carried out as speedily as possible.

4. I have the honour to observe that if any letter in future is addressed to an officer of the Native Police by the Bench at Surat it must not be written in the dictatorial style which characterised that received by Mr Marshall if that bench expects any notice to be taken of it. (QSL Reel A2.22 p 479)

Frederick Walker to Col. Sec. 10 March 1851

In January 1850 I did myself the honour to report to you the proceedings of the little police force under my command during the year 1849.

I now do myself the honour to submit for your information a report of the proceedings since the 1st January 1850 up to this date.

1. Having completed the purchase of the horses necessary for the members of the Native Police Force, I started from Sydney on the 25 January 1850 and arrived on the Edward River the last week in February. I stayed 10 days. I had 23 of the 30 recruits. I kept 7 vacancies to be filled up by blacks on the Murrumbidgee to whom I had previously promised that they should be admitted into the force if increased.

2. I had to wait until the 6th of May for the arrival of the police clothing, arms, saddlery and accoutrements. On the 13th I started Lieutenant Fulford with the police with instructions to wait for me at Kyatow (sic) on the Murrumbidgee and while there to fit out the 7 recruits mentioned in the 1st paragraph. I had to return to look (for) the stray horses all of which were found except one and having found Mr Fulford the whole party started for Callandoon on the 3rd June.

3. I have to observe that my reason for favouring volunteers from the Murrumbidgee District are that I have been acquainted with the blacks in that part of the colony for 7 years. I always placed implicit confidence in them and have never been deceived. In my opinion, also no blacks ought to be made use of as police in their own country as I know that if they are employed as such they will frequently attempt to avenge their own private animosities. The Sydney Native Police being now employed to the North and have no animosity.

4. After visiting all the stations along the Murray Darling River, the Native Police Force arrived at Callandoon on the 10 September, having suffered no hardships on this occasion because I had been so liberally supplied with means of carrying rations and tarpaulins. However, owing to the fearful drought on the Barwon I lost two police horses and 12 working bullocks.

5. On my arrival at Callandoon, I found the police left behind by me under Lieutenant Marshall were in a good state of discipline and had been employed on the Condamine, the Moonie and Wootu during my absence. The blacks of the Macintyre are so notorious I found had been perfectly quiet with the exception of a few ruffians who had previously been concerned in serious murders and especially Edward Bradley. These men joined with the Moonie blacks to kill cattle on the

Wootu and at some stations low down the Macintyre. The blacks on the Macintyre had nothing to do with a murder which was committed at Mr Williams, the man was killed by a black brought from near Warialda and I have little doubt that the white man was the aggressor.

6. The horses were too weak for the police to move for some time after their arrival and I made use of the time to get the men properly instructed in the use of their arms and accoutrements, to habits of regularity and cleanliness. Sergeant Major Whitmill was indefatigable in his exertions to attain that object and has been completely successful.

7. On the 4th November, I started Mr Marshall with the 1st Section of 11 men direct for the Burnett and Wide Bay (270 miles). He reached Gayndah on the 25th and started on the 27th to recover Mr Ferriter's sheep, 265 of which Police recovered after an arduous pursuit through a broken mountains and scrubby country. On the 17th December whilst Mr Marshall was out in search of several blacks who had committed murder, a large party of them came down upon the police with loud shouts and beating of spears. They were soon compelled to retire by the police but not before one horse was speared and one trooper speared and cut both temples with a nulla nulla. The blacks being on the ranges attempted to kill them by throwing stones down on the dismounted police but these missiles, however unpleasant to whites under such circumstances, are perfectly harmless when used against the Native Police. On the 8th January Mr Marshall joined me.

8. On the 14th November Mr Fulford started with the 3rd section of 11 men proceeded up the Wootu by the Moonie and then down the Condamine. On the Condamine, there had been no lives lost and no sheep stolen since the visit of the Native Police in 1849 but the blacks still continued to annoy the cattle on the station of the late Mr John Dangar. Mr Fulford crossed on then to the Dawson and arrived at Gayndah on the 12th December (409 miles). His party of police next went to Mr Walsh and Mt Corfield's and Mr Fulford having proceeded accompanied by some settlers who could identify several men accused on oath of murder to search for camps, the police came up to the blacks on the 28th December, some of the murders were immediately recognised and not surrendering an affray took place in which Mr Henry Walker had a spear through his shirt and Mr Corfield had a very narrow escape. On the

8th January, Mr Fulford joined me.

9. I had intended proceeding down the Macintyre and crossing over to the Balonne but I was obliged to alter this plan for I was forced to go round by Ipswich to procure the police clothing and ammunition. I therefore started on the 5th December visiting the port as such on my way and having received my supplies at Ipswich, I started up the Brisbane in hopes of being able to discover the murderers of Mr Balfour's man. In this I failed but Mr Simon Scott having informed me that some sheep of his had been stolen by an immense body of blacks camped near his residence, I proceeded in pursuit and on the 29th, I was rather surprised by a very large party of blacks issuing from a dense scrub and shouting at and defying the police under my command 22 in number. A charge without firing a shot, soon made the hostile blacks retreat into the vine scrub. When they reached that shelter, they however stood and the police who dismounted had to fire before they could retire, abandoning 50 of Mr Scott's sheep which he recovered. Some friendly blacks were sent by me the next day to invite the latterly dispersed to separate from the others and this had a very good effect as great numbers went into the different stations. In the different encounters, the blacks must necessarily have suffered some loss but it is difficult to arrive at what amount on account of the scrubby nature of the country into which they always retire. In any case, affidavits have been taken and forwarded to the Honourable Attorney-General. The number of white men murdered in the last twelve months in the District of Wide Bay and Burnett is 22.

10. On the 8th January, the whole force united and proceeded to Mr Balfour's in order that Mr Marshall and Mr Fulford two sections might receive their new clothing after which the police force returned into the Wide Bay District and proceeded to Maryborough where they arrived on the 16th July.

11. The blacks in the District of Wide Bay and Burnett have not shown any disposition of late to renew their aggressions but I am not satisfied yet that they will act in the same manner when the force (is) at present concentrated; separated in order to give the other Districts a share of protection; and as I know that several notorious murderers have taken refuge in Fraser's Island, I have delayed separating until I received answers to communications I sent by now to you relative to the necessity

of the police going to Fraser's Island. Mr Fulford returns however with the second Section immediately to Callandoon and 33 new recruits in that neighbourhood for the present. When the force ultimately separates, I proceed myself with two sections by the Dawson to the Maranoa District and Mr Marshall with the 1st Section will remain here.

12. I have the honour to inform you that there has been a great deal of sickness among the troopers of late owing to the excessive heat and the whole party having been exposed to a heavy rain during one night without cover, no less than 12 men have been laid up at a time from cold and fever but they are now recovering.

13. The officers of the Native Police have had an arduous duty to prepare in constantly attending to the discipline of the men and especially in making them look after their arms and accoutrements. Being so much in the bush and almost always travelling the men have a great deal of trouble in keeping everything in order. As His Excellency, the GG has allowed two white sergeants; the officers will be relived of a great deal of tasks and anxiety when they (sergeants) join. I do myself the honour to suggest that for 1852 there ought to be a white sergeant for every section.

14. It is a matter of great satisfaction to me to have to report that my endeavours to raise and form a police force have been successful. The men have behaved well and my expectations. There has never been a single case of insubordination and altho frequently exposed to great temptation no trooper has ever shown any symptoms of intoxication. I have so much confidence in the police in that respect that I can trust them anywhere. The devotalness (sic) they evince for their officers is one of the most pleasing traits in their character and that devotion is equally extended to the Sergeant Major who altho very strict, has shown so much temper and kindness that he has the confidence of all the men.

15. I have also to report that Messrs Marshall and Fulford have cordially and successfully assisted me in carrying out my plans. The arms and accoutrements of the new members, their orders are at any time fit for inspection and the discipline of their men has not withstanding the long journey never been relaxed. (QSL Reel A2.37 p 36)

Col. Sec. to Frederick Walker, 11 April 1851

In acknowledging the receipt of your letter of the 10th ultimo reporting the proceedings of the Native Police during the period from 1st January 1850 to 10th March 1851. I am desired by his Excellency the Governor to express to you the satisfaction of the government at the proof contained in your report of the efficiency of the officers, sergeant majors and troopers of the force under your command.

2. With respect to the suggestion contained in the 13th paragraph of your communication that an additional white sergeant should be appointed next year. His Excellency instructs me to say that your proposal shall be taken into consideration at the proper time. (SRNSW 4-3860 Reel2818 p 297)

Frederick Walker to Messrs Ferrett and Burnett, 2 June 1851

In answer to your questions as to my intentions relative to forming a Police Station on the Lower Condamine, I have to state:

1st. That it has never been proposed to have a fixed Station; that the section of twelve men intended for this part of the colony was to patrol through the Maranoa district, and Lower Condamine and Dawson country, not to be permanently stationed anywhere.

2ndly. That there are no funds provided by the Legislative Council for any buildings for the use of the Native Police, the buildings at Callandoon being erected at the expense of the force. However, I admit that it would be of great service to the force if, in each district over which the Police have to do duty, they had a station to which they could look as a home; especially this would be of advantage in case of sickness, and when any of the horses were not fit for work. Should the Settlers subscribe £30, I will point out a place at once, and find the remaining £20 required. At present, it is my intention to patrol in this part of the colony until the 10th day of July, when I return to Callandoon. Mr Fulford leaves Callandoon for this district on the 15th of this month and will meet me on the Balonne. He will not, however, make any long stay here. In August, the fourth section will come out here, and if the barracks are put up immediately, I will engage that a sergeant and a detachment is at the new Station not later than the 15th of August. P.S. I have forgotten to state that the station, if made, must be situated somewhere in the immediate vicinity of the junction of the Tannin, the Dogwood, and the Condamine. I need not remind you that occasionally you would have the benefit of the section that accompanies me in my rounds.[345]

Frederick Walker to Col. Sec. 6 July 1851

I had the honour yesterday of receiving the duplicate of your letter of 7 April 1851, N° 153 enclosing an opinion from the Honourable Attorney-General for my guidance in a proposed attempt to arrest sundry blacks charged on oath with murder and who are in the habit of retiring to Fraser's Island whenever they have committed any felonious outrage, and also authorising me to employ a coasting vessel for the purpose of proceeding with the native police to that island.

2. I do not regret that your letter did not reach me sooner as the state of my health and that of my men would have prevented me from acting on it.

3. I do myself the honour to state that the urgency for such a step is greater than ever, I fear that the blacks referred to, for years will keep up a system of murder and robbery and eventually themselves be great sufferers as in their frequent encounters with whites they would lose many lives; if this system is not put a stop to at once.

4. I shall therefore act upon the authority of his Excellency the Governor as soon as I can again gather a sufficient Force at Maryborough, which I hope to do before the end of September next. (QSL Reel A2.23 p 831)

Frederick Walker to Col. Sec. 1 August 1851

I etc. to report to you the duty of the Police force from the 10th March the date of my last report up to the 27th July being the date of my return to this place.

1. I regret to state that shortly after the despatching of my last report the illness among the men which I had hoped was on the decrease broke out with greater violence causing the death of two and laying up in time every man in the force.

2. This unfortunate circumstance did not however completely put a stop

345 *MBC* 14 June 1851 p 2.

to the duties of the force, as I went with a small detachment to afford protection to the settlers on the upper Burnett and Mr Marshall with a strong party visited the neighbourhood of Messrs Forster and Blaxland's stations as at both these places an outbreak had been expected; however, I am happy to say these expectations were not borne out although as a few sheep had been stolen at Mr Chas Archer's station and violence threatened to the shepherds, the timely arrival of the police was the cause of prevention.

3. On the 18th of April, I was joined by Sergeants Dolan and Skelton from Callandoon and the police force then concentrated in the vicinity of Gayndah separated.

4. Mr Marshall accompanied by sergeant Dolan and 13 native policemen proceeded to the station of Mr Tooth where the blacks had begun to destroy cattle, on the approach of the police they retired as usual to the sea coast.

5. Mr Marshall proceeded next to Maryborough where fears were entertained that the very large number of blacks assembled near the Boiling Establishment would commit some outrages; and it was already stated that they had stolen 3 sheep, however there was no evidence implicating any of them. Mr Marshall apprehended one man on suspicion of the murder of Mrs Shannon and Mr Gregor on the Pine River and attempted to capture two of the murders of the late Mr Blaxland they however took to the river and it not being possible to apprehend them they were fired at and I believe both killed. Mr Marshall expresses himself as much gratified at witnessing the peaceable demeanour of this very large number of blacks estimated at about 800.

6. Mr Marshall next proceeded to Mr Forster's on account of a threatened attack from the blacks, the alarm raised on this occasion proved to be as is frequently the case groundless and he therefore started according to my instructions for Callandoon it having been previously arranged that Lieutenant Fulford would relieve him in his duties which he had been so active in performing.

7. Upon leaving Gayndah, I proceeded to the Dawson where I found that the reports spread of drays having been attacked and Mr Stephen having been threatened were untrue. I would observe that it is a pity cre-

dence should be so easily given to every idle report of this nature as they only tend to increase the feeling of insecurity which was beginning to be allayed and in but too many cases I have found that when I investigated the matters the evidence on oath shewed these reports to be in some instances without foundation, in others much exaggerated.

8. The blacks however had again been at their old habits of cattle spearing and I regret that Mr Stephen should have suffered the losses he has through them. I did my best during fourteen days to secure some of those who were tracked by my men from when they had recently been killing cattle. They however not liking the vicinity of so large a force made off towards the Grafton range but four of them during pursuit having fallen across the native sergeant Willy alone, he was obliged to fire in his own defence and one was killed.

9. Upon leaving the Dawson, I visited the Lower Condamine not without success to check the cattle stealing which were being carried on there. On the subject of that portion of the Darling Downs, I have to state that I do not expect a reoccurrence of any aggressions of the serous nature, the depredations being now limited to stealing one sheep at a time and to the spearing of cattle by very small parties of blacks. I am convinced that the good feeling evinced of late by the settlers in that neighbourhood towards the blacks will tend more to keep it in a state of peace than any police force; a police station has at their request been established in the frontier of the District.

10. I next went to the Maranoa District and also attempted to put a stop to the hostility of the aboriginal natives in that District but the almost total want of grass and the heaviness of the ground from late rains completely knocked up all my horses and I found it best to return to Callandoon which I did direct through the scrub, having to walk a great part of the way to relieve the horses.

11. The state of the Maranoa is worse at present then many of the Northern Districts and the determined hostility of the blacks there must eventually lead to loss of life or the abandonment of the stations. Twenty-four troopers were therefore to proceed without delay to that District under the command of Lieutenant Fulford who will in future receive at the new police station Wandai Gumbal the clothing and other supplies for his Division.

12. It was with much regret I found that the police who had returned with Mr Fulford had not as I hoped escaped the sickness from which their comrades had suffered so much, Mr Fulford had inconsequence not been able to carry out my instructions for relieving Mr Marshall.

13. As the Burnett and Wide Bay Districts have been unavoidably left longer without protection than I could anticipate, I am using every exertion to get a party to proceed thereto as speedily as possible but the state of many of the horses is very bad.

14. I am glad to be able to state that the men are now in good health and great spirits and that they have been gratified by my having caused it to be known to them that His Excellency the Governor had been pleased to express his satisfaction with their services and good conduct.

16. At all the stations visited by Lieutenants Marshall and Fulford on their way into Callandoon, the accounts of the peaceable behaviour of the blacks were satisfactory except Mr McGeachie's on the Wootu where it is said they are killing cattle. The offenders I suspect are Moonie blacks.

17 The Macintyre country is reported by Lieutenant Fulford to have been remarkably quiet, a few head of cattle have been speared but not to a greater extent than in the Districts of acknowledged quietness such as that of the Murrumbidgee. (QSL Reel A2.23 p 668)

Col. Sec. to Frederick Walker, August 1851

In acknowledging the receipt of your letter of the 1st August reporting the proceedings of the Native Police from 10th of March to the 27th July last, I am directed to inform you that the Governor General is much gratified by your account of the continued good conduct of your force and His Excellency approves of your proposed arrangements for the disposition of the Native Police. (QSL Reel A2.23 p 678)

Frederick Walker to Troopers upon again going into the Bush, 4 August 1851

As the police will directly again go into the bush I have some things to say to you all:

1. No Policeman is to take grog or wine from anybody but his officer.

Any Sergeant or Corporal who does so will be broke and have the red cloth taken off his jacket and cap for 3 months. Any trooper will be soundly flogged. Altho' I tell you this, I am not afraid of any of you disobeying taking grog because you have before behaved so well and I know you will do so again. Never mind what any person says to you. When anybody tells you, I said he might give you grog, he tells you lies for neither I nor Mr Marshall or Mr Fulford ever will tell anybody to give you grog when we are not there.

2. I say nothing to you about fighting because anybody can fight but I want you to show everybody that I command a body of clean, sharp and good policemen not a lot of dirty, lazy charcoles (sic, charcoals) or stupid constables.
3. No policeman is to walk about without his carbine. If he does, he will be punished every time.
4. Every policeman must take care of his arms, his horse, his saddle & bridle, and his clothes. They belong to the Queen not to you.
5. The Governor has been very good to you and he will expect you to do your duty.
6. When a Policeman washes his shirt, he must not put it on again until it is quite dry. He is not to take off his cloak except (when) his officer tells him to do so and when it is warm, he will strap his jacket on the top of his cloak.
7. Keep away from gins when you are at a gunya; do what you like when you are in the bush. I will not be angry with you then.
8. When you are sick tell your officer directly.
9. Sergeants Dolan and Skilton are to you the same as officers.
10. Logan's policemen are never going to the Balonne and you will have some things to do, for the Balonne blacks are not old women. Old Simon can shew you how to fight if he likes; always close up directly. Mind, I must not have charcoles beat my Police.
11. What the Governor wants from you is to make charcoles quiet. He does not want them killed and he won't let white fellows do so. If they won't be quiet, you must make them that's all. But you will not

shoot unless your officer tells you. Mind, if the charcoles begin to throw spears or nulla nullas, then don't you wait but close up (and) knock them down.

12. I shall be quick after you and when the charcoles on the Balonne think that will do; I shall leave my troopers with Mr Fulford at Wandai Gumbal and take Logan and Willy's two sections to help Mr Marshall and Cobby's men to cramer (sic) the Island. Logan's men will then come back here to the Sergeant Major and the sections No 1 & 9, if the Governor says yes, will go with me to see Moreton Bay.

Now boys that is all I have to say to you except take care of yourselves. Don't get sick any more for it breaks my heart. When you bogey[346] don't stop long in the water. Mind, this is not your country. (QSA Series ID 14725/86133)

Frederick Walker to Col. Sec. 15 September 1851

I etc. that I started Lieutenant Fulford on the 10th August with 8 troopers his own native orderly and two supernumeraries, direct for Surat, Balonne.

2. From letters received from that quarter, I hear that Mr McPherson's station on the FitzRoy Downs had been burnt and that it was expected Mr Hall's station would be attacked on the 16th August, Mr Fulford would probably arrive there on the 15th.

3. Sergeant Skelton started on the 3rd August with a horse team and four troopers to take possession of the new Barracks at Wandai Gumbal, Lower Condamine.

4. The 1st Section 12 men under Lieutenant Marshall started for the Burnett and Wide Bay on Monday the 8th September.

5. The 1st Section under me and the 3rd under Sergeant Dolan were engaged from the 10th to the 30th August endeavouring to capture some blacks who had been pilfering at sheep stations. The greatest number of the culprits escaped through being warned in time by white persons. But during this time Cobby Jemmy the last of the murders of Edward

346 To swim or bathe.

Bradley was apprehended and delivered in safety to the lockup keeper at Warialda, one lad accused of pilfering called the fire boy who was apprehended and detained in custody for some time was discharged by me for want of sufficient evidence on oath. He however himself told me that he has stolen some flour from a Chinaman. The proper way to deal with such lads would be to give them a good horsewhipping and dismiss them. One black called Lippy accused on oath of a violent assault and robbing two Chainmen was killed by the Police in an attempt made by him to escape in the dark. Mr Marshall will hold the usual enquiry.

6. I start today with twenty men to reinforce Mr Fulford and shall probably return here about the 20th October in order to settle all the accounts up to the end of the year.

7. I then proceed to Gayndah at which place about the 10th November a force of 36 policemen will be concentrated. A meeting of Magistrates will then be required by me to consider again whether it is expedient that measures should be taken to apprehend felons on Fraser's Island.

8. The Sergeant Major proceeds tomorrow with his troopers and my white servant in order to endeavour to bring up the dray left by me on the Barwin at the Lawson's station. I have obtained the loan of a bullock team for that purpose. Two invalid troopers alone remain at Callandoon. (QSL Reel A2.21 p 25)

Frederick Walker to Col. Sec. 22 October 1851

In answer to your letter of the 27 September N° 51/234, I … state that Mr Marshall started on the 8th of that month for the Burnett and Wide Bay and that Sergeant Skelton had orders to start on the 5th October from the Condamine Barracks with 10 men for the Dawson which is in the Burnett District.

2. On the subject of the censure from certain stockholders in the Burnett District which you have annexed to your letter, I wish to make a few observations. This censure is signed by the most respectable people in the Burnett District and consequently must be hurtful to my feelings.

3. In my report of the 1 August, I stated in the 6th paragraph that Mr Fulford had instructions to relive Mr Marshall. The arrangement was

that both should start about the same time in order that neither District should be without a Police Force for its protection. This therefore is the arrangement which these persons stigmatise as injudicious.

4. In the 12th paragraph of the same report, I informed you of the unfortunate circumstances which had prevented Lieut. Fulford from following out my instructions. I was not aware of this until my return to Callandoon, 27 July.

5. To censure without being in possession of the facts is unfair but, in this case, it is still more unjust because two of the persons (Mr Reid & Mr Wilkin) signing the censure were aware of the arrangements which had been made.

6. The statement contained in the letter of those gentlemen that no part of the Police Force were in any District contiguous to the Burnett is to say the least of it rather outrageous.

7. Since forming the present Police Force, I have had little rest and much anxiety which was still more excited by the illness of all the men. I have been out in all weather, have never been home except for a few days at a time. I have incurred a great responsibility and damaged my health in endeavouring to make my small Force as available as possible and I have met with a very poor return.

8. I am aware that others persons have through the press been amusing themselves at my expense, but the opinion of these persons I believe not, as I knew that they would hunt to death any public servant if they only had the power.

9. His Excellency the Governor General is aware of all that has been done through my reports, which are substantiated by affidavits in the possession of the Honourable Attorney-General. His Excellency can alone judge whether my arrangements constituting the Force at my disposal are judicious or not and whether these arrangements have been carried out with energy. To him therefore alone I look for either approbation or disapprobation. Margin Notes: Commandant's observations appear reasonable & satisfactory – as long as he continues to perform the arduous & responsible duties with same zeal & efficiency, will have support of Government, CAF. (QSL Reel A2.21 p 20)

Frederick Walker to Col. Sec. 31 December 1851

I etc. to report the proceedings of the Native Police from the 1st August up to 31 December 1851.

1. Lt Fulford started with 11 men on the 10th August for the Maranoa District, he arrived at Mr Hall's station on the 16th in time to prevent any attack on the station he next proceeded to the spot where the blacks had burned down a hut of a Mr McEnroe and went in pursuit of these blacks; but without avail. He next proceeded to take possession of the new barracks at Wandai Gumbal.

2. The 1st Section under Mr Marshall started for the Burnett and Wide Bay Districts on the 8 September 1851.

3. On the 15th I started with 20 men for the Maranoa. I went out to check the cattle killing going on there and then went to the Barracks at Wandai Gumbal. I there arranged a system with Mr Fulford. He on one side started with a party to stop the cattle killing at Mr Blyth's and I went into the Maranoa District with another party. The blacks were caught 5 times in the act of cattle killing by these two parties of police and they refusing to surrender two or three lives were lost. The usual enquiry has not been held but will be on my return to Wandai Gumbal.

4. A man having been killed at Mr Ferrett's, Sergeant Skelton was on the spot within a few hours; but the rain made it impossible to track the murderers.

5. I next sent Sergeant Skelton, 8 October onto the Dawson where I had reason to expect an outbreak. After which I returned to Callandoon with 3 troopers. I arrived on the 20th October. The 4th Section rode with me during these last five weeks 700 miles. This could not be done at any other season of the year.

6. The unfortunate death of the Sergeant Major on the 21st was a great hindrance to the carrying out of my plans. I sent a despatch by three troopers to Mr Fulford and they went the 150 miles in three days in my horse track from Callandoon to the Burnett.

7. After having gone round several stations in the Upper Condamine to settle some amounts, I went down the Condamine to Wandai Gumbal. I was glad to find Mr Fulford had been indefatigable. The murderer of Mr Ferrett's man had been caught with a blanket stolen at the same time

but being well supported by a large armed body of aboriginal natives he resisted and was shot. Some evidence is yet required, when it is obtained, the depositions will be sent into the Attorney-General. The police had now patrolled from the 18th August up to 20th November in all directions the Lower Condamine country and the Maranoa District; every scrub had been penetrated and the numerous horse tracks of the police had caused the hostile tribes to believe that there was a much larger force employed than really was the case. Every settler that I met congratulated me on the success of my plan but Lt Fulford will not be able to carry it out completely until he has his sergeants.

8. I next went to the Dawson where I found Sergeant Skelton had been very active. A party of settlers headed by a Mr Coutts had proceeded a long way down the Dawson since I had been there in times past, and of this I was not aware. I had accordingly directed Sergeant Skelton into Mr Roach's as I believe that was the station the blacks intended to attack, and he dispersed a large body of them especially near it. It seems however that it was Mr Coutts who was attacked and I regret to hear that he has lost his men. A Mr Neil Ross had also been killed. Sergeant Skelton upon hearing the news immediately proceeded to the spot and some property was seized. The heavy rain made the ground so boggy that the police could not follow the murderers.

9. On this subject I do myself the honour to state that I might as well be expected to afford assistance at Cape York as to protect people who push out in such a manner before I have been able to carry out my plans and without giving me any notice.

10. I sent in Sergeant Skelton with the second section to assist Mr Fulford and took the third with me.

11. At Mr Livingston's station, Bungaban, serious affray with firearms had occurred between some Chinese and white servants. I was obliged to commit three of the Chinese for trial and two for twelve months in default of finding bail. I escorted the prisoners to Maryborough.

12. Ten miles before reaching Maryborough, Lt Marshall joined me with the 1st Section.

13. Sergeant Dolan had been sent on first by Mr Marshall in September to Mr Archer's station on the Burnett River. Mr Marshall having to re-

main behind on the Upper Condamine to look for horses.

14. On the 2nd October, Sergeant Dolan with his men apprehended one of the men accused on oath of being concerned in the murder of the late Mr Street. Three troopers were sent to escort the prisoner to the next station and there to await the arrival of Sergeant Dolan. About five miles from Mr Mackay's station the escort was attacked by a large party of blacks and the troopers seeing that the prisoner would escape shot him and one of the leaders of the hostile blacks, the three troopers chased them into the scrub.

15. On 7 October, information was given to Sergeant Dolan that 2000 sheep had been taken away from Mr Mackay and the shepherds nearly killed. The police went in pursuit and about 4 o'clock pm the same day they overtook the blacks. The Sergeant had warrants for six of them. They attempted to make their escape but two were killed. In the camp were found the coat of the late Mr Street, 4 axes, 6 shirts, 5 blankets and many other articles supposed to have been stolen when Mr Street was killed. It is also supposed that the black Jemmy mentioned in the warrant as one of the murderers of Mr Street was one of the two killed on this occasion.

16. Mr Marshall overtook the police at Mr Archer's on the 15 October. He then visited the stations of Mr Trevethan and of Mr Mackay. After having the horses shod at Gayndah, he went to Toomcul, Mr Ferrett's station as he had warrants for two blacks Ball and Devil on a charge of killing cattle at Mr Tooth's station, Widgee Widgee. Ball was apprehended but Mr Broadbent in his affidavit so completely satisfied Mr Marshall that Ball could not have been at Widgee Widgee for two days before, nor on the day nor for three weeks after the day upon which the offence was stated to have occurred that Mr Marshall discharged him. Devil was not apprehended because Mr Herbert had declared he was at his station on the day named at least 70 miles in a direct line from Widgee Widgee. A black called Millbong was killed on the 1st December 1851 in an attempt made by the police to apprehend him on a charge of sheep stealing. There is little doubt but this man is the man who has been mistaken for Devil as they have both but one eye and both had been wounded in the shoulder.

17. When Mr Marshall's party had joined me, I proceeded to Fraser's Island but of that proceeding I have made a separate report. Margin notes:

AG to peruse letter as great many blacks reported killed by police-trust depositions when received will prove these acts of severity to have been unavoidable [ref 52/4253]. CAF. (QSL Reel A2.23 p 680 to 693)

J Leith Hay and Frederick Walker to Col. Sec. 1 January 1852

We etc. to call your attention to the following circumstances.

1. The Commandant of the New South Wales Native Police having engaged a vessel for the purpose of conveying his force to and from Fraser's Island for the purpose of apprehending sundry felons, we deemed it necessary that some person should accompany the party who could identify one or more of the individuals accused.

2. The only case upon which we found we could act was the case of a murderous assault made on the person named in the margin, George Furber. The Commandant holds the warrant for the apprehension of the offender and we wished Mr Furber to accompany us, for the purposes of pointing out the man who did assault him.

3. But Mr Furber having the mail contract from Maryborough to Gayndah and as he had immediately to make his arrangements for the year 1852, we accepted his excuses especially as Mr Duncan Cameron told both of us that he could point out the man, as he had frequently seen him and Furber had shown him to him.

4. Mr Duncan Cameron was ready to go with us; but EB Uhr Esq JP who it seems is his employer not only refused to allow him to go but made use of threatening language to him if he did.

5. Mr Duncan Cameron was sure that he could point out the individual but Mr Uhr by his violent conduct prevented us from taking his deposition.

6. In conclusion, we most respectfully wish to state for the information of his Excellency the Governor General that in future we cannot act in concert with Mr Uhr as a magistrate. (QSL Reel A2.23 p 54)

Frederick Walker to Col. Sec. 5 January 1852

I do myself the honour to state for the information of his Excellency the Governor General the result of an attempt made by the force under my command to apprehend sundry felons accused on oath and supposed to have taken refuge on Fraser's Island.

2. I deemed it necessary that some person should accompany the force, who could point out one at least of the offenders, and Mr J Leigh Hay the only local magistrate who accompanied me was of the same opinion; the result of our endeavours to carry out that object is shewn in a letter from Mr Hay and myself.

3. Having engaged the *Margaret and Mary* schooner I considered it would be wrong if I did not go to the island and see if I could not do something to put a stop to the felonies of the Fraser's Island blacks. The force consequently started on the 24 December 1851 and the following is the result.

4. On our way down the Mary River, Captain Currie of the *Margaret and Mary* landed the police on the south bank of the river and whilst on shore I discovered a black's camp the remnant of some flour, several pieces of bark cut for making bread on and some books (stolen from the wharf at Maryborough) with the name of Mr Livingstone written in the first page.

5. 27 December, Captain Currie landed 20 troopers, the sergeant major, and one horse with James Leith Hay JP Esq, and myself at the point agreed upon which has since been distinguished by tree marked and painted N/P on Fraser's Island.

6. R P Marshall JP accompanied the boats, which were kindly put at my disposal by Messrs Wilmot and Norman Leith Hay each of these gentlemen manning one boat and having two troopers in each boat. Capt. Currie with his boat and crew all armed and sworn as Special Constables giving every assistance in their power.

7. Upon landing, the force under my command, I immediately visited a large camp which we had seen from the vessel. In this camp were found more flour and some more of Mr Livingstone's books. One small boat belonging to Mr Blackman at Maryborough and in the possession of the blacks tried to make off but was captured by the boats who were keeping vigilant guard.

8. Another large ship's boat full of blacks made it escape but the police fired into it and several balls struck. Unfortunately, the land force had got to such a distance from the boats that Mr Marshall's party could not hear the firing and the blacks escaped to a small island. It is possible as

this boat could not be found on our way back that it sunk. Two troopers jumped into the sea to try and capture it but it had got too far. They of course lost all their cartridges. [Margin: supposed to be the "Ebbert's?" "Effert's"?]

9. I camped on the spot the night of the 27th and during the night the blacks made frequent attempts to surprise the Native Police camp but without effect. Capt. Currie with his vessel and the boats dropped down to another point awaiting to a previous arrangement. Mr James Leith Hay with six troopers started in order to alter this arrangement; but it was too late.

10. Finding that in consequence of the large number of fresh water creeks, that the horse was an encumbrance. I sent Sergeant Major Dolan and five troopers to take it back to the rendezvous where he was also to meet with Mr Hay.

11. I started with the remaining troopers in pursuit of the blacks who had annoyed us during the night; whence we came up with them, they being on the top of the range escaped. We found a large fresh water lagoon on the table land. The rain was heavy all this day as well as the night previous. The scrubs were so dense that with difficulty the police forced their way, worn out with fatigue we returned to the rendezvous having walked and waded at least 25 miles.

12. Capt. Currie bought back his vessel to the rendezvous. Mr Marshall's party had captured several of the blacks and two of them Durobberee and Perika have been committed to take their trial for murderous assault on a Mr Furber.

13. The native sergeants Edgar and Willy asked me to allow them to pursue the hostile blacks. I considering it necessary and they followed them from the 31st December to the 2nd January inclusive never getting up to them until they reached the last side of the Island when the blacks took to the sea. Another book of Mr Livingstone's was recovered by the trooper Aladdin and one boat oar was found. The police found a fresh water lake which they described as about 4 miles circumference. The country was good on the East side. The police say that the blacks ate one of their party who was killed in the attack on the police camp on the night of the 27th December. The remains of the carcase being found cut

up in their bags which they threw away. I was too footsore to accompany the men.

14. It is difficult to explain to you the hardships from rain at one time, excessive heat at another and from myriads of mosquitoes and sand flies which the whole of the party have suffered. One half of the police are lame. The force employed is 24 men of the Native Police besides the gentlemen below mentioned.

15. Capt. Currie took the whole party safe up to Maryborough on the 3rd January. He will deliver to you the boat captured and the books which were recovered.

16. I do myself the honour to call the attention of His Excellency the Governor General to the valuable assistance which I have received from Messrs James Leith Hay JP, Norman Leith Hay and Wilmot. The services of Mr Marshall, I have so frequently directed the attention of the government to that it is needless for me to say more than that he acted with his usual energy and discretion. I have mentioned Capt. Currie in a separate letter. (QSL Reel A2.23 p 820)

Frederick Walker to Col. Sec. 5 January 1852

I etc. to call the attention of the government to the activity and real (support) evinced by the Master of the *Margaret and Mary* whilst engaged in the attempt lately made to apprehend several felons on Fraser's Island.

2. Everything that could possibly be done, to accommodate the troopers, land the force (and the horse a matter of some difficulty) and to cooperate with his vessel and crew, was done by Captain Currie.

3. I therefore suggest that a small reward be given to Captain Currie, the sum which I would wish to be given him is ten pounds. (QSL Reel A2.23 p 45)

Col. Sec. to Frederick Walker, 16 January 1852

Adverting to my letter of the 6th August last and previous correspondence respecting the capture of a number of aboriginal offenders who have congregated on Frazer's island, I have now the honour by direction of his Excellency the Governor to request that you will be good enough to report the present state of the natives. (SRNSW 4-3860 Reel2818 p 429)

Troop Orders, Callandoon, 7 March 1852

N° 1. The Sergeant on duty for the day will see the men up every morning and the blankets removed from the Barracks and placed on the fence or line. Weather permitting but on no case on the ground as that would endanger the health of the men.

N° 2. The Sergeant on duty will see that the men warned go for the horses immediately after they get up and not let them loiter about the Barracks then warn the other men for drill where he will attend himself.

N° 3 The Sergeant on duty will be present at the serving out of rations to the men morning and evening. See the Barrack's Armory and in front of the Commandant's quarters are cleaned the shelves dusted and the clothing neatly folded and put up.

N° 4. After breakfast, the horses will be taken from the yard and cleaned after which they will be walked back again to the yard. The brushes, curry combs and halters will be placed on the shelf in the Armory.

N° 5. The Sergeant on duty for the day will warn all parades and drills at the appointed hour and see the men for mounted duty ready to march in good time. He will visit the Barracks frequently in the day and if any blacks found there must be ordered the other side of the creek. He will call the roll every night and report the absentees if any to the Sgt Major. Gins will not be allowed at the Barracks without the Commandant's permission.

N° 6. The Sergeants of Sections will see their men turn out clean to parade and drill. The saddlery and accoutrements of their sections clean and in their proper place in the Armory. The sergeants will give all their assistance to the Sgt Major to get the new recruits drilled and ready for duty.

N° 7. The Sergeants of the Sections will make their men spread out their kit every Saturday for the Commandant's or Sgt Major's inspection and report all deficient after parade according to form. By Order James Dolan, Sgt Major.

Callandoon, 17 March 1852

N° 1 The sergeants in command of sections are warned that in no case are the Commandant's or officer's servants to be allowed in any matter whatever to interfere with or to give orders to the troopers of the Native Police.

N° 2 The sergeants are to attend themselves to the delivery of rations to the police and they are to see that the proper quantity is given them and that the rations are not wasted by the troopers. By order of the Commandant, James Dolan Sergeant Major. (QSA Series ID14733/86134)

Frederick Walker to Col. Sec. 1 March 1852

I have thought that you might wish to know from me what are the causes of difference between me and some of the northern settlers; they are, as far as I understand them, explained by the following:

Two settlers stated that the Government would not allow the squatters to shoot blacks but have sent up the Native Police to do so; a similar opinion was expressed in Sydney by a Mr Cowper, and many settlers have satisfied me that such were their views. One settler stated that it was necessary, and the duty of government, to evince a certain amount of vindictiveness against the blacks. One great cause of difference of opinion is the system, so much followed, of not allowing the blacks at the station.

Some of the settlers are quite indifferent as to that the consequences may be to the officers of Native Police. They still fancy that a system of warfare ought to be authorised by Government, and do not try to produce evidence upon which the police can legally act, and in some cases, have prevented the officers from obtaining such evidence. The object of these persons is to have it in their power to shut the mouth of Government, should any enquiries be made into their proceedings against the Aborigines, by saying that the officers of the Native Police are tarred with the same brush as themselves.

Previous to 1849, settlers in the outer districts, finding that they were beyond the protection of the law, and not being able to put up with the injuries done to life and property by the Aborigines, took up arms in their own defence, and attempted to put a stop by main force to a state of things which government had not been able to alter. In so doing, however justifiable the original motive may have been, yet each settler acted from a feeling of self-interest alone, not in the least with a view to the public good. It was impossible the settlers could act without showing, in some cases, motives of revenge and feelings of vindictiveness; and as most of their servants were men of no education, frequent instances of harshness and abominable cruelty were heard of. In many districts, the settlers succeeded in putting a stop to the hostilities of the Aborigines, but in some they signally failed; for instance, the Macintyre, where after nine years' warfare, the blacks were as far from subdued as ever. Many settlers, either from a wish not to have their comfort constantly disturbed, or perhaps, in some cases, from religious feelings, wished the Government to interfere, and by protecting their interests, render it no more necessary for them to protect themselves.

In 1848 the Government determined to interfere, and to attempt to protect the settlers, as well as provide that the blacks were not oppressed. It was resolved to try the experiment of a Native Police Force on a small scale, and the forming of such a corps was entrusted to me. When I undertook the raising of the police force, I saw all the difficulties, and I resolved upon my own plans. I knew that I would have to deal with men who had never been in the habit of reflecting, because they had nothing to reflect upon; and that they would, like all ignorant people, be fond of fighting for the mere fun; that the idea of duty was to them unknown. From the very first, therefore, having picked my experimental party from among men who for five years had known me well, and purposely from among blacks inhabiting a country one thousand miles from where the Native Police was to be at first employed, I lost no opportunity of improving the men morally, of practising their memories, teaching them to reflect, and argue among themselves; also in inculcating habits of regularity, obedience, and cleanliness. I think from the fact of there never having been one instance of insubordination, not one instance of intoxication, not one quarrel of a serious nature among them, and that no bad or obscene language has ever been heard from these men, since they have joined the police, and that during three years and a half they have been remarkable for their orderly and good conduct, is a pretty good proof that I have not failed in my endeavours; and I have been rewarded by receiving tokens of gratitude which far surpassed even my sanguine expectations. There is, however, room for further improvement, which I have not lost sight of.

During the four years in which I have held the command of this force, it has never acted unless I knew that a felony had been committed and I had reasonable grounds of suspecting the offenders, warrants had been issued, or affidavits clearly pointing out the offenders, sworn to. In every case depositions, have been forwarded to the Attorney-General of the proceedings of the Native Police, when a death has occurred through their endeavours to put a stop to hostilities; and he is the best judge whether I have acted legally or not. At all events, I have always thought that I was right, morally and legally. When mounted police had hostile encounters with armed felons, I presume that their officers had similar views.

The Government therefore never allowed any proceedings towards the Aborigines that were not warranted by law. It is remarkable that the persons, who were most clamorous against the Government for not interfering, should be the first to exclaim against them when they do. I have thus, I hope, disposed of the first cause of dissent. As for the second, although I can make allowance for the irritation, and perhaps, feelings of revenge, which may actuate a man at the time he sees his fellow creature cruelly murdered, or his property wantonly destroyed, I cannot but look with feelings of contempt and indignation on any person who can for any length of time feel vindictively towards such miserable and ignorant wretches as the Aborigines of this continent are in their natural state. And should any officer of the Native Police evince any vindictive feeling in his dealings with them, he would be unworthy of the confidence of the Government. The only object he must have in view is, by endeavouring to put the law into force against offenders, to intimidate others from committing crime.

I now come to the third cause of dissent. When the experimental force was raised, it was first sent to the Macintyre. With the exception of three stations, the blacks in that portion of the Darling Downs District were in a manner outlawed in their own country, being hunted from the river and creek frontages, and thus deprived of means of lawfully obtaining food. Driven to desperation, they carried on a constant war of retaliation with the whites and lived solely on cattle. So, accustomed were they become to this life that force had to be resorted to, to make the ringleaders submit. The Native Police arrived in May 1849; in October, the settlers laid aside their weapons; the blacks were admitted everywhere at the stations; and a run which would not have fetched £100 in May 1849, was disposed of in January 1850, for £500, so much had property risen in value by the increased security of life and property. One settler told me, that for eight years he had expended £150 per annum on his cattle station, and now for the first time had a return from it in the shape of fat stock. A class of men who for years, for the sake of profiting by the high rate of wages, endeavoured to keep up the old state of things, have disappeared from the neighbourhood, probably seeking in more disturbed districts for the employment which they saw they could no more get in a district getting daily more peaceable. It will be seen, therefore, that the principal cause of the success of the Native Police on the Macintyre, was that the settlers cordially co-operated with me in carrying out my plans, and the result is known; 55,000 sheep are now shepherded by blacks alone. So long as settlers carry on the system of preventing the blacks from obtaining their lawful means of livelihood and persist in not showing to them that all old grudges and vindictiveness are thrown on one side by the whites, which the blacks will believe when they are allowed at the stations, and not till then, so long will a system of depredations be carried on, which the Native Police may check, but cannot permanently put an end to. Such is the case in the districts of Burnett, Maranoa, and Wide Bay.

It has been argued that some settlers have shown the advantages of their system by not having incurred loss, but they have managed, however, to victimise their neighbours who acted more kindly towards the blacks. It is impossible to persuade me that a station is more safe because the Europeans do not see the blacks at it, for they may be, unknown to them, in a scrub only one mile from a sheep station, ready to pounce out at an advantage upon some unprepared and solitary shepherd. On the contrary, where they are seen it is known at least where some are, and it can generally be learned from them where the others are, and what their doings are. If every settler were to follow the system called "keeping them at a distance," a term adopted by settlers from convict stockmen, where would the blacks go for their food? One settler said he did not care, and his hearers seemed to admire the expression; but there cannot be many who could entertain such a selfish idea. If every settler were to allow to only ten Aborigines on his station, there would be such a small number of them in the bush that they would hardly be dangerous. It is the hostile bearing of the settlers that causes the blacks to keep in such large numbers, for they cannot continue the assemblies customary to them more than a few days at a time on account of the want of food (the bunya seasons are of course an exception). They supply this want from the herds of the settler and are compelled to do so.

The best argument I have heard yet in support of the system was that of a settler who said his reason for not admitting the blacks at his station was that he could not prevent quarrels between his servants and them, arising principally from the intercourse of the Europeans and the females. It is rather too bad that for such a reason the unfortunate Aborigines should be expelled from their own fatherland.

In conclusion, it is needless for me to say that everything in my power for the protection of the settlers will be done by me. His Excellency the Governor General has already shown that he has sufficient confidence in me.[347]

Lt G Fulford to Sgt RA Dempster, 20 April 1852

You will start this morning for the purpose of patrolling upon the Balonne River taking with you the men mentioned in the margin: Corporal Edward, Troopers Capita Simon, Rodney, Tom Thumb, Donald, Dick, Bunya Jimmy & Rinaldo.

2. From information I have received the blacks are killing and disturbing the cattle of Mr Ogilvie, you will visit that Station and any other that may be suffering from their depredations and I have no doubt that your presence will be sufficient to put a stop to their outrages.

3. You will keep up a constant patrol among the stations on the Balonne and neighbourhood for about three weeks or a month or longer if you consider it necessary unless the health of the men render it necessary to return. You have some of the men who are only recovering from fever and argue and as that is very prevalent at present and the men become unfit for duty you had better return immediately.

4. Should any collisions occur between the police under your command with hostile blacks, you will use every endeavour upon your part to pre-

---

[347] *SMH* 16 June 1852 p 1; *Maitland Mercury* 26 June 1852 p 4 & *MBC* 17 July 1852 p 4.

vent the unnecessary effusion of blood and sacrifice of life.

5. You will strictly adhere to the instructions issued by the Commandant to Sergeants in Command of Detachments and dated 17 March 1852. (QSA Series ID14733/86141p 70)

Lt G Fulford to Sgt RA Dempster, 13 May 1852

Understanding that you are unwell and cannot do duty likewise that you have been ill, I have to request that upon receipt of this that you will start at once and come on by short stages. Should you be unable to perform duty upon your arrival at Hall's Station you will proceed direct to the barracks. It is one of the most particular instructions I have, never to allow the Police to go after blacks with any white persons whatever unless they have one of their officers with them. You have committed a great fault in allowing them to go after the blacks with Mr. Johnson, as they have been induced to go into the Camp at Yamboukal, and from the evidence which I can get, I am sorry to say there is a very strong case which I should not be at all surprised, will lead both myself and you, with Mr. Johnson into a mess. The Police must not on any account whatever be permitted to go after blacks without an Officer with them, not even in the case of murder, because they may be induced by either foolish or designing persons to fire on blacks who are perfectly innocent of the offences laid to their charge.

I have left the men at Yamboukal but have sent down to you Donald and Rodney to fetch you the pack horse. I have likewise allowed two men to stop at Mr Hall's lower Station as I believe they expect to be attacked. You will bring them on with you when you come up and if you are unfit for duty you must return to the barracks at once and I must come down myself but you must if possible go out on Hall's run as there are a large number of blacks about in the neighbourhood who are … (damaged) to be disturbing the cattle, before you can attack those men you must have good proof that they are the actual offenders. I refer you to the instructions issued by the Commandant to Sergeants in Command of Detachments. I have sent you some Quinine enough to last you 4 days taking three doses per day. (QSA Series ID14725/86133 pp 23-25)

Lt G Fulford to Sgt RA Dempster, 8 June 1852

Bunya Jimmy and Rinaldo arrived here on Sunday.

You talk of being down the river for the last two or three months. I never expected that you would make the blacks perfectly quiet in about a fortnight. But as your section is the only disposable force I have at present to do the duty of the whole district, I cannot allow the people on the Balonne to monopolise the entire use of the Force.

I have not any shirts to send you but will endeavour to get some by the time you come home. As for white trousers this is the season in which the men ought to wear their blue ones and if their white ones are worn out they must do so.

I hope you will be very economical to enable me to make up for the extra rations I am obliged to use at the Barracks having so many gins and supernumeraries to keep.

You had better return to this when you again come up the river. You can see that the country is quiet as you come along and in places where it is not you can go out but I do not advise you to come up the river and then go back again.

I cannot send you any men as I have not a single man but is ill. I am glad to say that Larry is nearly well but if he was to go out in this damp weather he would most likely be taken ill again.

I have sent you down a dozen pipes by the Postman to be sent to Yamboukal. I suppose that you will be back at the Barracks in about a fortnight or three weeks from this at first hand. (QSA Series ID14733/86141 p 74)

Sgt RA Dempster's draft reports of his patrol of Balonne River, 20 April 1852[348]

My arrival at Werribon Mr Hall's Lower Station, I found the police with Mr Johnson who had followed the tracks of blacks within a few miles

[348] The following documents are included because they relate to the alleged misconduct of Sergeant R Dempster whilst on patrol of the Balonne River of 20 April 1852. The documents are incomplete, rough drafts of Dempster's report of that patrol. They are difficult to read and to reproduce with accuracy and precision.

of the Station. I proceeded to Yamboukal, Mr Hall's Upper Station. We experienced very heavy rain for the next 10 days and having received information from Mr Duncombe, the superintendent that the blacks were killing his cattle and greatly disturbing … (damaged). I was unable to proceed into the bush until the 31st May, the ground being so heavy that the horses were unable to travel. I then went out upon the run and found where the blacks had been running cattle. We followed their tracks which led us to a camp which contained a great number of bones freshly killed and which the blacks had only left about two days. We afterwards passed by two of their camps all of which contained the remains of recently slaughtered cattle. We came up to the camp in which the blacks were. The blacks heard the police before the police could come upon them and ran away. There were signs of beef having been eaten in the camp, but it was situated in such an impossible scrub that even if we had come upon them without their hearing us we should never have been able to have apprehended any of them. I then not being able to follow after these blacks for the want of rations, I returned to Yamboukal. Upon my arrival at Yamboukal, I found a letter for me from Mr Hazard, Mr Ogilvie's superintendent stating that the blacks were again amongst his cattle and that he had seen his … (damaged) of his hut and that the rest of the cattle had been driven off. After staying one day at Hall's to spell the horses, I then proceeded down to Mr Hazard's. I lost my horses on the first day. After my arrival at Wachoo, the next morning by sunrise some of the blacks from Warroo, Mr Fitzgerald's Station came and informed me that during the night myall blacks had come into the Warroo Station and speared two blackfellows, a boy and two gins and that these were dead and others were wounded, these were the blacks which were supposed to have been amongst Mr F's and Mr O's cattle. I ordered the men to saddle up immediately and proceeded in pursuit of these murderers.

After coming upon their tracks and following them for about 30 miles we came to the place where they were encamped in a nearly impassable Bindie Scrub the blacks either saw or heard us before we came upon the camp. We found in the camp a great quantity of fat and a lot of beef which had been only recently killed, we likewise got amongst them some (had) new knives and the police saw some of the blacks running away who had on nearly new white shirts. We followed on their tracks the next day but at night was obliged to leave them having been forced to tie the horses up the night before for want of food and water. We were three days before we could get out of the scrub and on the evening of the 4th day we arrived at Werribon. I then having patrolled about the run for nearly two months and the next day having received a letter from you desiring me to proceed to the Barracks as the section I had with me was the only available force at his disposal to return to the Barracks as soon as the quietness of the country would permit. I at once proceeded thither at which place I arrived on 19th June.

I have in conclusion to express to you my approbation of the conduct of the men throughout this journey as they have behaved and have been exceedingly well without any exception and I have had no occasion whatever to find fault with any of them (QSA Series ID14733/86141 pp 75-78)

Second Draft

According to Instructions received from you dated April 20, 1852 I started with the men mentioned in the margin for the purpose of patrolling the Balloon River.

On reaching Mr Ogilvie's Station (Wachoo) I had occasion to go out on the run when sickness (fever and ague) attacked me and three of the men which caused me to return to the station. The remainder of the men proceeded to Mr Hall's Station (Yamboukal) where I joined them in a few days after. I should have returned to the Quarters soon but the blacks being I did not think it prudent to leave the River just at that part under time in the until I was satisfied that the blacks had shifted out from the (rest of document missing) (QSA Series ID 14733/86141 p 79)

According to Instructions received from you on the 20 April 1852 I started with a detachment of Native Police for the purpose of patrolling on the Balonne River and the neighbouring stations. Upon my arrival at Mr Ogilvie's Station I received information that the blacks were destroying and hunting his cattle and had been for some time previous. I went out upon the run and saw where the blacks had killed and eaten some cattle and in surrounding places where they had been rushing the cattle upon the run only a few days previously. There having been a very great quantity of rain it was five days before we could find any tracks. When we did upon the fifth day we followed them the whole day but we did not come up with blacks at all. On the seventh day I and troopers Tom Thumb, Rodney and Dick were attacked with fever and ague. We then returned to the station at Wachoo. Rodney and Dick have recovered. I sent the police out to patrol upon the run to stop the depredations of the blacks as the stockman had brought word in that the blacks were still killing the cattle and I thought the sight of the police riding about might be the means of stopping their outrages. My Johnson who resides at Wachoo accompanied the police for the purpose of showing them the near ways thro the bush. I was much surprised after waiting at Wachoo for days that the police did not return. After having received a letter from Mr Duncombe, I started with troopers Tom Thumb, Bunya Jimmy.

2 requesting my immediate attendance as the …

6 and Rinaldo very nearly recovered

3 to be attacked by the … blacks who in the

7 for Hall's Station up the river upon my

4 immediate neighbourhood and had …

5 their intention of doing so (QSA Series ID14733/86141 p 80)

William Forster, Gingin to Frederick Walker, 26 April 1852

I have the honour to forward to you copy of a letter containing charges against you in your capacity of Commandant of the Black Police.

Copy: William Forster, Gingin to Col. Sec. 26 April 1852

I do myself the honour to report to you that three times within the last month my shepherds have been attacked by the natives their lives endangered and sheep taken from them.

I have not thought proper to advise the officer of the black police of these occurrences, because it has come to my knowledge that applications on the part of some of my neighbours for their assistance in similar cases have been lately disregarded and because last year when one of my flocks was taken by the natives and at the instance of my overseer, Mr Marshall visited the station ostensibly for the purpose of rescuing it, this gentleman finding the greater part of the sheep had been set free by the blacks and recovered previous to his arrival made no effort to capture the depredators though they are supposed to be the very parties concerned in the murder of the late Mr Gregory Blaxland. The reason for this conduct I am informed on good authority was that as the flock in question was not in possession of the blacks he could not believe it had been taken at all and that he considered himself to have been summoned without reason. I cannot but regard it is a great hardship and injustice that the officers of this corps should require our property to be left at the mercy of its plunderers as an evidence of whatever outrages have been committed and that not only are the lives of our servants put in peril but their statements discredited without this expensive corroboration which I confess it is altogether beyond my means to afford.

I beg also to refer to the postscript of your letter of the 19 May 1851 in which alluding to the murder of Mr Blaxland you did me the horror to acquaint me that "the Commandant of the Native Police has been instructed to afford assistance to the Police in the proceedings they may take for enforcing the law in this case." No such proceedings have hitherto been instituted and I continue to express my opinion that had the above instructions been attended to and the law properly enforced not only would the natives in this vicinity have been deterred from their late depredations on my property but much loss in other quarters would have been prevented and many valuable lives spared which have fallen as sacrifice to their unsurpassed hostility.

Nor can I quit this subject with making a last attempt to impress upon the government that the efficiency of the black police is by no means so great as it has been represented to be that by the mismanagement of its officers it is daily becoming less and that these gentlemen in many instances have neglected the duty and abused the authority entrusted to them. I am touching delicate ground and that His Excellency the Governor has already intimated his disapproval of what he judged to be the offensive language used by a former complainant on this very subject. But I trust while I disclaim any intentional disrespect; some allowance may be made for the want of opportunity afforded by a country life and its pursuits to culture that refined style of phraseology which is expected to characterise the official correspondence of the government.

I feel assured that the government has been deceived by erroneous information on this subject that it has become prejudiced in favour of their force by partial and interacted statements. That the black police might be useful I would not deny but I am convinced that they never will be so under their present system of management. A feeling is daily gaining ground in this and the adjacent District that they are even mischievous and that is vain to address any complaints against them to the authorities in Sydney. It is a remarkable fact that their sojourn on certain stations has been in many instances followed by aboriginal outrages, in some cases by the murder of white men. Mr Clarke was killed only a few days, Mr Trevethan not many weeks after the departure of the black police from the stations on which they respectively resided and it is undesirable that since the force was quartered in these two Districts the annual amount of murders and robberies committed by the natives has considerably increased.

I most respectfully solicit your attention to the following statements which I can if necessary substantiate. They seem to me to include among them some of the causes of that inefficiency of which I have complained and to contain abundant evidence of defective administration.

1. Promiscuous intercourse between the native women of the two Districts and the black police is, if not encouraged, not prevented by their officers. Not long since many of the troopers were infected with venereal disease. These women act as spies and messengers for various tribes and are commonly offered as bribes to conciliate the favour and mitigate the hostility of powerful antagonists. By their agency the intended movement of the black police are known and anticipated by the natives.

2. It has become a common practice of the officers of the black police to delegate their functions to their sergeants.

3. The commandant and his lieutenants take upon themselves to dispense with warrants and to decide whether they shall be executed or not. Mr Marshall lately apprehended a black on warrant and released him without formal enquiry. Mr Walker, when about to proceed to Frazer's Island, seized a number of blacks without charge of any kind and lodged them in the lock up at Maryborough, giving a written order to the chief constable to detain them a few days. These blacks were taken up while at work on board of a vessel which they had accompanied from the heads

4. The commandant has been intoxicated on several occasions.

5. The black police are in the habit of attaching themselves too constant-

ly to certain favoured localities or certain favourite stations and these are not in general situated in the disturbed portions of the two Districts. The Northern portion of Wide Bay has been visited but twice since their arrival and for a short time on both occasions. Individual preferences appear to influence their officers in these selections.

In conclusion, while I cannot help attributing to the present commandant the degradation of this corps, I would not be understood to infer that the evil would be certainly remedied by his removal. Some species of local control is in my opinion requisite to regulate the operations and guard against the caprices of such an officer who is in a great degree divested of responsibility by his distance from Sydney. Hoping that the government may be induced to take this suggestion into consideration. (QSA Series ID14733/86139)

Frederick Walker to Col. Sec. 5 May 1852

I etc. to represent to you that a letter from your office dated 26 April 1852 N° 52/132 has been forwarded to me transmitting for my report a communication from the Inspector General of Police and accompanied by a letter Mr Provincial Inspector Askins relative to the Native Police acting as auxiliaries to the regular constabulary.

Mr Askins simply states that that so many Chinese prisoners had been apprehended by the Native Police that the ordinary constables could not do the escort duty and he requires the Native Police force to do so. How can he request that force to be auxiliary? (Which I suppose means assisting). It strikes me that the deficiency is that the ordinary constabulary force is not in a position to be auxiliary. The Native Police force can never act in immediate concert with a constabulary force constituted as the present one, outside the limits. I cannot allow the men with whom I have taken so much pains to be subjected to the tyranny of men who like the constables outside the limits are so totally devoid of discipline. There is no esprit de corps among them at all. The Chief Constables almost everywhere are good men but they can do no good under such a system. You will observe also that in the Maranoa District, Mr Askins is completely at a stand (still). (QSL Reel A2.23 p 556)

Sol. Gen. to Col. Sec. 18 May 1852

In accordance with request contained in your letter of the 12th Instant N° 334, to the Attorney-General, I have the honour, in the absence of that officer, to return the report of the proceedings of the Native Police up to the end of December last. I have also the honour to transmit a similar Report of earlier date 31 August which I find amongst the paper's in the Attorney-General's office. Margin notes: Read 21st CAF. Should minute on 51/08113 be now communicated to Commandant? 25th. Yes, I have scratched out the word "proceedings" in the letter. 26th CAF. Mr Walker 31 May. 59/8113 The letter directed by the Governor's General Minute on the case is submitted herewith. But before that letter is despatched, I would suggest with deference that Mr Walker, Report should be referred for perusal of the Attorney-General. It would seem that at least three Aborigines have been shot by the Native Police; but it does not appear whether any enquiry was made, to show whether the shooting was justified by the circumstances of the case. 29 August. 51/3266 Commandant Native Police 10 March reporting proceedings of the police to 10 March 1851 open on register and not with records. 20 August. (SLQ Reel A23.23 p 662)

Col. Sec. to Frederick Walker, 18 May 1852

With reference to you letter of 1st March last reporting the cause of the difference that exists between yourself and certain of the settlers in the Northern Districts. I do myself the honour to inform you that his Excellency the Governor General entirely concurs in the views and opinions expressed by you relative to the policy that ought to guide the government and the Native Police Force towards the settlers and the Aborigines; and which I am to add you have hitherto carried out to the satisfaction of the government. (SRNSW 4-3860 Reel2818 p 494)

Col. Sec. to Frederick Walker, 22 May 1852

In transmitting to you the accompanying letter from William Forster Esq of the District of Wide Bay reporting that within a period of one month his shepherds have been attacked thrice by the Aborigines their lives endangered and their flocks taken from them and stating the reasons that induced him to refrain from advising the Officers of the Native Police of the occurrence of those outrages as also representing the inefficiency of that corps and submitting certain statements which seem to him to include many of the … (SRNSW 4-3860 Reel2818 p 495)

Frederick Walker to Col. Sec. 23 July 1852

Lieutenant Fulford reports that everything was quiet on the Lower Condamine, and, with the exception of some petty cattle stealing in the Maranoa District, I believe it to be in the same state.

I regret that a collision has again taken place between the Police and the petty cattle stealers above mentioned. I have not yet seen the affidavits taken before the magistrates at Surat but as the police had left Sergeant Dempster to accompany a Mr Johnson, I have written to Lieutenant Fulford, that it appeared to me that they must have had the Sergeant's consent or orders to do so, in which case he was unfit to be entrusted with a detachment or that the troopers had left without consent in which case he seemed to me to be unable to command them; and this I was not prepared to expect would be the case, as the men of the section entrusted to Sergeant Dempster had hitherto been noted for their steady obedient conduct. I have of course required a full explanation. The first clause of the written instructions given by me to all the European sergeants is that they are not to allow any person unconnected with the Native Police Force to interfere with or give orders to any of the troopers under their command.[349]

Lt G Fulford to Sgt RA Dempster, 3 August 1852

You will start from this today taking with you the men mentioned in the margin: Cpl Larry, Tprs Donald, Dick, Rodney, Capita Simon and Rinaldo.

2. The route you will follow is up this creek to Mr Blyth's dray track then by that track to the Yulebar and from thence on to the Fitzroy Downs. From information received the blacks are destroying the property of Mr Hall and Ogilvie. You will endeavour to put a stop to their outrages.

---

349 *SMH* 4 November 1857 p 2.

Upon your arrival on Fitzroy Downs I leave it to your judgement as to the road you take. But I would advise you proceed some way down the Coogoon towards Weribun. If I did see where the blacks were killing cattle, I would proceed across to the Maranoa.

3. It is my wish that you keep up a constant patrol as possible and visit all the stations on the river. After you have patrolled about and you find the country quiet you can return to the barracks.

4. You will as usual strictly adhere to the instructions issued by the Commandant to Sergeants in Command of Detachments. (QSA ID14733/86141 pp 87-88)

F Oliver O'Neill MD to Lt RP Marshall, 20 August 1852

In reply to your letter of the 18th inst., I have the honour to inform you that only one case of venereal disease among the troopers of the Native Police has come under my notice since the arrival of the force in these Districts. (QSA Series ID14733/86140)

Frederick Walker to Col. Sec. 28 August 1852

In your private letter of the 24 July 1852 you say that some dissatisfaction has been expressed at the practice started to prevail of obtaining recruits for the Native Police from among blacks employed in private service. How am I to answer this? I send you the roll of the 48 recruits. I cannot discontinue what I never began.

I now come to the case of Bungaree which you instance. I have never seen Bungaree. I have never met Mr Wilkie. The Auditor General and the Colonial Treasurer can prove to you that Bungaree has never been returned as a policeman. In 1849, I was informed that a black called Bungaree wished to join the Native Police and I was afterwards told that he had written two letters to me. I never received them. I was told that Bungaree was educated at the Sydney College by the late Mr Stephen Coxen and that that gentleman intended if his pecuniary affairs had not interfered with the arrangement to send Bungaree to one of the English universities. Bungaree having taken most of the prizes at school. In July 1851, Sergeant Skelton had instructions to take Bungaree with him to Callandoon if Bungaree was still wishing to serve the Queen. Skelton reported to me that Bungaree was a hired servant of Mr Colin McKenzie and he thought that Bungaree being an educated man could not come under the 15 clause of the Masters and Servants Act, 11 Vict[a] N° 9 and I concurred with the Sergeant in his opinion. Since that, it appears that Bungaree finished his agreement with Mr McKenzie and he afterwards I am told next to Mr Wilkie. Sergeant Major Dolan told me that on his way in, January last, he had seen Bungaree and that he bitterly complained that I had not answered his letters. I told Dolan to write to Bungaree and tell him he might join the police if he liked. I have not personally raised a single recruit. I cannot prevent my lads telling others that the Queen's service is preferable to any other. The same thing exists among European police and soldiers. If any man has the right to control the free British subject, Bungaree, Mr Charles Coxen is the man because he may properly be considered as his guardian; but Bungaree is well able to decide for himself. Bungaree, it seems has joined Mr Fulford on the Condamine and he must in fairness be protected by every magistrate of the territory in choosing his own way. I tell you plainly that Mr Wilkie's idea that Bungaree is his property is slavery.

I have no legal power to keep 96 men in the Queen's service. There is nothing to prevent them leaving that service at a moment. They are held and kept by the ties of gratitude to the government that has treated them so well and how can you wonder at their representing this to others.

I have gone into this matter in detail for I had been informed by Mr Crowder that a great deal of talk had been occasioned by Bungaree going to Mr Fulford. Before people come to a conclusion, it would be just as well if they heard both sides of a story. But all squatters are the same; they listen to the first yarn that is brought to them. (QSL Reel A2.25 p 507)

Sgt RA Dempster to Lt G Fulford, 10 September 1852

According to instructions received from you dated 3 August, I proceeded on patrol with the men mentioned in the margin, Cpl Larry, Tprs Donald, Dick, Rodney, Capita Simon and Rinaldo, for the Balonne River.

After encamping the first night on the Fanning Creek we struck across the Fitzroy Downs, on coming near to the Wallambilla Creek we observed late tracks of cattle with the tracks of blacks in pursuit of them;

every appearance of rain coming on we made on for the Creek but were obliged to encamp before we could reach it. At this place we had to stop two days and two nights, the whole of this time with the exception of one day was constant heavy rain. The next day we had gone between two or three miles when we came upon fresh blacks' tracks. We followed them about two miles and found their camp. They had not left long; we followed them up and soon came in sight of four gins, shortly after this we saw two blackfellows. They did not see us, during this time we heard a tomahawk at work. As these blacks were not committing themselves in any way neither were there any signs in their camp of their having done so, I of course did not disturb them. We then went down to the camp to see what blacks they were. Tpr Rinaldo being about the first man at the camp only just avoided a boomerang which was thrown at him by a blackfellow that bolted from the police at Callandoon. He was known by the name of Priam. Rinaldo seeing the black picking up his nulla nullas and spears immediately shot him. Another very powerful black threw a nulla nulla at Rodney which only just missed his head as he stooped on the horse. Rodney shoot him also. We then proceeded on our journey crossing the Bungil and Yalebone Creeks on to the Muckadilla. The whole of this country was in a fearful state with the late rain which compelled me to go to the Balonne as we were out of rations. We did not see any signs of blacks about this part.

I then went down to Mr Ogilvie's Station here the Culba Galoes were as busy as they could be killing cattle. I started out on the following day but that night the horses were startled in some manner and split into four or five mobs; here we were detained three days before we could find them again having lost so much time at the place I returned to Wachoo, Mr Ogilvie's from thence I proceeded down the Balonne River visiting the stations of Messrs Dangar, Loder, Baldwin's Ezzey and Grover at the last two mentioned stations the blacks have been doing great mischief lately especially at Mr Ezzey's among the cattle they have slaughtered some, several have been seen with spears in them on the adjoining run (his Uncle's) and at the time I was down there he assured me he could not find a beast on his run with the exception of a few crawlers which he turned out lately. These generally lay close to the hut. I was out with him for three days without seeing any fresh tracks of blacks when rain came on so heavily that I was obliged to return to his hut. There were very numerous old tracks of blacks to be seen on a body of cattle tracks, evidently hunting them.

Hearing that the Moonie Creek was quiet I did not go over there but made my way up the River again arriving at Mr Ogilvie's Station on the evening of the 2nd. I received information that the Culba Galoes were encamped about two hundred yards at the back of the hut. They had been in about four or five days. The second day after coming in they went out and brought in a quantity of fresh beef with them that they were very jolly, making the hut blacks very jolly also. That there were thirty-five counted by P … , Mr Fitzgerald's overseer; there being more at the back of the camp cutting bark. The following morning, I ordered the men to saddle up with the intention of capturing the notorious Oromondi. This being his mob. Upon coming up to the camp, several weapons were thrown at us. The blacks then immediately ran in various directions. I told the men to shoot Oromondi if they could not take him. Tpr Donald chased him when he turned and threw a boomerang. Donald lay flat down on the horse's back. The weapon grazing his back, he (Donald) then jumped off his horse and shot the offender; there were three more of these blacks shot. Larry spearing one in the back. During this time, I being then about ninety or one hundred yards at the back of the hut a blackfellow came to me and told me that there was a white fellow dead at the hut. There being only Johnson and Parker the stockman at the hut when I left it. I made haste to the hut and looked under the verandah which was full to excess with hut blacks, gins and picaninnies. There I saw Johnson. I asked him where Abraham was? He said he did not know. Then I said I think he is dead at the same time getting off my horse to go and see. I went to the other doorway of the hut where I saw the man laying dead. I then went out again to the police and in a few moments, we ceased firing. Most of the hostile blacks had by this time made their escape by the opposite end of the hut and crossed the river. In the afternoon of that day, I counted one hundred and twenty-two blacks including gins and children.

I beg to remark that the wounds of the deceased were caused ball and buck shot, thereby exonerating the police from any blame whatever as their ammunition is nothing more than powder and ball neither do I believe that either of them would put buck shot in even if they could obtain it without first asking me whether they might do so. I sent for Mr Hazard who was down the river at the time. he came up on Saturday night and we buried the man on Sunday. The following day I started on my journey up the river for headquarters where I arrived on the evening of Thursday last.

In conclusion I have to remark in this as on other previous occasions the conduct of the men with the exception of Larry has been exceedingly good much better than I expected as they could obtain nothing more than beef and milk at any station on the river everybody being short of rations. This I made known to them at Mr Ogilvie's Station and proposed to them to return and fetch rations from the barracks but they said they would go on and be satisfied with meat only.

Larry behaved very improperly nearly the whole of the time we were out repeatedly leaving his men both on the road and in the bush in spite of me speaking to him about it. He showed himself very sulky both with me and his men. The latter if they had been inclined to be riotous I could have done nothing with. On Sunday the 5th Larry for what reason I cannot say bought his two horses up to the camp with the intention of saddling up (this was after we had buried the man about 12 o'clock in the day) I asked him what he was going to do? He made no answer. I then was about taking the horses away from him when the remainder of the men who were in their camp said let him go sergeant, let him go. Thinking if he was stopped he might make some disturbance I took one of the horses from him but not without resistance being shown. He left me that day. I did not see anything more of him till we overtook at Mr Hall's lower station (Werribun) where he camped by himself about thirty yards from his men. Since then he remained with them till we arrived at the barracks. If we are to experience such conduct as this from the corporals I don't know what we may expect from the men? In fact, the sergeant's life is in danger, trusting you will make enquiries into this affair. (QSA ID14733/86141 pp 268-275)

Sgt RA Dempster's deposition, 3 September 1852

The information of Sergeant Richard Dempster of Wandy Gumble in the said Colony Sergeant of the Native Police taken on oath before me, Harry Whitty Esq CCL for the District of Maranoa one of her Majesty's

Justices of the Peace acting in and for the said Colony in the year of our Lord 1852 who saith as follows:

On Friday, 3rd September during the time I was engaged in the capture of several notorious blacks who were encamped at Mr Ogilvie's Station word was brought me by a blackfellow that a white man at the hut was shot. I immediately went to the hut where I saw Abraham Parker laying close to his own hut door dead. Mr Johnson was near and in front of his hut door. He had a double-barrelled gun in his hand. I asked Johnson had he fired a shot and he said he had. I did not see him fire. I examined the wounds. They appeared to me to be inflicted by a ball and buck shot. The charges went thro the muscle of the left arm fracturing the bone and entered the breast behind the left nipple and came out at the breast bone. The Native Police do not load with buck shot. I loaded my double-barrelled carbine with ball and buck shot. I had discharged one ball before I heard of the man being shot but in a different direction from the hut. The other barrel I had in reserve. Signed RA Dempster. Taken before me at Surat the day and month before mentioned H Whitty JP CCL. (QSA Series ID14733/86141 p 276)

Frederick Walker to Col. Sec. 4 October 1852

I have the honour to report, for the information of his Excellency the Governor-General, the proceedings of the Native Police Force, from the 1st March to the 30th September, 1852.

1. Lieutenant Richard P. Marshall, in his letter of the 29th March, reports the trouble that had been given to him through twenty-eight Chinese servants having absconded, leaving 20,000 of Mr Sandeman's sheep in the bush. The police, by forced marches, succeeded in overtaking the runaways, four of whom the police conveyed to the lock-up at Gayndah. He also reports that Mr Trevethan was murdered on the 29th March, and that the ringleader of his murderers was shot by the police on the 18th April. Both Lieutenants Marshall and Murray have been very active, and in my letter of the 2nd April I informed you of the result of Mr Murray's attempts to apprehend the blacks who had robbed Mr Trevethan's station, previous to the murder of that gentleman. Lieutenant Murray proceeded to the Dawson country on account of the murder of Mr Clarke in the middle of last April. Sergeant Skilton had arrived in that

neighbourhood. As I stated in my letter of the 28th of July, Lieutenant Marshall had, in June, a collision with the Wide Bay blacks, who were destroying Mr Tooth's cattle at Widgee Widgee.

On the 10th July, Wm. Dawson, the shepherd boy of Mr James Mackay, was murdered, and both Mr Marshall, and Mr Murray, having hastened to the spot. They met on Mr Mackay's run, Upper Burnett River, but were unsuccessful in their attempts to follow the tracks of the murderers. Since that, however, Lieutenant Murray reports that on the 29th August, three of these murderers had been shot by the Police. The affidavits relative to all the above occurrences have been forwarded to the Honourable the Attorney-General. Some blacks accused of outrages, have been forwarded to the lock up at Gayndah, but were discharged by the local magistrates, without the examination of the witnesses. Lieutenants Marshall and Murray report the continued good conduct of the men under their charge, but state that they had suffered much from ague. The trouble given by the Chinese servants seriously interfered with the attempts of the Police Force to protect the settlers from the outrages of the Aborigines.

2. Lieutenant Fulford reports that the Lower Condamine country is quiet, except that a small quantity of cattle had been speared. His account of the Maranoa district is not satisfactory; the heavy rains had given the blacks great opportunities for destroying cattle, which they had taken advantage of. They have evinced much obstinacy, which I have no doubt is principally caused by Mr Fulford having, according to my instructions, weakened his force by sending Sergeant Skilton to the Dawson.

In my letter of the 28th July, 1852, in the sixth clause, I stated that a collision had occurred at Yamboukal, between the police and hostile blacks. The police had been sent by Sergeant Dempster with a stranger.

The depositions which I have forwarded to the honourable the Attorney-General, and relative to this collision, are very unsatisfactory, and I have recommended the dismissal of Sergeant Dempster. Since that another affray had occurred at or near Mr Ogilvie's station on the Balonne, where the blacks were destroying much property. A storeman had been accidentally shot in the affray, which Mr Fulford has proceeded to investigate. I am informed that the unfortunate man was killed with a bullet and some buck shot. The native police had no buck shot. The eighth section of the native police started from here on the 27th September to reinforce Lieutenant Fulford.

3. Mr Fulford had been to the Dawson, to inquire into the murder of Mr Clarke, and of a Chinese servant of Mr Turnbull; and he has since learned that Sergeant Skilton had twice repulsed the blacks on the Dawson, but he had not received the particulars. I have no doubt that, when the usual enquiry is instituted, it will be found that Sergeant Skilton has behaved with his customary discretion. All Mr Fulford's division had suffered from ague.

4. In my letter of 28th July, I informed you of the state of the recruits at this place. Within ten days of my receipt of the saddlery, I started Sergeant McGrath, with the eighth section of twelve men. Lieutenant Blandford starts this day with sixteen men for the Dawson and Burnett. One-half of the clothing, saddlery and accoutrements have not yet arrived. I expect them on the 14th when Sergeant Major Dolan starts with eighteen men for the Burnett, and I leave this for the Ipswich and the Pine River; Sergeant Pincolt with the fourth section meeting me at Drayton.

5. A large party of Moonie blacks, and a few from the Balonne, came into the Macintyre, about thirty miles below this place, and commenced destroying the herd of Mr Tooth. I could only fit out two troopers and my orderly; notwithstanding, we succeeded in showing them the necessity of retiring from this neighbourhood. The Macintyre blacks had warned me previously. The affidavits are forwarded to the Honourable the Attorney-General.[350]

Frederick Walker to Col. Sec. 10 October 1852

In the sixth clause of my letter of the 23 July 1852, I had the honour of drawing your attention to what I feared was great mismanagement if not disobedience of my written orders by Sergeant Richard Dempster.

2. I now do myself the honour to recommend that Dempster may be discharged from the Native Police Force as it appears that notwithstanding his written instructions, he did order the native corporal Edward and his men to accompany Mr Johnson after blacks.

350 *MBC* 18 December 1852 p4; *SMH* 4 December 1852 p 4 & *Maitland Mercury* 4 December 1852 p 4.

3. I need not state that Dempster's offence is a very dangerous one; the affray at Surat ensuing from it, is of a doubtful nature and the native troopers complain of ill-usage from Europeans which could not have occurrence if their sergeant had not sent them away from the only protection they had as their evidence is not admissible in a Court of Justice.

4. I have the honour to observe that I regret I have not the power to remove the sergeant at once for it takes many weeks before I can learn the pleasure of his Excellency the Governor General and in some cases a sergeant ought not to be continued another hour in charge of a section.[351]

Frederick Walker to Col. Sec. 20 October 1852

I etc. to report upon a letter addressed to you from several settlers in the Wide Bay, Burnett Districts and dated Burnett River, 24 July 1852.[352]

1. I do not consider it necessary for me to name the settlers who expressed the opinions mentioned in the first two clauses of my letter of the 1st March. That letter was not written with the desire to cause any one but merely to convey my opinions to the government I serve. It is for the settlers signing this letter of 24 July to protest malignantly against an inference which my letter does not aim at. I have not said sanguinary news were generally entertained by Northern settlers.

2. The second clause of the letter alluded to contain the only charge these settlers have made in the letter against the Native Police Force. They state in that clause that warrants have been repeatedly placed in the hands of the officers and that they have generally failed to execute or even attempt enforcing them. On the Macintyre, every one of the five murders of Edward Bradley was either killed in the attempt to apprehend him or apprehended except Boney who died and many other men arrested on oath of murder or felony also but lost their lives when resisting the police.

On the Condamine, the murderers of Mr Ferrett's man was killed and the attempts to apprehend the men who previous to the arrival of the Native Police murdered eleven Europeans in 1849 are recorded in my re-

351 *SMH* 4 November 1857 p 2.

352 A copy of this letter may be found in Chapter 10—Letters to the Press.

ports and these reports are substantiated by the affidavits of the settlers who accompanied the police for the purpose of identifying the murderers.

You will remember that Mr Blaxland his two boys and the shepherds of Messrs Humphrey, Herbert, Corfield and Murray were murdered before the arrival of the Native Police. In the 7th & 8th paragraphs of my report of 10 March 1850, I give an account of the attempts by Lieutenants Marshall and Fulford to seize several blacks who had committed the murder of the shepherds of Messrs Corfield and Murray. Mr Corfield, Mr Mactaggart and if I am not mistaken, Mr Mactavish accompanied the police in these attempts and reported to me how well the police behaved.

The affidavits of these gentlemen were forwarded by me to the Attorney-General and yet now they state deliberately that no attempts were made. The affidavits of Mr Mactaggart and A M Thompson JP relative to an attempt to protect the property of Mr Tooth in June last were also in the possession of the Honourable the Attorney-General.

Three of the murderers of the shepherds of Mr Corfield was apprehended by Sergeant Major Dolan and was liberated by the local magistrates at Gayndah because Mr Corfield neglected to prosecute. I have already stated in a former letter that two of the men sworn to as Mr Blaxland's murderers have been killed by the Native Police.

The affidavits relative to the death of Mr Trevethan's murderers have been forwarded to the Attorney-General and in my efforts, I have given you an account of the numerous attempts made by the police to apprehend other offenders and affidavits sent to the Attorney-General will as I have before stated prove that these reports are true.

You are well aware how difficult it is sometime to apprehend Europeans who have committed felony or murder and that months have frequently elapsed before the offenders could be brought to justice. This difficulty is naturally much greater when the offenders are wild savages and it is possible that some may never be apprehended but there is no reason to accuse the Native Police of unwillingness to capture them. On the contrary, I affirm that their zeal and activity has never in this colony been surpassed if it has been equalled.

It appears to me strange that four magistrates of the territory should place their signatures to such misrepresentation. As to the challenge to particularise cases in which I have been prevented from obtaining evidence among others, I may mention one stated in the second clause of my report of 5 January relative to Fraser's Island and another stated in the 5th paragraph of my letter to the Attorney-General dated 1 August 1851 relative to a black called Sandy accused of sheep stealing.

3. In the third clause of the letter, these settlers solicit the government to institute an inquiry into the proceedings of the Native Police. These proceedings are well known to the government.

His Excellency the Governor General would I feel sure not consent to an inquiry being suddenly instituted when I would have to answer charges of which I previously had no idea and to prove which these settlers state they are prepared to produce disagreeable evidence. These settlers ought at least to make the charges first when His Excellency would be able to see whether an inquiry was requisite and if it is to give me timely notice. I feel the more confident in this matter because His Excellency cannot anticipate that he will be convinced of the necessity of reforming an organisation which during three years has been so completely successful in the Macintyre and Lower Condamine country.

4. The facts mentioned in the 4th clause of the letter do not prove the incorrectness if my opinion that the system of not allowing the natives at the stations is a principal cause of their outrages, they rather tend to prove the correctness of may statement that these persons who carried on that system had managed to victimise their neighbours who acted more kindly towards the blacks. As for the system not being general I differ with these settlers and I may point out that I have more opportunities of justifying of this matter than they have. In other Districts attempts have been made with success to conciliate the blacks of this colony.

The object I presume of the government is to make the blacks feel the strength of the law not that they should feel the strength of individuals. If it is justifiable for settlers to make the blacks feel their strength it is equally justifiable for the blacks to retaliate.The occupying of a country inhabited by savages must always be dangerous but I think that it is less dangerous to conciliate them, than to *(note page missing)*

As by Sergeant Major Dolan and Sergeant Skelton the zeal and activity of these officers have been repeatedly praised by several of the settlers. We can therefore put up with the hurtfulness of a few persons and the petty malice of a faction. (QSL Reel A2.24 p 675)

Frederick Walker to E Deas Thomson, 21 October 1852

Some time since a letter signed by a few of the Burnett and Wide Bay settlers and addressed to you appeared in the *Sydney Herald*, I expected that you would have sent that letter to me for explanation which possibly you have done, for I am aware that other letters have been sent to me by post which I have not received. As I am now on the point of starting for the Pine River, it is probable I should not receive any letters from you for a couple of months and I am anxious that you should have a refutation of the falsehoods contained in that letter. I have therefore included my answer to it to you hoping that if you approve of it you can make it official without waiting until I receive your letter. I think you will say that the answer is complete but there are many other circumstances which still shew in a still strange light the inconsistency of these persons. For instance, Mr Herbert one of the persons signing wrote to Mr Jones that everything that the Native Police force could do a legal force had been done by them. Mr Mactaggart wrote that the Police ought to be a military not a police force. It is evident that both those persons imagine that the police ought to act illegally but in the letter of accusation they state that the police have neglected their legal duty. There has I am told been a letter written accusing the Police and me especially of great crimes and misdemeanours. I have not seen it but I have seen a letter circulating it. All the letters against me are written by Forster, Walsh who is Mr Griffith's superintendent and the notorious Macintyre assassin Marks. I hope you will give directions about having the supplies for the police sent early the next year. The requisitions you will find moderate and the clothing I suppose is out from England by this. At last I have the saddles and bridles but not much more than half the clothing. Margin: The enclosed as requested, other papers herewith. No decision given on the above. 21 Dec. Yes. 52/10109 (SLQ A2.24 p 706)

Col. Sec. to Frederick Walker, 5 November 1852

Having laid before the Governor General your letter of the 10th ultimo, bringing under notice the disobedience of Sergeant Dempster and recommending he be discharged from the Native Police Force, I now do myself the honour to convey to you his Excellency's authority for the discharge of Dempster and to inform you that although the Governor General does not think it would be expedient to give you a general authority to dismiss non-commissioned officers from the Corps of Native Police at your own discretion, his Excellency sees no objection to you being authorised to suspend from duty at once any non-commissioned officer who may misconduct himself subject to the confirmation of the Governor General upon the case being reported.

Frederick Walker to Col. Sec. 25 January 1853

I have the honour to receive a letter from you relative to the recruiting of Native troopers. I have unfortunately left that letter at Traylan and cannot refer to the date.

2. I presume that it is the wish of His Excellency the GG that no blacks should be directly taken from the service of Europeans, if that is the case I have the honour to state that none have ever been taken with my consent unless with the consent or the request of settlers.

I am aware of one who has been recruited without my knowledge and he is named in the margin, Bendigo. When I did know that he had absconded, I did not discharge him for I had previously satisfied the cruel treatment he was subjected to.

3. This matter would never have been mooted were it not for an objection raised on what account I know not about an educated black called Bungaree. I explained as much as I know about this matter in a private letter to you; but the accompanying documents will throw some new light on the matter as it now appears that Mr Wilkie was himself desirous that Bungaree should join the police, that Mr Charles Coxen was Bungaree's last employer and not only did that gentleman give his consent to his joining the police but also furnished him with a horse to go to Mr Fulford.

4. I cannot suppose that His Excellency objects to blacks joining the

police because they had at one time been in the employment of some European (I mean that I have the right to enlist anyone I find out of employment) for if such should be the case and had such an order been given to me in 1848 it would have amounted to an order not to raise a Native Police Force.

5. I have also the honour to state that I have never departed from the plan originated by me of not employing blacks in their own country. (QSL Reel A2.25 p 499)

Frederick Walker to Lt G Fulford, 30 April 1853

I do myself the honour to state that I much disapproved of the policy carried on by the Settlers in the Maranoa District.

2. In 1849 & 1850, it was currently reported in the neighbouring District that Settlers had gone out in search of black cattle stealers or killers and that they were accompanied by some of the blacks belonging to the Ballem (sic) called station or hut blacks. Theses hut blacks as it was stated in the adjacent district were styled Native Police. In 1851 this policy was as I have been informed still carried on until I arrived July 1851.

3. I do myself the honour to draw your attention specially to the 2nd paragraph of my letter because I attribute to the matters mentioned in that paragraph all the mischief which has occurred in the Maranoa District since. I cannot mention a stranger case than the facts stated by you. If sixteen of the hut blacks having been murdered in 1852 by those which you are pleased to call Waddy jacks or some such name; in English, Outlaws. I do not understand by what right any British subject dare proclaim another British subject an Outlaw.

4. I have now stated my disapprobation of the settlers punishing, a punishing over which I have no control; but next I must allude to the punishing of a Force over which I think I have some control. I allude to mean the Division of Native Police under your command.

5. Four times the Native Police in the Maranoa District have fired at and killed Blacks at stations. The first time under Edward and Larry at Wamboukal (sic, Yamboukal) under circumstances which I am certain have evidence will have been satisfactory to the Honourable Attorney-General.

The second time at Yamboukal when the Native Police were instigated into an attack upon the blacks for no fault that I can see; except that one of your outlaws had quarrelled with a hut black about a bit of meat. The affidavits in that matter must be unsatisfactory to the Honourable Attorney-General. They are unsatisfactory to me for I perceive that the police that I have taken so much pains with have in that case been induced entrapped to commit murder.

The next case is that of Ouramundi; the lamentable death of Abraham Parker. I will not allude to unless it is to mention that he lost his life in through a flagrant disregard to Sergeant Dempster's orders; but I wish to be informed by what right had did Sergeant Dempster attempt to apprehend Ouramundi at all. (The cause of this accident.) He was simply told by Mr Hazard that Ouramundi was a notorious killer. This can be said of any black in the Maranoa District.

The fourth case is that of Sergeant Skelton at McEnroe's station. The evidence only shews (on one side) that there had been a common assault. In the 14th clause of my Instructions to the Sergeants it is stated. Also, if he sees an assault committed; but not if he hears of an assault having been committed (rest of letter missing) (QSA Series ID 14725/86133 p 27)

Frederick Walker to E Deas Thomson, 14 June 1853

The want of subalterns had thrown so much additional work on me that I have not been able to make out my usual reports and also the remittance to support such reports is not complete. I therefore thought you would like a private account of the state of the country and of the efficiency of the Police. I consider the Macintyre and Lower Condamine as not to be considered as disturbed country. The Maranoa accounts are still unsatisfactory and I have complained to Mr Fulford of the policing carried on by the sergeant under his command and Mr Marshall has gone there to inquire into matters and try and resolve them.

The Burnett District is quiet from one end to the other and nothing has occurred to disturb the peace except the murder of Mr Mackay's Chinese shepherd a matter which has given great satisfaction to certain parties, since the 1st January. This six months, peace is due to the indefatigable exertions of Messrs Marshall and Murrey, the same may be said of Wide Bay District with the exception of the supposed murder by the blacks of

Mr Uhr's Chinaman.

One matter that called our special attention was the great Bunya season and this I immediately attended to—I had great fears of the result as for six years there had never been such an assemblage. The murderer of Mr Balfour's Chinaman at it. It is remarkable that every alternate year a man is murdered at that station in the month of November. I know also (who) the murderers are but there is no legal evidence. I kept up a constant system of patrols, cut through the scrubs in all directions and so pursued the blacks that they dispersed at the end of the season without having done any damage whatever. Not a shot was fired. The difficulty of corresponding under such circumstances must have been great. I have been managing three sections at a time with only one white assistant. The greatest evil however under which we have suffered is that prostrating sickness fever and ague. It has knocked me up altogether and killed five of the men. Mr Marshall, Mr Murray and the Sergeant Major have been very ill and it is no joke shivering and shaking three or five hours one day and riding 25 miles the next. The cure is almost as bad, for the quinine quiet stupefies me. I was in hope that proceeding to Brisbane would relieve me and if I had taken Bigge's offer to go for three days to the Bay in his boat it is probable that I would have been; but I was called away on duty because the Chief Constable would not take six of my men for fear of the Attorney-General who it seems has given them a great fright. I must now go sick as I am to take a prisoner to Maryboro and give instructions to one Section and then to Traylan and afterwards *(unintelligible)*. I must have two months' spell. I have 300 miles' ride before me. I have a quiet fast walking horse luckily. At the last Assizes at Brisbane a black of the name of Mickie apprehended by the Native Police was convicted for the murder of Mrs Shannon and Mr Gregor (I presume as accessary after the fact). Now it is certain that he did rob the hut after the murder, but you must understand that he was a mere boy at the time and that the murderer made every boy, woman and child carry away the property. I can give the Attorney-General a half a dozen more under the same warrant all I have to do is to go round the different stations and take the boys who are tailing cattle, bullock driving or otherwise employed. There ought to be an amnesty for every one included in that warrant except Dundalli, who was an actual murderer. I hold several other absurd warrants such as two for blacks, names unknown and no description. The police all their sickness, all their hardships and the death of their comrades, have behaved admirably with the exception of the case of a sergeant having made some of them drunk and that's the eighth section had become masters of Sergeant McGrath. This section since under my own command is now equal to any except the 1st, 4th & 5th. (QSL Reel A2.23 p 364)

Col. Sec. to Frederick Walker, 18 June 1853

Referring to my letter of the 17th instant instructing you to raise a detachment of Native Police for service at Port Curtis, I do myself the honour by direction of His Excellency the Governor General to request that you will have the goodness to purchase nine draft horses for the use of the surveying party that has been despatched to Port Curtis and forward them to the Surveyor or Mr McCabe in charge of the Native Police. The Auditor General has been authorised to prepare warrants for advancing o you one hundred and eighty pounds to enable you to purchase the horses at an expense not exceeding twenty-five pounds each. P.S. In the event of you being unable to purchase draft horses at the usual price. You will be good enough to report what further service, you think will be necessary in order that a further advance may be made to you for the purpose. (SRNSW 4-3862 Reel 2818 p 162.)

Frederick Walker to Col. Sec. 30 June 1853

I regret to have to inform you that Lieutenant Morisset recent instructions to join me in the Burnett District and in consequence has not received my instructions addressed to Callandoon.

2. I have the honour to remark that the Burnett District is a very wide term and I cannot but express my surprise that Lieutenant Marshall should have given such vague orders and orders that upset my plans especially when it is stated that he knew that my principal object in going to Brisbane was to start the 5th Section to the Clarence and that Lieutenant Morisset was to take command.

When Mr Morisset was at Callandoon he was 300 miles nearer to Armidale than the Burnett District the most simple plan was to let him stop there until he received my answer to his letter, but even supposing that it was necessary that he should see me why could not Mr Marshall instruct him to join me at the Post Office Burnett Inn to which Mr Marshall addressed his letter to me and where I had appointed to be at a certain time to receive the abstracts etc. requisite to adjust the accounts for the quarter ending this day. Margin notes: 53/6057 Reporting departure of 5th Section to Clarence – Returned by Auditor General 13 July 1853. Appears to me a matter which Commandant should settle himself by reprimanding Lt Marshall if he considers necessary unless he wishes to make formal complaint against Mr M of wilful disobedience, CAF. (QSL Reel A2. 26 p 788)

Col. Sec. to Frederick Walker

... relative to instructions having been given to Lieutenant Morisset by Lieutenant Marshall to join you in the Burnett District instead of at Brisbane. I am desired to acquaint you that it appears to his Excellency that the present is a matter which you should yourself settle by reprimanding Lieutenant Marshall if you consider such a course to be necessary unless you wish to make a formal complaint against Mr Marshall for wilful disobedience of orders. (SRNSW 43860 Reel2818 p 175)

Frederick Walker to Col. Sec. 14 July 1853

I regret to have to inform you that the prices charged by the settlers have been so exorbitant that I can no longer procure rations for the police at the present rate of 1s 4d per diem.

2. I have made use of strong terms because the price of provisions do not justify such charges and this is very annoying to me because I have endeavoured to reduce the coast of the force under my command.

3. In no place does it appear to me that their charges are too high as much as at the Macintyre where the price is 1s 6d per diem for each man; and the settlers who would have been ruined without the aid of the Native Police have by their means some realised an independency, some made large fortunes.

4. I therefore do myself the honour to request that His Excellency the GG will be pleased to sanction that the Native Troopers may for the

present quarter ending the 30th September may be allowed 1s 6d per diem in lieu of rations. (QSL Reel A2.26 p 621)

Frederick Walker to Col. Sec. 14 July 1853

I do myself the honour to point out to you the impossibility of my carrying out at present the instructions contained in your circular N° 53/93, 20th May 1853.

1 I cannot see how I am to follow the instructions contained in the first paragraph considering that it takes sometimes three months before I can receive an answer from Sydney.

2 I will take the general instructions seriatim:

(1st) The only advance and allowances I receive are the amounts of pay for the whole force, which are duly accounted for at the end of the quarter and advances for the purchase of horses accounted for as soon as I can procure the receipts for any which may be brought; some at Brisbane some at Callandoon or other places from three to nine hundred miles apart and some of which have no postal communication.

You will observe that out of the advance for pay and allowances, the rations of the troopers must be paid some by me some by Mr Marshall and the other Officers. Consequently, the advance is all paid to my public account at the Bank of Australasia and I immediately transfer an amount to the credit of the Public Account of each Lieutenant's Bank of New South Wales sufficient to meet the pay of their detachments and to buy rations for their men during the current quarter.

(2nd) All our cheques are consequently on Public Account, except those for our own pay and allowances.

(3rd) This clause shows the impossibility of my carrying out this system on the face of it; as it is well known I have no clerks, and no office. Many of my letters are written both to you and the Auditor General under the following circumstances. The letter is brought to me at a station where everybody is hurrying about on his business no room or table is left for one half hour at my disposal and I have to refer back to papers. I consequently go into the bush; the troopers make a bark table and chair the answers are written and forwarded by an orderly.

(4th) As to the Auditor General getting my pass book periodically, he is welcome to inspect it as often as he can get it. I am very glad, if I can do so once a quarter and seldom have it more than three times a year. The Lieutenants complain that they can hardly ever get theirs.

(5th) The vouchers accounting for the advance are always sent at the end of the quarter unless some event preventing it. As for sending them monthly, it is impossible unless I am allowed a clerk and each Officer four orderlies to take them round for signature and return them to me. They would have each to travel about thirty miles a day and have four horses each. The quarterly account current might be carried out.

3 Even if the system were practicable, how long would it take before each officer was acquainted with this sudden alteration of our own simplified system?

4 I feel the hardship of the abrupt proceeding, because I expected a little rest after nine months' hard work in all weathers and I have no chance now of getting it as I must immediately carry out the instructions contained in your letters 53/149, 17th June and 53/152 18th June and which can only be done by me.

5 I have the honour to state that I am willing to follow out any instructions as to accounts which the Auditor General may give for the force under my command but his Excellency the GG will easily perceive that they must be very simple and only come into force 1st January 1854. (QSL Reel A2.26 p 605)

Frederick Walker to Col. Sec. 5 August 1853

I do myself the honour to state that matters have not being going on to my satisfaction at Wandai Gumbal. The horses are lost; the accounts of clothing, arms etc. and the horse list are in such confusion that I can make nothing of them. The troopers are in a very unsatisfied state and evidently neglect their duty or Mr Fulford would not have had to advertise for lost horses.

I do not believe that any newly appointed officer is sufficiently acquainted with my system, to carry it into my satisfaction and I should have to leave the station under the charge of one of the Sub Lieutenants in case of the inevitable absence of Lieutenant Fulford whose protracted illness is no doubt the cause of so much confusion.

3. Sergeant Major Dolan is the only person with me who is thoroughly acquainted with my system, that system in my absence is frequently interrupted by the newly appointed Lieutenants who have yet to learn their duty. This, Dolan as Sergeant Major could not prevent. I therefore do myself the honour to request that His Excellency the Governor General will be pleased to appoint him acting Adjutant as an experiment up to 31st December 1853 when, if it turns out successful, I will recommend that His Excellency should be please to appoint him permanently Adjutant.

4. This arrangement need make no alteration in salaries for 1853.

5. As the evil is every day increasing, I have given authority to Dolan to act in that capacity until the pleasure of His Excellency the Governor General be known and he starts tomorrow morning. He will inspect the Section on the Dawson under Sub lieutenant Bligh on his way to the station of Wandai Gumbal. I have written to Mr Fulford explaining Dolan's duty and I have no doubt it will be a great relief to him.

6. In the mean while I stop at Headquarters where I have sufficient to occupy me for some time in writing up the correspondence which is in arrears.

7. His Excellency will perceive that with a Force extended over such a large space, I cannot well get on without having some person to send round to inspect when I am occupied with other duty. Dolan is the only subaltern in the Force who has his accounts in unison with mine. (QSL Reel A2.28 p 357)

Col. Sec. to Frederick Walker, 22 August 1853

I have the honour to acknowledge the receipt of your letter of the 14th June last respecting the Aboriginal named in the margin, Mickie, who has been convicted at the last Brisbane Circuit Court of the murder of Mr Gregor.

2 In reply I am directed to transmit to you a copy of a communication I have received from His Honour Mr Justice Therry on the subject and to inform you that the Governor General quite concurs with His Honour in his remarks on the impropriety of the tone of your comments which appear to His Excellency to have been made without due caution or whilst labouring under feelings of excitement which He regrets to perceive you

have given way to in more than one of your recent communications with the Government. (SRNSW 4-3862 Reel 2818 p 197)

Frederick Walker to Col. Sec. 28 August 1853

In reply to your letter 53/173, dated 30th ultimo I have the honour to state that I considered it sufficient to express in a private letter to Lieutenant Marshal my dissatisfaction given by him to Lieutenant Morisset.

2. My only reason for stating my surprise at such instructions in my letter of 30th June was that I wished to show that I was not to blame for delays which had arisen in carrying out a measure on which you had so repeatedly written to me. (QSL Reel A2.26 p 786-787)

Col. Sec. to Frederick Walker, 22 September 1853

I am directed by the Governor General to transmit to you a copy of a letter from Mr HG Euston dated the 2nd ultimo and to request your report with reference to the necessity of erecting a Court House at Callandoon for the information of his Excellency. (SRNSW 4-3860 Reel2818 p 217)

Wm H Walsh, Degilbo to Frederick Walker, 29 September 1853

I shall feel obliged to you for an early settlement of the a/c lately rendered by me to your officer Mr Keens.

In consequence of observing in the *Sydney Morning Herald* for the 8th inst. that the allowances per diem to the Native Police troopers has been raised from 1s 4d to 1s 6d and that the Auditor General explained that the increase was caused by the exorbitant demands made by settlers for provisions for the force, altho it was established for their own protection. I have determined, should any of your men, from henceforth require rations from the Degilbo store to charge the full sum allowed by government for each. I point out to you that this alteration involves an advance of nearly 100 per cent over my previous charges.

Frederick Walker to Wm Henry Walsh, 13 October 1853

In answer to your letter of the 29th ulto I do myself the honour to state that the amount allowed to, by you as rendered to Sub Lieutenant Keen will be attended to as soon as I receive it.

2. With reference to your charging the full sum voted for any rations supplied by you to the Native Police in future, I have to answer that I shall not deem it my duty to pay a higher price than I may think reasonable.

3. I have to observe that although the Legislative Council may have voted 1s 6d per diem, it remains with his Excellency to decide what sum he will allow me to expend; for instance, 1s 8d was voted for one year but during six months I was authorised to expend 1s 4d only.

Should you consider yourself entitled to 1s 6d per diem who are resident within about 175 (sic) miles from a port those settlers who are at a distance of 300 miles will consider themselves fairly entitled to at least 2s per diem.

Also, I may point out that it is not because such a charge would be reasonable and fair on your part that you have come to determination which you will excuse me if I think unjust, for you yourself admit that hitherto you have charged 100 per cent under such an exorbitant price, but merely because the Honourable Auditor General made some observations which are unpalatable to you and yet which could not have alluded to any person who had charged 100 per cent under 1s 6d per diem. (QSL Reel A2.27 p 253)

Frederick Walker to Col. Sec. 14 October 1853

In enclosing correspondence between Wm Henry Walsh and me, I do myself the honour to state that I am unwilling to trouble the government with such matters; but as I know that the gentlemen alluded to will induce many of his neighbours to join with him in carrying out his system. I have thought it best to forward it to you for the information of his Excellency the GG. (QSL Reel A2.27 p 847)

Frederick Walker to Col. Sec. 14 October 1853

In answer to your letter of 22nd September, N° 52/7654 enclosing a long communication from Mr Easton,[353] I have the honour to state that it is rather difficult to make out what he really wants.

If it is a courthouse without a Court of Petty Sessions as I would sup-

---

353 Mr HE Easton's letter is set out at Chapter 7 under the sub-heading Sippy.

pose from the conclusion of his letter, I may say at once that the quarters of the Native Police at Callandoon are quite sufficient for any magistrate acting in his ministerial capacity and consequently that no courthouse is required.

2. But I believe that Mr Easton really wants a Court of Petty Sessions as in a previous paragraph he mentioned constabulary.

3. With regard to the observations made by Mr Easton as to the insufficiency of a Police Force which has been protecting him so long and so often in the stations he has occupied and which he still required although it is so useless, His Excellency the Governor General I have no doubt has already perceived that the reason why I did not act in the station clothed case was that Mr Easton brought me nothing but hearsay evidence. Sippy who is a boy of about 14 years of age is now in Brisbane gaol having been apprehended by the 2nd Section under Sergeant Graham. (QSL Reel A 2.28 p 230)

Frederick Walker to Col. Sec. 31 December 1853

I do myself the honour to state that a letter in the *Moreton Bay Courier* of the 17th December reflected upon two troopers of the Native Police and accusing Sub Lieutenant Bligh of refusing redress, is not consistent with the truth.

2. When the complaint was originally made Mr Bligh investigated the case and reported to me. It appears that Mr Bligh was on his way patrolling and at some distance behind him were two troopers bringing up the pack horses. Upon passing a sheep station one of them named in the margin, Jimmy McCann, got off his horse and walked (perhaps rather abruptly) into the hut to get a light for his pipe as well as for his mate. A newly arrived German woman who was not accustomed to the bush took alarm and fancied the trooper wished to take indecent liberties with her, which never entered his head. I know the man well; his brother and father are both in the force and I am satisfied that the explanation given to Mr Bligh was correct for I have since examined the man separately and there is no varying in their previous statements.

5. I would have taken no notice of this article if it bore on me only; but I have the honour to state that I consider it a most scandalous proceeding

to attempt to run down a young officer who like Mr Bligh has shown every disposition to do his duty and hitherto has done so completely to my satisfaction.

4. His Excellency the GG however, will not be surprised that such a proceeding should have taken place when I state that the document alluded to emanates from a person of the name of Marks an individual whose atrocities on the Macintyre I believe first induced His Excellency to raise the Native Police. There is also still a warrant in force for that person which warrant is under the hand and seal of Sub Lieutenant Bligh's brother and this alone would account for the animus. (QSL Reel A2.28 p 383)

Frederick Walker to Col. Sec. 20 January 1854

I do myself the honour to represent that in consequence of the high rate of carriage, I have supplied the native troopers at this and other stations by the Police drays two in number. One of which is driven by a European paid at the rate of £78 per annum by the troopers and the other by the supernumerary trooper Oliver likewise paid and rationed by the force. One of the drays cost the sum of £114 which was paid out of the provision allowance of the troopers.

2. I paid at the close of the year that the expense of rationing the men when on patrol so much excluded my calculation that although I have paid several out of my own salary rather than apply to the government I am not able to meet all demands. I therefore request that His Excellency the GG may be pleased to sanction the payment of the above dray and fourteen bullocks with tackling and tarpaulin complete at the price of one hundred and fourteen pounds. As the drays, will without any further charge, carry all the clothing and accoutrements there will be a saving in this item which amounts in 1853 to £37 12s.

3. His Excellency may perhaps be surprised at my having miscalculated the expense of rationing the men; but this arises from my having been so much from home doing duty which was forced on me for want of Officers and that I have not been able to get either of the officers or settlers to send in their accounts quarterly. The consequence being that a heap of them came on me at the end of the year of which I had no

idea. As I have now a gentleman, Mr John D L Ferguson, brother to the manager of the Union Bank at Goulbourn employed for the sole purpose of keeping my papers and accounts in order, I shall be better prepared in future.

4. I may observe that the request above mentioned and the list of articles enclosed purchased out of the men's provisions allowance for the use will convince His Excellency that the statement lately made by Forster in the Sydney Morning Herald to the effect that the Officers appropriated portion of the men's allowance as prerequisites was an infamous libel. Nearly every Officer has expended money out of his own funds in order to turn out his men in a neat manner. (QSL Reel A 2.28 p 518)

Colonial Secretary to Frederick Walker, 8 February 1854

In reply to your letter of 26th December last, I am directed to inform you that his Excellency the Governor General under your recommendation approves of Sergeant Major Dolan being continued in the appointment of Acting Adjutant of Native Police; and of his receiving pay and allowances similar to those received by a Sub Lieutenant of the Force. (SRNSW 43860 Reel2818 p 285)

Mrs Walker, mother, Dawlish to Frederick Walker, 16 February 1854

I was overjoyed this morning to receive a letter from you after such a long silence. But my joy was turned to sorrow when I read the contents. Indeed, I am grieved to death to think of your hard situation, and above all of your bad health and what would I give to be able to afford you any relief and comfort my dear son. Your fate presses son on my heart as you may believe. The only thing I can possibly think of to benefit you is for you to get leave of absence and come to England and live quietly with us for a year. Of course, this could only be affected by your being allowed some pay during your absence as is done for officers in India; for I am so poor now, with only £330 a year to exist on; after I have paid the allowances of Charles, John and poor Francis that it would be out of my power to pay your passage money, or indeed to support you at home with the comfort I would wish unless you had a little of your own. But you know that there is no sacrifice I would not make to restore you to health & peace of mind as far as possibilities go. I am therefore going to enclose you a letter to Sir Charles Fitzroy, which you will send if you think fit, and which will perhaps obtain for you what I most desire. God grant that he may consent and that I may see you once more before I leave this world of trials.

We are going to reside at Clifton next month; and shall take a small unfurnished house which Harriet will furnish out of the little money she has in the funds. This place would be too relaxing in the summer and we are told Clifton is very healthy. She has quite recovered her health here, and will I trust have no relapse. I myself are far from well, having repeated attacks of Influenza. But I get well again in time, till the next cold comes. I am so very sorry to hear you are unable to lay by anything. I had always hoped, with your pay, you might have managed to realize an independence. However, it seems all my hopes for my sons are ever to be disappointed. It is some consolation to know that our letters reach you and are any comfort to you. We do not hear from Edmund often now. His last letter was far from cheering. He could not save any more than yourself and wrote in low spirits. I had looked on him and you as the only sons who could afford me any consolation. Charles is still in Switzerland, and writes incessantly most tormenting letters, demanding what it is out of my power to give him. John is living at Kenilworth amongst his Roman Catholics and I hardly ever hear from him. As for poor Francis, he grows worse instead of better, being quite thin when last, I saw him. I am now seeking some place for a change for him, though I fear nothing could do his mind any good. But his health is excellent I believe. You will wonder I am still alive with so many miseries on every side, and it is a wonder indeed your letter today has not lessened them as you may imagine. Harriet is going to write to you and will tell you more news than I can. Robert Jones is married again, as I think I told you. Your Aunt Jones lives in London now, and your Aunt C at Bath with her daughter. She is very infirm & altered, you would not know her again - I dare not say I long for another… *page(s) missing, start of Harriet Walker's letter...* self in various ways. His health also has much improved, and at times he talks quite rationally and sensibly, but his mind is not collected many minutes together. He is quite tractable and good-humoured, and as he has a piano. He can amuse himself. God grant the present arrangement may continue as well as it promises now but should Mr and Mrs Adeline (sic) find him unmanageable, I don't know what we shall do, as of course they can only have moral control over him. I hope to re-join Mama in a few days, she has been quite ill during my absence, but I have no doubt when I get home, she will soon be well again. We heard from Edmund on the 7th of April. He was then well and doing well; he is at present head mathematical master at the College at Roorkee, but I fancy this is only a temporary employment. He is very anxious to know whether you received a letter from him, and why you do not answer him; his direction is Lieut. Edmund Walker, Bengal Engineers, Roorkee, India. I daresay you will see him some day, for he talks, if ever he has leave of taking a trip to Sidney. How I wish I could join you too and see what you are like now; the older I grow, the more my affections centre on my family, I seem to care for nothing else, but their welfare and happiness. My Aunt and Carolina are now at Bath, but they talk of coming to Clifton this summer. My Aunt is grown sadly infirm and cannot move now without assistance but her mind is still very active. Carolina is grown very fat, but very handsome still and sings as beautifully as she used to do. My music is really gone down; my long illness, having no piano for two years, … has been a great damper to my voice, but I am as fond of it as ever. Poor Francis was asking me the other day something about Leamington and I said, "Do you remember Frederick's beautiful voice?" He answered immediately, "O yes, what a beautiful voice he had." He has intervals of memory, and then I am amazed at what he says, but it never lasts many minutes. Now goodbye my dear Frederick, I am writing this in a hurry to be in time for the mail. Always direct to Messrs Drummonds and believe me your very affectionate sister. (QSA Series ID 14725/86134)

Frederick Walker to Col. Sec. 27 July 1853[354]

I do myself the honour to enclose a copy of a circular addressed by me to the Officers of the Native Police relative to the management of that force.

2. I have already by my reports informed his Excellency the Governor General of the practical success which has attended my endeavours to

[354] This letter is misdated and should read 1854.

maintain the Peace in the Districts committed to the protection of the Native Police and I am satisfied that success would have been complete if my work had not been destroyed in the manner pointed out by me in my circular and the exertions of some of the Officers as well as my own having been retarded by their having had to remedy the mischief caused by disregard of my instructions on the part of others. I may especially here mention Lieutenant John Murray as the most indefatigable of my assistants.

3. I may point out that success has attended during the period mentioned in my circular the attempts made by Mr Murray in conjunction with me to quell disturbances at the Bunya in the Wide Bay and Burnett Districts and to carry out the wishes of the government as regards the new settlements to the Northward; but during all that time a succession of mistakes had characterised the proceedings of the large force I had provided for the protection of the Lower Condamine a country reported as quiet in 1851 and the Maranoa District. I cannot but consider the murder of Mr Kettle within 18 miles of Wandai Gumbal as a slur on the Native police. There were two sections at that station and it is in every way the most complete establishment I possess.

4. I have also annexed a copy of regulations made out by me in May 1852 and which I submitted for the appraisal of Mr GR Nichols and he returned without altering. I would feel obliged if His Excellency the Governor General would favour me with his opinion both as regards the circular and the regulations.

5. In conclusion I trust that the hope I have expressed in the 8th paragraph of my circular may be realised. (SRNSW NRS906 4/719.2) Margin Note: As far as I can judge of the propriety of the circular and regulations herein referred to, I see no objection to them CAF 9th. Cmdt 15 August 54/9447.

Regulations—May 1852

Instructions to Sergeants when in command of detachments.

1. The sergeants are not to allow any person unconnected with the Native Police Force to interfere with or give orders to any of the troopers under their command.
2. They must be very careful of the men's health not to allow them to wear their jackets in hot weather; nor to allow them to put on their

newly washed clothes before they are dry; nor to stop too long in the water when bathing; nor to camp in low spots subject to fever and agues; nor to camp on ground wet through rain but cause them to strip back to put under them.

3. They are not to allow the cloaks to be unstrapped without orders nor except in extreme cases to be used for bed clothes.
4. The arms, clothes and accoutrements must be inspected as often as possible. No excuse will ever be admitted by the Commandant for dirty arms or accoutrements as with a very little trouble they are easily kept clean.
5. No cartridges are to be fired away without orders or unless under extraordinary circumstances such as in self-defence.
6. The backs of the horses must be carefully attended to and the saddles examined frequently. The saddle cloths kept clean. The horses' backs washed on dismounting and carefully rubbed down before saddling. The troopers never to be allowed to alter their stirrups from the length that must be fixed upon by the Sergeant Major.
7. In no case are any of the Native troopers to be allowed to take spirits from anyone except his officer or medical man. The Port Phillip Native Police have been noted for their drunkenness; and hitherto the New South Wales Native Police have been as noted for their sobriety. Much in this matter will depend on the example set by their Sergeants.
8. Whenever an opportunity occurs such as a day or two spell or a short stage the Sergeants are to practices the troopers in the drill taught them by the Sergeant Major and no other.
9. Before leaving the Police Station the Sergeants will carefully put in a safe and clean place such clothing as may not be wanted on patrol reporting to the officer in writing the state of the horses, arms and accoutrements and clothing before starting and upon their return.
10. The Sergeants will keep a daily account of all rations received in a book supplied for that purpose.
11. They will keep in a book a daily account of their journeys of the conduct of the men or of any other matter in which the officer in command may require information.
12. The Sergeants are not to punish any trooper but immediately report

any defaulter upon their return to the Police Station.

13. The object in sending out patrol parties is principally that the hostile blacks from the frequent visits of the Police may be deterred from murder and felony; this is the meaning of a Preventive Force.

14. It is however certain that occasionally the Sergeants will have to endeavour to apprehend persons who have committed felony during their absence. When the Sergeant holds a warrant, his duty is very clear, if he can identify the individual or has reasonable grounds to believe him to be the individual and if he must with resistance, he is justified in making use of force against the man he wishes to apprehend and any person assisting him. The Sergeant has no right to retreat. When he holds no warrant; if he can prove that a felony has been committed and that he has reasonable cause to suspect an individual, he is justified in using force if resisted. With white persons, it is not difficult to prove all this; but blacks are so much alike the evidence is generally so faulty that the Sergeants must be very cautious. The Commandant has frequently found that the statements made to him by individuals differed very widely from their affidavits when made on oath by the same persons. When a Sergeant sees, a felony being committed as a matter of course he is obliged to take all the offenders in charge. Also, if he sees an assault committed; but not if he hears of an assault having been committed. In any case the same law applies to blacks as it does to whites and if the Sergeants go beyond the law they do so at their own risk. A Sergeant has no power to disperse an illegally assembled body of men without an order of a magistrate or the Riot Act has been read, but if any of them commit a felonious act, he is bound to seize him; and any person assisting the offender does so at his own peril. Many persons will try to run the Sergeants to acts of aggression against the blacks and these persons would be the first to turn on them if they succeed in making them break the law. The blacks cannot be considered as men armed for illegal purposes, because their weapons are their principal means of obtaining food.

15. No person is more subject to abuse and no one has to keep a stronger guard over his troopers than a constable or any other Peace Officer. The Sergeant must be very particular in always keeping their troopers;

in always avoiding indiscreet discussions and causing the troopers to be careful in not allowing persons who anxiously seek for opportunities to pick quarrels with them or to find occasions for so doing.

16. Upon returning to the Police Station the Sergeants will report to the officer in command who is a magistrate everything concerning any collisions that may have taken place and give him full information in order that he may collect sufficient evidence.

17. In all cases when any person white or black makes use of indecent language to the Sergeant or one of the troopers in a public place, he is liable to be punished under Mr Nichols' new Vagrants Act; a copy of which will be supplied to every Sergeant. The evidence of the troopers cannot be admitted in a Court of Law.

18. No trooper is to be sent into Headquarters unless he is fully armed, accoutred and clothed and with a note to the Sergeant Major of what arms, clothes, horse etc., etc. he has with him and whether he has despatches. The trooper will receive orders to report himself to the Sergeant Major immediately on his arrival at Headquarters. (SRNSW NRS906 4/719.2)

Circular

Frederick Walker to the Officers of Native Police, 1 July 1854

Gentlemen, I do myself the honour to inform you that it is with deep regret I have to state that I am not satisfied with the manner in which my instructions and especially my verbal advice have been carried out since the month of May 1852. In doing so although I am sensitively hurt by so many blunders, I trust that in future the officers I now address will from experience be induced to follow a course more congenial to my feelings and better adapted to carry out the views of the government; which views must be very evident to all Officers as I have constantly requested them to read all correspondence belonging to the Native Police force in order themselves to understand how far the government have agreed with me or when they have expressed an opinion differing from mine, an opinion to which as a matter of course I could do so otherwise than submit.

2. The principal cause of complaint which I have to make is the mismanagement of the Wandai Gumbal Police Station, Lower Condamine; and the reasons I have for this complaint are.

N° 1 During my absence in Sydney from May 1852 until June 1852 sundry transactions with the Aborigines in the Maranoa District caused His Excellency the Governor General on my recommendations to dismiss Sergeant Dempster.

N° 2 After my return to Callandoon, I received information that the Native Corporal Larry had abandoned Sergeant Dempster; in consequence, I ordered N° 1 Section to join me.

N° 3 When I started the N° 8 Section from Callandoon under Sergeant McGrath in first rate order, I wrote to the officer at Wandai Gumbal, Lt Fulford, that it was imperative on him to proceed with that Section. The first patrol turn which it took it does not appear that this was done; the officer alluded to went with Mr Charles Blandford, recently appointed as third Lieutenant, to the Dawson although that officer had already received his instructions from me. Sergeant Small with N° 7 Section proceeded at the same time.

Having completed the business I had contemplated, I arrived at Traylan 20 December 1852 feeling confident that then everything was properly arranged. In five days, my hopes were suddenly disappointed. Sergeant Small had abandoned the N° 7 Section and had come into Gayndah with 2 Chinese prisoners, 1 native corporal and 2 troopers leaving the remainder of the Section without a guide, without protection, without control. Upon my enquiry, as to what orders had been given to the sergeant, I was informed the officer in command thought the senior officer had given his orders, the senior thought this had been done by the officer in command. The sergeant consequently had no orders.

N° 4 The N° 8 Section was sent out in the Maranoa District under Sergeant McGrath but I have no official document shewing that the officer in command at Wandai Gumbal had obeyed my imperative orders. The affidavits in all matters relative to the section are unsatisfactory and on one occasion one of the best troopers in the Section was wantonly fired at by a ruffian and no redress obtained for such a crime. I removed the N° 8 Section and certainly when I had put it on duty with me I reported it as completely disorganised. In a short time, afterwards I reported the N° 8 section as on a par with any except N°s 1, 4 & 5.

N° 5 In June 1853, I sent the N° 3 Section always considered as a good one and as there was no European officer I sent it under the command of the Native Sergeant Willy. The Section had not been here three weeks at Wandai Gumbal before letters reached me stating that six horses had been lost and that the two Native Corporals Tommy Hindmarsh and Coreen Jemmy had been guilty of mutiny a word previously unknown in the Native Police. I removed the N° 3 Section.

N° 6 In December 1853, I sent 25 pairs of blankets, purchased out of the small pay 3^d per diem of the Native Police, to station and it appears only 16 pairs were delivered. It is to be hoped that the officer, Lt Irving, whose negligence caused this deficiency, has himself remedied it, but it appears a strange fatality that with a temporary change of officers at Wandai Gumbal there should be no improvement. For by the last lamentable intelligence, I learn that the faithful, steady and gallant Native Sergeant Tom, N° 2 Section, had been guilty of a most outrageous act of mutiny.

3. The result is that I have successively removed N° 4, 8 & 3 Sections and now I am required to remove N° 2 and what is more that the settlers from personal interviews with me and by letter maintain that the country instead of prospering is retrograding and that my presence alone can remedy the matter that presence can only be temporary.

4. The troopers especially those who have been four and five years in the service complain of the excessive strictness amounting to tyranny with which they are treated at Wandai Gumbal especially they complain of the excessive and cruel punishment inflicted on Edwin and at night they are confined as prisoners to the Barracks. The dissatisfaction arising at Wandai Gumbal naturally spreads to Sections at other places and renders it difficult for other officers especially the newly joined and inexperienced to manage the men under them.

5. Of all grievances the most serious has been the unauthorised interference with my system of dividing the section into two subdivisions each under its own Native corporal. The native sergeants and corporals felt proud of their rank and command and it was gratifying to the men to be under the orders of their own countrymen. The morale ensuing from this system has been nearly destroyed; the officers instead of giving their orders through the sergeant or corporal and requiring their reports are constantly and needlessly interfering. The corporals are sent on

messages away from the men whom they ought to be superintending; on one occasion a corporal was sent to act as lackey to a European sergeant and they are sent without discrimination with the troopers to look for horses when in Barracks and made to assist in cleaning out the premises; thus, they have been deprived of the only privilege which their rank affords them. This grievance although carried onto a greater extent at Wandai Gumbal than elsewhere is felt in other sections also. The consequence over and above the bitter dissatisfaction of the men has caused a great hindrance to the properly carrying out of the police duty.

I will give one instance of that, on 25th July 1853, 23 horses were astray out of which 17 had been lost since the 24th October 1852.[355] The whole of these 17 horses had been lost from four sections commanded by 2 lieutenants, 1 sergeant major and 4 European sergeants. The other four sections under my command assisted by one officer and 2 sergeants did not lose one. It is evident many troopers must have been dismounted and unable to do duty; but this was not the worst evil, because many others instead of protecting the settlers were looking for stray horses and deteriorating their own.

The reason why there were no horses lost by the sections under my immediate command is simple that one corporal with his subdivision attended to the horses whilst his comrade saw that the baggage and cooking was attended to taking each duty every alternate morning. Every man knowing what he had to do, the duty was always done.

6. I have observed that many officers do not appreciate the character of the men. One Native Sergeant Boney no officer can agree with although I always find him a valuable assistant. I have frequently called for him to desire him to see that some duty I had overlooked was performed. He with the haughty look which is characteristic of his brother Larry as well as of him generally let me know that he had already attended to it. This haughty demeanour which the officers notwithstanding my remonstrance persist in calling sulk produces anger on their part when with me it produces only a smile of approbation.

---

355 Strayed from the Wandai Gumbal Native Police Station. *MBC* 2 July 1853 p 3, 9 July 1853 p 3, 16 July 1853 p 3, 23 July 1853 p 3 & 30 July 1853 p 1.

Very few of the men will stand driving although they are easily led, those who from natural insolence require driving, the officers, if they have tact, should cause the other men to drive and assist the appearance of it themselves. This can only be done by shewing need requiring proper respect to the Native sergeants and corporals. If the officers have not sufficient knowledge of human nature to find out the character of the men, the best they can do is to adopt my opinion and act accordingly. That opinion cannot be far wrong considering that during five years no man has been insubordinate to me and none have deserted. In 15 months, 10 men have deserted from the officers.

7. It is absolutely necessary that each officer should carry out my instructions. The neglect of these in one division causes confusion in others and it takes me some time to correct it. The worst cases of this neglect are few. The not properly carrying out of a constant patrol. The N° 3 complaint in my second paragraph, the 3rd Section having been sent on duty when a sanguinary encounter took place and the officer, Sub Lt Bligh, was not with his men and the marching of the N° 5 Section, Lt Morisset, from the Clarence to Traylan contrary to the orders of the Honourable Colonial Secretary and my instructions.

8. Having now pointed out where the officers have been wrong, I trust that in future the evil will be avoided and that I shall no more have to state that I fear to receive letters from officers especially when at Wandai Gumbal as they constantly bring one, news so unpleasant that they have rendered my life unhappy. (SRNSW NRS906 4/719.2)

Col. Sec. to Frederick Walker, 15 August 1854

Having laid before the Governor your letter of the 27th ultimo, forwarding copies of a Circular addressed by you to the Officers of the Native Police relative to their management of the Force and of Regulations drawn up by you for the guidance of Sergeants in command of a Detachments, and requesting to be favoured with His Excellency's opinion thereon, I am instructed to state that so far as His Excellency can judge of the propriety of the Circular and Regulations in question. He has no objection to either. (QSA Series ID14725/86134)

Col. Sec. to Lt G Fulford, 11 October 1854

Having laid before the Governor General your letter of the 14th ultimo complaining of the conduct of the Commandant of the Native Police I am instructed by his Excellency to inform you in reply that a Board has been appointed to investigate the charges brought against the Commandant by the Officers of the Native Police. (SRNSW 43860 Reel 2818 p 432)

Col. Sec. to Lt RP Marshall, 19 October 1854

I have the honour by direction of his Excellency the Governor General to acknowledge the receipt of your communication of the 2nd instant complaining of the conduct of the Commandant of the Native Police and to inform you in reply that your letter has been referred to the Board appointed for investigating the charges brought against the Commandant. (SRNSW 43860 Reel 2818 p 437)

Col. Sec. to Frederick Walker, 19 October 1854

I do myself the honour to inform you that your communication of the 26th ultimo relative to a complaint made by Sub Lieutenant Nicol concerning his pay and allowance has been forwarded to the Government Resident at Moreton Bay to be submitted to the Board directed to assemble to investigate the charges preferred against you by the officers of the Native Police. (SRNSW 4-3862 Reel 2818 p 437)

Col. Sec. to Frederick Walker, 1 November 1854

In reply to your letter of the 30th September reporting on the conduct of the Officers of the Native Police and stating that several of them had sent in their resignations, I am directed by his Excellency the Governor General to refer you to my communication of the 21st of the same month instructing you to proceed to Brisbane to receive further instructions on this subject from the Government Resident there. (SRNSW 43860 Reel 2818 p 443)

Col. Sec. to Frederick Walker, 2 November 1854

In acknowledging the receipt of your communication of the 11th ultimo reporting the probability of the Native Police corps being broken up should you be removed from the command, I am directed by his Excellency the Governor General to inform you that your communication has been referred to the Board appointed to investigate the complaints preferred by the Officers of the corps against you. (SRNSW 43860 Reel2818 p 443)

Col. Sec. to Frederick Walker, 2 November 1854

I do myself the honour by direction of his Excellency the Governor General to inform you that your communication of the 12th ultimo complaining of certain proceedings of Lieutenant Irving has been referred to the Board appointed to investigate the complaints preferred by the Officers of the Native Police against you. (SRNSW 4-3860 Reel2818 p 444)

Col. Sec. to Lt G Fulford, 2 November 1854

In acknowledging the receipt of your communication of the 11th ultimo reporting certain proceedings of the Commandant of the Native Police I am instructed by his Excellency the Governor General to inform you that a Board has been appointed to enquire into the charges preferred by the Officers of the corps against Mr Walker and that pending the investigation at Brisbane the Senior Lieutenant Mr Marshall has been appointed in charge of the corps. (SRNSW 4-3860 Reel2818 p 444)

JC Wickham to Lt RP Marshall, 7 November 1854

With reference to various communications from the Hon CS respecting certain charges preferred against the Commandant of the Native Police Force which are to be investigated at Brisbane by a Board appointed for that purpose, I have the honour to inform you that your evidence together with that of Lieutenants Fulford, Irving and Nicol and Acting Adjutant Dolan will be the first enquired by the Board.

2. I have therefore to request that you will make such arrangements as

you may deem necessary in order that as many of the above-named officers, as can be spared without detriment to the service, may proceed to Brisbane as soon as Mr Walker leaves the Police Station for the same purpose at the same time. I beg that you will be careful not to leave the Native troopers at either station without a sufficient number of officers to control them and preserve their discipline.

3. I may add that the Board are desirous that the officers should not be subject to any unnecessary expense and therefore do not require their attendance in Brisbane before Mr Walker's arrival. (SRNSW NRS906)

Col. Sec. to Lt RP Marshall, 19 January 1855

I am directed by his Excellency the Governor General to transmit to you for any observations you may desire to offer the enclosed communication from Mr Walker dated I January 1855, complaining of your conduct towards him. (SRNSW 4-3860 Reel2818 p 478)

RP Marshall to Col. Sec. 6 February 1855

I do myself the honour to acknowledge the receipt of your letter of 19 January N° 55/379, regarding me to make any observations I might desire, relative to the complaint preferred against me by Mr F Walker; and in reply by to state that Mr Walker has made most gross misstatements.

2. I do myself the honour to state that the two troopers named by Mr Walker were taken by him from their duties without my knowledge or sanction. In this step to say the least, Mr Walker was guilty of a great want of courtesy to me, and it was not until I received a letter from Sub Lt Bligh stating that Boonya James had been to Yabber with a message from Mr Walker to the troopers stationed at that place, saying that should the inquiry about to be held on his conduct turn out adverse to him, he would come back and take them all to their country; that I was aware but that they were at Dawson. On my arrival at Brisbane I saw Boonya James and Dick but neither directly or indirectly held any communication with them. I however found that Mr Walker was again making use of these men for the purpose of trying to disaffect the detachment in Brisbane with Sub Lt Bligh. Had Mr Walker not made a bad use of these men I should not have thought of taking the horses and firearms from them.

Over the men of course I had no legal control, and had they wished to remain with Mr Walker they were at perfect liberty to do so but the fact is the men brought their horses from South Brisbane where Mr Walker was staying and delivered them to Sub Lt Nicol, stating that they wished to be taken from attending on Mr Walker; that they were ashamed of his conduct in being so continually drunk and requested that an officer would go over with them to get their private property as they were afraid to go by themselves.

At the time, I was in South Brisbane taking possession of the arms, accoutrements etc. when this was told to me by the men. I returned with them and saw them take from the room in which they were staying what they claimed as their own property.

While taking possession of the government property held by Mr Walker, he drew a sword upon the party. Mr Walker states that this occurrence took place previous to the inquiry which is not correct. It was on the day of and subsequent to the inquiry. Previous to my taking possession of the arms etc., I consulted the Board of Inquiry as to the propriety of such a step and every member of the Board concurred with me and sent the Chief Constable and another at my request as I did not wish to come personally in contact with Mr Walker.

3. Mr Walker has informed you that Considine is his orderly. This is not correct. He has been receiving pay as a trooper for the last year a reference to the pay abstracts will show the truth of my statement.

4. I must decline employing troopers for the purpose spoken of by Mr Walker without instructions to that effect. And it will be for me to name the men employed on such duty, if His Excellency the GG sanctions Mr Walker's request.

5. The medical certificate accompanying Mr Walker's letter states that he was suffering from nervous debility, a fact self-evident to everyone who saw him and I am sorry that Mr Walker should have rendered it necessary for me to state that I saw him at Brisbane on five or six different days and that on such occasions he was much intoxicated. After having known Mr Walker for five years, I could not be mistaken as to the state he was in. (QSL Reel 2.31 p 406.)

Col. Sec. to RP Marshall, 7 February 1855

In acknowledging the receipt of your letter of the 23rd December last protesting in the names of yourself and brother officers against the remarks made by the Attorney-General in the Legislative Council on the 15th November last as reported in the *Empire* newspaper, I do myself the honour to state that the Attorney-General to whom your communication was referred has disclaimed any intention of casting any reflection on the officers of the Native Police. (SRNSW 4-3860 Reel2818 p 489)

Empire quote: "Although the pay which the officers received was too small to enable the Government to secure the services of very efficient and trust worthy men, still the greatest care should be exercised to prevent misconduct or abuse of power on the part of those entrusted with though immediate management of the force."[356]

Col. Sec. to RP Marshall, 9 February 1855

In acknowledging the receipt of your report of the 6th ultimo, N° 55/20 on certain charges preferred against you by Mr Walker late Commandant of the Native Police I am directed to inform you that the Governor General is perfectly satisfied with your explanation and his Excellency cannot accede to Mr Walker's request that Considine and another trooper be instructed to convey his private property to Ipswich. (NSW 4-3860 Reel2818 p 504)

Col. Sec. to Sub Lt J Bligh, 27 June 1855

With reference to the advances made to Mr Walker the late Commandant of the Native Police to pay with other expenses of the corps your salary and allowances which it appears he had withheld after obtaining your signature to the acquittances I am directed by his Excellency the Governor General to request that you state whether the authority given by you to Mr Walker for payment of your salary to the Commercial Bank was in writing and if so that you will forward to me a copy of the same if no written authority was given you are required to state the arrangement which you made with Mr Walker in respect to the payment of your salary etc. (NSW 4-3860 Reel 2817 p 493)

---

356 *Empire* 16 November 1854 p 4.

Proceedings at a Court of Enquiry respecting charges preferred by Officers of Native Police against Commandant Walker, 23 November 1854

Present: Captain Wickham R N – Colonel Gray, Police Magistrate – S Simpson, Commissioner of Crown Lands.

Commandant Walker was in attendance & had been previously furnished with copy of charges made against him – Letter N° 54/8216-8217-8218 was read [as it is – see also 54/08216, 54/08217, 54/08218] – Court adjourned until 4th December in order that Mr Marshall may attend.

Monday 4th day of December, 1854, Captain Wickham having opened Court at 11 o'clock pursuant to adjournment & Mr Walker the Commandant not being in attendance, or any of the Officers belonging to the Force, Court adjourned until Monday 11th inst. at 11 o'clock. Monday 11th day of December 1854, Court was further adjourned until Monday 18th inst. as none of the Officers of Force had arrived in Brisbane.

Monday 18th day of December 1854, the following Officers reported themselves: Lieutenant Marshall – Acting Commandant, Lieutenant Irving, Sub-Lieutenant Bligh, Sub-Lieutenant Nicol. Court adjourned until tomorrow at 10 o'clock for attendance of the other members of the Board – Mr Walker appeared.

Tuesday 19th day of December 1854, Present at 12 o'clock (noon): Captain Wickham – Colonel Gray – S Simpson. Captain Wickham stated to Board: That Mr Walker attended on Tuesday 5th December, so much in state of intoxication he could scarcely articulate, & on referring to his non-appearance on Monday (4th), Mr Walker informed Captain Wickham he had sent his blackfellow. Captain Wickham informed Mr Walker that Court was adjourned till following Monday (11th inst.) when Mr Walker did not appear, & on 18th December Mr Walker appeared, but was then in state of intoxication. Court waited until ½ past twelve o'clock, Mr Walker did not appear but had been told by Members of Board to be in attendance at 12 o'clock. Board then proceeded to business – Captain Wickham & Commissioner Simpson having seen Mr Walker at 11 o'clock in such a state it was not likely he would attend.

First Lieutenant Marshall, Acting Commandant called - With reference to your letter of 1st September 1854 to Colonial Secretary are these charges contained in that letter in concurrence with the rest of the Officers who have tendered their resignations? They are so, they generally concur with me in every charge. Did you personally submit copy of that letter to the different Officers? Felt it my duty to bring the charges & subsequently sent copies of the letter to Lieutenants Fulford & Murray. What opportunities have you had of observing Mr Walker's conduct? Have been nearly 5 years attached to Force. First 9 months after I joined, I did not see Mr Walker. I was then stationed with him a few days at Callandoon & then proceeded to the Burnett. In January 1851, Mr Walker came to Wide Bay where I was stationed & took Lieutenant Fulford & myself to "Colinton" Mr Balfour's station. [Board here remarked to Mr Walker who now made his appearance in state of intoxication, that they did not consider him in competent state to appear, requested him to retire, & as he continued to interrupt Board, it was determined to adjourn & report proceedings to Governor General.]

Wednesday 20th day of December 1854, Board met at request of Officers to hear their statements relative to pay due to them & to accounts unpaid.

Acting Commandant Marshall called – Will you state up to what period you have received pay? I have received pay up to 30th June last, have received nothing since. Wrote to Mr Walker 1st October requesting payment for the Quarter, Mr Walker returned my letter stating he had closed his accounts for resigned Officers & referred me to Auditor General – I believe nothing has been paid for ration money, & the men's pay, for Quarter ended 30th September last, & I believe the list now handed in which I received from Commandant's Secretary signed by me & marked "A" is statement of unpaid accounts for the Quarter ended 30th June last.

Senior Sub-Lieutenant Nicol called – With reference to your letter of 15th June to Colonial Secretary what portion of the pay which was then due to you have you since received? When Commandant arrived at Wandai Gumbal in August, he showed me his cheque book by which I saw that the amount due to me to 30 June had been paid into the Union instead of the Commercial, by which I was kept out of my pay till September when it was transferred. Have you received any portion of salary due to you since 30th June last? Not a farthing Are you aware if troopers under your immediate orders have received any portion of their pay since 22nd January last or any necessaries in lieu of pay? They received neither one nor the other – have expended more than £30 in purchasing [since I joined] clothing, blankets & flour for men, this was out of my own pocket to keep blacks alive & free from illness, has been no flour at Wandai Gumbal for last 3 months – I & Mr Fulford have been buying flour from Squatters for men during that time. We have bought 9 bags & kept the whole station. When I arrived at Wandai Gumbal in January last, there were only 5 quart & pint pots for 24 men, there have been none supplied since.

Lieutenant Irving called – Up to what date have you received pay? I have received pay up to 30th June with exception of £49 10s allowed me as an increase for the two first Quarters of 1853. I have received the increase for subsequent period, but the above sum is still due to me. Have you ever received any portion of your pay since? To the best of my belief none has been paid since, as my cheques have been returned from Sydney It is stated you have been overpaid £20 6d by Mr Ferguson's letter to Commandant. Do you know anything of that? I have been under necessity of purchasing rations for men & the amount, to the best of my belief, of about £40 & I considered the cheque for £20 I received from Commandant as an instalment in part payment of what I had advanced & having no reference to salary. Will you explain how this bill for £28 9s was incurred at Horton's Inn at Drayton for 5 men in September last? I arrived in Drayton with 5 sick men with orders from Mr Walker to take them to Horton's Inn & feed them well in the kitchen & give them plenty of vegetables – I remained there 13 days, men were sick during the whole time, 2 of them were very ill – wine was given men by orders of Doctor Bond; I paid Dr Bond's account for medical attendance out of my pocket. What do you consider due to you now? Up to end of this Quarter, there would be due to me £212 6s 3d for salary & forage, independent of amount due to me for rations purchased for men.

Sub-Lieutenant Bligh called: There is a letter signed by you dated November 1854 & addressed to Acting Commandant stating £141 due to you for salary. Have you received any portion of that since? I have not. You say in your letter that trooper named "Bunya Jimmy" was sent to your station "Yabba" with view to make men discontented by Mr Walker – upon what grounds was this statement made? Men told me Mr Walker had sent Bunya Jimmy to bring men down (in the event of this investigation turning out unfavourably to Mr Walker) to sign their resignation, & they told me that Mr Walker would come to Yabba & take them all away. Did you ever hear any of the men express their wish to leave Force before Mr Walker sent Bunya Jimmy? No! But after Bunya Jimmy was sent 2 of the oldest men said they would go with Mr Walker. Board adjourned until further instructions received from His Excellency the Governor General.

Unpaid Accounts

Account "A" referred to in letter from Board to Hon Colonial Secretary dated 20th December 1854, D Jones & Co - £206 11 10; Waugh & Cox - £17 19 6; H Buckley - £14 14 0; Philpott - £73 17 0; Berry & Holt - £10 3 8; Henry Palmer - £150; Markwell - £67 5 0; Atherton - £1 14 4; Emerson - £35 19 8; McDonald - £41 14 6; Scott - £10 14 10; Wilmott - £26 1 2; Wilmott – £3 18 0; Hourigan - £3-15-0; Leith Hay & Holt - £70 0 10; Leith Hay & Holt - £43 2 2; Leith Hay & Holt - £17 19 3; Leith Hay & Holt - £177 13 2; Corfield - £19 10; Swanson - £22 11 4; Wandai Gumbal - £81; R G Walkers & Co - £85; R G Walkers & Co - £17 2; R G Walkers & Co - £88; R G Walkers & Co - £18 2; Swift -£4; Sundry a/c - £10; Row - £10 14; Farquharson - £2 5; Fleming - £2 18; Durundar – £8 8 7; Haly - £4 8 1 [Total] £1347 2 11. Margin Note: I hereby certify that this List of Unpaid Accounts was handed to me by J D L Ferguson, Private Secretary to Mr Walker due up to 30 June 1854 – R P Marshall, Acting Commandant.[357]

Native Police Inquiry

The particulars of the inquiry instituted at Brisbane in the latter part of 1854, respecting the charges against Mr Walker, late Commandant of the Native Police, have just been published by the Government, and came to hand by last mail. The following was the Report of the Board:

"The Board of Inquiry to the Colonial Secretary, Brisbane, 20 December 1854.

Sir, In conformity with the instructions contained in your letter of the 23rd of September last, we have the honour to inform you that the Board of Inquiry for investigating the charges preferred against the Comman-

[357] QSL Reel A2.33 pp 683-694.

dant of the Native Police, assembled at Brisbane on the 23rd of November last, for the purpose of making preliminary arrangements, the Commandant having already reported his arrival to Captain Wickham. Notice having been forwarded to the Acting Commandant Marshall to attend the Board, with the necessary witnesses, and their arrival being notified, the Board assembled again at 12 o'clock, on the 19th instant, to proceed with the inquiry, when they were in attendance Acting Commandant Marshall, Lieutenant Irving, and Sub-Lieutenants Nicol and Bligh; Commandant Walker, however, failed to appear. After waiting half an hour, the Board proceeded with the examination of Mr Marshall; whilst so doing Mr Walker presented himself at the office, (it being about one hour after the time appointed for the meeting) accompanied by some eight or nine of the Native Police, which he was most desirous to bring into the Court with him. This, however, being resisted, they were left at the door, and Mr Walker took his seat, evidently in a state of intoxication, bordering on stupidity, so as not even to recognize his first Lieutenant, Mr Marshall, who was sitting at his side. Seeing the disgraceful condition of the Commandant, the Board requested him to retire; this, however, he declined to do, and conducted himself in such a haughty and insulting manner to the Board, that, without removing him by force, they had only one resource—to adjourn the Court. This being done, Mr Walker retired with the Troopers, and was proceeding with them across the river, when Mr Marshall, assisted by the other Officers, in the presence of one of the Board, prevented him; he carried off, however, two of the men; but the Officers, with the assistance of the Chief Constable, secured their arms and accoutrements, but not without some danger, as Mr Walker drew a sword, and threatened Mr Irving. In the evening the two Troopers who returned, bringing over their horses with them, having left their drunken Commandant in disgust. Under these circumstances, the Court met again this day, and, after examining the Officers present as regards the arrears due for pay and rations, and deeply regretting the embarrassments they are labouring under to pay even the ordinary expenses of their journey down, think it their duty to again adjourn the Court, and, without the slightest delay, to report it as their unanimous opinion,

1st. That Commandant Walker is in constant habits of intoxication, that render him totally unfit for any responsible post under Government, and particularly for that of Commanding the Native Police.

2nd. That the accounts of the Native Police Corps are in such a state of confusion, and the arrears due for pay and rations so heavy, (as shewn in an account for rations supplied by several persons for the use of the men, and marked A), that, in the opinion of the Board, immediate steps should be taken to stop the appropriation of any further sums on Mr Walker's orders.

3rd. That Mr Walker is tampering with the Police and endeavouring to render them disaffected to their Officers and the Government, the Board have ample evidence under their own eyes, although they have no fear for the result.

4th. That, in support of the above opinions, we have the honour to refer His Excellency the Governor-General to the accompanying minute of the proceedings of the Board during their inaction and waiting His Excellency's further orders in this matter, we have, &c., (Signed) J. C. Wickham, S. Simpson; Chas. Geo. Gray.

The Honourable the Colonial Secretary. The Board feel it their duty to express their approbation of the conduct of Lieutenant Marshall, the Acting Commandant throughout the inquiry, and think him worthy of the confidence of the Government. (Signed) J. C. Wickham; S. Simpson; Chas. Geo. Gray."

Acting upon this Report, the Colonial Secretary addressed a letter to Mr Walker informing him that he was dismissed from the post.[358]

PARLIAMENTARY PAPERS, ALLEGED KILLING OF STATION BLACKS BY NATIVE TROOPERS

By order of the Assembly the following return has been printed, to an address of the hon. The Legislative Assembly of New South Wales, dated 27 February 1857 requesting that his Excellency, the Governor General would be pleased to cause to be laid upon the table of the House, A return of all correspondence that may have taken place between the Government and any other parties relative to the suspension of a sergeant, and the killing of a lot of station blacks by native troopers as

[358] *Moreton Bay Courier* 5 January 1856 p 2.

stated in the evidence of RP Marshall Esquire taken before the Select Committee on the Native Police.

N° 1

Extract of a letter from "Commandant of the Native Police to the Colonial Secretary, reporting state of the Native Police Force; upon his return to Callandoon. Dated 23rd July 1853.

"Lieutenant Fulford reports that everything was quiet on the Lower Condamine, and, with the exception of some petty cattle stealing in the Maranoa District, I believe it to be in the same state.

I regret that a collision has again taken place between the Police and the petty cattle stealers above mentioned. I have not yet seen the affidavits taken before the magistrates at Surat but as the police had left Sergeant Dempster to accompany a Mr Johnson, I have written to Lieutenant Fulford, that it appeared to me that they must have had the Sergeant's consent or orders to do so, in which case he was unfit to be entrusted with a detachment or that the troopers had left without consent in which case he seemed to me to be unable to command them; and this I was not prepared to expect would be the case, as the men of the section entrusted to Sergeant Dempster had hitherto been noted for their steady obedient conduct. I have of course required a full explanation. The first clause of the written instructions given by me to all the European sergeants is that they are not to allow any person unconnected with the Native Police Force to interfere with or give orders to any of the troopers under their command. I have etc. F Walker Cmdt NP.

N° 2

Frederick Walker to Col. Sec. 10 October 1852

In the sixth clause of my letter of the 28th July 1852 I had the honour of drawing your attention to what I feared was great mismanagement if not disobedience of my written orders by Sergeant Richard Dempster.

2. I now do myself the honour to recommend that Dempster may be discharged from the Native Police Force as it appears that notwithstanding his written instructions he did order the native corporal Edward and his men to accompany Mr Johnson after blacks.

3. I need not state that Dempster's offence is a very dangerous one; the affray at Surat ensuing from it, is of a doubtful nature and the native

troopers complain of ill-usage from Europeans which could not have occurrence if their sergeant had not sent them away from the only protection they had as their evidence is not admissible in a Court of Justice.

4. I have the honour to observe that I regret I have not the power to remove the sergeant at once for it takes many weeks before I can learn the pleasure of his Excellency the Governor General and in some cases a sergeant ought not to be continued another hour in charge of a section.

N° 3

Colonial Secretary to Frederick Walker, 5 November 1852

Having laid before the Governor General your letter of the 10th ultimo, bringing under notice the disobedience of Sergeant Dempster and recommending he be discharged from the Native Police Force, I now do myself the honour to convey to you his Excellency's authority for the discharge of Dempster and to inform you that although the Governor General does not think it would be expedient to give you a general authority to dismiss non-commissioned officers from the Corps of Native Police at your own discretion, his Excellency sees no objection to you being authorised to suspend from duty at once any non-commissioned officer who may misconduct himself subject to the confirmation of the Governor General upon the case being reported.

N° 4

Frederick Waker to Col. Sec. 28 March 1857

I observed lately that Mr TG Rusden had in the Council asked you some question relative to an alleged attack upon Native Blacks on account of which a sergeant had been suspended. He also quoted Mr Marshall as his authority.

I suppose the matter refers to a case reported by me to your office either in August or September 1852 the result of which was the dismissal of Sergeant Richard Dempster.

The facts were as following: Sergeant Dempster being ill with ague improperly sent the men out on patrol with no responsible person in command; when they were out the police met with a Mr Johnson somewhere on the Balonne below Surat. This person opened a letter addressed to Sergeant Dempster which letter was to the effect that the police were immediately required at Yamboukal, a station of Mr Hall's only one mile from the Court of Petty Sessions at Surat. He persuaded the police to accompany him stating he had orders to that effect. Hence ensued the attack referred to. I am at a loss to conceive how Mr Marshall makes it out that they were Station Blacks. The letter from Yamboukal would show contrary to that. I do not know Mr Marshall asserted this, at all events he never saw any of the correspondence. The sergeant you will perceive was dismissed not as stated for being present but because he had not been.

The Bench of Magistrates at Surat held an inquiry the result of which is unknown to me unless that Mr Fulford wrote to me privately that Mr Johnson was nearly committing himself; it appeared strange to me how he could avoid doing so. This affair was quoted by me as one of my reasons for having no confidence in sergeants and is also again alluded to in the enclosure of my last letter to the Attorney-General, dated 25 September 1854.

N° 5

Colonial Secretary to RP Marshall, 20 March 1857

The Legislative Assembly having called for a copy of all correspondence that may have taken place between the Government and any other parties relative to the suspension of a sergeant and the killing of a lot of station blacks by native troopers as stated in your evidence taken before the Select Committee on the Native Police, I am directed to inform you that it is not clear on what occasion or at what place the transaction alluded to occurred and that the correspondence (if any exist) cannot at present be traced in this office; and to request therefore the favour of any further information on the subject which it may be in your power to afford.

N° 6

Colonial Secretary to RP Marshall, 19 June 1857

Not having received a reply to my letter of the 20th March last applying for information relative to the killing of Station Blacks by the Native Police as adverted to in your evidence before the select committee on Native Police I am directed to draw your attention to the subject and to request the favour of your early reply.

N° 7

RP Marshall to Col. Sec. 15 August 1857

I do myself the honour to acknowledge the receipt of your letter of the 20th March, LA 57-88, No 206 as also dated 19 June, 57-1667, No 485 and in reply have to state that in consequence of having no settled place of residence for the last twelve months, the letters were only received by me at this place a fortnight since.

2. Referring to the allusion made to my evidence before the Select Committee on the Native Police Force, I have to state that the correspondence spoken of by me was one that took place between the then Colonial Secretary and Commandant Walker as to the suspension of Sergeant Dempster who was in command of a detachment of native police stationed on the Balonne River.

3. In what I stated before the Select Committee, I never for a moment intended to infer that Mr Hely's question had reference to any statement in which there was a possibility of truth. I knew that a sergeant had been suspended and that a correspondence had taken place between the Colonial Secretary and the Commandant of the Force of the day on the subject and I again state that I know nothing of the real cause as to the officer being relieved from his duties for a period of I believe three months.

4. In conclusion, I have to point out for your consideration how easy it is for persons to make either malicious or absurd and ridiculous statements about such a force as the Native Police without the slightest foundation for such statements, and I have only to instance the words of the honourable member for Phillip, Brisbane and Bligh on the night passing the Estimates for the Force as quoted in the *Herald* of the ensuing day wherein it is stated "that the Native Police killed woman and children indiscriminately" or words to the same effect. Your letter of 23 July, 57-1667, 586, I received here last night. Warialda 22 August.[359]

[359] *SMH* 4 November 1857 p 2.

Between Frederick Walker Plaintiff

And

David Cameron Defendant

I Frederick Walker the above-named Plaintiff make oath and say as follows:

1. David Cameron the above-named Defendant is justly and truly indebted to me in the sum of Two thousand nine hundred ponds and upwards upon and by virtue of Articles of Agreement dated the fourteenth day of June in the year of Our Lord One thousand eight hundred and fifty nine whereby I the said Frederick Walker agreed to sell and transfer all my right and interest in and to six blocks of country on the Planet, Comet and Brown known as Planet N° 1, 2, 3, 4, 5 and 6 to David Cameron Esquire and to engage myself as superintendent to the said David Cameron to use my utmost endeavours to protect his property and increase his stock for the term of two years commencing at date of transfer of said runs or upon the said David Cameron being satisfied that such transfer would be completed . In consideration of such transfer being completed and at the expiration of the aforesaid two years the said David Cameron thereby agreed to make over to me the said Frederick Walker sixteen hundred ewes shorn and in lamb of the average ewes on the station, a team of six working bollocks with bows and yokes complete, one of the working drays of the station, one ton of flour, one chest of tea, six hundred and forty pounds of sugar and also two stock horses each and all of the average articles on the station. The said David Cameron also engaged to pay to the said Frederick Walker the sum of one hundred pounds sterling per annum with board and lodgings, washing and a comfortable private room and moreover to grant to the said Frederick Walker ten per cent of branded increase of horses and cattle and five per cent of the weaned lambs should such increase amount to above fifty per cent and be under seventy five per cent and ten percent should such increase amount to seventy five per cent or over during the term of the above Agreement. In the event of the un-fulfilment of the above Agreement in its integrity the amount which shall be allowed to the said Frederick Walker or his heirs shall be settled equitably by two practical settlers in the vicinity and their decision shall in such case be offered primarily to Mr David Cameron for which his bill at

three months shall be accepted. The said David Cameron upon his being satisfied that the transfer of the six Planet runs will be completed thereby agreed to give to the said Frederick Walker his Bill or note for three, six months and twelve months for One hundred and sixteen pounds thirteen shillings and four pence each being three hundred and fifty pound sterling in all and the said Frederic Walker thereby agreed to assign and make over to the said David Cameron all his right tile and interest to three runs contiguous to the Planet Runs known by the name of Comet No 1, 2 and 3 one of which is also known as Wongaleigh as security for the repayment of the said three hundred and fifty pounds. In the event of the tenders of Frederick Walker not being accepted David Cameron is thereby empowered to hold sheep to the value of three hundred and fifty pounds from the flock deliverable to Frederick Walker the above to be equitably valued by two settlers in the vicinity any charges incurred by David Cameron for rent etc. on the above Crescent Runs to be repaid to him at 12½ per cent interest added.

2. That I have been informed and verily believe that the said David Cameron has been making arrangements to remove his wife and family from his station and the Colony of Queensland.

3. That an execution for the amount of Two thousand nine hundred pounds with Three hundred and fifty pounds costs has been issued by the Sheriff of this Colony.

4. I have been informed and verily believe that David Cameron has secreted and concealed or otherwise secretly disposed of considerable sums of money and that by his leaving this Colony I shall be deprived of monies which I should otherwise recover by order of the Honourable Court from the said David Cameron the Defendant herein.

5. For the reasons aforesaid I verily believe that the said David Cameron is about to quit the Colony of Queensland unless he be forthwith apprehended.

6. This application is not made from malicious or improper purposes but solely to recover the amount due by the said defendant David Cameron to this Deponent.

7. I have caused a writ or summons to be sued out of this Honourable Court in this action at my suit against the above-named Defendant for

the above-named amounts. Frederick Walker, Signed and sworn by the above named Deponent Frederick Walker on the … day of July AD 1864 before me WH Wiseman PM, A Commissioner for Affidavits.

In the Supreme Court of Queensland
The seventeenth day of February
in the year of Our Lord one thousand
eight hundred and sixty-four
Cameron ats Walker}

The Defendant by Eyles Irwin Caulfield Browne his Attorney as to so much of the first count of the declaration as alleges that the Defendant did not nor would employ the Plaintiff as Superintendent nor provide him with board and lodgings and a comfortable private room says that the Plaintiff having engaged himself as superintendent to the Defendant for the term of two years commencing as in the said count mentioned, the Defendant took the Plaintiff into his service as such superintendent and was ready and willing to continue to employ him in such service and for such term as aforesaid and provided him with board, lodgings and a comfortable private room for as long as he remained in the Defendant's service and was ready and willing to continue to provide him therewith and for such term as aforesaid, yet, the Plaintiff nevertheless did not complete his said engagement and left the service of the Defendant before the expiration of the said term of two years and thereby discharged the Defendant from the further performance of so much of his said agreement as aforesaid. And for a second plea as to so much of the said first count as alleges that the Defendant would not pay the Plaintiff the sum of One hundred pounds per annum the Defendant says that all conditions were not fulfilled and all things did not happen and all times did not elapse necessary to entitle the Plaintiff to maintain this action in that behalf and to have the agreement in the said count mentioned performed in that behalf by the Defendant on his part in as much as the Plaintiff having engaged himself as superintendent to the defendant and to use his utmost endeavours to protect the property and increase the stock of the Defendant for the term of two years commencing as in the said count mentioned and the Defendant having taken the Plaintiff into his service as such superintendent and to perform such services and for such term as aforesaid the Plaintiff nevertheless did not complete his engagement and left the service of the Defendant before the expiration of the first year of the said term of two years.

And for the third plea as to so much of the said first count as alleges that the Defendant did not pay to the Plaintiff the sum of One hundred pounds per annum the defendant says that all conditions were not fulfilled and all things did not happen and all times did not elapse necessary to entitle the Plaintiff to maintain this action in that behalf and to have the agreement in the said count mentioned performed in that behalf by the Defendant in as much as the Plaintiff having engaged himself as superintendent to the Defendant to use his utmost endeavour to protect the property and increase the stock to his agreement in the said count mentioned or to abide by the decision of two settlers the Defendant says that he never refused to refer according to the said agreement or to abide by the decision of two settlers as in the said count mentioned.

And for an eight plea as to the second count of the Declaration the Defendant says that he did not agree as in the same count alleged.

And for a ninth plea as to said second count the Defendant says that all things did not happen and all times did not elapse and all conditions were not performed to entitle the Plaintiff to have the agreement in the said count mentioned performed by the Defendant in as much as the repayment of the sum of Three hundred and fifty pounds therein mentioned never was secured upon the said Planet Runs and upon the Plaintiff's interest thereon.

And for the tenth plea as to the common count of the Declaration of the defendant says that he never was indebted as alleged.

And for an eleventh plea to the whole declaration the Defendant says that the Plaintiff at the commencement of this suit was and still is liable in damages to the defendant in an amount equal to the Plaintiff's claim for that in consideration that the Defendant would deliver to the Plaintiff certain cattle, sheep, horses, stores and other goods and chattels to be safely kept and taken care of by the Plaintiff for the Defendant on request for reward to the Plaintiff the Plaintiff promised the Defendant to safely keep and take care of the said cattle, sheep, horses, stores and other goods and chattels while the same should be in the Plaintiff's care and keeping as aforesaid and to redeliver the same to the Defendant on request and the Defendant delivered the said cattle, sheep, horses, stores and other goods and chattels to the Plaintiff and the Plaintiff received and had the same in his care and keeping for the purpose and on the terms aforesaid and yet by the carelessness, negligence and improper conduct of the Plaintiff a great quantity of the said cattle, sheep, horses, stores and goods and chattels were wholly lost to the Defendant in respect whereof a right of cross action has accrued to the Defendant and the defendant is willing to set off the said amount against the Plaintiff's claim.

And for a further plea as to One thousand one hundred and fifty pounds parcel of the money claimed the Defendant says that the plaintiff the commencement of the suit was and still is indebted to the Defendant in an amount equal to the Plaintiff's claim for certain overdue promissory notes made and given by the Plaintiff to the Defendant and still unpaid for interest thereon and for money lent by the Defendant to the Plaintiff at his request and for money received by the Plaintiff for the use of the Defendant and for interest upon money due from the Plaintiff to the Defendant and forborne at interest by the defendant to the Plaintiff at his request and for money found to be due from the Plaintiff the Defendant on accounts stated between them which amount the Defendant is willing to set off against the Plaintiff's claim. Eyles Irwin Caulfield Browne, Defendant's Attorney.[360]

[360] QSA Series 5687 Writs ID 2321988.

Courtesy of the National Library of Australia
nla.obj-149661976

Frederick Walker's tree, Burke and Wills most northerly point, Camp 119, Northern Queensland circa. 1916

Bibliography

Newspapers

The Argus (Melbourne, Vic.: 1848 - 1957)
The Australian (Sydney, NSW: 1824 - 1848)
The Australian (National: 1964)
The Brisbane Courier (Qld.: 1864 - 1933)
The Courier (Brisbane, Qld.: 1861 - 1864)
Bell's Life in Sydney and Sporting Reviewer (NSW: 1845 - 1860)
The Dispatch (Sydney, NSW: 1843 - 1844)
Empire (Sydney, NSW: 1850 - 1875)
Geelong Advertiser and Squatters' Advocate (Vic.: 1845 - 1847)
The Goulburn Herald and County of Argyle Advertiser (NSW: 1848 - 1859)
Ipswich Herald and General Advertiser (Qld.: 1861)
The Maitland Mercury and Hunter River General Advertiser (NSW: 1843 - 1893)
Maryborough Chronicle, Wide Bay and Burnett Advertiser (Qld: 1860 – 1947)
The Moreton Bay Courier (Brisbane, Qld.: 1846 - 1861)
Morning Bulletin (Rockhampton, Qld.: 1878 - 1954)
The North Australian, Ipswich and General Advertiser (Ipswich, Qld.: 1856 - 1862)
North Australian and Queensland General Advertiser (Ipswich, Qld.: 1862 - 1863)
Northern Argus (Rockhampton, Qld.: 1865 - 1874
Queensland Times, Ipswich Herald and General Advertiser (Qld.: 1861 - 1908)
The Queenslander (Brisbane, Qld.: 1866 - 1939)
Rockhampton Bulletin and Central Queensland Advertiser (Qld.: 1861 - 1871)
The Shipping Gazette and Sydney General Trade List (NSW: 1844 - 1860)
The Sydney Gazette and New South Wales Advertiser (NSW: 1803 - 1842)
Sydney Mail (NSW: 1860 - 1871)
The Sydney Morning Herald (NSW: 1842 - 1954)
The Spectator (United Kingdom: 1828)
The Weekly Register of Politics, Facts and General Literature (Sydney, NSW: 1843 - 1845)

Books

Bride, Thomas, *Letter from Victorian Pioneers*, Melbourne 1898.
Burridge, Kenelm, *Encountering Aborigines: A Case Study: Anthropology and the Australian Aboriginal*, New York, 1973
Campbell, Judy, *Invisible Invaders*, Melbourne, 2002.
Coffey, Renee, *Frontier Violence in Gin Gin a History of Murder, Massacre and Myth*,

Brisbane, 2006.

Copland, Mark, *The Native Poole at Callandoon – A Blueprint for Forced Assimilation?* Brisbane, 1999.

Cracknell, WJ, *Report from the Superintendent of Electric Telegraphs on the condition of his department*, Brisbane, 1867.

Davidoff, Laura and Duhs, Alan, *Aboriginal Australia: An Economic History of Failed Welfare Policy*, Brisbane, 2008.

Graham, RH and Watson, HD, *Tumut and district sesqui centenary*, Tumut, 1974

Morgan, John, *The Life and Adventures of William Buckley*, Tasmania, 1852.

Morrill, James, *17 Years Wandering Among the Aborigines*, 2006.

Reynolds, Henry, *The Other Side of the Frontier*, Sydney, 2006

Richards, Jonathan, *"A Question of Necessity" The Native Police in Queensland*, Brisbane 2005

Sahlins, Marshall, *Stone Age Economics*, Chicago, 1972.

de Vaux Voss, Vivian, *The Morey Papers*, Emu Park, 1952.

Journals

Crommelin, Michael, *"Mabo: The Decision and the Debate"* Papers on Parliament No. 22, February 1994

McHugh, Michael, *Democracy and The Law*, The Australian Bar Association Conference, London, 5 July 1998,http://www.hcourt.gov.au/assets/publications/speeches/former-justices/mchughj/mchughj_london1.htm

Kirby, Michael, Sir Anthony Mason Lecture: *A F Mason - From Trigwell to Teoh*, [1996] MelbULawRw 20, p 1095.

Macintyre, Stuart, *On 'fabricating' history*, Evatt Journal, Vol. 3, No. 4, June 2003.

Sackville, Ronald, *"Why Do Judges Make Law? Some Aspects of Judicial Law Making"* [2001] UWSLawRw 5; (2001) 5(1) University of Western Sydney Law Review 59.

Taçon, P, and Chippindale, C, *Australia's Ancient Warriors: Changing Depictions of Fighting in the Rock Art of Arnhem Land, N.T.*, Cambridge Archaeological Journal, 4(2), pp. 211–248.

Williams, Alan N, Ulm, Sean, Cook, Andrew R, Langley, Michelle C, Collard, Mark, *Journal of Archaeological Science,* Volume 40, Issue 12, December 2013, pp 4612-4625.

www.ingramcontent.com/pod-product-compliance
Lightning Source LLC
Chambersburg PA
CBHW071939260326
41914CB00004B/676